WALES

THE COMPLETE WHO'S WHO
OF FOOTBALLERS SINCE 1946

DEAN P. HAYES

FOREWORD BY **TERRY YORATH**

SUTTON PUBLISHING

First published in the United Kingdom in 2004 by
Sutton Publishing Limited · Phoenix Mill
Thrupp · Stroud · Gloucestershire · GL5 2BU

British Library Cataloguing in Publication Data
A catalogue record for this book is available from the British Library.

ISBN 0-7509-3700-9

Author's note

Although every effort has been made and every care taken to ensure that this
book is statistically accurate, inevitably errors will creep in, for which I offer my
apologies in advance.

Typeset in 9.5/11.5 pt Joanna MT.
Typesetting and origination by
Sutton Publishing Limited.
Printed and bound in England by
J.H. Haynes & Co. Ltd, Sparkford.

Contents

Foreword

*T*he highs and lows of Welsh international football are all played out in the pages of this book through the lifeblood of the game – the players. Everyone knows how Pelé broke our hearts in 1958, but Dean Hayes has looked at the famous matches and beyond to trace the record of every player who has set foot on a pitch in Welsh colours since 1946. The team's most capped players – Neville Southall, Dean Saunders, Peter Nicholas, Ian Rush, Gary Speed, Mark Hughes – are here, of course, but so are all the others, even those who were capped once then internationally forgotten.

This unique, detailed and fascinating look at the national game traces the story from the early postwar struggles through the dramas of the 1950s, when one of the most unusual routes to qualification ever seen in the World Cup resulted in that match against Brazil. Moving on from the mixed fortunes of the 1960s, Wales hit the new decade with a new fighting spirit and a new optimism, becoming the sole British qualifiers for the European Championships in 1976 – a campaign in which I was privileged to win some of my 59 international caps.

The years since then have also seen some great international matches and some great players have taken to the pitch for Wales. Ian Rush and Neville Southall both won their first caps in the 1980s, and the team came tantalisingly close to qualification for the World Cup Finals in 1982 and 1986, and the European Championships in 1984. In the 1992 European Championships, when I was team manager, we finished only one point behind eventual finalists, Germany, in our qualifying group. The biggest news for many years was, of course, the near-miss for Euro 2004 in a campaign that saw a ten-game, 20-month unbeaten run, including that 2–1 defeat of Italy. It's a great foundation for the future.

Every one of the players from Bryn Jones in 1946 to Ben Thatcher in 2004 has earned his place in this dedicated celebration of Welsh football.

Terry Yorath, 2004

Introduction

Many great international footballers have come out of Wales to pull off results that have confounded the critics down the years. This book celebrates the players who have proudly worn the red dragon since the Second World War and revisits the triumphs and disappointments of nearly six decades.

The Welsh beat the odds to qualify for the 1958 World Cup Finals in Sweden and held Pelé's Brazil until the 70th minute. They also made it into the European Championship finals in 1976 but, despite a record of valiant effort, the team's recent history has been blighted by near qualification for major finals on a number of occasions. Under Mark Hughes, however, Wales earned themselves the title of most improved European national team.

A total of 264 players have appeared for Wales in the postwar period, among them Ivor Allchurch, John Charles, Neville Southall, Ian Rush and Ryan Giggs. They appear here in chronological order, that is, in the order that they made their international debut. Of course, in some matches a number made their debuts at the same time, and in such cases players are listed alphabetically. In a number of entries, reference is made to wartime caps. Though international games continued during hostilities, the Victory matches of 1946 and the wartime fixtures of 1939–45 were not recognised as full internationals, and therefore these appearances are not included in the total number of caps won. In the statistics section at the head of each player's entry, match dates are listed according to the years that marked the end of the season in which the game was played (e.g., September 1956 is shown under 1957). Every postwar game is included in the book up to the end of the 2003/04 season.

For each player I have aimed to provide the following information: full name, recognised position, period as a Wales player, height and weight, date and place of birth, date and place of death, career details, breakdown of appearances and goals scored for Wales, and biography. Heights and weights should be regarded only as approximate figures since they obviously varied throughout the player's career.

This book is a collection of statistics, biographies and games won and lost. But I hope it is more than that: it is a celebration of the great game.

Dean P. Hayes, Pembrokeshire, 2004

1946–49

Rebuilding

In October 1946, in the first full international after the Second World War, a full Racecourse Ground, plus the guest of honour, the great Billy Meredith, saw the Scots beaten 3–1 with goals from Trevor Ford, Bryn Jones and an own goal by James Stephen. In addition to Bryn Jones, two other Welshmen carried their pre-war international honours into the postwar years – Billy Hughes and Tommy Jones.

The new secretary of the Welsh Football Association (FA), Herbert Powell, had his first real taste of the trials and problems of getting a Welsh side together in the week leading up to the match against England at Maine Road on 13 November 1946. Trevor Ford and Bryn Jones were both unavailable and a number of other players were injured, requiring reserves to stand by. Three new caps were introduced and one of these, Alf Sherwood, went on to make 41 appearances for his country.

Ron Burgess began his international career during the Second World War and, when full internationals began again, he was the automatic choice for the left-half berth. Burgess was an excellent captain for both club and country, skippering the Spurs 'push and run' side to the League Championship in 1950/51. As well as representing Wales in the 1948 Great Britain side, he also became the first Welshman to play for the Football League XI.

Sadly, the 1940s were not distinguished by great success for Wales on the home international front – they were an attractive side but usually they found England too strong for them. In 1949 Wales embarked on their first tour abroad. They met Portugal, Belgium and Switzerland and, although they lost each match, they came back a little wiser about Continental football.

Almost ten years later, in the 1958 World Cup Finals Wales were to cause something of a stir not only on the Continent but throughout the football world.

Bryn JONES

Position	Inside-forward
Born	Brynmor Jones, Merthyr Tydfil, 14 February 1912
Died	Wood Green, London, 18 October 1985
Height	5ft 6in
Weight	10st 6lb
Clubs	Glenavon, Aberaman, Wolverhampton Wanderers, Arsenal, Norwich City
Welsh Caps	17 Goals 5

*1935 v N. Ireland (won 3–1)
1936 v Scotland (1–1), v England (won 2–1) 1 goal, v N. Ireland (lost 2–3)
1937 v England (won 2–1), v Scotland (won 2–1), v N. Ireland (won 4–1) 1 goal
1938 v Scotland (won 2–1) 1 goal, v England (lost 1–2), v N. Ireland (lost 0–1)
1939 v England (won 4–2), v Scotland (lost 2–3), v N. Ireland (won 3–1)
1947 v Scotland (won 3–1) 1 goal, v N. Ireland (lost 1–2)
1948 v England (lost 0–3)
1949 v Scotland (lost 1–3) 1 goal

INSIDE-FORWARD BRYN JONES worked down the pit while playing for his home-town club, Merthyr Amateurs, in the South Wales District League, before moving to Plymouth United. After being rejected by Southend United, he played for Glenavon in the Irish League before returning to Wales to play for Aberaman in the summer of 1933. However, he was soon on his way to Molineux for a fee of £1,500 and made his League debut against Everton at Goodison in a match that Wolves won 2–1. In his second season with the club, he won the first of 17 Welsh caps when he played against N. Ireland.

Jones stayed at Molineux for five seasons, scoring 57 goals in 177 games, including a hat-trick in a 4–2 home win over Preston North End on 20 April 1936. His best season in terms of goals scored was 1937/38, when he netted 15 in 36 League outings. At the end of that campaign he left to join Arsenal for a record fee of £14,000.

He scored Arsenal's first goal on his debut in a 2–0 win over Portsmouth and followed this by scoring twice in the next three League games. However, war was just around the corner and Jones was posted to Italy and North Africa while serving with the Royal Artillery.

On his return to Highbury, he helped the Gunners win the League Championship in 1947/48 and scored in the 4–3 Charity Shield victory over Manchester United. His Arsenal career finished while he was on the summer tour of Brazil in 1949. During a game against Vasco de Gama, spectators continuously ran on to the pitch and accidentally or not, Jones was hit on the head by a Brazilian policeman. Shortly after he became Norwich City's player-coach, his doctor advised him to retire from the game.

---

* Dates of International matches are listed according to the final year of the season in which they were played.

A wonderful ball player, Bryn Jones became the costliest footballer in Great Britain when he left Wolves for Arsenal for £14,000 in 1938. *(Getty Images)*

Billy HUGHES

Position	Full-back
Born	William Marshall Hughes, Llanelli, 5 March 1918
Died	Birmingham, 16 June 1981
Height	6ft 2in
Weight	12st 5lb
Clubs	Watchers Celtic, Birmingham City, Luton Town, Chelsea, Hereford United, Flint Town
Welsh Caps	10
	1938 v Scotland (won 2–1), v England (lost 1–2), v N. Ireland (lost 0–1)
	1939 v England (lost 2–3), v Scotland (lost 2–3), v N. Ireland (won 3–1), v France (lost 1–2)
	1947 v Scotland (won 3–1), v England (lost 0–3), v N. Ireland (lost 1–2)

BILLY HUGHES WAS A SOLID, dependable full-back for Wales either side of th
Second World War.

The Llanelli-born defender began his career with his home-town club befor
signing for Birmingham City in the summer of 1935. He was just 17 years old whe
he made his first-team debut for the St Andrew's club in an FA Cup third round repla
at home to Barnsley, which the Yorkshire club won 2–0. It was 1937/38 before h
established himself in the Birmingham side, his performances earning him the first o
ten full caps for Wales when he played against Scotland on 30 October 1937.

During the war years he appeared in a further 55 games for Birmingham an
guested for a number of clubs including Arsenal, Spurs and West Ham United. H
appeared in 14 unofficial internationals and in 1946 played for Great Britain agains
the Rest of Europe at Hampden Park. He was still a regular in the Birmingham sid
when League football resumed in 1946/47. Hughes had appeared in 110 League an
Cup games for the Blues when, in March 1948, he joined Chelsea for a fee o
£12,000.

By now, Hughes had matured into a highly skilled full-back, an effective ba
winner who always tried to be constructive, using the ball to excellent effect. H
looked upon this style of play with disdain and would always try to play his way ou
of difficulties whenever possible.

In the summer of 1951 Hughes went to Hereford United. Later, he played for Flin
Town, where he won a Welsh Cup winners' medal in 1954. But for the war, Hughe
would have made far more League appearances and won more international honour
for Wales. He later scouted for Chester.

Tommy G. JONES

Position	Centre-half
Born	Thomas George Jones, Connahs Quay, 12 October 1917
Height	6ft 0in
Weight	12st 6lb
Clubs	Llanerch Celtic, Wrexham, Everton, Pwllheli
Welsh Caps	17

1938 v N. Ireland (lost 0–1)
1939 v England (lost 2–3), v Scotland (lost 2–3), v N. Ireland (won 3–1)
1947 v Scotland (won 3–1), v England (lost 0–3)
1948 v England (lost 0–3), v Scotland (won 2–1), v N. Ireland (won 2–0)
1949 v England (lost 0–1), v N. Ireland (won 2–0), v Portugal (lost 2–3), v Belgium (lost 1–3),
    v Switzerland (lost 0–4)
1950 v England (lost 1–4), v Scotland (lost 0–2), v Belgium (won 5–1)

DESPITE HIS LIMITED CHANCES of first-team football at Wrexham, where he made just seven League appearances for the Robins, discerning judges spotted a future international in Tommy Jones, who was often regarded as one of the footballing 'scientists' of his day.

Tommy Jones left the Racecourse Ground in March 1936 to join Everton for a fee of £3,000. A footballing centre-half, he made his debut for the Blues six months later in a 1–0 defeat at Leeds United. It was his only game of the season. Jones established himself in the Everton side during the following campaign, at the end of which he won the first of his 17 Welsh caps when he played against N. Ireland.

During the war years he appeared in 142 games for the club and, when League football resumed in 1946/47, he was again the club's first-choice pivot. He scored his first League goal for the Merseyside club in a 3–3 home draw against Grimsby Town. In the summer of 1949 Jones was appointed club captain in place of Peter Farrell. A year earlier he could have joined the Italian giants AS Roma, who made several desperate attempts to sign him. Everton did in fact accept a considerable fee but the deal fell through after a row over the currency transaction.

Towards the end of his career with the Toffees, Jones upset the Everton board by publicly expressing his concerns at the way the club was being run. He had scored five goals in 175 League and Cup games when he left to join Pwllheli as the Welsh club's player-manager.

Cyril SIDLOW

Position	Goalkeeper
Born	Cyril Sidlow, Colwyn Bay, 26 November 1915
Height	6ft 1in
Weight	13st 10lb
Clubs	Colwyn Bay, Abergele, Flint Town, Llandudno Town, Wolverhampton Wanderers, Liverpool, New Brighton
Welsh Caps	7
	1947 v Scotland (won 3–1), v England (lost 0–3)
	1948 v England (lost 0–3), v Scotland (won 2–1), v N. Ireland (won 2–0)
	1949 v Scotland (lost 1–3)
	1950 v England (lost 1–4)

CYRIL SIDLOW PLAYED FOR the North Wales Coast FA representative XI while still a schoolboy and was later honoured by Wales at amateur level.

He began his career with his home-town club Colwyn Bay before appearing for a number of other North Wales sides in Abergele, Flint Town and Llandudno. He then joined Wolves as a professional in the summer of 1937. During the Second World War he served with the Duke of Wellington's Regiment and, while stationed in the North of England, he guested for Darlington, assisted Notts County and Wrexham, and appeared quite regularly for Wolves.

He received a wartime League Cup winners' medal in 1942 when Wolves beat Sunderland in the two-legged final. As well as winning seven full caps for his country he also played in 11 wartime and Victory internationals and twice represented the Northern Command.

On leaving Wolves, Sidlow joined Liverpool. He made 165 appearances for the club between 1946 and 1951, winning a League Championship medal and an FA Cup runners-up medal. He was a great favourite with the Anfield crowd. Although at times he could be inconsistent, he will always be remembered as one of the first goalkeepers to regularly throw the ball out of his area rather than simply kick it upfield.

In 1952 he joined New Brighton, but a year later he returned to Molineux as cover for Bert Williams, at the same time coaching the club's youngsters. Having been an apprentice carpenter before turning to football, he later returned to the building trade and retired in 1980.

Ray LAMBERT

Position	Full-back
Born	Raymond Lambert, Holywell, 18 July 1922
Height	5ft 10in
Weight	12st 3lb
Clubs	Liverpool
Welsh Caps	5
	1947 v Scotland (won 3–1)
	1948 v England (lost 0–3)
	1949 v Portugal (lost 2–3), v Belgium (lost 1–3), v Switzerland (lost 0–4)

RAY LAMBERT'S TALENT WAS recognised by Flintshire Schoolboys and in 1936, at the age of 13 years 189 days, he was signed by Liverpool on amateur forms – the youngest player ever to sign for a Football League club.

Lambert represented the Army against Portugal during the hostilities. But it wasn't until after the war, when he 'guested' for New Brighton and Reading, that Lambert's career got going. He went on to give Liverpool many seasons of dedicated service. He was originally a centre-half but developed into a solidly built defender who could play in either of the full-back positions. A cool and unruffled player, his main strength was his excellent positional play.

Lambert was a regular member of Liverpool's League Championship-winning side of 1946/47 and also appeared for the Reds in the 1950 FA Cup Final, where they lost 2–0 to Arsenal.

Ray Lambert was a strong, no-nonsense tackler. An outstanding servant to the

Anfield club, he made over 300 appearances. His son Wayne was at one time on Manchester City's books and played for several North Wales clubs. On hanging up his boots, Ray Lambert became a newsagent in Queensferry.

Doug WITCOMB

Position	Wing-half
Born	Douglas Frederick Witcomb, Ebbw Vale, 18 April 1918
Height	5ft 7in
Weight	11st 4lb
Clubs	Tottenham Hotspur, Northfleet, Enfield, West Bromwich Albion, Sheffield Wednesday, Newport County, Llandudno Town, Redditch
Welsh Caps	3
	1947 v Scotland (won 3–1), v England (lost 0–3), v N. Ireland (lost 1–2)

CAPPED BY WALES both during and after the war, wing-half Doug Witcomb began his career as a Spurs amateur in the mid-1930s, but found himself farmed out to Northfleet and Enfield. He moved to West Bromwich Albion in October 1937 and established his career there.

Newport County, Swansea Town, Leicester City, Lovells Athletic and Grimsby Town also benefited from Doug Witcomb's services during the war, but in March 1947, after appearing in 55 games for the Hawthorns club, he joined Sheffield Wednesday. Witcomb had made two appearances for Wales while with Albion and added a third cap to his collection a month after arriving at Hillsborough.

He made his Wednesday debut in a 5–1 defeat of his first club, Spurs, and helped the Owls avoid relegation to the Third Division. Witcomb was an important member of the Wednesday side that won promotion in 1949/50, missing just one match that season and two the following campaign, when they went straight back down. Midway through the 1951/52 season, Witcomb suffered a bad injury and was forced to miss much of the latter part of the campaign. He returned just in time to see the Owls clinch the Second Division title.

The arrival at Hillsborough of George Davis from non-League Oswestry meant that Witcomb lost his place. After making 230 first-team appearances for the Yorkshire club, he joined Newport County, where he took his total tally of League appearances for his three League clubs to 304.

Ron BURGESS

Position	Wing-half
Born	William Arthur Ronald Burgess, Ebbw Vale, 9 April 1917
Height	5ft 11in
Weight	11st 0lb
Clubs	Cwm Villa, Tottenham Hotspur, Swansea Town
Welsh Caps	32 Goals 1

1947 v Scotland (won 3–1), v England (lost 0–3), v N. Ireland (lost 1–2)

1948 v England (lost 0–3), v Scotland (won 2–1)

1949 v Scotland (lost 1–3), v England (lost 0–1), v N. Ireland (won 2–0), v Portugal (lost 2–3), v Belgium (lost 1–3), v Switzerland (lost 0–4)

1950 v England (lost 1–4), v Scotland (lost 0–2), v Belgium (won 5–1), v N. Ireland (0–0)

1951 v Scotland (lost 1–3), v N. Ireland (won 2–1), v Portugal (won 2–1), v Switzerland (won 3–2) 1 goal

1952 v England (1–1), v Scotland (won 1–0), v Rest of the UK (won 3–2), v N. Ireland (won 3–0)

1953 v Scotland (lost 1–2), v England (lost 2–5), v N. Ireland (won 3–2), v France (lost 1–6), v Yugoslavia (lost 2–5)

1954 v England (lost 1–4), v Scotland (3–3), v N. Ireland (lost 1–2), v Austria (lost 0–2)

ONE OF THE ALL-TIME GREATS, Ron Burgess had captained Spurs for only one season when he was appointed captain of Wales in 1947. The following year he was selected for the Great Britain team against the Rest of Europe in Glasgow.

He first caught the attention of Spurs' scouts while playing for local side Cwm Villa, for whom he once scored 59 goals in a season, mainly from the centre-forward position. He had signed amateur forms for Cardiff City but, with the promised trial not forthcoming, took a job as a pit boy. It was not the first time a player had taken the route from the Rhondda to White Hart Lane: Burgess followed Taffy O'Callaghan, Willie Evans and Jimmy Seed.

Burgess was taken on by the Spurs junior staff but, after less than 12 months with the club, was told he would not make the grade. Before returning home he popped into the ground to watch the Spurs 'A' team play. They were a man short and Burgess was asked to fill in at right-half. It was the first time he had played in anything but a forward position, but he did so well that Spurs offered him a place on the ground staff and an amateur contract at the famous Northfleet Nursery.

In his first season at Northfleet, Burgess was a member of the Spurs side that did the double, winning the Kent Senior League and the Kent Senior Cup. At the end of that campaign, Burgess turned professional and made his first-team debut for Spurs in February 1939 in a 2–1 win at Norwich City. It was an impressive debut and led to Burgess securing one of the half-back positions. For the next 15 years he was absent only due to injury, national service or international calls.

In fact, international honours were not long in coming, and he made the first of ten wartime appearances for Wales against England in November 1939. On the outbreak of war Burgess became a reserve policeman, later leaving to take work in a South Wales foundry. In 1940 he joined the RAF and became a physical training instructor. Throughout the Second World War, he won representative honours for the RAF, FA and Wales, turning out for both Spurs and Notts County when service demands allowed.

After 1945 Ron Burgess settled into the left-half position and became one of the finest attacking wing-halves the game has known. Burgess was an inspiring leader and the engine-room of Arthur Rowe's Spurs 'push and run' team that won the Second Division title in 1949/50 and the League Championship the following season. He was also the first Welshman to play for the Football League team and played for Great

Britain against the Rest of Europe. Burgess won 32 caps for Wales, many of them as captain. He possessed incredible stamina and never lost his attacking capability. Even late in his career, he played for Spurs on the left-wing.

In May 1954, after making his final appearance for Wales against Austria, Burgess left White Hart Lane to take up the post of player-coach with Swansea Town. He soon graduated to player-manager and then took over the manager's job on a permanent basis. After four years with Swansea, he moved to Watford and there discovered Pat Jennings, whom he later sold to Spurs. He took the Vicarage Road club to promotion to the Third Division in 1959/60 and to the fifth round of the FA Cup. After leaving Watford, he managed non-League Hendon, taking them to a 3–1 FA Amateur Cup Final victory over Whitby Town at Wembley.

In 1964 Burgess had unsuccessfully applied for the vacant position of Wales team boss, but he did assume control of the national side for a World Cup qualifying match against the USSR in October 1965, when Dave Bowen was absent because of a League commitment. For the record, Wales won 2–1.

Ron Burgess of Tottenham Hotspur and Wales (right) tussles with England and Blackpool legend Stanley Matthews during an FA Cup semi-final at Villa Park, 1948. *(Getty Images)*

George EDWARDS

Position	Outside-left
Born	George Edwards, Treherbert, 2 December 1920
Height	5ft 8in
Weight	10st 8lb
Clubs	Swansea Town, Birmingham City, Cardiff City
Welsh Caps	12 Goals 2

1947 v Scotland (won 3–1), v England (lost 0–3), v N. Ireland (lost 1–2)

1948 v England (lost 0–3), v Scotland (won 2–1), v N. Ireland (won 2–0) 1 goal

1949 v N. Ireland (won 2–0) 1 goal, v Portugal (lost 2–3), v Belgium (lost 1–3), v Switzerland (lost 0–4)

1950 v England (lost 1–4), v Scotland (lost 0–2)

GEORGE EDWARDS WAS ONE of football's outstanding wingers of the 1940s. He began his career as an amateur with Swansea and made his first-team debut towards the end of the 1938/39 season. Before the outbreak of the Second World War, Edwards had won a Welsh amateur cap against England. During the hostilities he continued to play for the Swans while studying for a degree at Swansea University. When he was called up for the RAF he was stationed in the Midlands and guested for Coventry City.

In 1945/46 he played for Wales in the Victory internationals and in October 1946 he won the first of 12 full caps in Wales's 3–1 defeat of Scotland.

By now George Edwards was a Birmingham City player, having helped the Blues win the League South title in 1945/46. He also helped the St Andrew's club win the Second Division Championship in 1947/48. Although he scored only nine goals in 99 games for the Blues, they were usually very crucial strikes.

In December 1948 he joined Cardiff City for a fee of £12,000, an ideal replacement for Roy Clarke who had left Ninian Park for Manchester City in 1947. Edwards was a member of the Bluebirds team that won promotion to the First Division in 1951/52, providing a number of chances for both Chisholm and Grant. He went on to score 34 goals in 194 League games. He netted hat-tricks in the 7–1 Welsh Cup win at Bangor in March 1951 and in a 6–1 win against the Jersey Saturday League in a friendly two months later.

When he decided to leave the game in 1955, he was still Cardiff's first choice left-winger and playing well. He was later invited to join the Ninian Park club's Board of Directors, a position he held for almost 30 years.

Trevor FORD

Position	Centre-forward
Born	Trevor Ford, Swansea, 1 October 1923
Died	Swansea, 29 May 2003
Height	6ft 0in
Weight	13st 4lb

Clubs	Swansea Town, Aston Villa, Sunderland, Cardiff City, PSV Eindhoven, Newport County, Romford
Welsh Caps	38 Goals 23

1947 v Scotland (won 3–1) 1 goal, v N. Ireland (lost 1–2) 1 goal

1948 v Scotland (won 2–1) 1 goal, v N. Ireland (won 2–0)

1949 v Scotland (lost 1–3), v England (lost 0–1), v N. Ireland (won 2–0) 1 goal, v Portugal (lost 2–3) 2 goals, v Belgium (lost 1–3) 1 goal, v Switzerland (lost 0–4)

1950 v England (lost 1–4), v Scotland (lost 0–2), v Belgium (won 5–1) 3 goals, v N. Ireland (0–0)

1951 v Scotland (lost 1–3), v England (lost 2–4) 2 goals, v N. Ireland (won 2–1), v Portugal (won 2–1) 1 goal, v Switzerland (won 3–2) 2 goals

1952 v England (1–1), v Scotland (won 1–0), v Rest of the UK (won 3–2) 1 goal, v N. Ireland (won 3–0)

1953 v Scotland (lost 1–2) 1 goal, v England (lost 2–5) 2 goals, v N. Ireland (won 3–2) 1 goal, v France (lost 1–6), v Yugoslavia (lost 2–5) 2 goals

1954 v Austria (lost 0–2)

1955 v Yugoslavia (lost 1–3), v Scotland (lost 0–1), v England (lost 2–3), v N. Ireland (won 3–2)

1956 v England (won 2–1), v Scotland (lost 0–2), v Austria (lost 1–2) v N. Ireland (1–1)

1957 v Scotland (2–2) 1 goal

TREVOR FORD WAS ONE OF THE leading forwards of his day. He became Wales's leading goalscorer of all time, netting a hat-trick in a 5–1 win over Belgium and two goals against England at Wembley in 1952. By the time he played the last of his 38 internationals against Scotland in 1957, he had a record 23 goals to his credit.

During the Second World War, Ford served in the Royal Artillery. With the unit team short of a centre-forward, his sergeant-major decided to try him up front.

Having signed for his home-town team of Swansea in 1942, Ford graduated into the Swans' first team during the latter stages of the hostilities. In 1945/46 he scored 44 goals in 41 games for Swansea and gained a place in the Welsh side for the Victory international of the season against N. Ireland at Ninian Park. Despite a disappointing debut, Ford kept his place in the side for the opening international of the following season and scored his first goal for his country in a 3–1 win over Scotland at Wrexham.

Not surprisingly, a number of First Division clubs began to show an interest in Trevor Ford. After scoring nine goals in the opening six games of the 1946/47 season, he joined Aston Villa for a fee of £12,000. He made his Villa debut in a 2–0 win at Highbury in January 1947 and, in nine games that season, scored nine goals. In terms of goals scored, his best seasons were 1947/48 and 1949/50, when he netted 18 in each campaign. On 27 December 1948 he scored four goals as Villa beat local rivals Wolverhampton Wanderers 5–1.

While with Villa, Ford received offers to play in Colombia, whose sides were out of the jurisdiction of the international football federation (FIFA) and so were able to pay much higher wages. He was definitely interested, but when Wales team-mate Roy Paul returned dissatisfied from a trip to South America, he decided against a move. Ford received another offer from a Portuguese club while on international duty in

Lisbon, but again rejected the overture.

However, in October 1950 Ford left Villa Park after scoring 61 goals in 128 games and signed for Sunderland for a fee of £30,000.

Ford scored a hat-trick on his home debut as the Wearsiders beat Sheffield Wednesday 5–1. He top-scored for the North-East club over the next two seasons, netting a hat-trick in a 4–1 home win over Chelsea in February 1952 and four goals in a 5–2 defeat of Manchester City at Maine Road in November 1952. He netted another treble at the start of the 1953/54 campaign when Arsenal were beaten 4–1, but a few weeks later, after scoring 70 goals in 117 games, he joined Cardiff City for what was then the Bluebirds' record fee of £30,000.

Ford became a firm favourite with the Cardiff supporters. Though not as prolific a scorer as in his early playing days, he did net four goals in two Welsh Cup games as Pembroke Borough were beaten 7–0 in 1954/55 and 9–0 in 1955/56. He had scored 59 goals in 119 outings for the Bluebirds when in 1955 he fell out with Trevor Morris following the City manager's decision to play him at inside-right.

Trevor Ford netted a hat-trick in a 5–1 win over Belgium in November 1949. *(Western Mail)*

After leaving Ninian Park, Ford was banned *sine die* by the Football League following his revelations about Sunderland Football Club in his autobiography *I Lead the Attack*, which was serialised in a Sunday newspaper. Although he was later reinstated, he was banned again when Football League secretary Alan Hardaker uncovered an illegal payment of £100 by Sunderland to Ford.

He went abroad and spent three successful years in Holland with PSV Eindhoven, where in 1957/58 he scored a remarkable 51 goals. He returned to these shores after the suspension was lifted to play for Newport County and later non-League Romford, but sadly a knee injury curtailed his playing career.

Ernie JONES

Position	Winger
Born	William Ernest Arthur Jones, Swansea, 12 November 1920
Height	5ft 9in
Weight	10st 13lb
Clubs	Bolton Wanderers, Swansea Town, Tottenham Hotspur, Southampton, Bristol City, Rhyl Town, Poole Town
Welsh Caps	4
	1947 v Scotland (won 3–1), v England (lost 0–3)
	1949 v Scotland (lost 1–3), v England (lost 0–1)

ERNIE 'ALPHABET' JONES started his career as an amateur with his home-town team of Swansea, but turned professional with First Division Bolton Wanderers. Unable to make the grade at Burnden Park, Jones returned to the Vetch Field midway through the hostilities to rejoin Swansea. During the war years, Jones quickly built up a reputation as a fast and clever attacking winger, able to play on either flank.

He won the first of four international caps for Wales in the first full international after the war as Wales beat Scotland 3–1 at the Racecourse Ground. He had collected a second against England before moving to join Tottenham Hotspur in the summer of 1947.

He spent only two full seasons at White Hart Lane, winning two more Welsh caps before finding his place taken by Les Medley. Jones had scored 16 goals in 65 first-team outings for Spurs. He then moved to Southampton in May 1949 as part of the deal that took Alf Ramsey to White Hart Lane.

Jones served the Saints for over two years before a transfer to Bristol City, where he finished his League career. He retired from first-class football at the end of the 1953/54 season and managed Rhyl Town, where he even helped design and erect the floodlights! He then played one game for Poole Town before spending two years coaching the juniors at The Dell.

Ernie Jones then moved back to Bolton, where he worked as an engineer for Hawker Siddeley. A member of the Association of Inventors and Innovators, he has since remained active in retirement designing water leisure products.

Aubrey POWELL

Position	Inside-forward	
Born	Aubrey Powell, Swansea 19 April 1918	
Height	5ft 5in	
Weight	10st 4lb	
Clubs	Cwm Wanderers, Swansea Town, Leeds United, Everton, Birmingham City, Wellington Town	
Welsh Caps	8	Goals 1
	1947 v Scotland (won 3–1), v England (lost 0–3)	
	1948 v England (lost 0–3), v Scotland (won 2–1), v N. Ireland (won 2–0)	

1949 v England (lost 0–1)
1950 v Belgium (won 5–1)
1951 v Scotland (lost 1–3) 1 goal

AUBREY POWELL WAS ONE of a number of players who successfully revived their League careers with Leeds United after the war, during which he served in Belgium. He soon gained recognition by Wales.

He had begun his career playing for Cwm Wanderers before joining Swansea as an amateur. His performances for the Vetch Field club soon attracted the bigger clubs, and in November 1955 Powell left South Wales to sign for Leeds United. On arriving at Elland Road, Powell made an immediate impact but, after breaking his leg in United's game at Preston North End in March 1937, he was told by the doctors that he would never play again.

Powell fought back to give the Yorkshire club stout service and collect full Welsh honours. On his return to the Leeds starting line-up, he formed a highly effective partnership with David Cochrane until the outbreak of war. During the hostilities, Powell appeared in 126 games for Leeds and for Wales in wartime internationals, winning his first official cap against Scotland.

In the summer of 1948, after he appeared in 119 League and Cup games for Leeds, the hard-up club sold him to Everton for a fee of £10,000. Injuries again hampered his progress at Goodison Park and, after a little over a season, he moved on to Birmingham. Powell was unable to settle at St Andrew's, where again injuries and a loss of form reduced his first-team appearances to just a handful.

He then tried his luck in non-League football with Wellington Town before hanging up his boots. He later worked as a carpenter before returning to Leeds to work as a representative for a confectionery company.

Ivor POWELL

Position	Wing-half
Born	Ivor Verdun Powell, Merthyr Tydfil, 5 July 1916
Height	5ft 8in
Weight	11st 6lb
Clubs	Bargoed, Queen's Park Rangers, Aston Villa, Port Vale, Barry Town, Bradford City
Welsh Caps	8
	1947 v England (lost 0–3)
	1948 v England (lost 0–3), v Scotland (won 2–1), v N. Ireland (won 2–0)
	1949 v Belgium (lost 1–3)
	1950 v Scotland (lost 0–2), v Belgium (won 5–1)
	1951 v Scotland (lost 1–3)

IVOR POWELL WAS ONE of the few Third Division players to win an international cap.

He played the last of his four wartime internationals for Wales against England in September 1943 before being posted to India, where he served as a PT instructor in the RAF. In this match, he had the misfortune to break his collarbone and was substituted by England's Stan Mortensen.

Ivor Powell began his Football League career with Queen's Park Rangers, whom he joined as an amateur in 1936 before signing professional forms the following year. He made his first-team debut for the Shepherd's Bush side in January 1939 and would obviously have played substantially more games for the club had the war not intervened.

A stocky, competitive wing-half, Powell made the first of his eight international appearances for Wales in the game against England, the first after the hostilities. He was an important member of the Rangers' side for the first two seasons of League football after the war, helping the club win the Third Division (South) Championship in 1947/48. However, in December 1948, after appearing in 157 games for the London club, he moved to Aston Villa for a fee of £17,000 – a record for both clubs.

Powell made his Villa debut in a goalless draw against Liverpool, and he appeared in 82 consecutive games for the Midlands club before he was ruled out by injury. He then joined Port Vale as player-manager but he was not well liked by the players at Vale Park, whom he is said to have tried 'to rule by fear'. His contract was terminated in November 1951 with Vale at the foot of the Third Division (South). He then moved to Barry Town before becoming the player-manager of Bradford City. The fans turned against him after he was forced into selling some of the club's best players. After a spell as Leeds United's trainer he took over as manager of Carlisle United.

He led the Cumbrians to their first-ever promotion before later serving as the coach of PAOK Salonika of Greece and the head football coach at the University of Bath.

Stan RICHARDS

Position	Centre-forward
Born	Stanley Verdun Richards, Cardiff, 21 January 1917
Died	Cardiff, 19 April 1987
Height	5ft 10in
Weight	11st 0lb
Clubs	Tufnell Park, Cardiff Corries, Cardiff City, Swansea Town
Welsh Caps	1
	1947 v England (lost 0–3)

STAN RICHARDS HEARD ABOUT his selection for Wales, in place of the injured Trevor Ford, in a telephone call to a Cardiff cinema. When he arrived at Maine Road for the match against England, he found that, in a rush to pack his kit, he had forgotten his boots.

Although he was born in Cardiff, Stan Richards played his early football in London with Tufnell Park before returning to South Wales to play for Cardiff Corries. Billy McCandless was alerted and, in the summer of 1946, Richards joined Cardiff City. He scored on his Football League debut in a 2–1 defeat at Norwich City, the first of 30 League goals in that 1946/47 season. His total, which included a hat-trick in a 6–1 home win over the Canaries on 28 December 1946, was a club record for the most League goals by an individual in a season until 2002/03, when it was beaten by Rob Earnshaw.

He was a great favourite with the Cardiff crowd, who would often shoot 'Open the score Richards and nod one in', illustrating the impact he had made in such a short space of time.

Surprisingly, he won only one Welsh cap, and that was against England in November 1946. In 1947/48 he suffered from a series of niggling injuries. At the end of that season, in which he had scored 40 goals in just 57 League games, he was allowed to join his former manager Billy McCandless at Swansea Town.

Although he was still experiencing problems with his knee, Richards made a magnificent contribution to Swansea's Third Division (South) Championship-winning season of 1948/49. He scored 26 goals in 32 games, including four in the defeat of Swindon Town at a muddy Vetch Field. Despite periods when his knees were so bad that he couldn't even train, Richards scored 35 goals in 65 games for Swansea before being forced to retire.

Alf SHERWOOD

Position	Full-back
Born	Alfred Thomas Sherwood, Aberdare, 13 November 1923
Died	Cowbridge, 12 March 1990
Height	5ft 8in
Weight	11st 0lb
Clubs	Aberaman, Cardiff City, Newport County
Welsh Caps	41

1947 v England (lost 0–3), v N. Ireland (lost 1–2)

1948 v Scotland (won 2–1), v N. Ireland (won 2–0)

1949 v Scotland (lost 1–3), v England (lost 0–1), v N. Ireland (won 2–0), v Portugal (lost 2–3), v Switzerland (lost 0–4)

1950 v England (lost 1–4), v Scotland (lost 0–2), v Belgium (won 5–1), v N. Ireland (0–0)

1951 v Scotland (lost 1–3), v England (lost 2–4), v N. Ireland (won 2–1), v Portugal (won 2–1), v Switzerland (won 3–2)

1952 v England (1–1), v Scotland (won 1–0), v Rest of the UK (won 3–2), v N. Ireland (won 3–0)

1953 v Scotland (lost 1–2), v England (lost 2–5), v N. Ireland (won 3–2), v France (lost 1–6), v Yugoslavia (lost 2–5)

1954 v England (lost 1–4), v Scotland (3–3), v N. Ireland (lost 1–2), v Austria (lost 0–2)

1955 v Yugoslavia (lost 1–3), v Scotland (lost 0–1), v England (lost 2–3), v N. Ireland (won 3–2)

1956 v England (won 2–1), v Scotland (lost 0–2), v Austria (lost 1–2), v N. Ireland (1–1)

1957 v Scotland (2–2), v England (lost 1–3)

ALF SHERWOOD WAS A MAGNIFICENT servant to Welsh football. Between 1949 and 1953 he made 23 consecutive appearances for his country, many as captain.

A master of the sliding tackle, Alf Sherwood had pace, tackling ability and positional sense that made him one of the best full-backs in the Football League and the one defender who could subdue the great Stanley Matthews.

Sherwood played for his home-town team of Aberaman, alongside wartime greats such as Dai Astley and Bryn Jones. He had gained Welsh schoolboy honours at both soccer and cricket. He appeared in the same side as Trevor Ford and Gilbert Parkhouse, the latter going on to play for Glamorgan and England as an opening batsman.

Sherwood played his early football as a wing-half and it was in that position that he first came to Cardiff City's attention. He was playing against the Bluebirds in a wartime game at Ninian Park and was so impressive that City manager Cyril Spiers signed him there and then. That was in 1941 and, over the next few years of wartime football, he turned out whenever he could get away from working down the pits.

During a game against Lovells Athletic, Cardiff found themselves short at the back. Sherwood agreed to have a go and, after performing as if he'd always played in this position, he stayed there for the rest of his career.

Sherwood played in 140 wartime games for Cardiff. He made his Football League debut in a 2–1 defeat at Norwich City on the opening day of the 1946/47 season. Missing just one game, he helped the Bluebirds win the Third Division (South) Championship campaign as they finished nine points ahead of runners-up Queen's Park Rangers.

Sherwood had played in an earlier Victory international against N. Ireland, but was given his first full Welsh cap when he was selected to play against England at Maine

Alf Sherwood (far left) of Cardiff and Wales sees the ball to safety in a match against England. (*Western Mail*)

Road in October 1946. Although his full-back partner in that match was captain Billy Hughes of Birmingham, it was Arsenal's Walley Barnes who was to become his partner for the next six years of international football.

Following Fred Stansfield's departure to Newport County, where he later became manager, Sherwood's defensive partner at Ninian Park was Ron Stitfall. Sherwood was appointed the Bluebirds' captain and in 1951/52 led the side into the top flight after finishing runners-up in the Second Division to Sheffield Wednesday.

He was also the stand-in goalkeeper for both Cardiff City and Wales. When the Bluebirds travelled to Anfield for an end-of-season game in April 1954, the home side had to win to keep their First Division status. City were 1–0 up when Sherwood, who had taken over in goal from the injured Ron Howells, had to face a penalty from Liverpool's Scottish international winger Billy Liddell. He saved it and Liverpool were relegated. For Wales he replaced the injured Jack Kelsey in what was his last international appearance in the match against England at Wembley in November 1956. Once again, he produced a series of magnificent saves but Wales lost 3–1.

Sherwood had appeared in 383 games for Cardiff City when it became apparent that he was no longer part of manager Trevor Morris's plans. He left Ninian Park in the summer of 1956 to join Newport County where he confounded his critics not only by playing in 205 games for the Somerton Park club but by winning two more caps for Wales.

In the early 1960s Sherwood spent three summers in New York in an attempt to promote the game in the United States. On his return to the British Isles, he had a brief spell as manager of Barry Town. After ending his involvement with the game he worked in insurance before being employed as a security officer with the National Coal Board.

Mal GRIFFITHS

Position	Outside-right
Born	William Malwyn Griffiths, Merthyr Tydfil, 8 March 1919
Died	Wigston Magna, Leicestershire, 5 April 1969
Height	5ft 9in
Weight	11st 2lb
Clubs	Merthyr Tydfil, Arsenal, Leicester City, Burton Albion
Welsh Caps	11 Goals 2
	1947 v N. Ireland (lost 1–2)
	1949 v Portugal (lost 2–3), v Belgium (lost 1–3)
	1950 v England (lost 1–4) 1 goal, v Scotland (lost 0–2), v Belgium (won 5–1)
	1951 v England (lost 2–4), v N. Ireland (won 2–1), v Portugal (won 2–1) 1 goal,
	v Switzerland (won 3–2)
	1954 v Austria (lost 0–2)

MAL GRIFFITHS WAS PLUCKED from Welsh junior football by Arsenal in May 1936. He spent seven months at Highbury before being loaned out to Margate, the Gunners' nursery club, for experience. On signing professional forms, he made his

League debut for the Gunners against Leicester City in February 1938, going on to score five goals in nine games as the North London club raced to the First Division title that year. However, rivalries for first-team places at Highbury were fierce, and only a bargain £800 transfer to Leicester City opened the door to regular first-team football.

This must have been one of the best investments made by any club, as Mal Griffiths was still a first-team regular at Filbert Street some 18 years later. Griffiths scored 76 goals in 409 League and Cup games for Leicester. He 'lost' one League appearance and one goal when the 1939/40 season was abandoned after only three fixtures. Griffiths became the first senior player to be automatically conscripted (into the Welsh Regiment), but the Foxes somehow contrived to lose touch with him during the war.

Given the list of clubs for whom he guested – Cardiff City, Aldershot, Fulham, Bournemouth, Chelsea, Brighton and Southampton – this was perhaps not so surprising. Eventually, a club director was sent to Wales to persuade Mal to resume his full-time career with Leicester.

Thereafter, Mal Griffiths's consistency made him an automatic choice in an ever-changing Leicester forward line. His steady record peaked at two critical times – he scored City's first-ever goal at Wembley in the 1949 FA Cup Final (they were ultimately defeated by Portsmouth), and he had his highest scoring season (11 goals) in 1953/54, helping Leicester take the Second Division Championship. At the end of their next promotion campaign, Leicester played an invited International XI in a testimonial for Mal Griffiths, who had represented his own country 11 times.

Mal Griffiths later ended his career with a spell at Burton Albion before becoming landlord of the Queen's Head in Wigston Magna, Leicestershire.

Jack HUMPHREYS

Position	Centre-half
Born	John Vaughan Humphreys, Llandudno, 13 January 1920
Died	Llandudno, 14 September 1954
Height	5ft 9in
Weight	11st 5lb
Clubs	Llandudno Town, Everton
Welsh Caps	1
	1947 v N. Ireland (lost 1–2)

JACK HUMPHREYS, THE SON OF A North Wales schoolmaster, was one of a number of Welsh international players produced by the Friars School in Bangor. The records show that in one school match Humphreys, playing at centre-forward, netted 12 goals!

After school he went to Loughborough College and trained to be a PE teacher. While at Loughborough, he captained the university Athletic Union before seeing service in France as a bombardier. Humphreys began his football career by playing in the Welsh League (North) for his home-town team of Llandudno, where his performances attracted the attention of a number of top-flight clubs.

Towards the end of the hostilities, Humphreys signed professional forms for Everton following a period at Goodison Park as an amateur. A powerful, defensive player, Humphreys was unfortunate to be a contemporary of Tommy G. Jones, and in four seasons on Merseyside made only 53 League appearances. He was eventually transfer-listed by the Blues and valued at £10,000, but he returned to his home-town club without a fee changing hands.

In June 1950 Humphreys repeatedly turned down an offer of a £4,000 signing-on fee and £100 a month from Millionaires Club of Bogota.

Jack Humphreys tragically died at the age of 34. His stepson Gerry Humphreys went on to play for Everton and Crystal Palace in the 1960s and 1970s and represented Wales at under-23 level.

Bill SHORTT

Position	Goalkeeper
Born	William Warren Shortt, Wrexham, 13 October 1920
Height	5ft 9in
Weight	13st 0lb
Clubs	Hoole Alexandra, Chester City, Plymouth Argyle
Welsh Caps	12
	1947 v N. Ireland (lost 1–2)
	1950 v Belgium (won 5–1), v N. Ireland (0–0)
	1952 v England (1–1), v Scotland (won 1–0), v Rest of the UK (won 3–2), v N. Ireland (won 3–0)
	1953 v Scotland (lost 1–2), v England (lost 2–5), v N. Ireland (won 3–2), v France (lost 1–6), v Yugoslavia (lost 2–5)

BILL SHORTT'S FIRST GAME FOR Wales was against Northern Ireland, when he deputised for Cyril Sidlow, who was touring the United States with his club Liverpool. Thereafter, he competed with Sidlow for the goalkeeping spot. In November 1952 Shortt realised his footballing ambition to play at Wembley when he was selected to face England.

Although Trevor Ford scored twice, Shortt conceded five goals as England romped home 5–2.

Shortt began his first-class career with Chester City, but the outbreak of the Second World War prevented him from making any League appearances for the then Sealand Road club. In February 1946 Shortt joined Plymouth Argyle and over the next ten seasons went on to appear in 342 League games for the Pilgrims.

Despite his rotundity, Shortt was a cool and confident goalkeeper. He was a loyal and most capable servant to the West Country club, and uniquely featured in the teams which won both the Home International Championship and the Third Division (South) title in the same season, 1951/52.

Weight was always a problem for Shortt and, prior to the start of that most successful of campaigns, the Plymouth physiotherapist advised 'a course of foam baths, dieting and hard training'. The strategy certainly paid off, as he slimmed down to 12 stone.

Shortt's international career came to an end after the close season tour of 1953 as he lost his place to Ron Howells and later Jack Kelsey after conceding 11 goals in two games.

Bill Shortt later became landlord of the Golden Hind in Hartley, Plymouth, where he had his international caps on display in the public bar.

Billy MORRIS

Position	Outside-left
Born	William Morris, Colwyn Bay, 30 July 1918
Died	Bodelwyddan near Rhyl, 31 December 2002
Height	5ft 4in
Weight	9st 7lb
Clubs	Llandulas, Llandudno Town, Burnley
Welsh Caps	5
	1947 v N. Ireland (lost 1–2)
	1949 v England (lost 0–1)
	1952 v Scotland (won 1–0), v Rest of the UK (won 3–2), v N. Ireland (won 3–0)

BILLY MORRIS WAS THE FIRST of Burnley's three full Welsh internationals since the war and the only one to spend his entire first-class career at Turf Moor.

He joined Llandudno Town of the Welsh League in 1938 from a junior club in Colwyn Bay, and almost immediately was the subject of much interest from scouts of the League's top clubs. Morris was also watched by the Welsh Amateur International electors but, although he was invited for trials, he was passed over. But Burnley realised his potential when in January 1939 he signed for the Clarets.

Although he went straight into the club's Second Division side, he hardly had time to get his League career off the ground before the war intervened and he was off overseas to serve his country in the conflict with Japan.

Billy Morris was one of just four Burnley players in the League side at the start of the 1946/47 season who had appeared for the club before the war. He was deceptively quick and around the six-yard box proved to be a valuable asset as he was in the right place when goalscoring opportunities arose. With the Clarets heading for both Wembley and promotion, he was playing so well that he could not be overlooked by his country again, and in April 1947 he made his full international debut against N. Ireland.

Like many other players, Billy Morris lost a number of important years because of the war and would most certainly have won many more than the five full caps he did win.

In 1952 he joined Burnley's coaching staff and was the 'A' team trainer for eight years before being released to take up the manager's position at Wrexham. The appointment was short-lived and, after a disappointing season in the Fourth Division, he left to run a guesthouse in Llandudno. After another brief spell back at the helm at the Racecourse Ground he left Wrexham and football, this time for good.

Walley BARNES

Position	Full-back
Born	Walley Barnes, Brecknock, 16 January 1920
Died	Hammersmith, 4 September 1975
Height	5ft 10in
Weight	11st 7lb
Clubs	Portsmouth, Southampton, Arsenal
Welsh Caps	22 Goals 1

1948 v England (lost 0–3), v Scotland (won 2–1), v N. Ireland (won 2–0)
1949 v Scotland (lost 1–3), v England (lost 0–1), v N. Ireland (won 2–0)
1950 v England (lost 1–4), v Scotland (lost 0–2), v Belgium (won 5–1), v N. Ireland (0–0)
1951 v Scotland (lost 1–3), v England (lost 2–4), v N. Ireland (won 2–1), v Portugal (won 2–1)
1952 v England (1–1), v Scotland (won 1–0), v Rest of the UK (won 3–2), v N. Ireland (won 3–0) 1 goal
1954 v England (lost 1–4), v Scotland (3–3)
1955 v Yugoslavia (lost 1–3), v Scotland (lost 0–1)

ONE OF ARSENAL'S GREATEST-EVER full-backs, Walley Barnes captained Wales on many occasions and always turned in a sound and reliable performance.

He was spotted while playing as an amateur inside-forward for Southampton, having played previously for the Saints' south coast rivals, Portsmouth. Arsenal signed him in the summer of 1943 and during the war years he played in every position except centre-forward, including a match in goal against Brighton which the Gunners won 3–1. Barnes served as a sergeant-major in the Army Physical Training Corps. At the end of the war he damaged his knee in a PT display and it was thought his career was over.

However, with guts and determination, he worked his way back to full fitness and in November 1946 he made his Football League debut for the Gunners in a 2–0 defeat at Preston North End. He was then 26 years old. Almost immediately, the popular full-back won a regular place in Arsenal's League side and in 1947/48 won a Championship medal as well as the first of 22 Welsh caps when he played against England at Ninian Park. Following the injury to Laurie Scott, Barnes switched from playing left-back to right-back.

During 1949/50 Barnes became the club's regular penalty-taker, scoring his first in a 2–1 win at West Bromwich Albion. That season saw Barnes captain Wales for the first time as well as winning an FA Cup winners' medal as Arsenal beat Liverpool 2–0. In 1951/52 he missed only one League game as the Gunners finished third in the First Division. He played a big part in helping the club reach the FA Cup Final, where they met Newcastle United.

In the 33rd minute of this match, Walley Barnes tore his knee ligaments when he caught his studs in the Wembley turf and twisted his leg. Though the ten-man Arsenal side battled gamely, the Magpies won 1–0, courtesy of a George Robledo goal.

The injury kept Barnes out of action for the entire 1952/53 season, but after working hard to regain full fitness he returned to the Arsenal side for the visit of

Chelsea to Highbury in September 1953. That season, Barnes scored his last penalty for the club in a 3–2 defeat of Preston North End, the club against whom Barnes had made his League debut. But his knee problems were to persist, and in September 1955 he eventually gave up his struggle, asking for his contract to be cancelled.

Barnes was appointed Wales team manager in May 1954, but resigned from his post in October 1956 to become the BBC's football adviser. He served the BBC in many capacities up to his untimely death at the age of 55 in September 1975.

George LOWRIE

Position	Centre-forward
Born	George Lowrie, Rhondda, 19 December 1919
Died	Bristol, 3 May 1989
Height	5ft 9in
Weight	11st 7lb
Clubs	Tonypandy, Swansea City, Preston North End, Coventry City, Newcastle United, Bristol City, Lovells Athletic.
Welsh Caps	4 Goals 2
	1948 v England (lost 0–3), v Scotland (won 2–1) 1 goal, v N. Ireland (won 2–0) 1 goal
	1949 v Portugal (lost 2–3)

DURING THE WAR YEARS, George Lowrie netted a headlining hat-trick for Wales against England at Wembley, scoring regularly in his nine wartime international appearances.

Lowrie played his early football with Swansea Town but, after being unable to break into the Vetch Field club's first team, he left to join Preston North End. He had played in only four League games for the Lilywhites when Coventry City manager Harry Storer paid £1,750 for his services in the summer of 1939.

During the Second World War he guested for Northampton Town and, while at the County Ground, won the first of his wartime caps. He returned to Highfield Road in 1942 and over the next few seasons of wartime football scored 48 goals in 74 games, including four goals in each of the games against Northampton Town (Home 5–0) and Notts County (Home 7–0).

When League football resumed in 1946/47, Lowrie was Coventry's leading goalscorer, with 29 goals in 36 games. His total included four goals in the 5–1 defeat of Sheffield Wednesday and hat-tricks against Newport County (Home 6–0), Swansea Town (Home 3–2), Bury (Home 3–1) and Newport County again in the FA Cup (Home 5–2).

He began the 1947/48 season in great style, scoring all four goals in a 4–1 win over Luton Town on the opening day of the season and a hat-trick in the club's third match as Brentford were beaten 4–1 at Griffin Park. Later in the season he netted another four goals in a 5–0 defeat of Bradford. But as First Division scouts flocked to Highfield Road to see his prolific marksmanship, his form dipped and he was rested.

He had scored 47 goals in 58 League games for Coventry when he left to join Newcastle United for a club record fee of £18,500. Unable to settle in the North-East, he moved to Bristol City. At Ashton Gate he had cruel luck with injury, a broken leg almost finishing his career. He later returned to Highfield Road to see out his League career with Coventry before playing non-League football for Lovells Athletic.

Sid THOMAS

Position	Winger
Born	David Sidney Thomas, Machynlleth, 12 November 1919
Height	5ft 6in
Weight	10st 5lb
Clubs	Treharris, Fulham, Bristol City
Welsh Caps	4
	1948 v England (lost 0–3), v Scotland (won 2–1), v N. Ireland (won 2–0)
	1949 v Scotland (lost 1–3)

DIMINUTIVE WINGER SID THOMAS played his early football for Welsh League club Treharris, his outstanding touchline displays attracting a number of the game's top clubs. It was Fulham manager Jack Peart who won the race for his signature, Thomas arriving at Craven Cottage in the summer of 1938.

Though he played in a handful of wartime games for the Cottagers, he had to wait eight years before making his Football League debut for the club – a 1–1 home draw against London rivals Tottenham Hotspur in November 1946. Though Sid Thomas was never a regular in the Fulham side, his performances when he did turn out for the Cottagers first team led to his winning four full caps for Wales. Thomas had scored four goals in 61 outings for Fulham when, in the summer of 1950, he was transferred to Bristol City for a fee of £9,000.

After playing in just 13 games for the Robins, Thomas was taken seriously ill with tuberculosis and forced to quit the game. Following a long dispute between Bristol City and Fulham over the transfer fee, the Ashton Gate club eventually paid up in full.

Billy BAKER

Position	Left-half
Born	William George Baker, Penrhiwceiber, 3 October 1920
Height	5ft 8in
Weight	11st 0lb
Clubs	Troedrhiw, Cardiff City, Ipswich Town, Ton Pentre
Welsh Caps	1
	1948 v N. Ireland (won 2–0)

BILLY BAKER WAS A REGULAR 12th man for Wales between 1946 and 1950, and many felt that he deserved greater international rewards than his solitary cap against N. Ireland in 1948.

A former coal miner, Billy Baker had trials with a number of clubs including Arsenal and Wolverhampton Wanderers before joining Cardiff City in the summer of 1938. Baker made his debut for the Bluebirds at outside-right in a 2–0 home win over Northampton Town in February 1939, but had made only three appearances when the Second World War intervened.

After appearing in 22 wartime fixtures in 1940/41, Baker went to fight for his country but was captured by the Japanese and was a prisoner of war for almost four years.

When League football resumed in 1946/47, Baker was converted to wing-half and, over the next nine seasons, went on to make 324 first-team appearances. In 1948 he was capped by Wales in the match against N. Ireland and in 1951/52 was instrumental in helping the Bluebirds win promotion to the First Division. His only goal in that campaign came in the 3–0 home win over South Wales rivals, Swansea Town.

Baker was the only Cardiff City player to have played before the Second World War and enjoy a lengthy career after it. He severed his ties with the Ninian Park club in June 1955, when he signed for Ipswich Town. He spent two seasons at Portman Road, making 20 League appearances before returning to Wales to play non-League football for Ton Pentre.

Billy LUCAS

Position	Wing-half/Inside-forward
Born	William Henry Lucas, Newport, 15 January 1918
Height	5ft 6in
Weight	11st 6lb
Clubs	Treharris, Wolverhampton Wanderers, Swindon Town, Swansea Town, Newport County
Welsh Caps	7
	1949 v Scotland (lost 1–3), v N. Ireland (won 2–0), v Portugal (lost 2–3), v Belgium (lost 1–3), v Switzerland (lost 0–4)
	1950 v England (lost 1–4)
	1951 v England (lost 2–4)

IN THE FIRST OF HIS EIGHT wartime international appearances for Wales in 1942, Billy Lucas scored the only goal of the game against England at Ninian Park before a crowd of 30,000.

Although he was on the books of Wolverhampton Wanderers, he failed to make the grade at Molineux and it was with Swindon Town that he began his League career. He had just established himself in the Robins' side when war broke out and interrupted his career. There was compensations, as he played in eight wartime and two Victory internationals for Wales. After the war ended he resumed his career with Swindon Town.

In March 1948, Swansea manager Billy McCandless paid a club record transfer fee of £11,000 to bring Lucas to the Vetch Field as the missing link in a side that would claim the Third Division (South) Championship the following season.

Lucas's early displays for the Swans led to the first of seven full caps for Wales when in October 1948 he played against Scotland at Ninian Park. He was able to play at both wing-half and inside-forward, and went on to score 35 goals in 20 League games for the Swans before leaving the Vetch in December 1953 to becom player-manager of Newport County. The value of his leadership qualities was onl realised when he left the club. At Somerton Park, Lucas was in charge of one of th smallest squads in the Football League and had to sell to survive. He resigned hi post in April 1961 but was reappointed less than a year later when Bobby Evan was sacked.

In February 1967 he returned to the Vetch as manager but the Swans wer struggling to avoid relegation from the Third Division. Unfortunately he was unabl to save them but he was instrumental in bringing a number of young players to th club.

He resigned in March 1969 but returned to Somerton Park for a third spell and i the first six months of this period worked without wages. In 1972/73 County misse out on promotion on goal average, but Lucas left in 1975 to give more time to hi business. He later became general manager at Newport County.

Roy PAUL

Position	Wing-half
Born	Roy Paul, Ton Pentre, 18 April 1920
Died	Treorchy, 21 May 2002
Height	5ft 10in
Weight	12st 0lb
Clubs	Ton Pentre, Swansea Town, Manchester City, Worcester City
Welsh Caps	33 Goals 1

1949 v Scotland (lost 1–3), v England (lost 0–1), v N. Ireland (won 2–0), v Portugal (lost 2–3), v Switzerland (lost 0–4)

1950 v England (lost 1–4), v Scotland (lost 0–2), v Belgium (won 5–1) 1 goal, v N. Ireland (0–0)

1951 v Scotland (lost 1–3), v England (lost 2–4), v N. Ireland (won 2–1), v Portugal (won 2–1), v Switzerland (won 3–2)

1952 v England (1–1), v Scotland (won 1–0), v Rest of the UK (won 3–2), v N. Ireland (won 3–0)

1953 v Scotland (lost 1–2), v England (lost 2–5), v N. Ireland (won 3–2), v France (lost 1–6), v Yugoslavia (lost 2–5)

1954 v England (lost 1–4), v Scotland (3–3), v N. Ireland (lost 1–2)

1955 v Yugoslavia (lost 1–3), v Scotland (lost 0–1), v England (lost 2–3)

1956 v England (won 2–1), v Scotland (lost 0–2), v Austria (lost 1–2), v N. Ireland (1–1)

ROY PAUL WAS ONE OF THE GREATEST footballers to hail from the Rhondda durin the 1940s. He was a forceful half-back who captained Manchester City to the FA Cu and made 33 appearances for Wales.

While working down the mines he played football at the weekends for a number c local sides. His performances attracted the attention of Swansea, who, after acquirin his services as an amateur, offered him professional terms. Although the Secon World War intervened before the strong-tackling Paul could make his League debu

oy Paul helped Wales to a 2–1 win over England in his final season of International
ootball. *(Lancashire Evening Post)*

he was a regular in the club's wartime games. In 1940 he was called up for National Service and, after being posted to Devon, guested for Exeter City. Following his particularly impressive display against Arsenal, his commanding officer sent him on a physical training course and he spent the rest of the war working as a PT instructor for the Marines in India.

At the end of the war Paul returned to the Vetch and was a member of the Swansea side that was relegated to the Third Division at the end of the 1946/47 season. However, two years later he was instrumental in the club winning the Third Division (South) Championship, his performances leading to his first full cap for Wales. While with Swansea, his career almost took on an unlikely turn. British stars Neil Franklin and Charlie Mitten were leading an exodus to Colombia, where big money was on offer, and this was soon extended to Roy Paul. He was offered £3,000 to join Colombian club Millionairos but decided against joining them. Swansea were not impressed by Paul's trip to South America and transfer-listed the Welsh international.

A number of top-flight clubs were interested in him, but it was Manchester City that paid £25,000 for his services in the summer of 1950.

Paul was immediately appointed club captain. He led City to the runners-up spot in the Second Division, behind champions Preston North End, and promotion to the top flight. After City won only two of their first ten matches in the First Division, manager Les McDowall signed Don Revie and Ivor Broadis and they, along with skipper Paul, were the main reason City remained in the First Division.

They reached the FA Cup Final at Wembley in 1955 only to lose 3–1 to Newcastle United. After the match, the City skipper vowed that they would be back the following year, and so it proved as the Maine Road club beat Birmingham 3–1. Thus Roy Paul became one of the few Welshmen to captain an FA Cup-winning side. In the close season he brought the FA Cup home to the Rhondda, fulfilling the promise he had made to take the trophy back to his native valleys. He woke one morning to find that he had left his car window open with the FA Cup lying on the back seat!

By the time of City's 1956 triumph, Paul's international career was over. His 33 caps included a single goal in a 5–1 win over Belgium, but the highlight had come in his final season of international football, when his eighth and last meeting with England brought a 2–1 win at Ninian Park, his only victory against the old enemy.

Paul eventually left Maine Road on the advice of a doctor because his son had a breathing disorder and it was felt that he would be helped by moving away from the heavily industrialised city of Manchester.

Paul's football career wound down with two seasons as player-manager of Worcester City. He guided the club to an FA Cup fourth-round tie with Sheffield United but found the strain of travelling from South Wales too great. On returning to the Rhondda he became player-manager of Garw Athletic and worked as a lorry driver until he retired in the mid-1980s.

red STANSFIELD

osition	Centre-half
orn	Frederick Stansfield, Cardiff, 12 December 1917
eight	5ft 10in
Veight	12st 0lb
lubs	Grange Athletic, Cardiff City, Newport County
Velsh Caps	1
	1949 v Scotland (lost 1–3)

ENTRE-HALF FRED STANSFIELD might have won more than his solitary cap for Vales against Scotland in October 1948 but for a broken leg sustained against arnsley some three months later.

Because of the Second World War, Fred Stansfield did not turn professional with ardiff City until he was 24 years old. He made his League debut at centre-half in a –1 defeat at Norwich City on the opening day of the 1946/47 season and missed st one game in that campaign as City won the Third Division (South) hampionship. His form the following season, as City pressed for another promotion, as so impressive that he was capped by Wales at full international level for the match gainst Scotland.

A month later, Stansfield scored his only League goal for the Bluebirds in a 4–3 ome defeat at the hands of Chesterfield. Then came the tragic injury in the match gainst Barnsley. Stansfield, who had played in 111 first team games, was unable to reak back into the side as Cyril Spiers, the Cardiff manager, had bought Stan Iontgomery from Southend United.

In September 1949, Stansfield joined Newport County and went on to play in 21 eague games for the Somerton Park club, later becoming their manager. He held this ost from March 1950 to December 1953, his best being 1951/52 when County nished sixth in the Third Division (South).

oy CLARKE

osition	Outside-left
orn	Royston James Clarke, Newport, 1 June 1925
eight	5ft 9in
eight	10st 11lb
lubs	Albion Rovers, Cardiff City, Manchester City, Stockport County, Northwich Victoria
Velsh Caps	22 Goals 5
	1949 v England (lost 0–1)
	1950 v Scotland (lost 0–2), v Belgium (won 5–1) 1 goal, v N. Ireland (0–0)
	1951 v Scotland (lost 1–3), v England (lost 2–4), v N. Ireland (won 2–1) 2 goals, v Portugal (won 2–1), v Switzerland (won 3–2)
	1952 v England (1–1), v Scotland (won 1–0), v Rest of the UK (won 3–2), v N. Ireland (won 3–0) 1 goal
	1953 v Scotland (lost 1–2), v England (lost 2–5)

Roy Clarke holds the unique record of playing in three different divisions of the Footba[
League in three consecutive games! *(Lancashire Evening Post)*

1954 v England (lost 1–4), v Scotland (3–3), v N. Ireland (lost 1–2)
1955 v Yugoslavia (lost 1–3), v Scotland (lost 0–1), v England (lost 2–3)
1956 v N. Ireland (1–1) 1 goal

ROY CLARKE'S FIRST TASTE of international recognition was as a member of the Welsh Schools baseball team in 1939. During the Second World War he worked in the coal mines but managed to play for local side Albion Rovers of Newport at the weekends.

Cardiff City won the race for his signature in 1942, and his early performances on the left wing were impressive enough to earn him a place in the Wales team for the Victory international of 1946 against N. Ireland. As it turned out, Clarke played less than one full season of peacetime football for the Bluebirds. His speedy hard-shooting forays down the left flank were a feature of the Cardiff side that won promotion to the Second Division in 1946/47. Towards the end of that season, Manchester City paid £12,000 for Clarke's services.

Roy Clarke holds the unique record of playing in three different divisions of the Football League in three consecutive League games. He played the last of his 39 games for the Bluebirds in the penultimate game of the 1946/47 season before he joined the Maine Road club. He played in Manchester City's last game of their Second Division promotion-winning season against his home-town club, Newport County, a game in which George Smith scored all five goals as City beat the Welsh side 5–1. Clarke's next game was at the start of the 1947/48 campaign with the Maine Road club in the top flight. They beat Wolves 4–3 at Molineux with Roy Clarke hitting the winner.

Clarke returned to Ninian Park in 1949 to win the first of 22 Welsh caps in a World Cup qualifying game against England (Wales lost 1–0). His last cap came some seven years later when he netted the goal in a 1–1 draw against Northern Ireland.

Plying his trade down the left wing, Roy Clarke provided many chances for the likes of Broadis, Westcott and Williamson as well as cutting in himself to score a number of vital goals during his stay at Maine Road.

Clarke was instrumental in City getting to Wembley at the end of the 1954/55 campaign. He hit both goals in the 2–0 win at Kenilworth Road as City disposed of Luton Town in the fifth round. He also hit the only goal of the semi-final against Sunderland at Villa Park, but unfortunately missed the final against Newcastle United due to injury. The following season, however, he picked up an FA Cup winners' medal after City beat Birmingham 3–1. Clarke's best season for the Maine Road club in terms of goals scored was 1956/57, when he scored 11 from 40 appearances.

The arrival of Ray Sambrook from Coventry City to contest the No.11 shirt along with Paddy Fagan, resulted in Clarke moving on to Stockport County on a free transfer as recognition of his sterling service. Clarke held the position of player-coach and then caretaker-manager at Edgeley Park before leaving to play non-League football for Northwich Victoria.

He returned to Maine Road in 1966 to run the City Social Club. After 22 years he retired, with hundreds of friends and colleagues paying tribute to him in a farewell party at the ground.

Archie HUGHES

Position	Goalkeeper
Born	William Arthur Hughes, Colwyn Bay, 2 February 1919
Died	Colwyn Bay, 11 March 1992
Height	6ft 2in
Weight	12st 13lb
Clubs	Colwyn Bay United, Larne, Newry Town, Huddersfield Town, Tottenham Hotspur, Blackburn Rovers, Nelson, Rochdale, Crystal Palace
Welsh Caps	5
	1949 v England (lost 0–1), v N. Ireland (won 2–0), v Portugal (lost 2–3), v Belgium (lost 1–3), v Switzerland (lost 0–4)

WITHIN WEEKS OF HIS TRANSFER from Spurs to Blackburn Rovers, goalkeeper Archie Hughes had gained his first Welsh cap in a 'masterly' display against England. However, his hold on the Wales goalkeeping jersey was short-lived, and he gave way to Cyril Sidlow and later Bill Shortt.

After starting his career with his home-town club, he tried his luck in N. Ireland with Larne and Newry Town before joining Huddersfield Town shortly before the outbreak of war. During the hostilities, he guested for a number of clubs, but it was at Tottenham Hotspur that his reputation grew. Such was Archie Hughes's success that, as football began to return to normality, the transfer from Huddersfield was made permanent. Although he played in most of the games in the transitional season of 1945/46, he was relegated to the reserves on the return of Ted Ditchburn.

Hughes was first of several keepers to experience the frustration of being Ted Ditchburn's understudy. The Spurs goalkeeper's remarkable consistency and freedom from injury meant that Hughes appeared in just two League games.

Clearly too good for continuous reserve-team football, he left White Hart Lane to play for Blackburn Rovers. Back on the League stage, he was once more able to display his considerable talents, being rewarded with five full caps for Wales. On losing his place to John Patterson, he played non-League football for Nelson before returning to League action with Rochdale and, later, Crystal Palace. Hughes then turned down a chance to rejoin Colwyn Bay, preferring a clean break from football.

He later worked as an engineer for the Hotpoint Company and then ran a gentlemen's clothing shop in Old Colwyn until his retirement.

Billy REES

Position	Inside-forward
Born	William Rees, Blaengarw, 10 March 1924
Died	Bridgend, 27 July 1996
Height	5ft 11in
Weight	12st 0lb
Clubs	Caernarvon Rovers, Cardiff City, Tottenham Hotspur, Leyton Orient, Headington United, Kettering Town

Welsh Caps   4

1949 v N. Ireland (won 2–0), v Belgium (lost 1–3), v Switzerland (lost 0–4)
1950 v N. Ireland (0–0)

BILLY REES, A COAL MINER for over seven years, was playing for Caernarvon Rovers when he was spotted by the Cardiff City manager Cyril Spiers. Principally an inside-forward but capable of playing in any of the forward positions, he turned out regularly for the Bluebirds during the war years and played for Wales against England in a wartime international in May 1945.

Rees was a regular member of the Cardiff side that won the Third Division (South) Championship in 1946/47, scoring 16 goals in 35 League appearances. He was the club's top scorer the following season with 11 goals. But, in the summer of 1949 after netting 33 goals in 101 League games, he left Ninian Park to join Tottenham Hotspur. Just before he left the Bluebirds, he won the first of four Welsh caps against N. Ireland.

Early on at White Hart Lane he suffered from a series of minor injuries and consequently it wasn't until December that he made his debut. He appeared in 14 games during Spurs' promotion-winning season of 1949/50 and played in the last of his internationals. With Peter Murphy signed from Coventry City in the summer of 1950, Spurs recouped their outlay as Rees was allowed to join Leyton Orient for a fee of £14,500.

He spent over five years at Brisbane Road, netting 66 goals in 198 appearances before moving into non-League circles with Headington United and Kettering Town. Later he worked as a plant operator and then for a pharmaceutical company in Bridgend.

Harry WILLIAMS

Position	Outside-right
Born	Harold Williams, Briton Ferry, 17 June 1924
Height	5ft 4in
Weight	8st 11lb
Clubs	Briton Ferry Athletic, Newport County, Leeds United, Bradford Park Avenue
Welsh Caps	4
	1949 v N. Ireland (won 2–0), v Switzerland (lost 0–4)
	1950 v N. Ireland (0–0)
	1951 v Scotland (lost 1–3)

HARRY WILLIAMS WON THE FIRST of his four Welsh caps after showing fine and consistent form, particularly during Newport County's FA Cup run of 1948/49 and in the Ironsides' 3–1 defeat of Leeds United. Against Leeds the Welsh minnows were inspired by Williams, who had been up in the early hours to complete his milk round.

As a boy, Harry Williams was rejected by Swansea Town after trials, but he made wartime guest appearances for Belfast Celtic and Cliftonville. When he was demobbed from the Royal Navy, where he served on destroyers, he signed for Briton Ferry Athletic. He joined Newport County in November 1946 where his performance, especially against Leeds, attracted much attention from the leading clubs.

It was Leeds United manager Major Frank Buckley who secured the services of the diminutive winger, paying Newport £12,000. With his size 5 boots Williams could dribble with both feet and was therefore employed on either wing. He already had two Welsh caps when he arrived at Elland Road, but soon added a couple more. He fought back from a broken leg sustained in a game against Everton in 1952 to reclaim his first-team place. In March 1957, after scoring 35 goals in 228 League and Cup games, he rejoined Newport County.

After just three months at Somerton Park, Williams left to join Bradford Park Avenue, where his career ended after a succession of injuries.

John H. ROBERTS

Position	Full-back/Inside-forward
Born	John Hopkin Roberts, Swansea, 30 June 1918
Died	20 June 2001
Height	5ft 11in
Weight	12st 0lb
Clubs	Cwmbwria, Bolton Wanderers, Swansea Town, Llanelli
Welsh Caps	1
	1949 v Belgium (lost 1–3)

JOHN H. ROBERTS, CAPTAIN of Bolton Wanderers, was on the fringe of the Welsh side in 1947. Walley Barnes and Alf Sherwood were in the driving seat and he had to wait until the 1949 tour of Portugal, Belgium and Switzerland for recognition. He gained his only cap when Sherwood was injured.

John H. Roberts joined Bolton Wanderers from his only junior club, Cwmbwria, in April 1936. After a series of outstanding displays in the club's Central League side, he made his Football League debut against Sunderland at Burnden Park. Roberts played at inside-forward in his first two seasons with the North-West club. He hit a purple patch midway through the 1938/39 season, scoring six goals in as many games. This total included a hat-trick in the 4–2 defeat of Everton.

During the war he served with the 53rd Field Regiment, playing a number of games abroad and guesting for Norwich City.

During 1946/47 he was switched to right-back when Lol Hamlett moved to centre-half. Roberts became such a success in that position that he was awarded the captaincy. In 1950, after scoring 19 goals in 171 games for the Wanderers, he left to join his home-town club, Swansea Town. He made 16 appearances for the Swans before joining Llanelli while continuing to work in a Swansea steel-works.

1950–59

The World Cup and Brazil

The great John Charles arrived with the 1950s, making his international debut in the first game of the new decade, on 8 March against N. Ireland at the Racecourse Ground. Aged 18 years and 71 days he was, at the time, the youngest player ever to represent the Welsh senior side. In their previous international, Wales had beaten Belgium 5–1 at Ninian Park. Yet the selectors, in an attempt to build for the future, made five changes.

Wales managed to achieve the elusive blend of youth and experience in the early 1950s. They beat a team representing the United Kingdom 3–2 in December 1951 in a match to celebrate the 75th anniversary of the Welsh FA. It was a good season for Wales, who went on to share the Home International Championship with England. In fact, between March 1951 and March 1952 Wales won five and drew two of the seven matches they played.

In 1954 Wales appointed their first team manager, Walley Barnes. The highly respected Barnes established the position of manager before handing over to Jimmy Murphy in 1955. Murphy's enthusiasm came to epitomise the efforts of Wales in the international field. It was around this time that Wales played two pairs of brothers – John and Mel Charles and Len and Ivor Allchurch. The four were in the team that beat Northern Ireland 3–2 in 1955, John Charles scoring a hat-trick.

The 1958 World Cup remains the only occasion on which all four Home Countries have qualified for the Finals, although Wales took the strangest route. Drawn in Group 4 with Czechoslovakia and East Germany, they lost both away games during a close-season tour in May 1957 and finished second behind the Czechs despite two home victories. However, they were given an unlikely second chance when mass withdrawals from the Asia/Africa group left Israel without any opponents. Some international teams refused to play Israel because of the political situation in the country at the time. FIFA ruled that Israel could not qualify without playing a match and so held a ballot of the eight European Group runners-up to provide some opposition. Wales came out of the hat and promptly beat Israel home and away to qualify as the unlikely representatives of Asia and Africa.

Wales kicked off the tournament with a 1–1 draw against Hungary. After losing an early goal, the Welsh defence, in which Jack Kelsey was outstanding, stood firm and John Charles equalised just before half-time. They put in a poor performance against Mexico and, despite leading through an Ivor Allchurch goal, conceded a late equaliser. Wales then faced Sweden, who had already qualified. A 0–0 draw ensured Wales a play-off against Hungary two days later in Stockholm. The Hungarians took the lead and then resorted to some dubious tactics, crudely fouling John Charles several times. But Charles provided the centre from which Allchurch volleyed a superb equaliser and, with 16 minutes to go, Terry Medwin cut inside from the right-wing and scored the winner. Wales had qualified for the quarter-finals.

In Gothenburg, Wales staged a heroic rearguard action against Brazil. It was not broken until the 70th minute, when Pelé's miss-hit trickled into the net from a deflection. Brazil went on to beat France and Sweden by 5–2 to win the World Cup in style, so Wales could be justly proud of holding them so close.

Frank SCRINE

Position	Inside-Forward
Born	Francis Henry Scrine, Swansea, 9 January 1925
Died	Swansea, 5 October 2001
Height	5ft 11in
Weight	12st 0lb
Clubs	Swansea Town, Oldham Athletic
Welsh Caps	2
	1950 v England (lost 1–4), v N. Ireland (0–0)

FRANK SCRINE'S INTERNATIONAL CAREER got under way during the 1949/50 season, when he played against England and N. Ireland. He then sustained a knee injury and was sidelined for 12 months.

The Swansea-born forward began his career as a rugby player, but the oval-ball game was not played during the Second World War and as a result he converted to football. Jock Weir, former Swansea scout and a member of the Swans' side in 1913/14, persuaded the young Scrine to appear in a trial for the Vetch Field club. In 1946 Scrine joined the club on professional terms, replacing Norman Lockhart, who left in October 1947 to join Coventry City. He made his debut against Leyton Orient that season. In his early days with Swansea, Scrine was an out-and-out left-winger whose tremendous body swerve fooled many an opposing full-back.

He helped the club win promotion to the Second Division in 1948/49, netting a hat-trick against Bristol Rovers, Scrine had an outstanding season in the higher grade of football and scored the Swans' goal in the 2–1 FA Cup fourth-round defeat by Arsenal at Highbury. Also that season, he netted a hat-trick in the club's Welsh Cup Final win over Wrexham. It was this kind of form that led to his winning two full international caps.

Having made a number of transfer requests, Scrine was allowed to leave the club in October 1953 and joined Oldham Athletic. He had scored 45 goals in 142 League games for the Vetch Field club and continued to score on a regular basis for Oldham, finding the net 21 times in 78 games.

Keith JONES

Position	Goalkeeper
Born	Keith Jones, Nantyglo, 23 October 1928
Height	5ft 10in
Weight	12st 0lb
Clubs	Stourport Swifts, Kidderminster Harriers, Aston Villa, Port Vale, Crewe Alexandra, Southport
Welsh Caps	1
	1950 v Scotland (lost 0–2)

THOUGH WALES LOST 2–0 to Scotland on Keith Jones's full international debut for his country, the selectors were satisfied with his form and called on him for the next match against Belgium. Three days before the match, his promising international career was halted by injury in Aston Villa's match with Sunderland.

Jones began his career with non-League Kidderminster Harriers, where his displays between the posts attracted the attention of the leading clubs. He was signed by Aston Villa in the summer of 1946 and given his League debut in the local derby against Wolverhampton Wanderers in December of that year. Unfortunately he did not have the best of games, as Villa went down 4–1, but he held his place for the rest of the season.

After recovering from the injury that had halted his progress at international level, he found it difficult to hold down a regular place in the Villa side and asked to be placed on the transfer list. However, he won his place back halfway through the 1952/53 season and went on to appear in 199 first-team games. Following the arrival of Nigel Sims from Wolverhampton Wanderers, Jones left Villa to join Port Vale.

He was a regular in the Valiants side for a season and a half but in December 1958, after appearing in 68 League and Cup games, he moved to Crewe Alexandra. He ended his career with Southport, where he failed to make a League appearance.

John CHARLES

Position	Centre-half/Centre-forward
Born	William John Charles, Swansea, 27 December 1931
Died	21 February 2004
Height	6ft 2in
Weight	13st 12lb
Clubs	Swansea Town, Leeds United, Juventus, AS Roma, Cardiff City, Hereford United

Welsh Caps   38   Goals 15
1950 v N. Ireland (0–0)
1951 v Switzerland (won 3–2)
1953 v N. Ireland (won 3–2), 2 goals, v France (lost 1–6), v Yugoslavia (lost 2–5)
1954 v England (lost 1–4), v Scotland (3–3) 2 goals, v N. Ireland (lost 1–2) 1 goal,
    v Austria (lost 0–2), v Yugoslavia (lost 1–3)
1955 v Scotland (lost 0–1), v England (lost 2–3) 2 goals, v N. Ireland (won 3–2) 3 goals
1956 v England (won 2–1), v Scotland (lost 0–2), v Austria (lost 1–2), v N. Ireland (1–1)
1957 v Scotland (2–2), v England (lost 1–3) 1 goal, v N. Ireland (0–0), v Czechoslovakia
    (won 1–0), v E. Germany (lost 1–2), v Czechoslovakia (lost 0–2)
1958 v Israel (won 2–0), v Israel (won 2–0), v Hungary (1–1) 1 goal, v Mexico (1–1),
    v Sweden (0–0), v Hungary (won 2–1)
1960 v Scotland (1–1) 1 goal
1962 v England (1–1), v Brazil (lost 1–3), v Brazil (lost 1–3), v Mexico (lost 1–2) 1 goal
1963 v Scotland (lost 2–3) 1 goal
1964 v Scotland (lost 1–2)
1965 v Scotland (won 3–2), v USSR (lost 1–2)

FEW WOULD ARGUE WITH the description of John Charles as the greatest Welsh player of all time. Many Welshmen would go further and describe 'the gentle giant' as simply the greatest player of all time.

After leaving school, he joined the Swansea ground staff and soon began to show ability beyond that of his fellow apprentices. However, his stay at the Vetch Field was brief and Leeds United manager Major Frank Buckley persuaded the young Charles to go to Elland Road. In April 1949, three months after turning professional, Charles made his League debut at centre-half in the game against Blackburn Rovers. The following season he did not miss a League game and on 8 March 1950 he became the youngest Welshman ever to represent his country when, at 18 years 71 days old, he played against N. Ireland.

As the Yorkshire side bid for more goal power in an effort to climb out of the Second Division, Charles was switched to centre-forward with devastating effect. In 1953/54, Charles scored 42 goals to become the first Welshman to top the Football League scoring lists, establishing a club scoring record that is unlikely to be beaten. Only a leaky defence prevented promotion, so Charles temporarily returned to the back line to plug the gap. But he was later restored to the attack and netted 29 goals in the promotion season of 1955/56. In the First Division, Charles continued to score with great regularity and Leeds were tagged 'Charles United' !

On 19 April 1957 he was chosen as captain of Wales for the first time and led them in a goalless draw against Northern Ireland. But this was a milestone in Charles's career, for in the crowd was Umberto Agnelli, wealthy president of Juventus, and so began one of the most talked-about of all transfers.

Within a week of the Belfast international, Leeds and Agnelli had agreed terms. It took Charles a little longer – months of negotiation, in fact. But he signed in August in time for the Italian season and for the sort of money English footballers only dreamed about up to that time. The cost to Juventus was £65,000, a record fee for a British player. Within a year, a poll by the Italian football paper *Il Calcio Illustrato*

John Charles, 'the gentle giant', was considered by many to be the greatest Welsh player of all time. *(Liverpool Daily Post & Echo)*

elected Charles the best player in the country. Charles enjoyed the limelight. He bought a share in a restaurant and acquired a villa on the Italian Riviera as well as one in Turin. Helped by Charles's 28 goals, Juventus won the Championship that year and two years later won both the Championship and the Cup.

In the 1958 World Cup in Sweden, Charles was at centre-forward in the Wales team that drew with Hungary, Mexico and Sweden before beating Hungary in a play-off for the quarter-finals. Sadly, the savage treatment he had received ruled him out of the match against Brazil. In all, Charles collected 38 caps for his country and could have had far more had he been available.

After five successful years he decided to return to these shores, rejoining Leeds United. However, life under Don Revie's management was very different, and after just three months he returned to Italy and AS Roma. Injuries and a loss of form limited his appearances for Roma and he was dropped by Wales. Charles finally signed for Cardiff City for £20,000 at the end of that season.

By now, Charles had slowed down and reverted to a defender's role at Ninian Park. In 1966 he was transferred to non-League Hereford United, for whom he scored 130 goals in 243 appearances. He left Hereford in 1971 just before the club achieved their ambition of Football League status. After a spell as manager of Merthyr Tydfil, Charles became youth coach at Swansea in 1973 but left soccer three years later to become a publican in Leeds. He later ran the toy department in a children's shop.

Bryn ALLEN

Position	Inside-forward
Born	Brynley William Allen, Gilfach Goch, 23 March 1921
Height	5ft 9in
Weight	11st 0lb
Clubs	Gilfach Welfare, Swansea Town, Cardiff City, Newport County, Reading, Coventry City
Welsh Caps	2
	1951 v Scotland (lost 1–3), v England (lost 2–4)

ALTHOUGH ON THE BOOKS OF Swansea Town, inside-forward Bryn Allen guested for the Swans' local rivals Cardiff City during the Second World War. His transfer to the Ninian Park club was eventually made permanent and he made his Football League debut in a 2–1 defeat at Norwich City on the opening day of the 1946/47 season.

That season, he went on to score 17 goals in 39 League games for Cardiff, including a hat-trick in a 6–2 home win over Northampton Town, as the Bluebirds went on to win the Third Division (South) Championship. He had played in just two games at the start of the following season when he was transferred to Newport County. He spent just under a year at Somerton Park before he returned to Cardiff. In 17 League games, he scored five goals, including four in a five-game spell midway through the 1948/49 season.

Allen had taken his tally of goals to 22 in 58 League games in his two spells at Ninian Park before he left the club for a second time in the summer of 1949.

He joined Reading but left to play for Coventry City after just nine months at Elm Park. He had a successful period as a Coventry player, scoring 26 goals in 88 League outings.

He won two full international caps for Wales in the 1950/51 season.

Jack PARRY

Position	Goalkeeper
Born	Brinley John Parry, Pontardawe, 11 January 1924
Height	5ft 9in
Weight	12st 0lb
Clubs	Clydach, Swansea Town, Ipswich Town
Welsh Caps	1
	1951 v Scotland (lost 1–3)

JACK PARRY'S FORM FOR HIS first League club, Swansea, impressed the Welsh FA selectors. But he had an unhappy debut for Wales against Scotland – the team lost 3–1. Despite showing great consistency over the following seasons, he was overlooked thereafter.

Parry joined the Swans from local team Clydach in September 1946 and made his League debut in 1946/47, the first season of League football after the Second World War. Over the next four seasons, Parry went on to appear in 98 League games. He won a Third Division (South) Championship medal in 1948/49 when he appeared in 22 games.

Jack Parry earned a reputation for being a brave and agile goalkeeper, never afraid to dive at the feet of an onrushing forward. His performances for the Swans not only won him selection at full international level for Wales, but also attracted a number of the game's leading clubs. However, it was Third Division Ipswich Town's manager Scott Duncan who finally persuaded Parry to leave the Vetch Field. He was the Portman Road club's first-choice keeper for four seasons, appearing in 138 League games and winning another Third Division (South) Championship medal in 1953/54.

Ivor ALLCHURCH

Position	Inside-forward	
Born	Ivor John Allchurch, Swansea, 16 December 1929	
Died	Monmouth, 10 April 1997	
Height	5ft 10in	
Weight	11st 10lb	
Clubs	Plasmarl, Swansea Town, Newcastle United, Cardiff City, Worcester City, Haverfordwest,	
	Pontardawe	
Welsh Caps	68	Goals 23
	1951 v England (lost 2–4), v N. Ireland (won 2–1), v Portugal (won 2–1), v Switzerland	
	(won 3–2)	

1952 v England (1–1), v Scotland (1–0) 1 goal, v Rest of the UK (won 3–2) 2 goals,
v N. Ireland (won 3–0) 1 goal

1953 v Scotland (lost 1–2), v England (lost 2–5), v N. Ireland (won 3–2), v France (lost 1–6)
1 goal, v Yugoslavia (lost 2–5)

1954 v England (lost 1–4) 1 goal, v Scotland (3–3) 1 goal, v N. Ireland (lost 1–2), v Austria
(lost 0–2)

1955 v Yugoslavia (lost 1–3) 1 goal, v Scotland (lost 0–1), v England (lost 2–3), v N. Ireland
(won 3–2)

1956 v England (won 2–1), v Scotland (lost 0–2), v Austria (lost 1–2), v N. Ireland (1–1)

1957 v Scotland (2–2), v England (lost 1–3)

1958 v Israel (won 2–0) 1 goal, v Israel (won 2–0) 1 goal, v N. Ireland (1–1), v Hungary
(1–1), v Mexico (1–1) 1 goal, v Sweden (0–0), v Hungary (won 2–1) 1 goal, v Brazil
(lost 0–1)

1959 v Scotland (lost 0–3), v England (2–2) 1 goal, v N. Ireland (lost 1–4)

1960 v England (1–1), v Scotland (1–1)

1961 v N. Ireland (won 5–1) 1 goal, v Spain (lost 1–2), v Spain (1–1) 1 goal, v Hungary
(lost 2–3) 1 goal

1962 v England (1–1), v Scotland (lost 0–2), v Brazil (lost 1–3) 1 goal, v Brazil (lost 1–3),
v Mexico (lost 1–2)

1963 v Scotland (lost 2–3) 1 goal, v Hungary (lost 1–3), v England (lost 0–4), v Hungary
(1–1), v N. Ireland (won 4–1)

1964 v England (lost 0–4)

1965 v Scotland (won 3–2), v England (lost 1–2), v Greece (won 4–1) 2 goals, v N. Ireland
(won 5–0) 1 goal, v Italy (lost 1–4), v USSR (lost 1–2)

1966 v England (0–0), v USSR (won 2–1) 1 goal, v Scotland (lost 1–4) 1 goal, v Denmark
(won 4–2), v Brazil (lost 1–3), v Brazil (lost 0–1), v Chile (lost 0–2)

IVOR ALLCHURCH WAS KNOWN as the 'golden boy' of Welsh football. He was one of the most gifted players ever to emerge from Wales.

Despite having appeared in only 30 League games for Swansea, he was capped by Wales in November 1950 against England at Roker Park. The selectors decided that Allchurch was the man to fill the role vacated by Bryn Jones, who had played his last international two years before. Wales lost 4–2, with Trevor Ford scoring both the Welsh goals, but the match was to be the first of 27 consecutive games that Allchurch played for his country during the next six seasons.

During the 1950/51 season Allchurch became the youngest Swansea Town player to have appeared in all 42 League matches during the campaign. The following season he was selected to play for the Welsh League against the Irish League, scoring two and making three in an easy win at Windsor Park. First Division clubs were now beginning to take an interest in the blond youngster, and Wolves made an abortive £36,000 offer for the gifted inside-forward.

Allchurch was a fixture in the Welsh team, missing only a handful of games through injury. One of his best games for Wales was against a combined United Kingdom side for the 75th anniversary of the Football Association of Wales, when he scored twice in a 3–2 win.

For Swansea, Allchurch netted seven hat-tricks including four goals in a 5–0 win

Ivor Allchurch jumps for the ball against Hideraldo Bellini and Nilton De Sordi of Brazil during Wales's World Cup quarter-final match in Gothenburg, 21 June 1958. *(Getty Images)*

over Sunderland in August 1958, following the Wearsiders' relegation from the First Division.

Although Ivor was a more gifted player than his brother Len, the two of them wore Welsh shirts against Northern Ireland in 1955 in a game which also saw Wales field another pair of brothers, John and Mel Charles. That year also saw Ivor Allchurch play his part in Wales's 2–1 win over England at Ninian Park as they gave one of their best-ever team displays. After he had appeared for Wales in the 1958 World Cup Finals in Sweden, he received great praise from the world's press and it was obvious that he would soon get the chance to show what he could do in the top flight.

Newcastle United signed him for £28,000 in October 1958 and he made a great start for the Magpies, scoring twice in a 3–1 win over Leicester City. When he arrived on Tyneside, Newcastle were struggling, and the Welsh international was assigned to a striker's role where his creative talents were largely wasted. Newcastle were relegated to the Second Division and in August 1962 Allchurch returned to South Wales for a fee of £18,000 to play for Cardiff City.

Allchurch scored on his Bluebirds' debut in a 4–4 draw against Newcastle and was the club's top scorer for the next three seasons, including netting a hat-trick in the South Wales derby as Cardiff beat Swansea 5–0.

In May 1966, Allchurch played his 68th and last game for Wales in Chile, a record that stood for 20 years, until Joey Jones overtook him.

Having moved back to Swansea, he found himself a member of the team that attracted the record gate to the Vetch Field. The FA Cup match against Arsenal in February 1968, which the Gunners won 1–0, was watched by 32,786. This was his last FA Cup match. It is an interesting fact that he played his first and last games in the competition against Arsenal – though they were separated by 18 years!

The Queen presented him with the MBE for his services to Welsh football. In 1967/68, his last season of League football, he netted his seventh and final hat-trick for the club against Doncaster Rovers. Remarkably, the then 38-year-old ended the campaign as the club's leading scorer with 21 League and Cup goals.

After leaving Swansea he played non-League football for Worcester City, Haverfordwest and Pontardawe, turning out until past his 50th birthday before finally hanging up his boots.

Ray DANIEL

Position	Centre-half
Born	William Raymond Daniel, Swansea, 2 November 1928
Died	7 November 1997
Height	6ft 1in
Weight	12st 5lb
Clubs	Swansea Town, Arsenal, Sunderland, Cardiff City, Hereford United
Welsh Caps	21
	1951 v England (lost 2–4), v N. Ireland (won 2–1), v Portugal (won 2–1)
	1952 v England (1–1), v Scotland (won 1–0), v Rest of the UK (won 3–2), v N. Ireland (won 3–0)

1953 v Scotland (lost 1–2), v England (lost 2–5), v N. Ireland (won 3–2), v France (lost 1–6),
   v Yugoslavia (lost 2–5)
1954 v England (lost 1–4), v Scotland (3–3), v N. Ireland (lost 1–2)
1955 v England (lost 2–3), v N. Ireland (won 3–2)
1957 v Scotland (2–2), v England (lost 1–3), v N. Ireland (0–0), v Czechoslovakia
   (lost 0–2)

THE WELSH SELECTORS HAD no qualms about picking Ray Daniel, even though he wasn't a regular in the Arsenal side. He won his first full cap in November 1950 when he gave an impressive display against Jackie Milburn in a 4–2 defeat by England at Roker Park. Daniel went on to win 21 caps for Wales, building up a fine understanding with Ron Burgess and Roy Paul. Although he was later displaced by John Charles, the flamboyant defender won his place back in the side when Charles moved to play centre-forward.

Although he attended the same school as the young Ivor Allchurch, it was Ray's brother, Bobby, who was very much the local soccer starlet. He not only captained Swansea Schools but won Welsh Schoolboy international honours in 1938. Sadly, just after he had been signed by Arsenal, Bobby was killed while on active service with the RAF. This terrible tragedy spurred Ray on to consider a career in the game and during the latter stages of the Second World War he played as an amateur for Swansea.

In October 1946 he too was offered a chance at Highbury and signed for the Gunners without any hesitation. His early days with the North London club were spent in the reserves at Hendon, where he was groomed as a successor to the club's ageing first-team centre-half Leslie Compton. Called up for National Service in January 1947, he returned to Highbury and made his League debut against Charlton Athletic as Compton ended the season early to play cricket for Middlesex. Daniel's first five seasons at Highbury were spent in the club's reserve side; it was 1951/52 before he made the position his own.

Although he had broken a wrist, which was set in plaster, Daniel passed a late fitness test to line up in the Arsenal side to play Newcastle United in the 1952 FA Cup Final. Early in the game, Daniel clashed with Milburn, the Magpies' centre-forward, and the partly knitted bone was broken again. He battled on bravely but the Gunners lost 1–0. Daniel was a regular in the Arsenal side again the following season, missing only one match as the Highbury club won the League Championship on goal average from Preston North End. It was thought that Daniel would be the next Arsenal captain but, after yet another disagreement with manager Tom Whittaker, he was allowed to leave Highbury in the summer of 1953, joining Sunderland for a record £30,000.

Daniel teamed up with fellow Welsh international Trevor Ford was a virtual ever-present in the Sunderland side. But by and large he and other great individuals like Bingham, Ford and Shackleton failed to blend as a team. During his time at Roker Park, allegations regarding illegal bonuses paid to a number of players were reported to the Football League and Daniel was one of those suspended. Sadly, it not only cost him a fine but also restricted his appearances for Wales.

His last game for his country came in May 1957, when he was rushed to Czechoslovakia to play in a World Cup game, just days after the suspension had been lifted.

Daniel later had a short spell with Cardiff City before ending his League career with his home-town club, Swansea. After playing part-time non-League football for Hereford United, he worked as an area manager for Courvoisier Brandy and then became postmaster at Cockett Post Office.

Iorwerth HUGHES

Position	Goalkeeper
Born	Iorwerth Hughes, Abergele, 26 May 1925
Died	16 June 1993
Height	5ft 10in
Weight	12st 8lb
Clubs	Llandudno Town, Luton Town, Cardiff City, Worcester City, Newport County, Hastings United
Welsh Caps	4
	1951 v England (lost 2–4), v N. Ireland (won 2–1), v Portugal (won 2–1), v Switzerland (won 3–2)

IORWERTH HUGHES'S BRILLIANT goalkeeping display against England in an amateur international in January 1949 led to a three-month chase by Luton Town for his signature. Although he was in the company of England internationals Ron Baynham and Bernard Streten, Hughes won four full caps for Wales while with the Hatters, though he almost missed his first with an ankle injury.

On leaving school, Iorwerth Hughes went to work in the village shop while awaiting call-up. He served with the Royal Welch Fusiliers and Royal Corps of Signals and first played in goal when a team-mate was injured in an Army match in Germany. Following demob he was recommended to Llandudno Town and, after a series of outstanding displays, he was signed by Luton Town.

Hughes went on to play in 36 League games over the next two seasons for the Kenilworth Road club before, in August 1951, Cardiff City signed him for what was then a record fee for a goalkeeper. Unfortunately a spate of niggling injuries reduced his first-team appearances during his time at Ninian Park. In 1953, after a brief spell with non-League Worcester City, he moved to Newport County, where he became a part-time professional.

He clocked up 106 League appearances in four seasons at Somerton Park before moving to Hastings United. A broken arm prompted him to retire from the game to concentrate on his work as an electronics engineer.

Noel KINSEY

Position	Inside-forward
Born	Noel Kinsey, Treorchy, 24 December 1925
Height	5ft 8in
Weight	10st 9lb
Clubs	Treorchy Amateurs, Cardiff City, Norwich City, Birmingham City, Port Vale, King's Lynn, Lowestoft Town.
Welsh Caps	7
	1951 v N. Ireland (won 2–1), v Portugal (won 2–1), v Switzerland (won 3–2)
	1952 v England (1–1)
	1954 v N. Ireland (lost 1–2)
	1956 v England (won 2–1), v Scotland (lost 0–2)

NOEL KINSEY WAS A MEMBER of the Welsh side that beat England 2–1 in October 1955.

His career began with a couple of wartime games for Cardiff City after his goalscoring feats for Treorchy Amateurs had attracted the attention of the Ninian Park club. However, the Bluebirds didn't pursue their interest and in the summer of 1947 he joined Norwich City.

Always alert around the penalty area, he top-scored for the Canaries in 1949/50 with 17 goals in 42 League and Cup games, including eight in the first seven games of the season. He reached double figures in the next two seasons as the Carrow Road club finished second and third respectively in the Third Division (South). He had scored 65 goals in 243 games for Norwich when, in the summer of 1953, he was allowed to join Birmingham City.

In his second season at St Andrew's, he won a Second Division Championship medal, scoring 13 goals in 35 games, and in 1956 he netted the Blues' goal in the 3–1 FA Cup Final defeat by Manchester City at Wembley.

Kinsey had been capped four times while with the Canaries but added another three caps to his collection while at St Andrew's. After scoring 56 goals in 174 games for Birmingham, he joined Port Vale.

He was a regular in the club's Fourth Division Championship side of 1958/59, and then appointed player-coach. On leaving Vale Park he had a short spell with King's Lynn before becoming a successful player-coach to Lowestoft Town.

Glyn WILLIAMS

Position	Right-back
Born	Glyndwr James John Williams, Maesteg, 3 November 1918
Height	5ft 10in
Weight	10st 8lb
Clubs	Caerau, Cardiff City
Welsh Caps	1
	1951 v Switzerland (won 3–2)

GLYN WILLIAMS WAS A RESERVE for the Welsh side against Portugal on 12 May 1951 but gained his one cap the following Wednesday when he replaced Walley Barnes, who had left with Arsenal for their tour of Brazil.

A hard-tackling defender, Glyn Williams began his career with his home-town club Caerau and in 1946 helped them win the Welsh Amateur Cup. Even though he had only played a handful of games, his form had been impressive and Cardiff had no hesitation in signing him.

He made his debut for the Bluebirds in a 1-0 win at Aldershot in January 1947 during the club's Third Division (South) Championship-winning season. In the seven games in which he played in that campaign, the opposition failed to score in five of them. Since he was able to play in either full-back position or at wing-half, he missed very few games over the next six seasons. In 1950/51, as Cardiff just failed in their bid for promotion to the First Division, his form led to his being selected for Wales's close season tour, during which he won his only full international cap.

In 1951/52 he played his part in helping the Bluebirds reach the top flight. But at the end of the following season he was released after appearing in 160 first-team games. Although he failed to score at Football League level, he did get on the score sheet in an FA Cup third-round tie against West Bromwich Albion in January 1950.

Billy FOULKES

Position	Outside-right
Born	William Isaiah Foulkes, Merthyr Tydfil, 29 May 1926
Died	Hoole, nr Chester, 7 February 1979
Height	5ft 7in
Weight	11st 6lb
Clubs	Cardiff City, Winsford United, Chester, Newcastle United, Southampton, Hyde United
Welsh Caps	11 Goals 1
	1952 v England (1-1) 1 goal, v Scotland (won 1-0), v Rest of the UK (won 3-2), v N. Ireland (won 3-0)
	1953 v Scotland (lost 1-2), v England (lost 2-5), v France (lost 1-6), v Yugoslavia (lost 2-5)
	1954 v England (lost 1-4), v Scotland (3-3), v N. Ireland (lost 1-2)

BILLY FOULKES SCORED with his first kick of the ball after just four minutes of his international debut for Wales against England in October 1951.

After a spell as an amateur on Cardiff's books, Billy Foulkes had moved north to play non-League football for Winsford United. He then became a regular in the Chester side, appearing in 118 League games for the then Sealand Road club. In October 1951 Newcastle United paid £11,500 for his services and, within three days of putting pen to paper, he made his First Division debut.

Foulkes scored on his international debut and continued making headlines. In that 1951/52 season, he ended a quite amazing six months by helping the Magpies lift the FA Cup at Wembley – an ever-present in United's cup run.

Foulkes was a compact, strong and stocky forward, possessed a stinging shot, and was versatile, operating on the wing or at inside-forward. Yet, after that bright opening, his face never seemed to fit at St James Park.

He moved on to Southampton but suffered a back injury soon after his arrival at The Dell. The Saints complained to the Football League, requesting that the transfer be reversed, but the dispute was ruled in Newcastle's favour. Foulkes soon moved back to Chester, serving the team well in over 170 games. He then ran a milk bar in Chester's tourist centre.

Reg DAVIES

Position	Inside-forward
Born	Ellis Reginald Davies, Glyncorrwg, 27 May 1929
Height	5ft 8in
Weight	11st 0lb
Clubs	Cwm Athletic, Southampton, Southend United, Newcastle United, Swansea Town, Carlisle United, Merthyr Tydfil, King's Lynn
Welsh Caps	6
	1953 v Scotland (lost 1–2), v England (lost 2–5)
	1954 v England (lost 1–4), v Scotland (3–3)
	1958 v E. Germany (won 4–1), v England (lost 0–4)

REG DAVIES WAS A slightly built inside-forward who played on both flanks to equal effect. He had a sudden burst of speed over ten yards which could prove devastating in the opposition's penalty area and provide an inventive, telling pass.

As a former soprano choirboy with the Steffans Silver Singsters, he had toured with the Great Britain choir before beginning his football career as an amateur with Southampton. In 1949, after a spell in the Army, he joined Southend United. In April 1951, after scoring 18 goals in 41 games for the Shrimps, he left to play for Newcastle United, who paid £9,000 for his services.

Davies scored on his First Division debut as the Magpies beat Wolverhampton Wanderers 3–1, but he was first and foremost a team man. He won his six international caps while on Tyneside, but never quite clinched a permanent place in the Newcastle side in his seven seasons with the club. He was 12th man for the 1952 FA Cup Final but unluckily missed out in 1955. Athough picked to play, he developed tonsillitis and had to step down. He had scored 50 goals in 170 League and Cup games for United when, in October 1958, he moved to Swansea in a cash and player exchange deal involving Ivor Allchurch.

On 27 December 1958 he netted a hat-trick for the Swans in a 4–4 draw with Derby County. He went on to score 29 goals in 108 League outings for the Vetch Field club before being transferred to Carlisle United just prior to the start of the 1962/63 season.

He later played for Merthyr Tydfil before becoming player-manager of King's Lynn. Davies emigrated to Perth in 1971, appearing for Western Australia against New Zealand at the age of 47 and playing on until his 50th year.

Arthur LEVER

Position	Full-back
Born	Arthur Richard Lever, Cardiff, 25 March 1920
Height	5ft 11in
Weight	12st 4lb
Clubs	Cardiff Corinthians, Cardiff City, Leicester City, Newport County
Welsh Caps	1
	1953 v Scotland (lost 1–2)

FULL-BACK ARTHUR LEVER, popularly known as 'Buller', joined Cardiff City in 194
and made 104 wartime appearances for the club before making his League debut in
2–1 reversal at Norwich City on the opening day of the 1946/47 season. He went o
to become the club's only ever-present that season as the Bluebirds won the Thir
Division (South) Championship.

He was ever-present again the following season when he scored in both matche
against the Second Division runners-up, Newcastle United, from his position at righ
back. Lever went on to make 114 consecutive appearances from his debut until he wa
injured in City's 1–0 win at Tottenham Hotspur in March 1949.

The full-back had made 168 appearances for the Ninian Park club when i
September 1950 he joined Leicester City for a fee of £17,000. Ever was entrusted b
manager Norman Bullock with the team captaincy. He exhibited a cool defensiv
acumen, though for his last two seasons at Filbert Street he faced stiff competition fc
places, especially from the up-and-coming Stan Milburn.

He won his sole Welsh cap against Scotland at the beginning of the 1952/5
season. He returned from Leicester City to his homeland to assist Fred Stansfield a
Newport County. On retirement from the game, he worked as a market gardener.

Ron STITFALL

Position	Full-back
Born	Ronald Frederick Stitfall, Cardiff, 14 December 1925
Height	5ft 9in
Weight	12st 4lb
Clubs	Cardiff City
Welsh Caps	2
	1953 v England (lost 2–5)
	1957 v Czechoslovakia (won 1–0)

FULL-BACK RON STITFALL WON only two full international caps for Wales, the fir
against England in November 1952 and the second almost five years later in Ma
1957 in a World Cup qualifier against Czechoslovakia. It could be argued that h
should have won more.

In a playing career which spanned two decades, Ron Stitfall joined his home-tow

lub Cardiff City as a schoolboy during the Second World War and played his first
game for the club in wartime competition when only 14 years of age.

He appeared in a number of wartime games for the club before serving in the Army
for four years. It was 1947 when he returned to Ninian Park. In October of that year
he made his League debut at left-back in place of Alf Sherwood, who was away on
international duty. The match at Brentford ended in a goalless draw thanks to Stitfall's
last-minute goal-line clearance. For the next 18 seasons, Ron Stitfall was virtually ever
present in the Bluebirds side

During his first few seasons with the club Stitfall played in ta variety of positions. In
1949/50 he had a spell playing centre-forward and scored in each of his first five
appearances in the No. 9 shirt. Given that he scored only eight goals in the 454 first-
team games in which he played, it was a remarkable performance. Much of that time
he spent partnering Alf Sherwood, the two of them making the best full-back pairing
outside of the top flight.

After hanging up his boots, Ron Stitfall left Ninian Park and joined Newport
County's training staff.

Harry GRIFFITHS

Position	Outside-right
Born	James Henry Griffiths, Swansea, 4 January 1931
Died	Swansea, 25 April 1978
Height	5ft 7in
Weight	10st 10lb
Clubs	Swansea City, Merthyr Tydfil
Welsh Caps	1
	1953 v N. Ireland (won 3–2)

HARRY GRIFFITHS MADE HIS international debut for Wales against Northern Ireland
in April 1953. It wasn't until the latter part of his career, when he enjoyed something
of an Indian summer, that his form as a full-back was good enough to spark talk of a
recall to the Wales squad.

One of Swansea's most popular and loyal servants, Harry Griffiths joined the Vetch
Field club's ground staff at the age of 15 and signed professional forms two years
later. He made his Football League debut against Chesterfield in 1948/49 at outside-
right. After establishing himself as a first-team regular in 1951/52, he rarely missed a
game over the next 11 seasons.

Griffiths was one of the club's greatest utility players, appearing in every position
for the Swansea side except centre-half and goalkeeper. He left the club in 1964 after
scoring 68 goals in 424 League games, including hat-tricks against Leicester City in
March 1956 and Doncaster Rovers some seven months later.

He became player-manager at Merthyr Tydfil and remained there for two seasons
before returning to Swansea as the club's first-team trainer under manager Billy Lucas.
Griffiths was appointed the Swans manager in January 1975 and almost led the club
to promotion from the Fourth Division in 1976/77, missing out by just one point

after a fine run-in. He left the club as a result of ill-health before the Swans went up the following season.

He returned to help out at Vetch Field but died at the early age of 47 while working in the treatment room prior to Swansea's match against Scunthorpe United on 25 April 1978.

Terry MEDWIN

Position	Winger
Born	Terence Cameron Medwin, Swansea, 25 September 1932
Height	5ft 9in
Weight	11st 8lb
Clubs	Swansea City, Tottenham Hotspur
Welsh Caps	30 Goals 6

1953 v N. Ireland (won 3–2), v France (lost 1–6), v Yugoslavia (lost 2–5)
1957 v Scotland (2–2) 1 goal, v England (lost 1–3), v N. Ireland (0–0), v Czechoslovakia (won 1–0), v E. Germany (lost 1–2), v Czechoslovakia (lost 0–2)

1958 v England (lost 0–4), v Scotland (1–1) 1 goal, v Israel (won 2–0), v Israel (won 2–0),
    v N. Ireland (1–1), v Hungary (1–1), v Mexico (1–1), v Hungary (won 2–1) 1 goal, v Brazil
    (lost 0–1)
1959 v Scotland (lost 0–3), v England (2–2), v N. Ireland (lost 1–4), v England (1–1)
1960 v Scotland (1–1), v N. Ireland (3–2) 2 goals
1961 v Republic of Ireland (won 3–2), v Scotland (won 2–0), v England (lost 1–5), v Spain
    (lost 1–2)
1963 v Hungary (lost 1–3) 1 goal, v England (lost 0–4)

ERRY MEDWIN FORMED A deadly partnership with John Charles in the World Cup
inals of 1958. During the vital play-off against Hungary, Medwin scored the
vinning goal that took Wales into the quarter-finals, where, despite Medwin again
aving an outstanding game, they lost 1–0 to Brazil.

Terry Medwin was one of the heroes of Tottenham Hotspur's League and Cup
ouble winning side of 1960/61. He spent his childhood at Swansea prison, where
is father, who was on Southampton's books in the 1920s, was a prison officer.
Vhile playing for the Welsh Schoolboys, his performances as a goalscoring winger
ttracted the attention of a number of top-flight clubs, but it was no real surprise

when he joined the Vetch Field club next door to the
prison.

After a few seasons of reserve-team football, he made
his League debut for the Swans in January 1952, scoring
inside the first minute against Doncaster Rovers. He held
his place for the rest of the season, alternating between the
right-wing and centre-forward.

His form the following season led to his winning the
first of 30 full caps for Wales when he played in a 3–2
win over N. Ireland in Belfast in April 1953. Despite
scoring regularly for the Swans over the next couple of
seasons, he lost his place in the Welsh side. Medwin was
one of the game's most versatile players, having occupied
all the front-line positions with the Vetch Field club. He
joined Tottenham Hotspur on the last day of the 1955/56
season for £25,000. Medwin scored 60 goals in 148
League games for Swansea, and scored twice on his Spurs
debut in a 6–0 home win over Leicester City.

His form in the First Division in 1956/57 led to an
international recall for the match against Scotland in
October 1956. He scored in that game as Wales drew 2–2
and over the next five years became a regular in the side.

Medwin, who was a Tottenham regular for four years,
was most unfortunate to lose his first-team place to Terry

Tottenham Hotspur and Wales footballer Terry Medwin is
seen here on his knees as he scores against West Ham
United. Bobby Moore (left) looks on as goalkeeper Lawrie
Leslie dives, 25 August 1962. *(Getty Images)*

Dyson during the club's dramatic 1960/61 double winning season; but, with 15 outings as deputy for either Dyson or Cliff Jones, he did qualify for a League Championship medal. The following season he appeared on a more regular basis and was a member of the Spurs side that retained the FA Cup, beating Burnley 3–1 Injuries sadly caused him to miss the club's European Cup Winners' Cup success over Athletico Madrid, but he regained his fitness to tour South Africa with Spurs during the summer of 1963. It was on this trip that Medwin suffered a broken leg against a Nation States American Football League (NSAFL) Invitation XI.

After a long fight to regain full fitness, Terry Medwin eventually had to admit defeat. Having scored 96 goals in 247 games for the White Hart Lane club, he retired to take up the manager's post at Athenian League Enfield. He later coached League sides, Cardiff City, Fulham and Norwich City, as well as helping Dave Bowen with the Welsh team during the 1970s. Medwin's last appointment was back at the Vetch Field, where he became assistant manager to John Toshack. He helped the Swans reach the top flight but in 1983 ill-health forced his premature retirement from the game.

Derrick SULLIVAN

Position	Wing-half
Born	Derrick Sullivan, Newport, 10 August 1930
Died	Newport, 23 September 1983
Height	5ft 10in
Weight	11st 0lb
Clubs	Cardiff City, Exeter City, Newport County, Hereford United, Ebbw Vale
Welsh Caps	17
	1953 v N. Ireland (won 3–2), v France (lost 1–6), v Yugoslavia (lost 2–5)
	1954 v N. Ireland (lost 1–2)
	1955 v England (lost 2–3), v N. Ireland (won 3–2)
	1957 v Scotland (2–2), v England (lost 1–3)
	1958 v N. Ireland (1–1), v Hungary (1–1), v Sweden (0–0), v Hungary (won 2–1), v Brazil (lost 0–1)
	1959 v Scotland (lost 0–3), v N. Ireland (lost 1–4)
	1960 v England (1–1), v Scotland (1–1)

A WHOLE-HEARTED PLAYER, Derrick Sullivan was a member of the Welsh team that did so well in the 1958 World Cup Finals, having made his international debut five years earlier against N. Ireland.

He was one of the most versatile Cardiff City players. He worked his way up through the ranks to make his League debut for the Bluebirds in a 1–1 home draw against Newcastle United on 10 April 1948 at the age of 17 years 243 days. He played on the left-wing in that game but, over the next few seasons, he played in all the forward positions before settling into a half-back position in 1952/53. However, he still went on to play in almost every outfield shirt for the Bluebirds in a career that saw him score 21 goals in 305 League and Cup games. His best season in terms of goals scored was the club's promotion-winning run in 1959/60, when he netted eight times in 30 appearances.

Sullivan left Ninian Park in September 1961 and joined Exeter City. But after 44 League appearances for the Grecians, he returned to South Wales to play for Newport County. He ended his League career at Somerton Park and, after a season playing for Hereford United, he signed for Welsh League club Ebbw Vale.

Ron HOWELLS

Position	Goalkeeper
Born	Ronald Gilbert Howells, Llanelli, 12 January 1927
Height	5ft 11in
Weight	12st 0lb
Clubs	Swansea City, Barry Town, Cardiff City, Worcester City, Chester City
Welsh Caps	2
	1954 v England (lost 1–4), v Scotland (3–3)

IT WAS HIS CONSISTENT DISPLAYS between the posts for Cardiff City, where he was a first-team regular for six years, that earned Ron Howells two full caps for Wales. However, he conceded seven goals in those two games.

Howells began his career with his home-town club Swansea but had made only eight appearances for the Vetch Field club before he was released and joined non-League Barry Town. His performances for the Welsh League side led to Cardiff City signing the keeper in the summer of 1950. With Iorwerth Hughes as the club's first-choice keeper, he had to wait until Boxing Day 1951 before making his first-team debut. He gave a near-faultless display in a 3–0 home win over his former club, and after that was a virtual ever-present for the next six seasons.

In that time, he played in 172 games for the Bluebirds and won his two full international caps for Wales.

After leaving Ninian Park he went to Worcester City, but returned to League action in September 1958 with Chester City and went on to appear in 80 games for the Cestrians.

Jack KELSEY

Position	Goalkeeper
Born	Alfred John Kelsey, Llansamlet, 19 November 1929
Died	19 March 1992
Height	6ft 0in
Weight	12st 0lb
Clubs	Winch Wen, Arsenal
Welsh Caps	41
	1954 v N. Ireland (lost 1–2), v Austria (lost 0–2)
	1955 v Yugoslavia (lost 1–3), v Scotland (lost 0–1), v N. Ireland (won 3–2)

1956 v England (won 2–1), v Scotland (lost 0–2), v Austria (lost 1–2),
    v N. Ireland (1–1)
1957 v Scotland (2–2), v England (lost 1–3), v N. Ireland (0–0), v Czechoslovakia
    (won 1–0), v E. Germany (lost 1–2), v Czechoslovakia (lost 0–2)
1958 v England (lost 0–4), v Scotland (1–1), v Israel (won 2–0), v Israel (won 2–0),
    v N. Ireland (1–1), v Hungary (1–1), v Mexico (1–1), v Sweden (0–0), v Hungary
    (won 2–1), v Brazil (lost 0–1)
1959 v Scotland (lost 0–3), v England (2–2)
1960 v England (1–1), v Scotland (1–1), v N. Ireland (won 3–2)
1961 v Scotland (won 2–0), v England (lost 1–5), v N. Ireland (won 5–1), v Spain (lost 1–2),
    v Spain (1–1), v Hungary (lost 2–3)
1962 v England (1–1), v Scotland (lost 0–2), v N. Ireland (won 4–0), v Brazil (lost 1–3),
    v Brazil (lost 1–3)

FROM HIS FIRST CAP AGAINST NORTHERN IRELAND in 1954 until his retirement, Jack Kelsey's magnificent form made him an almost permanent fixture in the Wales side. Kelsey's status was confirmed by his selection to represent Great Britain against the Rest of Europe in the FIFA Anniversary match at Belfast in August 1955.

Jack Kelsey was a one-club man. He was unlucky to be at Highbury at a time when the club's fortunes were at a really low ebb. Although one of a long line of excellent custodians who have graced the Arsenal side over the years, he won just one club honour, a League Championship medal in his first full season. His distinguished career was ended prematurely by injury at the age of 32.

Kelsey's early football career was spent with Swansea League club Winch Wen, and after a trial with Llanelli he was given a private trial with Arsenal in the summer of 1949. Still only a teenager, Kelsey signed professional forms for the Gunners in August of that year and began an association with the North London club that was to last virtually up to his death in March 1992.

His early days were spent under the tuition of coach George Male at Hendon as he worked his way up the ranks. He had to wait quite a while for his first-team break. George Swindin was the club's regular keeper and Ted Platt his natural deputy. But in February 1951 Kelsey was given his chance in the Arsenal first team for the match against Charlton Athletic. Sadly, this game resulted in Arsenal's heaviest home defeat for 22 years as they lost 5–2. He was given a second chance at Manchester United the following week. He played better, but he still let in three. So it was back to the reserves until he returned to the first team for 29 matches during the 1952/53 League Championship-winning season.

The following season, Kelsey became the London club's first-choice keeper, his displays winning him the first of 41 international caps in March 1954. Displacing Plymouth Argyle's Bill Shortt as Wales's premier keeper, he missed just four of his country's matches between his debut and his final game in May 1962. During that time he shared in the victory over England at Ninian Park in 1955, and the following year he saw the other side of the coin when he was injured at Wembley and replaced by Alf Sherwood as Wales lost 3–1.

The highlight of Jack Kelsey's international career was helping Wales to the quarter-finals of the World Cup in Sweden in 1958, where they lost 1–0 to the

Wales and Arsenal goalkeeper Jack Kelsey gets his body behind the ball and makes a save, 13 October 1952. *(Getty Images)*

ventual winners Brazil. Tragically, it was while playing for Wales against Brazil in ao Paulo in May 1962 that Kelsey collided heavily with Brazilian centre-forward 'ava, damaging his spine. At a subsequent medical examination it was discovered that e had a deformity of the spine which, had it been noticed earlier, would have revented him from ever playing League football. After a six-month fight to regain is fitness, he was forced into retirement. He had played in 352 League and Cup ames for the Gunners.

Arsenal played a testimonial game for him with Glasgow Rangers in 1963, but the eeper was sufficiently well-regarded at Highbury to be retained on the staff. For over quarter of a century he worked in the club's commercial department, where he was n accessible and popular figure right up to his death.

Bill HARRIS

Position	Inside-forward/Wing-half
Born	William Charles Harris, Swansea, 31 October 1928
Died	Middlesbrough, 16 December 1989
Height	5ft 11in
Weight	11st 7lb
Clubs	Swansea Town, Llanelli, Hull City, Middlesbrough, Bradford City
Welsh Caps	6
	1954 v Austria (lost 0–2)
	1957 v E. Germany (lost 1–2), v Czechoslovakia (lost 0–2)
	1958 v E. Germany (won 4–1), v England (lost 0–4), v Scotland (1–1)

BILL HARRIS BEGAN HIS CAREER with his home-town club, Swansea. But, having failed to make the grade with the Vetch Field club, he was released following his National Service. After a short spell with Welsh League club Llanelli, he joined Hull City, who were more than happy to pay out £2,000 for his services. Harris stayed at Boothfery Park for four seasons, appearing in 145 games for the Tigers before being transferred to Middlesbrough for £15,000 in March 1954.

Harris's first game for Boro was in a 3–3 home draw against Chelsea, and although he played in nine of the remaining ten games that season, he couldn't prevent the Teesside club from being relegated to Division Two.

It wasn't long before Bill Harris was converted from wing-half to inside-forward and with great success. He stayed at Ayresome Park for 11 seasons, being ever present in 1955/56 and 1956/57. His performances for Boro led to his winning six full caps for Wales over four years – the first against Austria just a couple of months after he joined the Teesside club. Harris went on to score 72 goals in 378 games with a best of 14 in 1961/62. This total included a hat-trick in a 4–3 win at Newcastle United.

On leaving Middlesbrough he joined Bradford City as player-manager, but after just one unsuccessful season at Valley Parade he returned to Teesside to manage Stockton.

Cliff JONES

Position	Winger
Born	Clifford William Jones, Swansea, 7 February 1935
Height	5ft 7in
Weight	10st 7lb
Clubs	Swansea Town, Tottenham Hotspur, Fulham, King's Lynn, Bedford Town, Wealdstone, Cambridge City
Welsh Caps	59 Goals 16
	1954 v Austria (lost 0–2)
	1956 v England (won 2–1) 1 goal, v Scotland (lost 0–2), v Austria (lost 1–2), v N. Ireland (1–1)

Flying winger Cliff Jones of Spurs and Wales, scored a hat-trick in a 4–1 defeat of Northern Ireland in April 1963. *(Lancashire Evening Post)*

1957 v Scotland (2–2), v England (lost 1–3), v N. Ireland (0–0), v Czechoslovakia (won 1–0),
    v E. Germany (lost 1–2), v Czechoslovakia (lost 0–2)

1958 v E. Germany (won 4–1) 1 goal, v England (lost 0–4), v Scotland (1–1), v Israel
    (won 2–0), v Israel (won 2–0) 1 goal, v N. Ireland (1–1), v Hungary (1–1), v Mexico (1–1),
    v Sweden (0–0), v Hungary (won 2–1), v Brazil (lost 0–1)

1959 v N. Ireland (lost 1–4)

1960 v England (1–1), v Scotland (1–1), v N. Ireland (won 3–2)

1961 v Republic of Ireland (won 3–2) 2 goals, v Scotland (won 2–0) 1 goal, v England
    (lost 1–5), v N. Ireland (won 5–1) 2 goals, v Spain (1–1), v Hungary (lost 2–3) 1 goal

1962 v England (1–1), v Scotland (lost 0–2), v N. Ireland (won 4–0), v Brazil (lost 1–3),
    v Brazil (lost 1–3), v Mexico (lost 1–2)

1963 v Scotland (lost 2–3), v Hungary (1–1) 1 goal, v N. Ireland (won 4–1) 3 goals

1964 v England (lost 0–4), v Scotland (1–1), v N. Ireland (lost 2–3)

1965 v Scotland (won 3–2), v Denmark (lost 0–1), v England (lost 1–2) 1 goal,
    v Greece (lost 0–2), v Greece (won 4–1), v N. Ireland (won 5–0) 1 goal, v Italy (lost 1–4),
    v USSR (lost 1–2)

1967 v Scotland (1–1), v England (lost 1–5)

1968 v England (lost 0–3), v Scotland (lost 2–3), v W. Germany (1–1)

1969 v Italy (lost 0–1), v Rest of the UK (lost 0–1)

CLIFF JONES WAS ONE OF Wales's greatest players. He won the first of his 59 caps against Austria in May 1954. He had a disappointing debut and had to wait another 18 months before being given another chance against England at Ninian Park. This time it was a completely different story: Wales won 2–1 and Cliff Jones scored a memorable winner. The flying winger is also remembered for netting a hat-trick in a 4–1 defeat of Northern Ireland in 1963.

Cliff Jones was the fourth member of his family to make his name in professional football. He followed his father, Ivor, who played for Swansea Town West Bromwich Albion and Wales; his uncle Bryn, who played for Wolverhampton Wanderers, Arsenal, Norwich City and Wales; and his brother Bryn, who played for Swansea Town, Newport County, Bournemouth, Northampton Town and Watford.

In his youth, Cliff played for both Swansea and Wales Schools sides, and in 1949/50 captained the Swansea schoolboys team that won the English Schools Shield for the second time since the war. Though he was taken on to the staff at the Vetch Field, he was wise enough to learn a trade outside football, that of a sheet-metal worker at Swansea Docks.

His performances for both club and country led to a number of top sides making inquiries about him. Just when it seemed he would leave the Vetch, he had to do two years National Service, who had been deferred because of his apprenticeship in the Royal Horse Artillery (King's Troop). On returning to Swansea, he was eventually signed by Tottenham Hotspur which, after a long series of negotiations paid £35,000 to take him to White Hart Lane. After just three months with Spurs he was off to Sweden with Wales for the 1958 World Cup Finals.

On his return to White Hart Lane for pre-season training, Jones broke a leg in a practice game. Although it was a major blow for both player and club, it allowed him recharge his batteries. When he did return to first-team action four months later, he became an indispensable member of the team, capable of playing on either wing and at inside-forward. There were few more exciting sights in the game than Cliff Jones leaving his marker for dead with a great burst of speed. Jones was always alert to the possibility of cutting inside with the ball to shoot for goal, and he was also an accomplished header of the ball.

He was an important member of the Spurs double-winning side of 1960/61 and the team that won the FA Cup in 1962 and the European Cup Winners' Cup in 1963. Jones also picked up a third FA Cup winners' medal in 1967 as the first non-playing substitute in an FA Cup Final. Throughout his career with Spurs, he continued to represent his country and also represented the Football League on three occasions, quite an achievement for a non-English player.

In October 1968 he was allowed to leave White Hart Lane and join Fulham for £5,000. But in his two years at Craven Cottage he found himself occupying a completely different role from the one he had at Spurs, a role that involved him doing more running.

After winding down his career with a number of non-League clubs, he opened a butcher's shop in Tottenham High Road. Unfortunately it wasn't a success and he returned briefly to the sheet-metal-working trade before becoming a games instructor at Highbury Grove School.

Derek TAPSCOTT

Position	Centre-forward
Born	Derek Robert Tapscott, Barry, 30 June 1932
Height	5ft 9in
Weight	10st 12lb
Clubs	Barry Town, Arsenal, Cardiff City, Newport County, Cinderford Town, Carmarthen
Welsh Caps	14 Goals 4

1954 v Austria (lost 0–2)
1955 v Yugoslavia (lost 1–3), v Scotland (lost 0–1), v England (lost 2–3),
    v N. Ireland (won 3–2)
1956 v England (won 2–1) 1 goal, v Scotland (lost 0–2), v Austria (lost 1–2) 1 goal,
    v N. Ireland (1–1)
1957 v N. Ireland (0–0), v Czechoslovakia (won 1–0), v E. Germany (lost 1–2)
1959 v England (2–2) 1 goal, v N. Ireland (lost 1–4) 1 goal

ALTHOUGH DEREK TAPSCOTT'S first match as a full international was classed as a friendly, it was anything but, and Tapscott's continual barging of the Austrian goalkeeper had a lot to do with the general atmosphere on the pitch. Although it wasn't illegal, barging was not a tactic favoured by Continental sides. Tapscott came close to scoring on a number of occasions but the Austrians won 2–0.

Derek Tapscott was one of the Football League's most consistent goalscorers of the mid- and late 1950s. Tapscott hailed from a family of 17. On leaving school he had a variety of jobs including working on a building site. He also played football for his

Derek Tapscott was a consistent scorer, but injury and loss of form cost him his place in the 1958 World Cup Finals. *(Lancashire Evening Post)*

home-town side Barry Town in the Welsh and Southern Leagues, where he built up reputation as a prolific goalscorer.

In October 1953, Arsenal manager Tom Whittaker gave him the chance to sign for one of the most famous teams in the country. He didn't need asking twice and although he had to take a pay cut from his combined football and building labourer' wages, he soon put pen to paper. He made his League debut alongside Tomm Lawton in the match against Liverpool at Highbury towards the end of the 1953/5 season and celebrated by scoring twice in a 3–0 win. Then, following his inter national debut, he scored twice in a 3–0 win at Portsmouth and ended the seaso with five goals in as many matches. The following season saw him win a regular plac in the Arsenal side, scoring 13 goals in 37 games. In 1955/56 Tapscott was the Gunners leading scorer with 21 goals, and the next season he scored 25 goals, the most since Ronnie Rooke netted 33 in 1947/48. In the early part of the 1957/58 season, when he seemed to be at his peak, he had to undergo a cartilage operation. The injury cost him his place in the Welsh side for the 1958 World Cup Finals in Sweden. When he did regain full fitness, Arsenal decided that he had no future in the top flight and sold him to Cardiff City for £15,000.

He was the Bluebirds' leading scorer in 1959/60 with 20 goals as the Ninian Park club won promotion to the First Division. He was top scorer again the following season with 21 goals in 39 games, including his first hat-trick for Cardiff in a 3–1 win over West Bromwich Albion. Despite City being relegated in 1961/62, Tapscott netted his second hat-trick for the club in a 3–2 home win over Birmingham City. The following season he netted his third in a 4–2 win at Charlton Athletic. Tapscott continued to score on a regular basis and, in seven years at Ninian Park, he netted 99 goals in 233 first-team games, including six in the 16–0 Welsh Cup defeat of Knighton in 1960/61 – still the individual scoring record of any Cardiff player in a first-team fixture.

In July 1965 he joined Newport County before later moving into non-League football with Cinderford Town and Carmarthen. After retiring from the game he took up the position of a sportswear representative.

Stuart WILLIAMS

Position	Full-back
Born	Stuart Grenville Williams, Wrexham, 9 July 1930
Height	5ft 9in
Weight	12st 12lb
Clubs	Wrexham, West Bromwich Albion, Southampton
Welsh Caps	43

1954 v Austria (lost 0–2)
1955 v England (lost 2–3), v N. Ireland (won 3–2)
1956 v England (won 2–1), v Scotland (lost 0–2), v Austria (lost 1–2)
1958 v England (lost 0–4), v Scotland (1–1), v Israel (won 2–0), v Israel (won 2–0),
    v N. Ireland (1–1), v Hungary (1–1), v Mexico (1–1), v Sweden (0–0), v Hungary
    (won 2–1), v Brazil (lost 0–1)
1959 v Scotland (lost 0–3), v England (2–2), v N. Ireland (lost 1–4)
1960 v England (1–1), v Scotland (1–1), v N. Ireland (won 3–2)
1961 v Republic of Ireland (won 3–2), v N. Ireland (won 5–1), v Spain (lost 1–2),
    v Spain (1–1), v Hungary (lost 2–3)
1962 v England (1–1), v Scotland (lost 0–2), v N. Ireland (won 4–0), v Brazil (lost 1–3),
    v Brazil (lost 1–3), v Mexico (lost 1–2)
1963 v Scotland (lost 2–3), v Hungary (lost 1–3), v England (lost 0–4), v Hungary (1–1)
1964 v England (lost 0–4), v Scotland (1–1)
1965 v Scotland (won 3–2), v Denmark (lost 0–1), v England (lost 1–2)
1966 v Denmark (won 4–2)

STUART WILLIAMS, THE SON OF A Wrexham director, was the most capped of all West Bromwich Albion's international players, winning 33 of his 43 caps for Wales while at the Hawthorns.

He began his footballing career as an amateur with his home-town team Wrexham making his League debut for the Robins against Rochdale in April 1949. He joined the Albion ground staff in November 1950 and stayed at the club for 12 years. Initially, rather unsuccessfully, he played as an inside-forward, but then mainly as a fine full-back in nearly 300 games for the club. He was particularly unlucky in 1954 when, according to some versions of the official FA Cup Final programme, he was down to replace injury victim Stan Rickaby for the final against Preston North End. Instead, at the last minute, manager Vic Buckingham decided to bring in an out-of-position Joe Kennedy.

Released by the Baggies in September 1962, Williams moved to Southampton for a fee of £15,000 and made another 200 or so appearances for the south-coast club. Williams's first goal for the Saints came in the local derby against Portsmouth as Southampton won 4–2.

On hanging up his boots, he returned to the Hawthorns as the club's trainer in time for the 1968 FA Cup Final against Everton. In 1971 he went back to The Dell as assistant manager to Ted Bates before other coaching jobs followed at Aston Villa and Stavanger in Norway.

Dave BOWEN

Position	Wing-half
Born	David Lloyd Bowen, Maesteg, 7 June 1928
Died	Northampton, 25 September 1995
Height	5ft 9in
Weight	10st 8lb
Clubs	Northampton Town, Arsenal
Welsh Caps	19 Goals 1

1955 v Yugoslavia (lost 1–3), v Scotland (lost 0–1)
1957 v N. Ireland (0–0), v Czechoslovakia (won 1–0), v E. Germany (lost 1–2)
1958 v E. Germany (won 4–1), v England (lost 0–4), v Scotland (1–1), v Israel (won 2–0)
   1 goal, v Israel (won 2–0), v N. Ireland (1–1), v Hungary (1–1), v Mexico (1–1), v Sweden
   (0–0), v Hungary (won 2–1), v Brazil (lost 0–1)
1959 v Scotland (lost 0–3), v England (2–2), v N. Ireland (lost 1–4)

IT WAS ONLY AFTER BECOMING an Arsenal regular that Dave Bowen made an international impact and captained Wales to the quarter-finals of the 1958 World Cup.

Bowen signed for Arsenal from Northampton Town in the summer of 1950 as an understudy to Joe Mercer. Although he made his League debut for the Gunners against Wolves in March 1951, he had to wait until the end of the 1954/55 season before winning a regular place in the Arsenal League side. By this time, he had won the first of his 19 Welsh caps against Yugoslavia in September 1954.

Dave Bowen was a motivator supreme, whose storming, passionate performances throughout the mid- and late 1950s did much to lift a rather ordinary Arsenal side. He was appointed captain of the North London club. With his fist clenched and vocal chords straining, he was a formidable adversary. He went on to appear in 162 League and Cup games for the Gunners before rejoining Northampton Town in July 1959 as their player-manager.

He was a very successful manager, leading the Cobblers from the Fourth Division to the top flight in the space of five seasons. He later served as general manager and director. There are still those who maintain that Arsenal need have looked no further than Dave Bowen when, in the 1960s, they sought a leader to restore them to their former glories.

Billy REED

Position	Outside-right
Born	William George Reed, Rhondda, 25 January 1928
Died	16 January 2003
Height	5ft 8in
Weight	10st 0lb
Clubs	Rhondda Town, Cardiff City, Brighton and Hove Albion, Ipswich Town, Swansea Town
Welsh Caps	2
	1955 v Yugoslavia (lost 1–3), v Scotland (lost 0–1)

BILLY REED WAS CAPPED TWICE BY WALES, and became the first player to receive full international honours while on the books of Ipswich Town.

The Rhondda-born winger played his early football with his home-town club before joining Cardiff City. Unable to make the grade at Ninian Park, the former Welsh amateur moved to Brighton and Hove Albion in the summer of 1948. But he had to wait until Christmas Day before making his League debut in a 1–1 draw at Exeter City.

Reed found himself in and out of the Brighton side over the next couple of seasons. However, in 1951/52 he was not only ever-present but the club's top scorer with 19 goals, a total which included a hat-trick in a 5–1 win over Ipswich Town. Reed was leading the south-coast club's scoring charts again the following season when he was transferred to Ipswich, having scored 37 goals in 132 games for the Seagulls.

At Portman Road, Reed was considered the best right-winger in the lower divisions. Possessing exceptional dribbling skill, he was dubbed the 'Stanley Matthews' of the Third Division. In 1953/54 he helped Ipswich win the Third Division (South) Championship, pipping his former club by three points. In fact, Reed scored in both matches against Brighton, including the winner in a 2–1 victory at the Goldstone Ground. Although the club were relegated in 1954/55, Reed was one of Ipswich Town's best players, scoring 12 goals, including a hat-trick in a 5–2 home win over Walsall. He won another Third Division (South) Championship medal in 1956/57 but played the last of his 171 League and Cup games in which he scored 46 goals the following season Reed ended his career with Swansea Town.

Johnny KING

Position	Goalkeeper
Born	John King, Ferndale, 29 November 1933
Died	Australia, 30 November 1982
Height	6ft 0in
Weight	12st 0lb
Clubs	Swansea Town
Welsh Caps	1
	1955 v England (lost 2–3)

BEFORE THE EMERGENCE of Swansea goalkeeper Roger Freestone, Johnny King held the Vetch Field club appearance record with 368 League games under his belt between 1950 and 1964.

King made his Swansea debut as a 17-year-old amateur in a 5–0 defeat at Birmingham City in December 1950. Just as he began to establish himself, he was called up to do two years' National Service. On his release, King proved himself to be one of the best keepers outside the top flight. During the course of the 1954/55 season he won the only full cap of his career when he played for Wales in their 3–2 defeat by England at Wembley.

Up until the arrival of Noel Dwyer from West Ham United in the summer of 1960, Johnny King was a virtual ever-present in the Swansea side but, following the Irishman's performances when he deputised for King, he had to be content to share the goalkeeping duties. In February 1961, King was deservedly awarded a £1,000 benefit following a superb performance against Preston North End in the fourth round of that season's FA Cup.

The popular keeper later emigrated to Australia, where he died aged only 49 in 1982.

Len ALLCHURCH

Position	Outside-right
Born	Leonard Allchurch, Swansea, 12 September 1933
Height	5ft 8in
Weight	11st 0lb
Clubs	Swansea Town, Sheffield United, Stockport County, Haverfordwest
Welsh Caps	11
	1955 v N. Ireland (won 3–2)
	1956 v Austria (lost 1–2)
	1958 v E. Germany (won 4–1), v Scotland (1–1), v Israel (won 2–0), v N. Ireland (1–1)
	1959 v Scotland (lost 0–3)
	1962 v Scotland (lost 0–2), v N. Ireland (won 4–0), v Brazil (lost 1–3)
	1964 v England (lost 0–4)

LEN ALLCHURCH WAS JUST 21 years old when he made his international debut for Wales against Northern Ireland in Belfast, forming a left-wing partnership with

On his debut Len Allchurch formed a left-wing partnership with his brother Ivor and helped John Charles score a hat-trick against Northern Ireland. *(Lancashire Evening Post)*

brother Ivor and helping to provide the service that enabled the legendary John Charles to score a hat-trick.

Although he made his debut for Swansea Town at the age of 17, it was not until the end of his National Service at the age of 20 that he established himself in the Swans' first team. Allchurch was not a 'push and run' winger but relied upon guile and close ball control before providing crosses for his forwards. In March 1961 he moved to Sheffield United for £18,000 and was immediately involved in helping the Blades win promotion to the First Division. He made 123 League appearances for the Yorkshire club before, just one week short of his 32nd birthday in 1965, he joined Stockport County for a fee of £10,000.

His four seasons at Edgeley Park were highly successful, County winning the Fourth Division Championship in Allchurch's second season and performing creditably in the Third Division. Allchurch's teasing skills were of particular benefit to County's twin-strike force of Atkins and Fryatt but, after they had both left Edgeley Park, Allchurch's talents went to waste. In September 1969 he returned to the Vetch Field to take his tally of goals in his two spells to 60 in 342 League games.

On leaving the first-class scene, he joined his brother Ivor at Welsh League club Haverfordwest. He later ran a hotel in Swansea and established a successful leather goods business.

Mel CHARLES

Position	Centre-half/ centre-forward
Born	Melvyn Charles, Swansea, 14 May 1935
Height	6ft 1in
Weight	13st 10lb
Clubs	Leeds United, Swansea Town, Arsenal, Cardiff City, Porthmadoc, Port Vale, Haverfordwest
Welsh Caps	31 Goals 6

1955 v N. Ireland (won 3–2)
1956 v England (won 2–1), v Scotland (lost 0–2), v Austria (lost 1–2)
1957 v England (lost 1–3), v N. Ireland (0–0), v Czechoslovakia (won 1–0), v E. Germany (lost 1–2) 1 goal, v Czechoslovakia (lost 0–2)
1958 v E. Germany (won 4–1), v England (lost 0–4), v Scotland (1–1), v Israel (won 2–0), v Israel (won 2–0), v Hungary (1–1), v Mexico (1–1), v Sweden (0–0), v Hungary (won 2–1), v Brazil (lost 0–1)
1959 v Scotland (lost 0–3), v England (2–2)
1961 v N. Ireland (won 5-1) 1 goal, v Spain (lost 1–2), v Spain (1–1), v Hungary (lost 2–3)
1962 v England (1–1), v Scotland (lost 0–2), v N. Ireland (won 4–0) 4 goals, v Brazil (lost 1–3)
1963 v Scotland (lost 2–3), v Hungary (lost 1–3)

MEL CHARLES WAS VOTED THE best centre-half in the 1958 World Cup tournament. He had made his international debut in April 1955 when he played right-half in a 3–2 win over Northern Ireland in Belfast and showed his versatility by scoring all four goals against the same opposition seven years later when Wales won 4−0 at Ninian Park.

The versatile Mel Charles scored all four goals as Wales beat Northern Ireland 4–0 at Ninian Park in April 1962. *(Getty Images)*

He showed early promise when he played for the Swansea Schools team that won the English Schools' Football Association (ESFA) Trophy in 1950. After a trial with Leeds United, he signed professional forms for Swansea Town in May 1952. Over the next seven seasons, Charles played in 233 League games for the Vetch Field club, scoring 69 goals.

Like his brother John, he became very much sought after and in March 1959 he joined Arsenal for a Highbury club record fee of £42,750 plus Gunners' youngsters Peter Davies and David Dodson. Charles was seen as the player around whom manager George Swindin could build a title-winning side. After alternating between centre-half and centre-forward in his first season with the club, the multi-gifted Welshman's Highbury career was devastated by two cartilage operations, and in his first two seasons with the club he started less than half the Gunners' games. Even when he did turn out, he often played carrying injuries. He started the 1961/62 season as the club's first-choice centre-forward and scored two goals against Everton and a hat-trick in the defeat of Blackburn Rovers. Charles was majestic in the air and possessed intricate skills for such a big man. He netted 17 goals in 23 League and Cup games that season before returning to Wales to sign for Cardiff City for £28,500 in February 1962.

For the Bluebirds he scored 24 goals in 81 League games and took his total of international appearances to 31 before being displaced by his brother John on his return from Italy.

He then played non-League football for Porthmadoc in the Welsh League (North) before returning to League action with Port Vale at the end of the 1966/67 season. He later played for Haverfordwest before hanging up his boots.

On retirement he went into business in his home town of Swansea before becoming involved in a Swansea Council scheme providing sport for the unemployed. Along with his brother John, he guided the fortunes of his son Jeremy, who played League football for Swansea City, Queen's Park Rangers and Oxford United and won 19 caps for Wales.

Alan HARRINGTON

Position	Full-back
Born	Alan Charles Harrington, Penarth, 17 November 1933
Height	5ft 9in
Weight	11st 2lb
Clubs	Cardiff Nomads, Cardiff City
Welsh Caps	11
	1956 v N. Ireland (1–1)
	1957 v Scotland (2–2), v England (lost 1–3)
	1958 v Scotland (1–1), v Israel (won 2–0), v Israel (won 2–0), v N. Ireland (1–1)
	1961 v Scotland (won 2–0), v England (lost 1–5)
	1962 v England (1–1), v Scotland (lost 0–2)

ALAN HARRINGTON WON 11 full caps for Wales, his last six years after he made his debut against Northern Ireland in April 1956.

He joined his home-town club, Cardiff City, from local side Cardiff Nomads in the autumn of 1951, but he had to wait until midway through the 1952/53 season before being given a chance in the Bluebirds' first team. Playing at wing-half, he made an impressive debut in a goalless draw against Tottenham Hotspur at Ninian Park. He went on to make ten League appearances that season and, in his first six matches for the South Wales club, the opposition failed to score. However, it was in the 1954/55 season that Alan Harrington established himself as a first-team regular and, with the exception of the entire 1963/64 campaign because of a broken leg, he was a virtual ever-present in the Cardiff side for the next 12 seasons.

Harrington was strong in the tackle and a good distributor of the ball. He had played in 405 first-team games for the Ninian Park outfit when he was forced to give the game up following another broken leg sustained in a 1–1 draw against Leyton Orient at Brisbane Road in January 1966.

Mel HOPKINS

Position	Full-back
Born	Melvyn Hopkins, Ystrad, 7 November 1934
Height	5ft 11in
Weight	10st 6lb
Clubs	Tottenham Hotspur, Brighton and Hove Albion, Ballymena United, Canterbury City, Bradford Park Avenue
Welsh Caps	34

1956 v N. Ireland (1–1)
1957 v Scotland (2–2), v England (lost 1–3), v N. Ireland (0–0), v Czechoslovakia (won 1–0), v E. Germany (lost 1–2), v Czechoslovakia (lost 0–2)
1958 v E. Germany (won 4–1), v England (lost 0–4), v Scotland (1–1), v Israel (won 2–0), v Israel (won 2–0), v N. Ireland (1–1), v Hungary (1–1), v Mexico (1–1), v Sweden (0–0), v Hungary (won 2–1), v Brazil (lost 0–1)
1959 v Scotland (lost 0–3), v England (2–2), v N. Ireland (lost 1–4)
1960 v England (1–1), v Scotland (1–1)
1961 v N. Ireland (won 5–1), v Spain (lost 1–2), v Spain (1–1), v Hungary (lost 2–3)
1962 v N. Ireland (won 4–0), v Brazil (lost 1–3), v Brazil (lost 1–3), v Mexico (lost 1–2)
1963 v Scotland (lost 2–3), v Hungary (lost 1–3), v N. Ireland (won 4–1)

MEL HOPKINS WAS A FIRST-CHOICE player for Wales for several years and made 23 successive international appearances for his country. He played for Wales throughout the World Cup Finals of 1958, helping them reach the quarter-finals, where he gave a near-faultless display against the Brazilian winger Garrincha.

He grew up in a Rhondda rugby stronghold where as a boy he had to form his own team to get a game of soccer. He was spotted by both Spurs and Manchester United playing for the Ystrad Boys Club in Glamorgan and was offered the chance to join the ground staff of either club. He chose the North London club and, after developing rapidly, made his League debut against Derby County in October 1952, six months after signing professional forms. It was another two years before he was able to

Melvyn Hopkins played in 23 consecutive internationals following his debut. He gave an outstanding display against Brazil's Garrincha in the 1958 World Cup quarter-finals. (Getty Images)

replace the ageing Arthur Willis and Charlie Withers as first-choice left-back, but by the mid-1950s Hopkins was recognised as one of the best full-backs in the country. Hopkins was fast, tenacious and strong in the tackle, and liked nothing better than joining the attack, but he was always able to recover quickly when circumstances required it.

It was while playing for Wales against Scotland at Hampden Park in November 1959 that Mel Hopkins's nose was horrifically smashed in a collision with the home side's Ian St John. The injury not only cost Hopkins his place in the Welsh side but also his position in Bill Nicholson's side, who were on the threshold of greatness. His place in the Tottenham side was taken by Ron Henry, who took his chance so well that he wore the No. 3 shirt throughout the club's 1960/61 League and Cup double winning season

Although he remained at White Hart Lane for a further five seasons, Hopkins was never able to get back into the Spurs team on a regular basis. His only goal for the club in 240 first-team appearances came in his only European encounter as Spurs beat Slovan Bratislava 6–0 in March 1963. Although he was primarily a reserve during his last few seasons with the White Hart Lane club, he was still first choice for Wales and won 34 caps in total.

In October 1964 he followed Spurs striker Bobby Smith to Brighton and Hove Albion and played an important role in helping the Seagulls win that season's Fourth Division Championship. On leaving the Goldstone Ground, Hopkins played for Ballymena, Canterbury City and later Bradford Park Avenue, where he took his total of Football League appearances for his three clubs to 307.

He later became a sports instructor for Brighton Education Authority and then sports officer at Horsham Sports Centre.

Trevor EDWARDS

Position	Full-back
Born	Leonard Trevor Edwards, Rhondda, 24 January 1937
Height	5ft 8in
Weight	11st 3lb
Clubs	Charlton Athletic, Cardiff City, Hakoah (Australia)
Welsh Caps	2
	1957 v N. Ireland (0–0), v E. Germany (lost 1–2)

TREVOR EDWARDS WON THE FIRST of his two full international caps for Wales at the age of 20 while he was doing his National Service in the RAF. The young full-back had appeared in just a handful of Football League matches for Charlton Athletic when he was selected for Wales as a replacement for Alf Sherwood. After appearing in two full international matches, he then took part in Wales's first-ever under-23 match.

Edwards was a nephew of Dai Astley, who made 13 full international appearances for Wales before the Second World War. He was taken on to the Charlton Athletic ground staff as a youngster and turned professional in 1955. He had been recommended to Athletic's manager Jimmy Seed by Haydn Price, the former Walsall and Welsh international.

He was a quick-tackling defender whose pace enabled him to cover well, and he could play in either full-back position and distributed the ball well. His consistent performances in the Addicks' defence attracted attention from Liverpool, but nothing came of it. Edwards had appeared in 64 games for Charlton when, in the summer of 1960, he was transferred to Cardiff City.

While he was with the Bluebirds he had a spell in the forward line, scoring three goals, but after appearing in 73 League games for the Ninian Park club he lost his first-team place. In April 1964 he decided to emigrate to Australia, where he continued his soccer career playing for Hakoah.

Roy VERNON

Position	Inside-forward
Born	Thomas Royston Vernon, Prestatyn, 14 April 1937
Died	4 December 1993
Height	5ft 9in
Weight	10st 2lb
Clubs	Blackburn Rovers, Everton, Stoke City, Halifax Town, Great Harwood
Welsh Caps	32 Goals 8

1957 v N. Ireland (0–0), v Czechoslovakia (won 1–0) 1 goal, v E. Germany (lost 1–2), v Czechoslovakia (lost 0–2)
1958 v E. Germany (won 4–1), v England (lost 0–4), v Scotland (1–1), v Sweden (0–0)
1959 v Scotland (lost 0–3)
1960 v N. Ireland (won 3–2)
1961 v Republic of Ireland (won 3–2), v Scotland (won 2–0) 1 goal, v England (lost 1–5)
1962 v N. Ireland (won 4–0), v Brazil (lost 1–3), v Brazil (lost 1–3), v Mexico (lost 1–2)
1963 v Scotland (lost 2–3), v Hungary (lost 1–3), v England (lost 0–4)
1964 v England (lost 0–4), v Scotland (1–1)
1965 v Greece (won 4–1) 1 goal, v N. Ireland (won 5–0) 2 goals, v Italy (lost 1–4)
1966 v England (0–0), v USSR (won 2–1) 1 goal, v Scotland (lost 1–4), v Denmark (won 4–2) 2 goals, v N. Ireland (lost 1–4)
1967 v N. Ireland (0–0)
1968 v England (lost 0–3)

ROY VERNON WAS A MEMBER of the Wales team that participated in the 1958 World Cup Finals in Sweden. He had made the first of his 32 international appearances against Northern Ireland in Belfast in April 1957, aged 19.

It was a friend of Johnny Carey the Blackburn Rovers' manager who saw Roy Vernon playing for Mostyn YMCA and recommended him to the Ewood Park club. Vernon had already been invited to Everton for a trial but opted to join the Rovers' ground staff.

The Prestatyn-born inside-forward made his League debut for Blackburn as an 18-year-old in September 1955. On that day he played on the right-wing against

Roy Vernon was a creative player who could strike a dead ball with tremendous power. *(Lancashire Evening Post)*

Liverpool and in direct opposition was his fellow countryman, Ray Lambert. Vernon retained his amateur status so that he could represent Wales at both youth and amateur levels. By the time he was 19, he had won his first Welsh cap in the goalless draw against Northern Ireland.

Vernon was a regular member of the Blackburn side, displaying maturity far beyond his years. He was a creative player who could strike a dead ball with tremendous power. He was also more than capable of producing breathtaking wizardry on the pitch, although he was also temperamentally unpredictable. Having helped Blackburn win promotion to the First Division in 1957/58, he began to grow increasingly disillusioned with life at Ewood Park. He continually clashed with Rovers new manager Dally Duncan and decided to follow his mentor, Johnny Carey, to Everton. He joined the Toffees in a £27,000 deal that took Eddie Thomas to Blackburn in exchange.

Vernon went on to captain Everton and was the club's leading scorer in four of his five seasons at Goodison Park. He was a member of the side that won the League Championship in 1962/63. He formed a prolific goalscoring partnership with Alex Young, scoring 24 goals in that campaign, including a hat-trick in a 4–1 win over Fulham on the final day of the season to clinch the title.

At Goodison there were occasional brushes with Carey's successor, Harry Catterick and, in March 1965, after scoring 110 goals in 199 League and Cup games, Vernon left Everton and joined Stoke City. After five productive seasons with the Potters, Vernon left the Victoria Ground to spend a short time playing in South Africa. He had taken his total of international appearances to 32 and had a brief spell on loan with Halifax Town.

In September 1970 he returned to the North-West to join former Blackburn colleagues Ronnie Clayton and Bryan Douglas at Great Harwood. Together all three former internationals took the little Northern Premier League club into the first round of the FA Cup for the first time in its history. Vernon retired from the game in 1972 and later ran an antiques business in Blackburn, but began to suffer from arthritis of the hip and spine. He died in 1993 at the age of 56.

Colin WEBSTER

Position	Centre-forward
Born	Colin Webster, Cardiff, 17 July 1932
Died	Swansea, 1 March 2001
Height	5ft 9in
Weight	11st 0lb
Clubs	Cardiff City, Manchester United, Swansea Town, Newport County
Welsh Caps	4
	1957 v Czechoslovakia (won 1–0)
	1958 v Hungary (1–1), v Mexico (1–1), v Brazil (lost 0–1)

COLIN WEBSTER WON THREE of his four Welsh caps playing in the 1958 World Cup Finals in Sweden, and was on the books of three of Wales's four Football League clubs.

He joined his home-town team Cardiff City as a 17-year-old in 1949, but failed to make the grade with the Bluebirds. Jimmy Murphy's contacts put Manchester United in touch with the youngster, and in May 1952 he signed for the Old Trafford club. He was too old to take part in the club's FA Youth Cup success and had to serve his apprenticeship in the Central League.

After making his League debut at Portsmouth towards the end of the 1953/54 season, the versatile forward, who was also able to play at wing-half, played enough games in the club's League Championship winning side of 1955/56 to qualify for a medal. After the Munich air disaster, he established himself as a first-team regular and played in United's 1958 FA Cup Final defeat against Bolton Wanderers. The following October, having scored 31 goals in 79 League and Cup games, he joined Swansea Town for a fee of £6,000.

Webster soon made an impact at the Vetch Field and in 1959/60 was the club's leading scorer with 21 goals. Included in his total were hat-tricks against Plymouth Argyle and Charlton Athletic. He was the Swans' top scorer in 1960/61, when he found the net 18 times. In March 1983, after scoring 65 goals in 159 League games, he left the club to see out his career with Newport County.

Des PALMER

Position	Inside-forward
Born	Desmond Frederick Palmer, Swansea, 23 September 1931
Height	5ft 9in
Weight	11st 7lb
Clubs	Swansea Town, Liverpool, Durban City (South Africa), Derby County
Welsh Caps	3 Goals 3
	1957 v Czechoslovakia (lost 0–2)
	1958 v E. Germany (won 4–1) 3 goals, v England (lost 0–4)

DES PALMER MADE HIS INTERNATIONAL debut for Wales against Czechoslovakia in May 1957 and scored a hat-trick in only his second full international when Wales beat East Germany 4–1 in 1958.

He made his Swansea debut against Hull City in September 1952, but although he had a scoring record of almost one goal every other game, he never really established himself as a first-team regular at the Vetch Field. He ended the 1956/57 season as the club's top scorer with 18 goals, after which he was capped by Wales, but he never netted a hat-trick for the Swans in his total of 38 goals in 83 League games.

He left the club in March 1959 to join Liverpool in return for a fee of £4,000 and wing-half Ron Saunders. Sadly for Palmer, his move to Anfield turned into a disaster when he suffered knee ligament damage playing for the club's Central League side before he had made his first-team debut.

On leaving Merseyside he tried his luck in South Africa before Derby County manager Harry Storer signed him for the Rams. Although he scored six goals in 18 first-team outings, the move didn't work out and he was released.

Dai THOMAS

Position	Full-back/Inside-forward
Born	David Thomas, Abercregan, nr Port Talbot, 1 August 1926
Height	5ft 7in
Weight	11st 5lb
Clubs	Abercregan, Swansea Town, Newport County
Welsh Caps	2
	1957 v Czechoslovakia (lost 0–2)
	1958 v E. Germany (won 4–1)

DAI THOMAS HAD BEEN selected for Wales as a reserve on a number of occasions before winning the first of two full caps against Czechoslovakia in May 1957.

He began his footballing career with local Welsh League side Abercregan before being given his chance at Football League level with Swansea Town. He started life at the Vetch Field as an inside-forward but was soon converted to full-back, and over the next 11 seasons with the Swans he was one of the club's most consistent performers.

Thomas was one of the game's best club men. Throughout his time at the Vetch he missed games only through injury or illness, and he was never dropped. He went on to score 16 goals, many of them vital, in 298 League appearances for the Swans. In the summer of 1961, he was unexpectedly made available for transfer at a nominal fee and joined Newport County.

The popular defender went on to appear in 58 League games for the Somerton Park club before hanging up his boots.

Graham VEARNCOMBE

Position	Goalkeeper
Born	Graham Vearncombe, Cardiff, 28 March 1934
Died	Cardiff, 25 April 1993
Height	5ft 10in
Weight	12st 3lb
Clubs	Cardiff City, Merthyr Tydfil
Welsh Caps	2
	1958 v E. Germany (won 4–1)
	1961 v Republic of Ireland (won 3–2)

CARDIFF-BORN GOALKEEPER Graham Vearncombe was capped twice at full international level by Wales, and played his first game for the Bluebirds on the final day of the 1952/53 season in a 2–0 defeat at Aston Villa.

However, over the next two seasons, he appeared in only 17 League games as he understudied Ron Howells. He eventually became the Ninian Park club's first-choice keeper midway through the 1955/56 campaign. That season also saw him win a Welsh Cup winners' medal as Swansea Town were beaten 3–2 in the final. In

1957/58 he shared the goalkeeping duties with Ken Jones, but the following season he played only in the final game of the campaign as the club's cricketing keeper Ron Nicholls took over between the posts. However, he was the club's keeper in all bar one of the games in their run to lifting the Welsh Cup again, and won his second medal in that competition as Lovell's Athletic were beaten 2−0.

Vearncombe became the club's No. 1 custodian again in 1959/60 and went on to appear in 238 first-team games, making his last appearance in the 2−0 Welsh Cup final replay win over Bangor City in May 1964 to win his third such medal.

Vearncombe left the Bluebirds in the close season to play part-time football for Merthyr Tydfil.

Ron HEWITT

Position	Inside-forward
Born	Ronald Hewitt, Flint, 21 June 1928
Died	23 September 2001
Height	5ft 8in
Weight	10st 3lb
Clubs	Wolverhampton Wanderers, Walsall, Darlington, Wrexham, Cardiff City, Coventry City, Chester City, Hereford United, Northwich Victoria, Witton Albion, Caernarvon.
Welsh Caps	5 Goals 1
	1958 v Israel (won 2−0), v N. Ireland (1−1) 1 goal, v Sweden (0−0), v Hungary (won 2−1), v Brazil (lost 0−1)

RON HEWITT MADE THREE appearances for Wales in the 1958 World Cup Finals.

He had started his career as a junior with Wolverhampton Wanderers but, after failing to make the grade at Molineux, he had short spells with Walsall in 1949 and Darlington in 1950. A move to Wrexham in 1951 saw the Flint-born player embark on a six-year stay at the Racecourse Ground.

In 1951/52, his first season with the Robins, he topped the club's scoring charts with 16 goals in 38 games. After netting 13 the following season, he topped the club's scoring lists for a second time in 1953/54. His best season in terms of goals scored was 1956/57, when he scored 22 goals in just 31 League appearances, including hat-tricks against Barrow and Carlisle United. That campaign also saw him represent the Third Division (North) team against the South, but in the summer of 1957 he left the Racecourse Ground to join Cardiff City for £7,000. Within months of his arrival at Ninian Park, Hewitt won the first of his five Welsh caps in the World Cup play-off second leg against Israel.

He led the Bluebirds' goal charts for two successive seasons, which included a hat-trick in a 4−3 home win over Blackburn Rovers in March 1958.

He returned to Wrexham in 1959 two years after joining Cardiff City. After a further season in which he took his Wrexham goal tally to 111 in 267 first-team games, he joined Coventry City for £4,500. He later ended his League career with Chester before playing non-League football for Hereford United, Northwich Victoria, Witton Albion and Caernarvon.

Colin BAKER

Position	Wing-half
Born	Colin Baker, Cardiff, 18 December 1934
Height	5ft 9in
Weight	11st 4lb
Clubs	Cardiff Nomads, Cardiff City
Welsh Caps	7
	1958 v Mexico (1–1)
	1960 v Scotland (1–1), v N. Ireland (won 3–2)
	1961 v Republic of Ireland (won 3–2), v Scotland (won 2–0), v England (lost 1–5)
	1962 v Scotland (lost 0–2)

COLIN BAKER WON SEVEN full Welsh international caps. He played his first Wales match against Mexico in the 1958 World Cup Finals in Sweden.

He was one of the greatest wing-halves in the history of Cardiff City. He joined the Ninian Park club from Cardiff Nomads. Replacing his namesake Billy Baker in the Bluebirds' side, he made his League debut in a 2–2 draw at home to Sheffield Wednesday on the final day of the 1953/54 season. He had to wait until the 1955/56 season before winning a regular place in the City side and over the next ten seasons or so, made 352 first-team appearances including being an ever-present in 1961/62.

Although he was not a prolific goalscorer, finding the net on just 19 occasions during his Bluebirds' career, he did come close to scoring a hat-trick in the 5–1 home win over Charlton Athletic on 2 January 1960. He had scored two of Cardiff's goals when his long-range shot took a wicked deflection and hit the foot of the Addicks keeper's post.

Colin Baker very rarely suffered from injuries, but he was the injured player who had to come off when David Summerhayes became the club's first substitute in the opening match of the 1965/66 season against Bury.

Phil WOOSNAM

Position	Inside-forward
Born	Philip Abraham Woosnam, Caersws, 22 December 1932
Height	5ft 10in
Weight	10st 10lb
Clubs	Bangor University, Manchester City, Sutton United, Leyton Orient, West Ham United, Aston Villa
Welsh Caps	17 Goals 3
	1959 v Scotland (lost 0–3), v England (2–2)
	1960 v England (1–1), v Scotland (1–1), v N. Ireland (won 3–2) 1 goal
	1961 v Republic of Ireland (won 3–2) 1 goal, v Scotland (won 2–0), v England (lost 1–5), v N. Ireland (won 5–1), v Spain (lost 1–2) 1 goal, v Hungary (lost 2–3)
	1962 v England (1–1), v Scotland (lost 0–2), v N. Ireland (won 4–0), v Brazil (lost 1–3)
	1963 v Hungary (1–1), v N. Ireland (won 4–1) 1 goal

PHIL WOOSNAM APPEARED for Wales at schoolboy, amateur and youth levels before playing for Manchester City as an amateur. During his four years at Maine Road he studied at Bangor University and appeared in only one League game for the club.

After his National Service he joined Leyton Orient, and in four seasons with the Brisbane Road club scored 19 goals in 108 League games.

In November 1958 he joined West Ham United for a fee of £30,000. At that time only three British players had commanded a higher fee in the transfer market. During his four years at Upton Park, he won 14 full Welsh caps to add to the one he had won while with Leyton Orient. After scoring 27 goals in 147 first-team games, he was allowed to leave Upton Park, and in November 1962 he moved to Aston Villa for a fee of £27,000.

Although never a prolific scorer, he scored 20 in 40 League and Cup appearances for the Villans in 1965/66 before unexpectedly leaving the club in the close season to become manager-coach of theAmerican club the Atlanta Chiefs.

In 1969 he was appointed Commissioner of the North American Soccer League (NASL) and the following year he coached the United States World Cup side.

Vic CROWE

Position	Wing-half
Born	Victor Herbert Crowe, Abercynon, 31 January 1932
Height	5ft 10in
Weight	11st 4lb
Clubs	West Bromwich Albion, Aston Villa, Peterborough United
Welsh Caps	16
	1959 v England (2–2), v N. Ireland (lost 1–4)
	1960 v England (1–1), v N. Ireland (won 3–2)
	1961 v Republic of Ireland (won 3–2), v Scotland (won 2–0), v England (lost 1–5), v N. Ireland (won 5–1), v Spain (lost 1–2), v Spain (1–1), v Hungary (lost 2–3)
	1962 v England (1–1), v Scotland (lost 0–2), v Brazil (lost 1–3), v Mexico (lost 1–2)
	1963 v Hungary (lost 1–3)

VIC CROWE WAS BORN IN South Wales. He was just two years old when he moved with his family to Handsworth, Birmingham. After playing with Erdington Albion, West Bromwich's nursery side, he signed professional forms for Aston Villa in the summer of 1952.

He made his League debut for Villa at Manchester City in October 1954, a match in which Tommy Thompson scored a hat-trick in his side's win. In 1959/60 he missed just one game as Villa won the Second Division Championship. He was capped 16 times by Wales, winning his first against England at his home ground of Villa Park in November 1958. Crowe made an impressive debut as Wales drew 2–2.

In 1960/61, he was instrumental in Villa winning the first-ever League Cup and in 1963 won a runners-up prize in the same competition. Crowe left Villa Park in 1964 to join Peterborough United, having made 351 League and Cup appearances.

He played in just 56 League matches for Posh before becoming assistant-coach to NASL-side Atlanta Chiefs. He returned to Villa Park in 1969 and in January 1970 became the club's manager. He took them to the League Cup Final in 1971 and a year later led the club back into the Second Division. He left Villa in 1974 to coach Portland Timbers and returned to these shores to coach at a number of non-League clubs.

Dai WARD

Position	Inside-forward
Born	David Ward, Barry, 16 July 1934
Died	12 January 1996
Height	5ft 8in
Weight	10st 4lb
Clubs	Barry Town, Bristol Rovers, Cardiff City, Watford, Brentford, Worcester City, Bath, Cambridge United
Welsh Caps	2
	1959 v England (2–2)
	1962 v England (1–1)

DAI WARD WAS A BORN OPPORTUNIST, an inside-forward of pace, skill and bravery who was most unlucky not to make more than two appearances for Wales.

He started his career with his home-town team Barry Town, where his goalscoring exploits alerted a number of clubs. Ward joined Bristol Rovers in November 1954 but had to wait until the spring of 1956 before being called up to deputise for the injured Geoff Bradford. He responded by scoring nine times in eight outings and, if the Pirates had beaten Leeds United and Liverpool in their last two games, they would have won promotion to the top flight.

In December 1956, in the match against Doncaster Rovers, Ward scored a hat-trick in the space of just four minutes – in goal for the Belle Vue club that day was Northern Ireland international keeper Harry Gregg. Ward's best season in terms of goals scored was 1958/59, when he found the net 27 times in 38 matches. This form led to the first of his two international caps. Unfortunately an injury to Dave Bowen prompted a late reshuffle in which Ward was switched to left-half. Although he created a goal for Ivor Allchurch, he lost his place.

After disagreeing on a number of occasions with Bristol Rovers' boss Bert Tann Ward embarked on a bitter battle to leave the club, which he criticised for lack of ambition. At one time he threatened to quit the game and actually took a job as an ice-cream salesman. The unhappy saga eventually ended in February 1961, when he signed for Cardiff City.

Predictably, he continued to score at a higher level and won a second Wales cap But he fell out of favour at Ninian Park too, and saw his playing days out with Watford and Brentford, an anti-climax to a career that could and should have hit the heights.

Vic ROUSE

Position	Goalkeeper
Born	Raymond Victor Rouse, Swansea, 16 March 1936
Height	6ft 0in
Weight	11st 10lb
Clubs	Millwall, Crystal Palace, Northampton Town, Oxford United, Leyton Orient
Welsh Caps	1
	1959 v N. Ireland (lost 1–4)

VIC ROUSE HAS GONE DOWN in football's annals as the first international player to be chosen from the ranks of the Fourth Division. He appeared for Wales against Northern Ireland in Belfast on 22 April 1959.

Unable to make the grade with Millwall, Rouse joined Crystal Palace in the summer of 1956 and over the next seven seasons was the club's first-choice goalkeeper. Palace fans knew that his selection for his country was fully deserved, for he had impressed many with his splendid performances and was in a run of 143 consecutive League appearances with just a single absence. Rouse succeeded Roy Bailey between the posts before going on to set up a club record of 238 Football League goalkeeping appearances (since exceeded by the invincible John Jackson). It then took Bill Glazier – another goalkeeper destined for the First Division – to oust him.

Rouse was ever-present throughout Palace's promotion-winning season of 1960/61. A feature of his game that season was an accurate and powerful throw by which he frequently set up a fast Palace counter-attack.

He left Selhurst Park in April 1963 to join Northampton Town, but had left the County Ground before the new season began to spend a couple of seasons with Oxford United. He later ended his involvement with the first-class game by playing for Leyton Orient.

He then went to play in America for Atlanta Chiefs, where he also became coach for several years. On his return to England, he became manager and coach to the Metropolitan Police team.

Tony ROWLEY

Position	Inside-forward
Born	Antonio Camilio Rowley, Porthcawl, 19 September 1929
Height	6ft 0in
Weight	12st 3lb
Clubs	Wellington Town, Birmingham City, Stourbridge, Liverpool, Tranmere Rovers, Bangor City
Welsh Caps	1
	1959 v N. Ireland (lost 1–4)

TONY ROWLEY BEGAN HIS CAREER with Wellington Town, where his goalscoring feats prompted Birmingham City to offer him terms. However, he failed to make any League appearances while at St Andrew's and was transferred to non-League Stourbridge.

Liverpool picked him up in October 1953 and he scored a hat-trick on his debut for the Reds. His tally of 38 goals in 60 appearances over four seasons at Anfield is quite impressive but Rowley had his critics. There were some who said he was too slow and consequently he drifted in and out of the Liverpool team.

Tranmere manager Peter Farrell paid a club record fee of £3,500 for his services in March 1958. In his first full season at Prenton Park, he was the club's joint top scorer with Keith Williams, both players netting 26 goals. Included in Tony Rowley's total were four goals in a 9–0 home win over Accrington Stanley and a spell in which he scored eight goals in six consecutive games. It was his form this season that led to him being capped by Wales against Northern Ireland in Belfast.

At the end of the 1960/61 season, by which time he had scored 49 goals in 108 games, he left Prenton Park to play non-League football for Bangor City.

Graham MOORE

Position	Midfielder
Born	Graham Moore, Hengoed, 7 March 1941
Height	6ft 0in
Weight	13st 2lb
Clubs	Cardiff City, Chelsea, Manchester United, Northampton Town, Charlton Athletic, Doncaster Rovers
Welsh Caps	21 Goals 1

1960 v England (1–1) 1 goal, v Scotland (1–1), v N. Ireland (won 3–2)
1961 v Republic of Ireland (won 3–2), v Spain (1–1)
1962 v Brazil (lost 1–3)
1963 v Hungary (1–1), v N. Ireland (won 4–1)
1964 v Scotland (lost 1–2), v N. Ireland (lost 2–3)
1966 v N. Ireland (lost 1–4), v Chile (lost 0–2)
1969 v Scotland (lost 3–5), v England (lost 1–2), v N. Ireland (0–0), v Rest of the UK (lost 0–1)
1970 v Italy (lost 1–4), v England (1–1), v Scotland (0–0), v N. Ireland (won 1–0)
1971 v Romania (0–0)

GRAHAM MOORE WON THE FIRST of his 21 Welsh caps against England at Ninian Park in October 1959. He scored with a last-minute header to earn his side a 1–1 draw.

He had begun his playing days with Bargoed YMCA in 1956 and joined Cardiff City the following year. After some impressive displays for the Ninian Park club's reserve side, he made his first–team debut at Brighton and Hove Albion in September 1958 and scored a last-minute equaliser to make the score 2–2.

In 1959/60 Moore scored in the first three games of the season and went on to find the net 13 times in 41 League games as the club won promotion to the First Division. The following season he had the misfortune to break a leg but still managed to score four of City's goals in their 16–0 Welsh Cup win over Knighton. In

his Wales debut Graham Moore scored with a last-minute header in a 1–1 draw with
ngland. *(Getty Images)*

December 1961 Chelsea manager Tommy Docherty paid £35,000 to take Moore, the 'golden boy' of Welsh football, to Stamford Bridge.

He had scored 32 goals in 101 first-team outings for Cardiff, but in his first few weeks with Chelsea he struggled to find his form as the club were relegated. He led them back to the top flight in 1962/63 but in November 1963 he was transferred to Manchester United for £35,000.

Unable to make much of an impression at Old Trafford, he moved on to Northampton Town before later playing for Charlton Athletic and Doncaster Rovers.

Mel NURSE

Position	Centre-half
Born	Melvyn Tudor George Nurse, Swansea, 11 October 1937
Height	6ft 2in
Weight	12st 12lb
Clubs	Swansea City, Middlesbrough, Swindon Town, Bury Town, Merthyr Tydfil
Welsh Caps	12
	1960 v England (1–1), v N. Ireland (won 3–2)
	1961 v Republic of Ireland (won 3–2), v Scotland (won 2–0), v England (lost 1–5),
	v N. Ireland (won 5–1), v Spain (lost 1–2), v Spain (1–1), v Hungary (lost 2–3)
	1963 v Hungary (lost 1–3), v England (lost 0–4)
	1964 v Scotland (1–1)

MEL NURSE, A WELSH SCHOOLBOY centre-half, began his League career with his home-town club, Swansea City, signing professional forms in June 1955. Over the next seven seasons Nurse gave many outstanding performances at the heart of the Swansea defence. In 1960, after winning two Welsh under-23 caps, he made his full international debut against England at Wembley. It was the first of 12 full caps for his country, nine of them won while he was with the Swans.

He proved himself to be an inspirational leader, captaining the Swans during his last few seasons with the club. However, as the Welsh club struggled in the lower reaches of the Second Division, Nurse requested a transfer on a number of occasions, on all of which he was turned down. But eventually the Swans had to release him, and in September 1962 he joined Middlesbrough for a fee of £25,000.

It wasn't long before his performances led to his appointment as club captain at Ayresome Park. Over the next three seasons, Nurse was a virtual ever-present, and although he scored only nine goals in 124 games for the Teesside club, many were spectacular efforts. One of his strikes while a Boro player was against his former club and sent them spiralling into the Third Division. In the summer of 1965 Nurse joined Swindon Town and spent three seasons at the County Ground before returning to Swansea in the summer of 1968.

He scored 11 goals in 256 League games in his two spells with Swansea before entering non-League football with Suffolk club, Bury Town. He later ended his career with Merthyr Tydfil, for whom he was playing when he suffered a broken leg.

1960-69

Ups and Downs

The fortunes of the Welsh international side fluctuated through the 1960s. After Jimmy Murphy relinquished his position as team manager in 1964 because of the pressure of his work at Old Trafford, the Welsh FA appointed the former Welsh skipper Dave Bowen.

His first match in charge saw Wales beat Scotland 3–2, with Ken Leek netting two of the goals; but the game was sadly notable as John Charles's last for Wales. Fortunately for Bowen, the Welsh tradition of finding outstanding centre-halves was to continue, as Mike England proved his worthiness to fill the No. 5 red shirt as convincingly as the many great Welshmen before him. Among the other players Bowen had at his disposal were Gary Sprake, Peter Rodrigues and the inspirational Terry Hennessey, while up front he could call on the evergreen Ivor Allchurch, Roy Vernon and the two Davies, Ron and Wyn. He also had Cliff Jones, who had played an important role in the great Spurs team who did the League and FA Cup double in the early 1960s.

There should have been great deeds to report, but, while there were good displays – Russia were beaten 2–1 at Ninian Park in 1965 – the Nations Cup and World Cup passed and Wales failed to qualify. Matches that would once have packed both Ninian Park and the Racecourse Ground failed to attract the crowds. The major problem was that Dave Bowen had trouble in freeing his players from club duty.

Even in 1969, when Wales were trying to qualify for the World Cup, the problem of player release put an intolerable strain on those responsible for getting the team together. Then in April of that year Wales flew to Dresden for a World Cup qualifier against East Germany with only ten players. Gil Reece had to relinquish his seat on the plane because it was overbooked, and he and several other players had to follow a day later to make up the squad. Not surprisingly, Wales lost 2–1.

These were not the brightest days for Wales, and the struggles emphasised the difficulties faced by a small country fighting to preserve its footballing identity and reputation.

Graham E. WILLIAMS

Position	Left-back
Born	Graham Evan Williams, Denbigh, 2 April 1938
Height	5ft 8in
Weight	10st 0lb
Clubs	Rhyl, West Bromwich Albion, Weymouth
Welsh Caps	26 Goals 1

1960 v N. Ireland (won 3–2)
1961 v Republic of Ireland (won 3–2), v Scotland (won 2–0), v England (lost 1–5)
1963 v Hungary (1–1), v N. Ireland (won 4–1)
1964 v England (lost 0–4), v Scotland (1–1), v N. Ireland (lost 2–3)
1965 v Scotland (won 3–2), v Denmark (lost 0–1), v England (lost 1–2), v Greece (lost 0–2), v Greece (won 4–1), v N. Ireland (won 5–0) 1goal, v Italy (lost 1–4), v USSR (lost 1–2)
1966 v N. Ireland (lost 1–4), v Brazil (lost 1–3), v Brazil (lost 0–1), v Chile (lost 0–2)
1967 v Scotland (1–1), v England (lost 1–5), v N. Ireland (0–0)
1968 v N. Ireland (won 2–0)
1969 v Italy (lost 0–1)

GRAHAM E. WILLIAMS CAME UP through West Bromwich Albion's youth team set-up as a left-winger. However, he was soon converted to left-back and took over that position in the club's first team from fellow Welsh international Stuart Williams, although both men shared the two full-back positions on occasions for both club and country. Graham E. Williams also played in a number of his 26 international appearances in his former position of left-winger.

He spent 18 years with the Albion, being granted a fully deserved testimonial in 1966. That year he captained the Hawthorns side to success in the League Cup and in 1968 to success in the FA Cup as Everton were beaten 1–0. Williams, who appeared in almost 400 League and Cup games for Albion, was partnered at right-back for the majority of those games by England defender Don Howe. Howe later became Albion's manager and released the popular Welsh international in the summer of 1972.

Williams then joined Weymouth as player-manager before coaching in Greece and Kuwait. He also had a three-month spell as 'chief coach and manager' at Cardiff City.

Ken LEEK

Position	Centre-forward
Born	Kenneth Leek, Ynysybwl, nr Pontypridd, 26 July 1935
Height	5ft 10in
Weight	11st 6lb
Clubs	Pontypridd, Northampton Town, Leicester City, Newcastle United, Birmingham City, Bradford City, Rhyl, Merthyr Tydfil, Ton Pentre.
Welsh Caps	13 Goals 5

1961 v Scotland (won 2–0), v England (lost 1–5) 1 goal, v N. Ireland (won 5–1) 1 goal, v Spain (lost 1–2), v Spain (1–1), v Hungary (lost 2–3)
1962 v Scotland (lost 0–2), v Brazil (lost 1–3) 1 goal, v Mexico (lost 1–2)

1963 v England (lost 0–4)
1965 v Scotland (won 3–2) 2 goals, v Greece (lost 0–2), v Greece (won 4–1)

KEN LEEK, WHO SCORED TWICE in the last three minutes of Wales's 3–2 win over Scotland in 1965, began his Football League career with Northampton Town. He had scored 29 goals in 77 games for the Cobblers when he left the County Ground to join Leicester City in May 1958.

The hard-working centre-forward continued to find the net for the then Filbert Street club, so much so that he had, in fact, scored in every round during the Foxes' run to the 1961 FA Cup Final. On the morning of the match against double-chasing Tottenham Hotspur, however, he was dropped. Not surprisingly, he left Leicester in the summer after having scored 43 goals in 111 League and Cup games to join Newcastle United.

Unable to settle at St James Park, he joined Birmingham City in November 1961. Although he played in only 24 games that season, he was the club's top scorer, with 18 goals including a spell of 12 goals in 12 games. In 1962/63 he again headed the club's goalscoring charts with 30 League and Cup goals, including two in the first leg of the League Cup Final when the Blues beat Aston Villa 3–1. After scoring 61 goals in 120 games for the St Andrew's club, he returned to Northampton Town, where he took his tally of goals to 33 in 93 games before signing for his last League club, Bradford City.

After leaving Valley Parade he played non-League football for Rhyl, Merthyr Tydfil and Ton Pentre before settling in the Daventry area, working for Ford Motors.

Graham G. WILLIAMS

Position	Outside-left
Born	George Graham Williams, Wrexham, 31 December 1936
Height	5ft 5in
Weight	10st 4lb
Clubs	Oswestry Town, Bradford City, Everton, Swansea Town, Wrexham, Wellington Town, Tranmere Rovers, Port Vale, Runcorn.
Welsh Caps	5 Goals 1
	1961 v N. Ireland (won 5-1), v Spain (lost 1–2), v Spain (1–1), v Hungary (lost 2–3)
	1962 v England (1–1) 1 goal

GRAHAM 'FLICKA' WILLIAMS scored his one goal for Wales in his last international appearance to hold England to a 1–1 draw at Ninian Park in October 1961.

He had been introduced into League football by Bradford City following spells with Wrexham and Oswestry Town as an amateur.

In March 1956, towards the end of his first season at Valley Parade, Williams was transferred to First Division Everton, becoming the Goodison Park club's first big money signing in seven years. A bright future was predicted for him, but during his three years with the Merseyside club he failed to do himself justice.

However, after moving to Swansea in February 1959 for a fee of £5,000, he became an instant favourite of the Vetch Field crowd, who admired the diminutive winger's bravery and willingness to take on defenders. Although one of the smallest players in the game, he was a brave, tricky and elusive customer. After achieving under-23 honours, he won the first of five full caps against Northern Ireland and would undoubtedly have won many more but for a broken leg that kept him out of action for two seasons. Williams scored 20 goals in 89 League games, a number of them spectacular, before returning to North Wales to play for his home-town club.

He re-established himself with the Robins and then had a brief period playing non-League football for Wellington Town. A productive spell at Tranmere followed before he ended his League career with Port Vale. Williams, who had scored 47 goals in 249 games for his five League clubs, then joined Runcorn, where he ended his playing days.

Mike ENGLAND

Position	Centre-half
Born	Harold Michael England, Holywell, 2 December 1941
Height	6ft 2in
Weight	13st 3lb
Clubs	Blackburn Rovers, Tottenham Hotspur, Cardiff City
Welsh Caps	44 Goals 3

1962 v N. Ireland (won 4–0), v Brazil (lost 1–3), v Mexico (lost 1–2)
1963 v Hungary (1–1), v N. Ireland (won 4–1)
1964 v England (lost 0–4), v Scotland (1–1), v N. Ireland (lost 2–3)
1965 v Denmark (lost 0–1), v England (lost 1–2), v Greece (lost 0–2), v Greece (won 4–1) 1 goal, v N. Ireland (won 5–0), v Italy (lost 1–4), v USSR (lost 1–2)
1966 v England (0–0), v USSR (won 2–1), v Scotland (lost 1–4), v Denmark (won 4–2), v N. Ireland (lost 1–4)
1967 v Scotland (1–1), v England (lost 1–5)
1968 v England (lost 0–3), v N. Ireland (won 2–0), v W. Germany (1–1)
1969 v E. Germany (lost 1–2), v Rest of the UK (lost 0–1)
1970 v E. Germany (lost 1–3), v Italy (lost 1–4) 1 goal, v England (1–1), v Scotland (0–0), v N. Ireland (won 1–0)
1971 v Romania (0–0)
1972 v Finland (won 3–0), v England (lost 0–3), v Scotland (lost 0–1), v N. Ireland (0–0)
1973 v England (lost 0–1), v England (1–1), v Scotland (lost 0–2), v England (lost 0–3)
1974 v Poland (lost 0–3)
1975 v Hungary (won 2–0), v Luxembourg (won 5–0) 1 goal

MIKE ENGLAND WAS ONE OF the few Welshmen to have both played for and managed his country. He began his career in the same Ysgol Dinas Basing team as his future international team-mate Ron Davies. At the age of 15 he was offered the choice of joining Blackburn Rovers or Glamorgan County Cricket Club. He accepted the Ewood Park club's offer and was a member of Blackburn's FA Youth Cup-winning side of 1959.

Mike England of Blackburn Rovers and Wales was one of the few players to both captain
and manage his national team. *(Lancashire Evening Post)*

He played for Rovers at outside-right, half-back and centre-forward before settling in central defence. England's versatility was used by his country at under-23 level when he was played at inside-forward as well as in the half-back line. He went on to play in a record 11 games at this level, many of his appearances coming after he had made his full international debut against Northern Ireland in April 1962, a match Wales won 4-0.

England soon became Blackburn's first-choice centre-half. His height made him dominant in the air, while on the ground his strength and speed made him a daunting prospect for even the quickest of opposition forwards. However, England's game was not based just on power; his deft touches, instant control and accurate distribution put him in a class of his own. Eventually he became disenchanted with the Ewood Park club who, it seemed, lacked ambition as they let a number of their better players join top clubs. Rovers refused to let him go and England, who was a stubborn and fiercely ambitious player, threatened to quit the game altogether. England made a series of transfer requests. Having scored 21 goals in 184 games, he left Ewood Park to join Tottenham Hotspur in August 1966.

The fee of £95,000 was a British record for a defender and it wasn't long before he became a great favourite with the White Hart Lane crowd. In his first season with Spurs he helped the club lift the FA Cup. Despite missing the 1971 League Cup Final with an ankle injury, he helped the North London club win the 1972 UEFA Cup and the 1973 League Cup. He also appeared and scored in the 1974 UEFA Cup Final.

In March 1975, aged 33, he was troubled by ankle problems. With Spurs struggling against relegation, he quite suddenly announced his retirement after scoring 20 goals in 434 games for the White Hart Lane club.

However, he re-emerged the following August to play one season for Cardiff City, having spent the summer with Seattle Sounders. He helped the Bluebirds win promotion from the Third Division and then spent four further summers playing for Seattle.

Following Mike Smith's decision to take up a club appointment, Mike England was successful with his application to become Wales's team manager. In his first game in charge in May 1980, Wales beat England 4-1 at the Racecourse Ground. Despite the limited resources at his disposal, England took Wales close to qualification for both the World Cup and the European Championships. He helped to guide the international careers of Mark Hughes, Ian Rush, Neville Southall and Kevin Ratcliffe. In 1984 England, was awarded the MBE for his services to Welsh soccer.

In February 1988 Mike England was controversially sacked after Wales had yet again just missed qualification for a major championship. As with all major football decisions, opinions were divided on the wisdom of this move. Though some questioned his tactical approach, most recognised his great qualities as a motivator of players.

Terry HENNESSEY

Position	Central defender/Wing-half
Born	William Terence Hennessey, Llay, 1 September 1942
Height	5ft 11in
Weight	11st 5lb
Clubs	Birmingham City, Nottingham Forest, Derby County
Welsh Caps	39

1962 v N. Ireland (won 4–0), v Brazil (lost 1–3), v Brazil (lost 1–3)

1963 v Scotland (lost 2–3), v Hungary (lost 1–3), v England (lost 0–4), v Hungary (1–1)

1964 v England (lost 0–4), v Scotland (1–1)

1965 v Scotland (won 3–2), v Denmark (lost 0–1), v England (lost 1–2), v Greece (lost 0–2), v USSR (lost 1–2)

1966 v England (0–0), v USSR (won 2–1), v Scotland (lost 1–4), v Denmark (won 4–2), v N. Ireland (lost 1–4), v Brazil (lost 1–3), v Brazil (lost 0–1), v Chile (lost 0–2)

1967 v Scotland (1–1), v England (lost 1–5)

1968 v England (lost 0–3), v Scotland (lost 2–3), v N. Ireland (won 2–0)

1969 v W. Germany (1–1), v E. Germany (lost 1–2), v Rest of the UK (lost 0–1)

1970 v E. Germany (lost 1–3), v England (1–1), v Scotland (0–0), v N. Ireland (won 1–0)

1972 v Finland (won 3–0), v Czechoslovakia (lost 0–1), v England (lost 0–3), v Scotland (lost 0–1)

1973 v England (lost 0–1)

TERRY HENNESSEY WAS A cultured player who won 39 caps for his country. He was given his Birmingham City debut by the club's new manager Gil Merrick in March 1961 in a 3–2 home win over Manchester City. In 1962/63 he won a League Cup winner's medal and was voted Midland Footballer of the Year. In that season he was the club's only ever-present, and over the next six seasons that he played at St Andrew's he missed very few matches. Having appeared in 202 games for Birmingham, he left St Andrew's in November 1965 to join Nottingham Forest as the eventual replacement for long-serving Jeff Whitefoot.

His Forest debut was unusual in that both the club's goals in a 2–1 win over Blackpool were scored by the opposition in the dying minutes of the game. Hennessey was only 23 when he arrived at the City Ground, but he looked much older because of his receding hairline. Showing a great maturity in his play, he was soon appointed Forest's captain and in 1966/67 led the Reds to the FA Cup semi-final, where they lost 2–1 to Spurs, and to runners-up in the First Division.

Hennessey was one of the players that Matt Gillies allowed to leave. He joined Derby County in February 1970 as the Rams' first £100,000 signing and in 1971/72 won a League Championship medal. After injury cut short his playing career the following season, he managed non-League Tamworth and Kimberley Town before coaching Tulsa Roughnecks in the NASL.

Mal LUCAS

Position	Wing-half
Born	Peter Malcolm Lucas, Wrexham, 7 October 1938
Height	5ft 8in
Weight	11st 6lb
Clubs	Bradley Rovers, Leyton Orient, Norwich City, Torquay United
Welsh Caps	4
	1962 v N. Ireland (won 4–0), v Mexico (lost 1–2)
	1963 v Scotland (lost 2–3), v England (lost 0–4)

MAL LUCAS WAS A FORMER WELSH schoolboy international. He had also won recognition at under-23 level before making the first of his four full international appearances for Wales against Northern Ireland in April 1962.

After having trials with Bolton Wanderers and Liverpool, Mal Lucas joined Leyton Orient. In six years with the Brisbane Road club he made 157 League appearances. His Football League debut for the London club came in November 1958, but it was another two seasons before he established himself as a first-team regular. In 1961/62 he helped Orient win promotion to the First Division. However, after they were relegated the following season, he was allowed to leave the club and joined Norwich City.

His debut for the Canaries came in a 4–1 home win over Manchester City in September 1964, after which he played in the remaining 35 games to help the club finish sixth in the Second Division. In 1967/68 he missed just one game, the nearest he came to being ever-present. Two seasons later he played the last of his 204 League and Cup games for the club and moved on to Torquay United, to whom he gave four seasons' loyal service.

On hanging up his boots he became an account executive/collector for Brent Leisure Services Ltd.

Dave HOLLINS

Position	Goalkeeper
Born	David Michael Hollins, Bangor, 4 February 1938
Height	6ft 0in
Weight	11st 9lb
Clubs	Merrow, Brighton and Hove Albion, Newcastle United, Mansfield Town, Nottingham Forest, Aldershot, Portsmouth, Romford
Welsh Caps	11
	1962 v Brazil (lost 1–3), v Mexico (lost 1–2)
	1963 v Hungary (1–1), v N. Ireland (won 4–1)
	1964 v England (lost 0–4)
	1965 v Greece (won 4–1), v N. Ireland (won 5–0), v Italy (lost 1–4)
	1966 v Scotland (lost 1–4), v Denmark (won 4–2), v Brazil (lost 1–3)

DAVE HOLLINS CAME FROM a well-known footballing family: his father Bill was a goalkeeper for Wolves; his brother John was a household name at Chelsea and

Arsenal; and another brother, Roy, turned out for Brighton. Strangely, Dave and John Hollins played international football for different countries with John appearing for England!

After signing for Brighton as a replacement for Bryan Harvey, his displays led to a number of top clubs making enquiries. In March 1961 he joined Newcastle United.

He had a remarkable opening few weeks as a Newcastle player. He saved a penalty on his Magpies' debut against eventual double winners Spurs and then saw Chelsea score six goals past him on his St James's debut. Four weeks later, United were relegated to the Second Division.

Agile and acrobatic, Dave Hollins made a series of breathtaking saves that earned him international recognition for Wales. Sadly, he failed to maintain such a high standard week in week out and, following a dispute with new manager Joe Harvey over wages, he left the North-East to play for Mansfield Town.

He served the Stags with distinction, being part of their FA Cup giant-killing line-up that reached the sixth round in 1968/69. Hollins then played for Aldershot and had loan spells with Nottingham Forest and Portsmouth before playing non-League football for Romford.

After leaving the game, Hollins settled in Guildford, running a decorating business. He also played bowls for the London Welsh club

Barrie JONES

Position	Outside-right
Born	Barrie Spencer Jones, Swansea, 10 October 1941
Height	5ft 7in
Weight	11st 4lb
Clubs	Swansea City, Plymouth Argyle, Cardiff City
Welsh Caps	15 Goals 2

1963 v Scotland (lost 2–3), v Hungary (lost 1–3), v England (lost 0–4), v Hungary (1–1),
      v N. Ireland (won 4–1)
1964 v Scotland (1–1) 1 goal, v N. Ireland (lost 2–3)
1965 v Denmark (lost 0–1)
1969 v Italy (lost 0–1), v W. Germany (1–1) 1 goal, v E. Germany (lost 1–2), v Scotland
      (lost 3–5), v England (lost 1–2), v N. Ireland (0–0), v Rest of the UK (lost 0–1)

SWANSEA-BORN BARRIE JONES began his career with his home-town team as a winger in the traditional mould. In five years at the Vetch Field he was capped eight times at Welsh under-23 level. He won the first of 15 full caps when he played against Scotland at Ninian Park in October 1962.

Jones possessed pace and a powerful shot. He had scored 23 goals in 166 games when he was transferred to Plymouth Argyle for £45,000 in September 1964. It was then the Devon club's highest-ever payment for a player. It was Jones's exceptional ball control which Argyle manager Malcolm Allison was seeking to incorporate into his team plans. In three seasons at Home Park, Jones scored nine goals in 99 games. However, in March 1967 the fair-haired winger returned to South Wales and to Cardiff City for a fee of £25,000.

Shortly after his arrival at Ninian Park, he switched from the wing to midfield. His play improved so much that he went on to win a further seven international caps while with the Bluebirds. He was ever-present in the 1967/68 and 1968/69 seasons, playing in 107 consecutive League games from his debut. On 4 October 1969 he broke his leg in the last minute of Cardiff's 3–2 defeat at Blackpool. Although he attempted a number of comebacks in the club's reserves, he never regained full fitness and had to hang up his boots at League level. Though never a prolific scorer with the Ninian Park club, netting 18 goals in his 107 games, he did once score a hat-trick in the club's 5–0 win over Mauritius in May 1969.

He then had a number of seasons playing non-League football before going into business in the Swansea area.

Tony MILLINGTON

Position	Goalkeeper
Born	Anthony Horace Millington, Hawarden, 5 June 1943
Height	5ft 10in
Weight	11st 8lb
Clubs	West Bromwich Albion, Crystal Palace, Peterborough United, Swansea City
Welsh Caps	21
	1963 v Scotland (lost 2–3), v Hungary (lost 1–3), v England (lost 0–4)
	1965 v England (lost 1–2), v USSR (lost 1–2)
	1966 v Brazil (lost 0–1), v Chile (lost 0–2)
	1967 v England (lost 1–5), v N. Ireland (0–0)
	1968 v N. Ireland (won 2–0), v W. Germany (1–1)
	1969 v Italy (lost 0–1), v E. Germany (lost 1–2)
	1970 v England (1–1), v Scotland (0–0), v N. Ireland (won 1–0)
	1971 v Czechoslovakia (lost 1–3), v Finland (won 1–0)
	1972 v Finland (won 3–0), v Czechoslovakia (lost 0–1), v Romania (lost 0–2)

GOALKEEPER TONY MILLINGTON began his Football League career with West Bromwich Albion, where his displays between the posts led to his winning the first of 21 full caps for Wales against Scotland in October 1962.

Millington made 40 League appearances for the Baggies before leaving the Hawthorns for Crystal Palace in the autumn of 1964. The Hawarden-born keeper failed to establish himself at Selhurst Park and in March 1966 signed for Peterborough United. Millington went on to appear in 118 League games for the Posh and there set the club record for international caps (a total of 8), a record he still holds today. He joined Swansea City in the summer of 1969 and made his debut in a goalless home draw at home to Chesterfield on the opening day of the club's Fourth Division promotion-winning season of 1969/70, a campaign in which he kept 20 clean sheets.

A brave and agile goalkeeper, Tony Millington had very few bad games during his five seasons at the Vetch Field, and his performances won him a further eight caps. During the 1971/72 season he equalled Jack Parry's record sequence of remaining unbeaten in five consecutive games, a record that was broken only by Dai Davies in 1981/82. Tony Millington was a great Vetch Field favourite and appeared in 178 League games for the Swans before later helping his brother Grenville run the Wrexham disabled supporters club.

Cliff SEAR

Position	Left-back
Born	Reginald Clifford Sear, Wrexham, 22 September 1936
Height	5ft 10in
Weight	10st 8lb
Clubs	Oswestry Town, Manchester City, Chester City
Welsh Caps	1
	1963 v England (lost 0–4)

CLIFF SEAR HAD JUST CAPTAINED the Wales under-23 side when he was called into the full squad and made his international debut against England at Wembley in October 1962. In what turned out to be his only full international appearance, he didn't have the best of games: Wales lost 4–0.

He was working as a miner at Bershaw Colliery when he was first on Manchester City's books as an amateur before being offered professional terms in January 1957. After some impressive performances in the club's Central League side, he was given his first-team debut at Birmingham City in April of that year in a match the Blues drew 3–3. Early the following season he settled into the City side and, over the next few seasons, Cliff Sear was one of the club's most consistent performers.

Sear went on to appear in 279 League and Cup games for Manchester City before leaving Maine Road in April 1968 to join Chester City. He appeared in a further 51 League games for the then Sealand Road club before becoming the club's youth team coach, working alongside his former Manchester City colleague Alan Oakes, who had become Chester's manager.

Ollie BURTON

Position	Wing-half
Born	Alwyn Derek Burton, Chepstow, 11 November 1941
Height	5ft 11in
Weight	12st 0lb
Clubs	Newport County, Norwich City, Newcastle United
Welsh Caps	9
	1963 v Hungary (1–1), v N. Ireland (won 4–1)
	1964 v England (lost 0–4)
	1969 v Italy (lost 0–1), v E. Germany (lost 1–2), v Scotland (lost 3–5), v England (lost 1–2), v N. Ireland (0–0)
	1972 v Czechoslovakia (lost 0–1)

MARKED OUT BY HIS GINGER HAIR and a high-pitched yell on the field, Ollie Burton was a tough footballer but one who could play a bit too. He also possessed a tremendous drive that was never used to its full potential during his international career – he won nine full caps for Wales over nine years.

He began his League career with Newport County before joining Norwich City in March 1961 after the Canaries had paid £11,000 for his services. During his time at Carrow Road his displays led to a number of top-flight clubs chasing his signature. In the summer of 1963 Newcastle manager Joe Harvey paid the East Anglian club £37,500 to bring Burton to St James Park – one of United's costliest purchases at the time. Signed as a wing-half, the Welshman eventually operated as a defensive stopper when the style of football changed after the 1966 World Cup.

A versatile player for the Magpies, Burton also played right-back, in midfield and even at centre-forward. He took his time to settle in the North-East and didn't win a permanent place in the Newcastle side until the end of the 1964/65 season. Although he faced stiff competition for a place at the heart of the Magpies' defence from the likes of Iley, McNamee and Moncur, it was Burton who wore the No. 5 shirt when the Magpies won the Inter Cities Fairs Cup.

He was on Newcastle's books for over ten years. He was the club's first substitute and the first substitute to score for the club. However, he was unlucky with injuries and a knee problem forced his early retirement in January 1972.

Barrie HOLE

Position	Wing-half
Born	Barrington Gerard Hole, Swansea, 16 September 1942
Height	5ft 10in
Weight	10st 4lb
Clubs	Cardiff City, Blackburn Rovers, Aston Villa, Swansea City
Welsh Caps	30
	1963 v N. Ireland (won 4–1)
	1964 v N. Ireland (lost 2–3)
	1965 v Scotland (won 3–2), v Denmark (lost 0–1), v England (lost 1–2), v Greece (lost 0–2), v Greece (won 4–1), v N. Ireland (won 5–0), v Italy (lost 1–4), v USSR (lost 1–2)
	1966 v England (0–0), v USSR (won 2–1), v Scotland (lost 1–4), v Denmark (won 4–2), v N. Ireland (lost 1–4), v Brazil (lost 1–3), v Brazil (lost 0–1), v Chile (lost 0–2)
	1967 v Scotland (1–1), v England (lost 1–5), v N. Ireland (0–0)
	1968 v England (lost 0–3), v Scotland (lost 2–3), v N. Ireland (won 2–0), v W. Germany (1–1)
	1969 v Italy (lost 0–1), v W. Germany (1–1), v E. Germany (lost 1–2)
	1970 v Italy (lost 1–4)
	1971 v Romania (0–0)

BARRIE HOLE'S FATHER BILLY, a Swansea Town player, had been a pre-war Welsh international winger. His older brothers Colin and Alan both followed in their father's footsteps and played for their home-town club. Barrie, however, did not follow the family tradition, preferring to join neighbours and rivals Cardiff City. He made his League debut for the Bluebirds as a 17-year-old in a 4−3 win at Leyton Orient in February 1960, a season in which the Ninian Park club won promotion to the First Division. He soon established himself as a creative wing-half and inside-forward, although occasionally he turned out at centre-forward in an injury crisis. Hole rarely missed a game, being ever-present in 1964/65. While at Ninian Park, Hole won five Welsh under-23 caps and the first of 30 full caps when he played against Northern Ireland in April 1963.

During the summer of 1966 Hole was allowed to leave Cardiff and joined Blackburn Rovers for a fee of £40,000. He was the Lancashire club's first specialist midfielder in the days when tactics were changing in the wake of England's World Cup triumph. Tall and slight in build, Hole was an extraordinarily gifted ball player. His intelligent positioning and constructive use of the ball made him one of the most exciting midfield players of his era. Not affected by pre-match nerves, he had the ability to ghost into the opposing penalty area completely unmarked, enabling him to score a number of important goals.

In September 1968 Hole was on the move again, this time to Aston Villa for £60,000. Although he admitted to a fear of flying, Hole rather surprisingly put his international career in jeopardy when he flew to play in America with the Villa Park club rather than represent Wales in the 1970 Home International Championships. Hole's time at Villa Park was not a happy one. Midway through the 1969/70 season he quit the club following a stormy time under Tommy Docherty's management. At this point Hole turned his back on the game and went into his father's business. However, during the summer of 1970 Roy Bentley, the Swansea manager, persuaded him to make a comeback, willingly paying Villa £20,000 to bring Hole to the Vetch Field. He was an important member of the Swans' midfield for a couple of seasons, but he left the game in May 1972 and became a newsagent in Swansea, like his father before him.

Wyn DAVIES

Position	Forward
Born	Ronald Wyn Davies, Caernarfon, 20 March 1942
Height	6ft 1in
Weight	12st 5lb
Clubs	Caernarfon, Wrexham, Bolton Wanderers, Newcastle United, Manchester City, Manchester United, Blackpool, Crystal Palace, Stockport County, Crewe Alexandra, Bangor City, Arcadia Shepherds.
Welsh Caps	34 Goals 6

1964 v England (lost 0−4)
1965 v Scotland (won 3−2) 1 goal, v Denmark (lost 0−1), v England (lost 1−2), v Greece (lost 0−2), v N. Ireland (won 5−0), v USSR (lost 1−2) 1 goal
1966 v England (0−0), v USSR (won 2−1), v Scotland (lost 1−4), v Denmark (won 4−2) 1 goal, v N. Ireland (lost 1−4) 1 goal, v Brazil (lost 1−3), v Brazil (lost 0−1), v Chile (lost 0−2)

Wyn Davies of Manchester City and Wales had stunning aerial power, winning 34 caps for Wales. (*Manchester Evening News*)

1967 v Scotland (1–1), v England (lost 1–5) 1 goal
1968 v Scotland (lost 2–3), v N. Ireland (won 2–0), v W. Germany (1–1) 1 goal
1969 v Italy (lost 0–1), v Scotland (lost 3–5), v England (lost 1–2), v N. Ireland (0–0)
1970 v E. Germany (lost 1–3)
1971 v Romania (0–0), v Czechoslovakia (lost 1–3)
1972 v England (lost 0–3), v Scotland (lost 0–1), v N. Ireland (0–0)
1973 v England (lost 0–1), v Scotland (lost 0–2), v N. Ireland (lost 0–1)
1974 v Poland (lost 0–3)

WYN DAVIES WAS AN important member of the Welsh side for ten years. During that time he made 34 full international appearances for his country.

It was while playing for his home-town team Caernarfon in the Welsh League that he was spotted by a Wrexham scout. After scoring on his debut, Davies went on to become a member of the Robins' side that enjoyed a lengthy run in the League Cup. In his last match for Wrexham before signing for Bolton Wanderers, Davies was one of three players who scored a hat-trick in a 10–1 win over Hartlepool United. He joined Bolton in a transfer deal worth £20,000 in cash plus Ernie Phythian, who was valued at £10,000, moving to the Racecourse Ground.

During his time at Bolton, Wyn Davies became affectionately known as 'Wyn the Leap' due to his amazing heading talents in the centre-forward position. Quickly installed into the No. 9 shirt, he was a regular in the Wanderers' side for four and a half years. He ended the 1964/65 season as the Wanderers' top scorer with 25 goals, including a hat-trick against Southampton. His performances for Bolton led to his name being linked with a number of top clubs, and in October 1966 he left Burnden Park to join Newcastle United for a club record fee of £80,000.

He was the Magpies' first superstar of the modern game, although a reluctant one, being a somewhat remote character. Twenty-four hours after joining Newcastle, he made his debut in the local derby against Sunderland. Although his ball skills never matched his aerial ability, he held the ball up well and controlled the forward line. Very much a provider of chances, the target man up front, he was never lethal in front of goal. Yet he did grab his share of goals, mostly with powerful headers that found the back of the net. As the Magpies surged into European competition, Davies became one of the most feared strikers on the Continent, scoring ten goals in 24 games and helping the club win the Inter Cities Fairs Cup in 1969. However, after suffering an injury, Davies found it difficult to get back into the side and returned to the north-west to team up with long-time admirer Joe Mercer at Manchester City.

His stay at Maine Road was brief - he moved across the city to Old Trafford. Given that he was playing in a struggling team and alongside another non-established striker, Ted MacDougall, any hope of an Indian summer disappeared with the appointment of Tommy Docherty as manager. After a short spell with Blackpool he headed south for an equally brief stint with Crystal Palace before later playing for Stockport County and Crewe Alexandra.

He later played non-League football for Bangor City and also in South Africa's National Football League for Pretoria club Arcadia Shepherds.

Gary SPRAKE

Position	Goalkeeper
Born	Gareth Sprake, Swansea, 3 April 1945
Height	6ft 0in
Weight	13st 3lb
Clubs	Leeds United, Birmingham City
Welsh Caps	37

1964 v Scotland (1–1), v N. Ireland (lost 2–3)
1965 v Scotland (won 3–2), v Denmark (lost 0–1), v Greece (lost 0–2)
1966 v England (0–0), v USSR (won 2–1), v N. Ireland (lost 1–4)
1967 v Scotland (1–1)
1968 v England (lost 0–3), v Scotland (lost 2–3)
1969 v W. Germany (1–1), v Scotland (lost 3–5), v England
    (lost 1–2), v N. Ireland (0–0), v Rest of the UK (lost 0–1)
1970 v E. Germany (lost 1–3), v Italy (lost 1–4)
1971 v Romania (0–0), v Scotland (0–0), v England (0–0),
    v N. Ireland (lost 0–1)
1972 v Finland (won 3–0), v England (lost 0–3), v Scotland
    (lost 0–1), v N. Ireland (0–0)
1973 v England (lost 0–1), v England (1–1), v Poland (won 2–0),
    v Scotland (lost 0–2),
    v N. Ireland (lost 0–1)
1974 v Poland (lost 0–3), v Scotland (lost 0–2), v N. Ireland
    (won 1–0)
1975 v Austria (lost 1–2), v Hungary (won 2–0), v Luxembourg
    (won 5–0)

GARY SPRAKE, WHO LIVED next door but one to Arsenal and Wales goalkeeper Jack Kelsey, became the international side's youngest-ever goalkeeper when he made his debut against Scotland in November 1963 aged 18 years 231 days.

Sprake had left school at the age of 15 to take an apprenticeship as a fitter and turner, playing in goal for the works team. He was spotted by Leeds United's Welsh-based scout Jack Pickard, who also discovered John Charles playing for Swansea Schools.

In March 1962 Sprake made an unexpected first-team debut for the Elland Road club. He was enjoying a lie-in when frantic Leeds officials contacted him on the morning of United's Second Division game at Southampton. The club's first-choice keeper Tommy Younger had been taken ill, and so 16-year-old Sprake was rushed to Manchester Airport and flown to the south coast in a two-seater plane for a dramatic League debut. The game kicked-off 15 minutes late because of United's predicament. Although the Saints won 4–1, Sprake had impressed enough and the following season won Younger's place on merit. Leeds manager

Don Revie thought very highly of Sprake. When the young keeper abandoned Elland Road after feeling homesick and losing his confidence, to return to South Wales, Revie followed him to convince the blond-haired six-footer that he had a future in the game.

Sprake eventually made the breakthrough into the Leeds first team in September 1962 in the match against Swansea at the Vetch Field, a game the Yorkshire club won 2–0. He was the Leeds first-choice keeper for the next ten seasons, during which time he won a League Championship medal, a League Cup winners' medal, two Inter Cities Fairs Cup medals and a Second Division Championship medal.

When Leeds won the League Championship in 1968/69, Sprake was an ever-present as the Elland Road club won the title with the fewest number of goals

When Gary Sprake of Leeds United and Wales made his debut against Scotland in November 1963 he became Wales's youngest-ever goalkeeper. *(Lancashire Evening Post)*

conceded by any champions. At the start of that season Sprake produced heroics to keep out Ferencvaros of Hungary and help Leeds secure a goalless draw and so win the Inter Cities Fairs Cup for the first time.

A member of the phenomenal Leeds United side of the 1970s, Sprake played in 507 first-team games, more than any other Elland Road goalkeeper. Although Sprake was an acrobatic and exciting keeper, he was also prone to lapses of concentration, more often than not when the TV cameras were present. One famous Sprake incident came at Anfield, where he literally threw the ball into his own net. Yet in spite of these occasional blunders Gary Sprake was a goalkeeper of the highest class.

On losing his Leeds place to David Harvey, Sprake was transferred to Birmingham City in October 1973 for a fee of £100,000. He had made just 16 League appearances for the St Andrew's club when injury and illness forced his premature retirement from the game.

Ron DAVIES

Position	Centre-forward
Born	Ronald Tudor Davies, Holywell, 25 May 1942
Height	6ft 0in
Weight	11st 6lb
Clubs	Chester City, Luton Town, Norwich City, Southampton, Portsmouth, Manchester United, Millwall
Welsh Caps	29 Goals 9

1964 v N. Ireland (lost 2–3) 1 goal
1965 v England (lost 1–2)
1966 v Brazil (lost 1–3) 1 goal, v Brazil (lost 0–1), v Chile (lost 0–2)
1967 v Scotland (1–1) 1 goal, v England (lost 1–5), v N. Ireland (0–0)
1968 v Scotland (lost 2–3) 1 goal, v N. Ireland (won 2–0) 1 goal, v W. Germany (1–1)
1969 v Italy (lost 0–1), v W. Germany (1–1), v Scotland (lost 3–5) 2 goals, v England (lost 1–2) 1 goal, v N. Ireland (0–0), v Rest of the UK (lost 0–1)
1970 v England (1–1), v Scotland (0–0), v N. Ireland (won 1–0)
1971 v Czechoslovakia (lost 1–3) 1 goal, v Scotland (0–0), v England (0–0), v N. Ireland (lost 0–1)
1972 v Romania (lost 0–2), v England (lost 0–3), v Scotland (lost 0–1), v N. Ireland (0–0)
1974 v England (lost 0–2)

RON DAVIES WAS ONE OF THE postwar period's most consistent goalscorers and there was a time when his heading ability made him probably the most sought after player in the top flight. His success at Southampton turned him into a valuable commodity for his country, and in May 1969 he established himself as a striker of true international worth with three spectacular headers in the Home International Tournament.

Determined to succeed, he trained by hurdling in Army boots to build up his strength and leaping powers. Spotted by Chester manager John Harris, he continued to work in the local steelworks as an apprentice moulder. However, five weeks later he was employed as a ground-staff boy, the first Chester ever had. Although he had

Ron Davies, one of the most consistent postwar goalscorers, found the net on his international debut against Northern Ireland in 1963. *(Manchester Evening News)*

made his League debut the previous season, it was 1960/61 when he really established himself in the Cestrians side, scoring 23 goals in 39 games. In the last game of the season at Hartlepool United, Chester needed to win to avoid the humiliation of being bottom of the League. Davies helped his side score four times, grabbing two fine goals himself. However, as his team's defence let in four, Chester were last. Still a teenager, he topped the club's goalscoring charts again the following season and in 1962/63 netted four goals in a 6–1 win over Luton Town.

A few weeks later he joined Luton Town for a fee of £10,000. Although the Hatters were relegated to the Third Division in Davies's first season at Kenilworth Road, he more than repaid his transfer fee, scoring 21 goals in 29 games for his new club.

In September 1963 Davies joined Norwich City for a record transfer fee of £35,000. His first season at Carrow Road brought him 27 goals as he relished the service he was given by two wingers whose task it was to find Davies's blond head. Although he continued to score goals, Norwich weren't winning anything, and so Davies left to play for First Division Southampton.

Not even the most enthusiastic Saints' fan expected Davies to make the impact he did. In 1966/67 he scored 38 First Division goals to become the Football League's top marksman. Five further efforts in cup-ties made him the leading goalscorer in Europe. In 1967/68 he scored another 28 goals to retain his title as the League's leading scorer, sharing the honour with George Best.

Davies's heading powers were awesome, and in August 1969 he scored four goals at Old Trafford, prompting Matt Busby to say that he had no peer in Europe. In fact, United headed a whole host of clubs eager for his signature, but the Saints were determined to hold on to him. However, injuries then began to take their toll, and in April 1973 he was allowed to join south-coast rivals Portsmouth. Davies later played for Manchester United and Millwall before hanging up his boots.

Roy EVANS

Position	Full-back
Born	Royston Sidney Evans, Parkmill, 5 June 1943
Died	Ebbw Vale, 20 January 1969
Height	5ft 8in
Weight	11st 3lb
Clubs	Swansea City, Hereford United
Welsh Caps	1
	1964 v N. Ireland (lost 2–3)

AT THE END OF THE 1962/63 season, his first at the Vetch Field, full-back Roy Evans played for the Wales under-23 side, later making two more appearances at that level. Evans went on to win one full cap for Wales when he played against Northern Ireland at the Vetch Field in April 1964, a match the Welsh lost 3–2.

Roy Evans was a strong-tackling full-back, whose positional play and distribution were second to none. He was a virtual ever-present in the Swansea side in the early 1960s. When Vic Gomersall left Manchester City to join the Swans, the two defenders formed one of the Vetch Field club's best full-back pairings since the Second World War.

He went on to appear in 217 League games for the Swans, scoring seven goals, many of them long-range spectacular strikes. He left the Vetch in 1967 to join then non-League Hereford United. He was a firm favourite with the Edgar Street club's fans.

Roy Evans and former Swansea player Brian Purcell were tragically killed in a car crash in January 1969.

Brian GODFREY

Position	Inside-forward
Born	Brian Cameron Godfrey, Flint, 1 May 1940
Height	5ft 8in
Weight	11st 2lb
Clubs	Flint Alexandria, Everton, Scunthorpe United, Preston North End, Aston Villa, Bristol Rovers, Newport County
Welsh Caps	3 Goals 2
	1964 v N. Ireland (lost 2–3) 1 goal
	1965 v Denmark (lost 0–1), v Italy (lost 1–4) 1 goal

A CREATIVE MIDFIELDER, Brian Godfrey was a provider of numerous openings for his colleagues. He was always eager to burst through from the middle to shoot for goal, doing so twice in the three full international matches he played for Wales.

Although he started his League career with Everton and later played for Scunthorpe United, it was with Preston North End that Godfrey first came to prominence. He scored the goal that took North End to the 1964 FA Cup Final but was 12th man at Wembley. That was two years before substitutes were introduced, and to his disappointment he did not receive a medal. During his time at Deepdale, Godfrey proved himself a prolific scorer and in 1964/65 he teamed up with Alex Dawson, the two of them scoring 53 of North End's 80 goals. Godfrey's share was 26 and included a hat-trick in a 5–1 win at Ipswich Town. The following season Godfrey was the club's leading scorer with 20 goals, and in the last game of the campaign he netted the club's fastest-ever hat-trick – his three goals coming in just five minutes as North End beat Cardiff City 9–0.

Having joined Aston Villa in October 1967, Godfrey continued to score goals as though they were going out of fashion. He achieved his greatest moment in football when he returned to Wembley as captain of Villa in the Football League Cup Final. His midfield generalship had inspired the Third Division club to victory over Manchester United in the semi-final. But there was no fairy-tale ending, and Tottenham Hotspur defeated Villa in the final. After four years at Villa Park, he joined Bristol Rovers, one of the teams they beat on their way to the final, in a £58,000 deal that took Ray Graydon to Villa Park.

In 1973 Newport County manager Billy Lucas laid out a club record fee of £10,000 to secure Godfrey's services, seeing him as an experienced general who could steer the Ironsides towards promotion. The midfielder linked up with his fellow former Evertonian Brian Harris, Newport's captain and assistant manager. He made an indifferent start but gradually settled down to give Newport some good service before leaving the playing side in 1975.

He then embarked on his own management career, taking in Bath City, Exeter City, Weymouth and Gloucester City. It has surprised many observers that the Welsh international did not remain in the profession at League level.

Mike JOHNSON

Position	Centre-half
Born	Michael George Johnson, Swansea, 13 October 1941
Height	6ft 0in
Weight	11st 6lb
Clubs	Swansea City
Welsh Caps	1
	1964 v N. Ireland (lost 2–3)

MIKE JOHNSON'S WHOLEHEARTED performances at the heart of the Swansea defence won him two Welsh under-23 caps. He secured his one and only full international cap against Northern Ireland at the Vetch Field in April 1964.

Johnson was a former Swansea Schoolboys player, and worked his way up through the ranks at the Vetch Field to make his first-team debut midway through the 1959/60 season. His early years at the Vetch were spent as understudy to Mel Nurse. However, whenever he did play for the Swans the powerful centre-half always gave a committed and polished performance, and in view of this the club let Nurse join Middlesbrough in September 1962.

By the time he had won full international honours, Johnson had not only become the Swans' regular centre-half but had been appointed club captain. In his first game as skipper he led the Swans to a 4–1 win over Barrow. Johnson scored only one goal for the South Wales club during his 168 League appearances, but his defensive displays certainly reduced the opportunities for the opposition forwards to score.

Ronnie REES

Position	Winger
Born	Ronald Raymond Rees, Ystradgynlais, 4 April 1944
Height	5ft 8in
Weight	10st 12lb
Clubs	Coventry City, West Bromwich Albion, Nottingham Forest, Swansea City
Welsh Caps	39 Goals 3

1965 v Scotland (won 3–2), v Denmark (lost 0–1), v England (lost 1–2), v Greece (lost 0–2), v Greece (won 4–1), v N. Ireland (won 5–0), v Italy (lost 1–4), v USSR (lost 1–2)
1966 v England (0–0), v USSR (won 2–1), v Scotland (lost 1–4), v Denmark (won 4–2) 1 goal, v N. Ireland (lost 1–4), v Brazil (lost 1–3), v Brazil (lost 0–1), v Chile (lost 0–2)
1967 v England (lost 1–5), v N. Ireland (0–0),
1968 v England (lost 0–3), v Scotland (lost 2–3), v N. Ireland (won 2–0) 1 goal, v W. Germany (1–1)
1969 v Italy (lost 0–1), v W. Germany (1–1), v E. Germany (lost 1–2), v Scotland (lost 3–5), v Rest of the UK (lost 0–1)
1970 v E. Germany (lost 1–3), v Italy (lost 1–4), v England (1–1), v Scotland (0–0), v N. Ireland (won 1–0) 1 goal
1971 v Romania (0–0), v Czechoslovakia (lost 1–3), v England (0–0), v N. Ireland (lost 0–1), v Finland (won 1–0)
1972 v Czechoslovakia (lost 0–1), v Romania (lost 0–2)

Ronnie Rees could play on either wing, and made 39 appearances for Wales. *(Lancashire Evening Post)*

ABLE TO PLAY ON EITHER WING, Ronnie Rees won international recognition in 1962 when he took Welsh under-23 honours. He secured the first of 39 caps in a 3–2 defeat of Scotland in October 1964.

Rees began his Football League career with Coventry City and made his debut for the Sky Blues against Shrewsbury Town in September 1962. After that he became a fixture in the Highfield Road club's first team and was never seriously threatened in six years with the club. An ever-present in 1963/64, when the Sky Blues won the Third Division Championship, his total of 15 goals included a hat-trick in an 8–1 home win over Shrewsbury Town. Rees went on to score 52 goals in 262 games for Coventry before being transferred to West Bromwich Albion for £65,000 in March 1968.

After just one season at the Hawthorns, he had a brief spell with Nottingham Forest before moving to Swansea City in January 1972 for what was then a club record fee of £26,000.

This was his final stopping place in League football. Although it has to be said that he never really made the impact for which all Swansea fans had hoped, he went on to make 89 League appearances before leaving the club. He then worked behind the scenes at Cardiff City before taking a job with a large car manufacturer in Bridgend.

Peter RODRIGUES

Position	Right-back
Born	Peter Joseph Rodrigues, Cardiff, 21 January 1944
Height	5ft 8in
Weight	11st 0lb
Clubs	Cardiff City, Leicester City, Sheffield Wednesday, Southampton, Romsey Town
Welsh Caps	40

1965 v Greece (lost 0–2), v Greece (won 4–1), v N. Ireland (won 5–0)
1966 v England (0–0), v USSR (won 2–1), v Scotland (lost 1–4), v Denmark (won 4–2),
    v N. Ireland (lost 1–4), v Brazil (lost 1–3), v Brazil (lost 0–1), v Chile (lost 0–2)
1967 v Scotland (1–1)
1968 v England (lost 0–3), v Scotland (lost 2–3), v N. Ireland (won 2–0)
1969 v E. Germany (lost 1–2), v England (lost 1–2), v N. Ireland (0–0), v Rest of the UK
    (lost 0–1)
1970 v E. Germany (lost 1–3), v England (1–1), v Scotland (0–0), v
    N. Ireland (won 1–0)
1971 v Romania (0–0), v Czechoslovakia (lost 1–3), v Scotland (0–0), v England (0–0),
    v N. Ireland (lost 0–1)
1972 v Finland (won 3–0), v Czechoslovakia (lost 0–1), v Romania (lost 0–2),
    v England (lost 0–3), v N. Ireland (0–0)
1973 v England (lost 0–1), v England (1–1), v Poland (won 2–0), v Scotland (lost 0–2),
    v England (lost 0–3), v N. Ireland (lost 0–1)
1974 v Poland (lost 0–3)

A FAST, ATTACKING FULL-BACK, Peter Rodrigues enjoyed nothing more than mounting spectacular overlapping raids down the wing. He was particularly quick in

A fast, attacking full-back, Peter Rodrigues of Southampton and Wales won 40 caps for the national side. *(Getty Images)*

recovery. Rodrigues made his under-23 debut for Wales just three months after his League debut for his home-town club, Cardiff City.

Rodrigues was a former Welsh schoolboy and youth international. He was almost transferred to Newport County during his early days at Ninian Park. At the time, Rodrigues hadn't made his League debut for the Bluebirds, but they wisely turned down the £500 offer from the Somerton Park club.

After making his Cardiff debut in a 3–3 draw at Sunderland in September 1963, Rodrigues was a virtual ever-present in the Bluebirds side for the next few seasons, appearing in both full-back positions. However, the Ninian Park club were unable to offer him the standard of football he required, and in December 1965 Rodrigues was sold to Leicester City for £42,500, a club record fee. He had won the first of 40 Welsh caps against Greece earlier that year.

At Filbert Street his pace, his overlapping inclinations and his undisputed mastery of the sliding tackle brought a new dimension to perceived notions of full-backs at the Midlands club. His career with the Foxes would surely have stretched much further had it not been for the emergence of Steve Whitworth. Only one disappointing incident – a missed close-range good chance in the 1969 FA Cup Final defeat by Manchester City – remotely overshadowed his stay at Leicester. But he firmly obliterated that particular Wembley memory later in his career. Rodrigues left Filbert Street in October 1970 when Danny Williams paid £50,000 to take him to Sheffield Wednesday.

The Owls, who had just been relegated to the Second Division, had started badly and Williams hoped that Rodrigues's arrival would help to turn the tide. In the event, Williams survived in office for only three more months while Rodrigues remained to serve two more successors, Dooley and Burtenshaw. However, although Rodrigues held his form and added 17 more caps to his collection while at Hillsborough, he was unable to halt the Yorkshire club's gradual slide. After being released on a free transfer in 1975, Rodrigues's lengthy and distinguished career climaxed in remarkable fashion. He probably felt that he had achieved all he could in the game when he joined Lawrie McMenemy's Southampton, yet twelve months later he captained the unfancied south-coast club to a shock FA Cup Final win over Manchester United.

Herbie WILLIAMS

Position	Midfielder
Born	Herbert John Williams, Swansea, 6 October 1940
Height	6ft 0in
Weight	11st 9lb
Clubs	Swansea City
Welsh Caps	3
	1965 v Greece (lost 0–2), v Greece (won 4–1)
	1972 v Romania (lost 0–2)

HERBIE WILLIAMS WAS AN IMPORTANT member of the Swansea side that reached the FA Cup semi-finals of 1964. His performances the following season led to his winning two Welsh caps when he played in both matches against Greece. Seven years later against Romania he added another cap to his collection.

He had been a member of the Swansea Schoolboys team that beat Manchester in the final of the English Schools' Trophy in 1954, a year in which the side also won the Welsh Shield. In 1955 Williams captained the Swansea Schoolboys as they won the Welsh Shield for a second time.

After leaving school he was apprenticed at Swansea Docks but decided to give this up when he was offered professional terms by the Swans. He was just 17 when he made his debut for the club in a 5–0 home win over Sunderland in September 1958. It was in this match that Ivor Allchurch scored four of Swansea's goals. His first goals for the club came at Leicester City when he scored twice in a 6–3 win for the Swans.

Williams was a great club man, and when Roy Bentley became manager in 1969 he was appointed captain. He went on to appear in 513 League games, scoring 104 goals including four goals against York City, a hat-trick against Southampton from left-half and a magnificent hat-trick in a 4–0 win over Oldham Athletic during the club's promotion-winning season of 1969/70. Later in his career he settled at centre-half, although he played in a variety of positions for the club.

Herbie Williams was a skilful and wholehearted player who played under seven managers at Swansea. He left the Vetch Field in January 1975 for a new life in Australia.

Cyril LEA

Position	Wing-half
Born	Cyril Lea, Wrexham, 5 August 1934
Height	5ft 9in
Weight	11st 0lb
Clubs	Bradley Rovers, Leyton Orient, Ipswich Town
Welsh Caps	2
	1965 v N. Ireland (won 5–0), v Italy (lost 1–4)

ORIGINALLY A FULL-BACK, Cyril Lea's career blossomed when he was converted to wing-half. He established himself in Leyton Orient's team from 1960/61 and went on to make 205 League appearances for the Brisbane Road club. He helped the Os into the First Division in 1962 but, after losing his place, he joined Ipswich Town in November 1964.

After making his first-team debut in a 1–1 home draw against Charlton Athletic, he played in the remaining 24 games of the season, captaining the side on six occasions. That season his form was such that he was capped twice by Wales at full international level – against Northern Ireland in Belfast and Italy in Florence.

Appointed club captain at Ipswich, he missed very few games over the next two seasons, the latter of which saw Town finish fifth in the Second Division. In 1967/68, when Ipswich won the Second Division Championship, Lea made just four appearances, and only one as substitute the following season when the club were in the top flight. Lea had played in 123 games for the Blues. On retiring he joined the club's coaching staff, although he did have a short spell as caretaker manager when Frank O'Farrell left the club.

He later coached the Welsh national side and was assistant to Alan Durban at Stoke City. Lea also had three good seasons at Colchester United when they just missed promotion in each of the campaigns conducted when he was in charge. However, despite his relative success he was sacked.

Colin GREEN

Position	Full-back
Born	Colin Robert Green, Wrexham, 10 February 1942
Height	5ft 8in
Weight	10st 8lb
Clubs	Everton, Birmingham City, Wrexham, Tamworth
Welsh Caps	15
	1965 v Italy (lost 1–4), v USSR (lost 1–2)
	1966 v England (0–0), v USSR (won 2–1), v Scotland (lost 1–4), v Brazil (lost 1–3), v Brazil (lost 0–1)
	1967 v England (lost 1–5)
	1968 v England (lost 0–3), v Scotland (lost 2–3), v N. Ireland (won 2–0), v W. Germany (1–1)
	1969 v Scotland (lost 3–5), v N. Ireland (0–0), v Italy (lost 0–1)

FULL-BACK COLIN GREEN BEGAN his Football League career with Everton. On his debut he marked the legendary Stanley Matthews in a 4–1 win for the Toffees at Blackpool. He had made only 15 League appearances for the Goodison Park club when Birmingham paid £12,000 for his services in December 1962.

Green made his City debut in a 2–0 home defeat at the hands of Tottenham Hotspur later that month. At the end of his first season at St Andrew's, he won a League Cup winners' medal after the Blues had beaten neighbours Aston Villa in the two-legged final. As a result of Green's performances over the next few seasons he won 15 full caps for Wales, the first against Italy in May 1965.

His full-back partners were numerous – Stan Lynn, Ray Martin and Bobby Thomson – but, no matter who it was, he always formed a fine understanding. Green, who suffered a broken leg in 1966, was a regular in the Birmingham side until the end of the 1968/69 season, when another injury cost him his first-team place. His only goal in 217 appearances for the club was the winner in a 3–2 victory at Carlisle United in September 1968. After leaving St Andrew's he had a short loan spell with Wrexham before ending his playing career with non-League Tamworth.

Gil REECE

Position	Winger
Born	Gilbert Ivor Reece, Cardiff, 2 July 1942
Height	5ft 7in
Weight	9st 9lb
Clubs	Cardiff City, Ton Pentre, Pembroke Borough, Newport County, Sheffield United, Swansea City.
Welsh Caps	29 Goals 2

1966 v England (0–0), v USSR (won 2–1), v Scotland (lost 1–4), v N. Ireland (lost 1–4)
1967 v Scotland (1–1)
1969 v Rest of the UK (lost 0–1)
1970 v Italy (lost 1–4)
1971 v Scotland (0–0), v England (0–0), v N. Ireland (lost 0–1), v Finland (won 1–0)
1972 v Finland (won 3–0) 1 goal, v Romania (lost 0–2), v England (lost 0–3), v Scotland (lost 0–1), v N. Ireland (0–0)
1973 v England (lost 0–1), v N. Ireland (lost 0–1)
1974 v Poland (lost 0–3), v England (lost 0–2), v Scotland (lost 0–2), v N. Ireland (won 1–0)
1975 v Austria (lost 1–2), v Hungary (won 2–0), v Luxembourg (won 5–0), v Hungary (won 2–1), v Luxembourg (won 3–1) 1 goal, v Scotland (2–2), v N. Ireland (lost 0–1)

GIL REECE JOINED CARDIFF CITY as a part-timer in May 1961 while continuing his trade as a plumber. He graduated to the club's reserve side and had a loan spell with Welsh League Ton Pentre. Towards the end of the 1962/63 season he was released and left to see out the season with Pembroke Borough. After turning in some useful displays, he was offered the chance to join Newport County and in 1964/65 he became one of the club's most consistent goalscorers.

At the end of that season he joined Sheffield United for a fee of £10,000. As a result of his performance during the early part of the 1965/66 campaign he won his first Welsh cap against England at Ninian Park. Apart from

Gil Reece of Sheffield United, 1970. Having won 29 caps, his international career was ended when he broke a leg. (*Lancashire Evening Post*)

minor injuries he held his place in the Wales side for the next few seasons, winning 29 caps, until he suffered a broken leg against Blackpool while playing for the Blades. He went on to score 58 goals in 210 appearances for the Bramall Lane club before leaving to rejoin Cardiff City in September 1972.

He became club captain and played in a variety of roles for the Bluebirds. In his first season he scored a hat-trick in a 5–0 Welsh Cup Final second leg win over Bangor City. He repeated the feat the following season when he scored the only goal of the Welsh Cup Final second leg against Stourbridge. Although the club were relegated in 1974/75, Reece was the top scorer with nine goals. The following season he helped the Bluebirds win promotion to the Second Division at the first attempt and won his third Welsh Cup winners' medal. He scored 35 goals in 114 games for City before returning to the Vetch Field for a short spell.

Keith PRING

Position	Winger
Born	Keith David Pring, Newport, 11 March 1943
Height	5ft 9in
Weight	11st 4lb
Clubs	Newport County, Rotherham United, Notts County, Southport
Welsh Caps	3
	1966 v Denmark (won 4–2), v Chile (lost 0–2)
	1967 v N. Ireland (0–0)

KEITH PRING MADE THREE FULL international appearances for Wales, but he had attended a rugby-playing school where he represented Cardiff Schools at the handling game. On leaving school he became an apprentice draughtsman. He joined Newport County as a part-time professional footballer. He was a fast-raiding winger able to play on either flank, and turned full-time at the age of 21.

Pring made 61 League appearances for the Ironsides. In October 1964 he joined Rotherham United for £10,000, and his form for the Millers in the Second Division prompted Wales's manager Dave Bowen to include him against Denmark in place of the injured Gil Reece.

Pring was transferred to Notts County as part of the deal that took Dave Watson to Millmoor. In 1969 he moved on to his last League club, Southport. In August 1971 his career was ended when he broke a leg in the match against Brentford. His comeback twelve months later was abortive and he decided to retire on medical advice.

After recovering to play rugby for Southport, where he set a club record of 263 points, he joined Wigan Athletic as coach. He worked for a number of years as a representative in the North-West for the Bass Charrington brewery.

Glyn JAMES

Position	Centre-half
Born	Edward Glyn James, Llangollen, 17 December 1941
Height	5ft 11in
Weight	12st 5lb
Clubs	Blackpool
Welsh Caps	9
	1966 v Brazil (lost 1–3), v Brazil (lost 0–1), v Chile (lost 0–2)
	1967 v N. Ireland (0–0)
	1968 v Scotland (lost 2–3)
	1971 v Czechoslovakia (lost 1–3), v Scotland (0–0), v England (0–0), v N. Ireland (lost 0–1)

GLYN JAMES, ONE OF Blackpool's longest-serving and most loyal players, was appointed captain not long after his debut for the club in 1960. His leadership qualities earned him nine Welsh caps, although he was never on the winning side.

James made his Blackpool debut as a replacement for the injured Roy Gratrix in a 2–0 defeat at Preston North End in October 1960. But, because of Gratrix's domination of the role, the Llangollen-born defender had to wait four seasons before replacing him on a regular basis.

Following Blackpool's relegation from the First Division in 1966/67, James was outstanding at the heart of the Seasiders' defence, leading the club back into the top flight in 1969/70. When Blackpool won the Anglo-Italian Cup against Bologna in 1971, James was missing through injury. But, when they played AS Roma in the 1972 final, he had an outstanding game, holding the defence together as the Italian giants threatened to overpower the Seasiders. At the beginning of the 1971/72 season, manager Bob Stokoe found himself facing an injury crisis and tried Glyn James at centre-forward. He responded with six goals in his first five games, including two in each of the opening games against Swindon Town and Cardiff City. Three games later he hit another brace in a 3–1 win at Portsmouth. However, when Keith Dyson arrived from Newcastle United, he returned to his normal position of centre-half.

James played his last game against Fulham in January 1975 and scored 25 goals in 446 League and Cup games. He was rewarded with a testimonial game after 15 seasons with the Bloomfield Road club.

Alan DURBAN

Position	Midfielder	
Born	William Alan Durban, Bridgend, 7 July 1941	
Height	5ft 9in	
Weight	10st 11lb	
Clubs	Cardiff City, Derby County, Shrewsbury Town	
Welsh Caps	27	Goals 2
	1966 v Brazil (lost 0–1)	
	1967 v N. Ireland (0–0)	

1968 v England (lost 0–3), v Scotland (lost 2–3) 1 goal, v N. Ireland (won 2–0),
   v W. Germany (1–1)
1969 v W. Germany (1–1), v E. Germany (lost 1–2), v Scotland (lost 3–5), v England (lost 1–2)
   v N. Ireland (0–0)
1970 v E. Germany (lost 1–3), v Italy (lost 1–4), v England (1–1), v Scotland (0–0),
   v N. Ireland (won 1–0)
1971 v Romania (0–0), v Czechoslovakia (lost 1–3), v Scotland (0–0), v England (0–0),
   v N. Ireland (lost 0–1), v Finland (won 1–0)
1972 v Finland (won 3–0) 1 goal, v Czechoslovakia (lost 0–1), v England (lost 0–3),
   v Scotland (lost 0–1), v N. Ireland (0–0)

ALAN DURBAN WAS THE ONLY Welsh international soccer player to have compete
in the All England Tennis Championships at Wimbledon. He could also quite easil
have made the grade at cricket or rugby union. However, by the time he left Po
Talbot Grammar School, a number of soccer scouts were competing for his signature.

Durban joined Cardiff City in September 1958 and made his League debut a year late
in a 2–1 win at Derby County, the club with which he was to make his name. After a
in-and-out period at Ninian Park, Durban was transferred to Derby County for a fee c
£10,000. It was certainly money well spent, for Durban was one of the few players
the Baseball Ground to survive and play a significant role in the Brian Clough era.

Durban had two distinct phases at Derby County, the first as a goalscoring insid
forward and the second as an intelligent midfield player. In his first role, he scored 2
goals in 1964/65, a total equalled by his partner Eddie Thomas, who had joined th
Rams from Swansea Town. Durban went on to score 112 goals in 403 first-tea
outings for Derby County, including four hat-tricks, but there is no doubt that his be
days at the club were when he played in midfield.

Although he lacked pace and was not a particularly good tackler, he had a great fir
touch and a wonderful feel for the flow of the game. Perhaps his greatest attribute wa
his ability to find space in crowded penalty areas, often arriving late to score a larg
number of his goals from close range.

Durban spent ten years at the Baseball Ground and was a major influence in th
team's rise to the First Division and, in 1971/72, its capture of the Leagu
Championship. On leaving Derby, he joined Shrewsbury Town, later becoming th
Gay Meadow club's player-manager. He steered the club out of the Fourth Division i
1974/75 and to Welsh Cup success. When he hung up his boots, Durban had playe
in more than 550 League games and appeared at all 92 grounds!

In February 1978 Durban was appointed manager of Stoke City, where h
introduced more discipline into the club and appointed Howard Kendall as his chi
coach. The Potters won promotion to the First Division in 1978/79 but then struggle
to avoid relegation in their first season in the top flight.

He left for Sunderland, taking on the task of restoring the Wearsiders to some of the
former greatness. However, after three troubled years he was sacked. Six months lat
he was back with Cardiff City as manager, but it turned out to be a bad move. Whe
the Bluebirds suffered relegation in two successive seasons, Durban was dismissed.

Disillusioned with the game, he became manager of the Telford Indoor Tenni
Centre.

Alan Durban was the only Welsh international soccer player to have competed in the All England Tennis Championships at Wimbledon. *(Getty Images)*

Frank RANKMORE

Position	Centre-half
Born	Frank Edward John Rankmore, Cardiff, 21 July 1939
Height	6ft 1in
Weight	13st 4lb
Clubs	Cardiff Corinthians, Cardiff City, Peterborough United, Northampton Town
Welsh Caps	1
	1966 v Chile (lost 0–2)

SIGNED BY CARDIFF CITY from local club Cardiff Corinthians, centre-half Frank Rankmore found himself mainly in the Bluebirds' reserve side at Ninian Park and at the end of the 1959/60 season he was placed on the transfer list. However, when the club's regular centre-half Danny Malloy left the Bluebirds, Rankmore was re-signed and came off the transfer list. In his first full season, in which he made 37 League appearances, Cardiff was relegated to the Second Division. He was powerfully built defender, full of determination and enthusiasm. Rankmore lost his place when John Charles arrived at Ninian Park, and was sold to Peterborough United for a fee of £10,000.

Rankmore was at home in the lower divisions. He gained his only full international cap against Chile as a substitute for Glyn James, when the Wales side toured South America in the summer of 1966.

In June 1968 he moved to Northampton Town after Wrexham dropped out of the race for his signature. At the County Ground he became a great crowd favourite, a player renowned for his skill and power in the air. But in 1971 an injury led to his retirement and probably cost the Cobblers promotion to the Third Division. He later returned to Cardiff to work as a publican.

Alan JARVIS

Position	Midfielder
Born	Alan Leslie Jarvis, Wrexham, 4 August 1943
Height	5ft 8in
Weight	11st 9lb
Clubs	Everton, Hull City, Mansfield Town
Welsh Caps	3
	1967 v Scotland (1–1), v England (lost 1–5), v N. Ireland (0–0)

IN HIS THREE APPEARANCES at full international level for Wales, Alan Jarvis was selected by Dave Bowen as one of six forwards but operated in midfield alongside Barrie Hole.

Jarvis was also capped by Wales at youth and amateur levels. He had a successful trial for Preston North End in 1959, but shortly afterwards accepted an invitation to join Everton. He played in the Merseyside club's Central League side at the age of 16 but despite a number of impressive displays he failed to win a place in their first team

By 1964 Cliff Britton, who had been manager at Preston North End, was in charge t Hull City. When Jarvis was transfer-listed by the Toffees he snapped him up on a ree transfer. Jarvis spent his first-season at Boothferry Park in the club's reserve side, ut after winning a first team place he missed just one game between 1965 and 970.

Jarvis was a master of the accurately weighted pass. He was Mansfield Town's most xpensive signing when he left Hull to join the Stags in March 1971. He had studied o become a quantity surveyor while playing for the Tigers, and followed that rofession after hanging up his boots.

Rod THOMAS

Position	Right-back
Born	Roderick John Thomas, Glyncorrwg, 11 January 1947
Height	6ft 2in
Weight	13st 0lb
Clubs	Gloucester City, Swindon Town, Derby County, Cardiff City, Newport County
Welsh Caps	50
	1967 v N. Ireland (0–0)
	1968 v W. Germany (1–1)
	1969 v Italy (lost 0–1), v W. Germany (1–1), v England (lost 1–2), v N. Ireland (0–0),
	v Rest of the UK (lost 0–1)
	1970 v E. Germany (lost 1–3), v Italy (lost 1–4), v England (1–1), v Scotland (0–0),
	v N. Ireland (won 1–0)
	1971 v Romania (0–0), v Czechoslovakia (lost 1–3), v Scotland (0–0), v England (0–0),
	v N. Ireland (lost 0–1)
	1972 v Finland (won 3–0), v Czechoslovakia (lost 0–1), v Romania (lost 0–2), v England
	(lost 0–3), v Scotland (lost 0–1), v N. Ireland (0–0)
	1973 v England (lost 0–1), v England (1–1), v Poland (won 2–0), v Scotland (lost 0–2),
	v England (lost 0–3), v N. Ireland (lost 0–1)
	1974 v Poland (lost 0–3), v England (lost 0–2), v Scotland (lost 0–2), v N. Ireland (won 1–0)
	1975 v Hungary (won 2–0), v Luxembourg (won 5–0), v Hungary (won 2–1), v Luxembourg
	(won 3–1), v Scotland (2–2), v England (2–2), v N. Ireland (lost 0–1)
	1976 v Austria (won 1–0), v Yugoslavia (lost 0–2), v England (lost 0–1)
	1977 v Czechoslovakia (won 3–0), v Scotland (0–0), v England (won 1–0), v N. Ireland (1–1)
	1978 v Kuwait (0–0), v Scotland (lost 0–2), v Czechoslovakia (lost 0–1)

A COOL, UNHURRIED DEFENDER, Rod Thomas was discovered by Swindon Town laying for Gloucester City in the Southern League as an inside-forward. During his ears at the County Ground, Thomas made the Welsh full-back position his own and was surprising that he was not signed by a First Division club earlier than his move o Derby County.

Thomas made his League debut for Swindon against Scunthorpe United in May 966 and went on to give eight seasons' service to the Wiltshire club. He was a member of the Swindon side that won the League Cup in 1969, a season in which ey also achieved promotion to the Second Division. Thomas scored his first goal for

Rod Thomas could play anywhere in the back four. He won 50 caps for Wales
(Lancashire Evening Post)

he club at the start of the 1969/70 season as the Robins won 2–0 at Aston Villa. An
ver-present in 1970/71, Thomas went on to score five goals in 296 League games
or Swindon before being signed by Derby County for £80,000 in November 1973.

Although he had to wait to make his mark at Derby, an injury to Ron Webster let
od Thomas into the Rams' side. In the second half of the club's 1974/75 League
hampionship winning season, he was at last able to play anywhere in the back four
ith equal efficiency.

In October 1977 he joined Cardiff City for £10,000 and, although injury problems
ampered his progress at Ninian Park, he made 96 appearances in four years before
ejoining Gloucester City in 1981. He had a short spell with Newport County before
eaving Somerton Park to work for Francis Lee's paper empire. He later ran a pub in
heltenham.

ohn MAHONEY

osition	Midfielder
orn	John Francis Mahoney, Cardiff, 20 September 1946
eight	5ft 8in
Veight	11st 4lb
lubs	Ashton United, Crewe Alexandra, Stoke City, Middlesbrough, Swansea City
Velsh Caps	51 Goals 1

1968 v England (lost 0–3)
1969 v E. Germany (lost 1–2)
1971 v Czechoslovakia (lost 1–3)
1973 v England (lost 0–1), v England (1–1), v Poland (won 2–0), v Scotland (lost 0–2),
    v England (lost 0–3), v N. Ireland (lost 0–1)
1974 v Poland (lost 0–3), v England (lost 0–2), v Scotland (lost 0–2), v N. Ireland (won 1–0)
1975 v Austria (lost 1–2), v Hungary (won 2–0), v Luxembourg (won 5–0), v Hungary
    (won 2–1) 1 goal, v Luxembourg (won 3–1), v Scotland (2–2), v England (2–2), v N. Ireland
    (lost 0–1)
1976 v Austria (won 1–0), v Yugoslavia (lost 0–2), v England (lost 0–1), v N. Ireland
    (won 1–0), v Yugoslavia (1–1)
1977 v W. Germany (lost 0–2), v Czechoslovakia (won 3–0), v Scotland (0–0), v England
    (won 1–0), v N. Ireland (1–1)
1978 v Kuwait (0–0), v Kuwait (0–0), v Scotland (lost 0–2), v Czechoslovakia (lost 0–1),
    v Iran (won 1–0), v England (lost 1–3), v Scotland (1–1), v N. Ireland (won 1–0)
1979 v W. Germany (lost 0–2), v Scotland (won 3–0), v England (0–0), v N. Ireland (1–1),
    v Malta (won 2–0)
1980 v Republic of Ireland (won 2–1), v W. Germany (lost 1–5), v Turkey (lost 0–1)
1982 v Iceland (2–2), v USSR (lost 0–3)
1983 v Yugoslavia (4–4), v England (lost 1–2)

OHN MAHONEY WAS BORN IN Cardiff. His father was a rugby player who moved
orth to become a Rugby League professional, so John started his football at Ashton
Jnited before moving to Crewe Alexandra. He later joined Stoke City, where the
oaching staff worked on his initial ungainly style and turned him into a fine

John Mahoney was a fine midfielder whose 51 caps were spread over a period of 15 years
(Lancashire Evening Post)

idfielder who won 51 caps for Wales. The first of these came against England in ctober 1967 and the last against the same country some 15 years later.

At Stoke he won a Football League Cup winners' medal in 1972 and went on to ore 25 goals in 284 League games before joining Middlesbrough for a fee of 90,000. After two seasons at Ayresome Park he linked up with his cousin John oshack at Swansea and played a major role in the Welsh club's renaissance.

Despite a series of niggling injuries during his first few weeks with the club, he oon settled down and in 1980/81 he won a Welsh Cup winners' medal and helped e club win promotion. He was outstanding as the Swans played top-flight football or the first time in their history. He had appeared in 110 League games for the Vetch eld club when a broken leg against Brighton and Hove Albion ended his playing reer in March 1983.

After a spell on Swansea's commercial staff, he went into management with Bangor ty and took them into Europe. He later managed Newport County until the merton Park club were wound up. He then took charge at Bangor for a second time.

David POWELL

osition	Central defender
orn	David Powell, Dolgarrog, Vale of Conway, 15 October 1944
eight	5ft 10in
eight	10st 2lb
ubs	Gwydyr Rovers, Wrexham, Sheffield United, Cardiff City
elsh Caps	11 Goals 1

1968 v W. Germany (1–1)
1969 v Italy (lost 0–1), v W. Germany (1–1), v Scotland (lost 3–5), v England (lost 1–2),
    v N. Ireland (0–0)
1970 v E. Germany (lost 1–3) 1 goal, v England (1–1), v Scotland (0–0), v N. Ireland
    (won 1–0)
1971 v Romania (0–0)

ENTRAL DEFENDER DAVID POWELL began his playing career with Gwydyr Rovers, d during his spell at the club he was capped by Wales at youth level. In January 962 Wrexham took him on to their ground staff. After working his way up through e ranks and making an impression in the club's reserve side, he was given his first-am debut while still an amateur.

Three days after that game at Bristol Rovers, he signed professional forms. Over the ext couple of seasons it became clear that the strong-tackling defender was destined or greater things. Although his only club honour with the Robins was a Welsh Cup nners-up medal, he gained four under-23 caps and made his full international ebut against West Germany at Ninian Park in May 1968.

In September of that year he signed for Sheffield United. Powell continued to epresent his country. He spent three seasons at Bramall Lane before returning to Vales to play for Cardiff City. Sadly, he had to finish his career prematurely through jury and in 1974 he joined the South Wales Police, working at their training centre Bridgend.

Steve DERRETT

Position	Full-back
Born	Stephen Clifford Derrett, Cardiff, 16 October 1947
Height	5ft 8in
Weight	12st 4lb
Clubs	Cardiff City, Carlisle United, Aldershot, Rotherham United, Newport County, Barry Town, Bridgend
Welsh Caps	4
	1969 v W. Germany (1–1), v Scotland (lost 3–5)
	1970 v Italy (lost 1–4)
	1971 v Finland (won 1–0)

AFTER WORKING HIS WAY UP through the ranks with his home-town team Cardiff City, Steve Derrett made his first-team debut for the Bluebirds in Holland in European Cup Winners' Cup match. He was equally at home at full-back or in sweeper's role, where his quick powers of recovery were used to advantage. He won four full international caps during his time with the Ninian Park club. Two of these appearances saw the national side suffer heavy defeats at the hands of Scotland and Italy.

In April 1972 Derrett left the Bluebirds to join Carlisle United. But he was unable to settle at Brunton Park, and after a loan spell with Aldershot he moved to Rotherham United. He had a lengthy stay at Millmoor, scoring his first-ever Football League goal.

In the summer of 1976 he returned to South Wales to join Newport County. After a knee injury ended his full-time career, he went into non-League football with Barry Town and later Bridgend.

While at Somerton Park he obtained an FA Coaching qualification and was appointed assistant warden at a Cardiff youth club. He later worked as a Development Officer for the Probation Service before becoming a sales representative for a safety equipment firm in Cardiff.

John TOSHACK

Position	Forward
Born	John Benjamin Toshack, Cardiff, 22 March 1949
Height	6ft 1in
Weight	12st 0lb
Clubs	Cardiff City, Liverpool, Swansea City
Welsh Caps	40 Goals 13
	1969 v W. Germany (1–1), v E. Germany (lost 1–2) 1 goal, v Scotland (lost 3–5) 1 goal, v England (lost 1–2), v N. Ireland (0–0), Rest of the UK (lost 0–1)
	1970 v E. Germany (lost 1–3), v Italy (lost 1–4)
	1971 v Scotland (0–0), v England (0–0), v N. Ireland (lost 0–1), v Finland (won 1–0) 1 goal
	1972 v Finland (won 3–0) 1 goal, v England (lost 0–3)
	1973 v England (lost 0–1), v England (1–1) 1 goal, v Poland (won 2–0), v Scotland (lost 0–2) v England (lost 0–3)

John Toshack scored 12 goals in 40 international matches for Wales, and later spent just 44 days in charge of the national team. (*Lancashire Evening Post*)

1975 v Austria (lost 1–2), v Hungary (won 2–0) 1 goal, v Luxembourg (won 5–0) 1 goal,
   v Hungary (won 2–1) 1 goal, v Luxembourg (won 3–1), v Scotland (2–2) 1 goal, v England
   (2–2) 1 goal
1976 v Yugoslavia (lost 0–2), v England (lost 0–1), v Yugoslavia (1–1)
1977 v Scotland (lost 0–1)
1978 v Kuwait (0–0), v Kuwait (0–0), v Scotland (lost 0–2), v Czechoslovakia (lost 0–1)
1979 v W. Germany (lost 0–2), v Scotland (won 3–0), 3 goals, v England (0–0), v N. Ireland
   (1–1), v Malta (won 2–0)
1980 v W. Germany (lost 1–5)

JOHN TOSHACK ONCE SCORED a hat-trick for Wales against Scotland. But he had shown an early aptitude for cricket. Perhaps this isn't surprising: a distant relative Ernie Toshack, was an Australian Test cricketer who played against England nine times in the years immediately after the Second World War. John played for the Welsh Schoolboy XI. However, when it came to making a choice football was his first love, and he went to his home-town club Cardiff City as an apprentice.

At just 16 years 236 days old, he was the youngest player to appear in a League match for the Bluebirds when he came off the bench on 13 November 1965 to score the final goal in a 3–1 win over Leyton Orient. He had always had a talent for goals, scoring a hat-trick against Northern Ireland in a schools international and 47 goals in 22 games for Cardiff Schools. Over the next few seasons he continued to find the net, hitting his first hat-trick for the club in January 1968 as Ebbw Vale were beaten 8–0 in a Welsh Cup game. After teaming up with Brian Clark, he netted 31 goals in 1968/69 including scoring in both legs of the Welsh Cup Final as Swansea were beaten 5–1 on aggregate, and he was the Second Division's leading scorer. In 1969/70 he scored his first League treble for Cardiff in a 4–2 defeat of Queen's Park Rangers and followed it up with another early the following season as Hull were beaten 5–1.

It wasn't long before Liverpool persuaded Cardiff to part with him. Bill Shankly paid out a then club record fee of £110,000. At Liverpool Toshack quickly endeared himself to the Kop by helping to erase a two-goal deficit against Everton in the Merseyside derby, climbing high above Everton and England centre-half Brian Labone to head the equaliser before nodding down Alec Lindsay's cross for Chris Lawler to score the winner.

The partnership he established with Kevin Keegan made the pair of them the most feared attacking force in the First Division. Some of the more imaginative newspapers of the day claimed that they had some strange telepathic understanding. During their period together, Toshack carried off two UEFA Cup winners' medals, three League Championships and the FA Cup. Sadly, he was forced to sit out Liverpool's first European Cup victory on the substitute's bench. Following Keegan's departure, recurring injuries were limiting Toshack's appearances, as indeed they had throughout his time at Anfield. The writing was on the wall and in March 1978 Toshack left Liverpool to become player-manager of Swansea City.

By the end of his first season at the Vetch he had helped the Swans clinch third place and promotion to the Third Division. In a three-year spell with Toshack at the helm, Swansea climbed from the Fourth Division to the First – a feat unrivalled in

League history. At one time, when Swansea were top of the First Division, Toshack was being tipped as the next manager at Anfield. But then it all started to go wrong and the team he had built began to disintegrate at an alarming rate. The break came in March 1984, but he was out of work for only a couple of months before he was invited to manage Sporting Lisbon. He later managed Real Sociedad and in his first season with the club they beat favourites Atletico Madrid in the Spanish Cup Final.

Tosh, who had been awarded the MBE in 1982 for his services to soccer, took over as manager of Real Madrid in 1989. He guided them to the League Championship with a record number of points and goals in his first season with the club, yet that did not prevent him being sacked in November 1990 following a run of indifferent results. He then managed Real Sociedad. In March 1994 he had a spell as Welsh national team boss, but it lasted a mere 44 days and one game. He later took over at Deportivo La Coruna, before, in 1999–2000, having a second spell in charge of Real Madrid.

1970–79

Moving On

*I*n 1974 Mike Smith was appointed as the first full-time manager of the Wales team. This and other changes helped send Wales into their centenary year, 1976, at a peak of achievement and ambition. They emerged from the difficulties of the previous decade and equipped themselves for the urgent development of the modern era.

However, the early years of the decade were not without problems. On 26 September 1973 Trevor Hockey became the first Welsh international to be sent off in a game against Poland that his team lost 3–0.

Matched against Austria, Hungary and Luxembourg, the Welsh turned in some worthy performances in the 1976 European Championship qualifiers. Despite losing 2–1 in Austria, they beat Hungary 2–0 and Luxembourg 5–0 to move to the head of the table. The Welsh completed the double over Hungary and Luxembourg and then sat back to see whether Austria could overtake them in their match against Hungary. The Hungarians won 2–1, which meant Austria had to take two points off Wales at Wrexham while the home side required just one point to ensure qualification. Arfon Griffiths scored the only goal of the match, ensuring that Wales became the sole British quarter-finalists.

Their opponents were Yugoslavia, but in the first leg in Zagreb Wales concentrated on defence and lost 2–0. The return leg developed into a bad-tempered affair and came close to being abandoned. Yugoslavia took the lead from a penalty before Ian Evans equalised just before half-time. Then, 20 minutes into the second-half, the East German referee disallowed a Welsh 'goal'; spectators invaded the pitch, beer cans were thrown and play was suspended for five minutes. When play was resumed, another Welsh 'goal' was disallowed and a Terry Yorath penalty saved. At the final whistle the police were needed to escort the referee from the field – a disgraceful end to a distasteful game.

Scotland and Czechoslovakia were in Wales's qualifying group for the 1978 World Cup, and the battle was on between the British pair when Wales beat the Czechs 3–0 in March 1977. Then Scotland beat Czechoslovakia 3–1, putting themselves in the driving seat. If they could beat Wales away in October, they were through. A draw would mean that Wales would need a win in Prague, while a defeat would require Wales to draw against the Czechs. The crucial match was played at Anfield because none of the Welsh stadiums met the requisite safety standards. Despite playing a 'home' game away, the Welsh were much better and looked more likely to score. A disputed penalty for handball gave the Scots the lead just 12 minutes from time, before Kenny Dalglish put the result beyond doubt. Mike Smith was crestfallen. 'None of my players handled the ball. Words cannot describe how we feel losing a match after putting up such a historic fight.'

Dick KRZYWICKI

Position	Winger
Born	Richard Lech Krzywicki, Penley, 2 February 1947
Height	5ft 10in
Weight	11st 1lb
Clubs	West Bromwich Albion, Huddersfield Town, Scunthorpe United, Northampton Town, Lincoln City
Welsh Caps	8 Goals 1
	1970 v E. Germany (lost 1–3), v Italy (lost 1–4), v England (1–1) 1 goal, v Scotland (0–0), v N. Ireland (won 1–0)
	1971 v Romania (0–0), v Finland (won 1–0)
	1972 v Czechoslovakia (lost 0–1)

IN WHAT WAS HIS THIRD FULL international appearance for Wales, Dick Krzywicki scored a superb goal against England to help Wales towards a share of the 1970 Home International Championships.

Dick Krzywicki was born a short distance from Wrexham, where his father, a Polish soldier, was serving. When he was three years old the family moved to Leek.

In 1962 he was taken on to the West Bromwich Albion ground staff and made his League debut two years later at the age of 17. While never a regular first teamer, he was an important squad member and could play at inside-forward as well as on the wing. Quick off the mark, he was at one time one of the fastest players in the First Division.

In March 1970 Huddersfield Town manager Ian Greaves signed him for a club record fee of £45,000. He scored on his debut, and a few weeks later the club were promoted to the First Division. Injuries and a loss of form while Krzywicki was with Huddersfield Town led to spells on loan with Scunthorpe United and Northampton Town before he eventually joined Lincoln City. After helping the Imps win the Fourth Division Championship, he left League football, severing all his ties with the game. He had scored 30 goals in 182 League outings for his five clubs.

Eight times-capped Dick Krzywicki in the colours of Huddersfield Town. *(Lancashire Evening Post)*

Terry YORATH

Position	Midfielder
Born	Terence Charles Yorath, Cardiff, 27 March 1950
Height	5ft 11in
Weight	10st 12lb
Clubs	Leeds United, Coventry City, Tottenham Hotspur, Vancouver Whitecaps, Bradford City, Swansea City
Welsh Caps	59 Goals 2
	1970 v Italy (lost 1–4)
	1971 v Scotland (0–0), v England (0–0), v N. Ireland (lost 0–1)
	1972 v Czechoslovakia (lost 0–1), v England (lost 0–3), v Scotland (lost 0–1), v N. Ireland (0–0)

1973 v England (1–1), v Poland (won 2–0), v Scotland (lost 0–2)

1974 v Poland (lost 0–3), v England (lost 0–2), v Scotland (lost 0–2), v N. Ireland (won 1–0)

1975 v Austria (lost 1–2), v Hungary (won 2–0), v Luxembourg (won 5–0) 1 goal, v Hungary (won 2–1), v Luxembourg (won 3–1), v Scotland (2–2)

1976 v Austria (won 1–0), v England (lost 1–2), v Yugoslavia (lost 0–2), v Scotland (lost 1–3), v England (lost 0–1), v N. Ireland (won 1–0), v Yugoslavia (1–1)

1977 v W. Germany (lost 0–2), v Scotland (lost 0–1), v Czechoslovakia (won 3–0), v Scotland (0–0), v England (won 1–0), v N. Ireland (1–1)

1978 v Kuwait (0–0), v Kuwait (0–0), v Scotland (lost 0–2), v Czechoslovakia (lost 0–1), v W. Germany (1–1), v Iran (won 1–0), v England (lost 1–3), v Scotland (1–1), v N. Ireland (won 1–0)

1979 v Turkey (won 1–0), v W. Germany (lost 0–2), v Scotland (won 3–0), v England (0–0), v N. Ireland (1–1)

1980 v Republic of Ireland (won 2–1), v Turkey (lost 0–1), v England (won 4–1), v Scotland (lost 0–1), v N. Ireland (lost 0–1), v Iceland (won 4–0)

1981 v Turkey (won 4–0), v Czechoslovakia (won 1–0), v Republic of Ireland (won 3–1) 1 goal, v Turkey (won 1–0), v USSR (0–0)

TERRY YORATH IS ONE OF Wales's most capped players. His entry into the game of football was quite by accident. He was noted at school for his ability as a rugby union scrum-half and had trials with the strong schoolboy side in Cardiff at the handling game. Then one day he went to watch his brother play football against Rhondda Valley Boys. The Cardiff boys were a player short and so Terry Yorath borrowed a pair of boots and went on to give a fine performance. He won four Welsh Schoolboy caps as a left-winger and, after turning down Cardiff City and the two Bristol clubs, joined Leeds United as an apprentice.

He turned professional in April 1967 and a year later made his League debut against Burnley. This was his only League appearance before he made the first of his 59 international appearances against Italy in 1969.

Yorath was an aggressive hard-tackling competitor, and in nine seasons at Elland Road he proved himself a fine clubman. A substitute in Leeds' 1973 FA Cup Final team, he made the starting line-ups for the 1973 European Cup Winners' Cup and 1975 European Cup Finals, but in all three only picked up a losers' medal. During the club's League Championship winning season of 1973/74, Yorath played in 28 games and occupied five different positions. Towards the end of his time at Elland Road, Yorath was an automatic choice, occasionally captaining the club. However, in August 1975, after scoring 12 goals in 196 games, he joined Coventry City for a fee of £125,000.

At Highfield Road, Yorath was immediately appointed captain. In his first season with the club his leadership qualities did much to steer the Sky Blues clear of relegation. After that he was plagued by injuries and in the summer of 1979 he joined Tottenham Hotspur for £225,000.

Yorath was signed to add steel to a midfield that boasted the talents of Glenn Hoddle, Ossie Ardiles and Ricky Villa, and performed the task admirably for a season. But, when he recovered from an injury sustained early in the following campaign, he found his place in the side had been taken by Graham Roberts. Yorath was allowed to

An aggressive, hard-tackling midfielder, Terry Yorath captained Wales in 42 of his 59 appearances. *(Lancashire Evening Post)*

leave White Hart Lane, and joined Vancouver Whitecaps during which time he won his final three caps for Wales. Yorath captained Wales on 42 occasions. If he hadn't moved to North America, where Welsh manager Mike England found it difficult to check on his form, he may well have added more caps to his collection.

Returning to these shores, he joined Bradford City as assistant manager and helped the Bantams win the Third Division Championship in 1984/85. He then joined Swansea and led them to promotion to the Third Division in 1987/88. Shortly afterwards he walked out to become Bradford City's new boss. The move sparked a tremendous row between the two clubs over compensation, which was resolved when Yorath bought out his own contract. Things didn't work out and he returned to Swansea before leaving a second time to become manager of Wales.

He took Wales close to qualification for the 1992 European Championships, but the following year his contract was not renewed, since Wales failed to qualify for the 1994 World Cup. He later worked in Beirut as the Lebanese national team manager before taking charge of Bradford City and Sheffield Wednesday. He is currently at Huddersfield Town as the Yorkshire club's assistant manager.

Leighton PHILLIPS

Position	Central defender/Midfielder
Born	Leighton Phillips, Neath, 25 September 1949
Height	5ft 10in
Weight	10st 11lb
Clubs	Cardiff City, Aston Villa, Swansea City, Charlton Athletic, Exeter City
Welsh Caps	58

1971 v Czechoslovakia (lost 1–3), v Scotland (0–0), v England (0–0), v N. Ireland (lost 0–1)

1972 v Czechoslovakia (lost 0–1), v Romania (lost 0–2), v Scotland (lost 0–1), v N. Ireland (lost 0–0)

1973 v England (lost 0–1)

1974 v Poland (lost 0–3), v N. Ireland (won 1–0)

1975 v Austria (lost 1–2), v Hungary (won 2–0), v Luxembourg (won 5–0), v Hungary (won 2–1), v Luxembourg (won 3–1), v Scotland (2–2), v England (2–2), v N. Ireland (lost 0–1)

1976 v Austria (won 1–0), v England (lost 1–2), v Yugoslavia (lost 0–2), v England (lost 0–1), v N. Ireland (won 1–0), v Yugoslavia (1–1)

1977 v W. Germany (lost 0–2), v Scotland (lost 0–1), v Czechoslovakia (won 3–0), v Scotland (0–0), v England (won 1–0)

1978 v Kuwait (0–0), v Kuwait (0–0), v Scotland (lost 0–2), v Czechoslovakia (lost 0–1), v W. Germany (1–1), v England (lost 1–3), v Scotland (1–1)

1979 v Malta (won 7–0), v Turkey (won 1–0), v W. Germany (lost 0–2), v Scotland (won 3–0), v England (0–0), v N. Ireland (1–1), v Malta (won 2–0)

1980 v Republic of Ireland (won 2–1), v W. Germany (lost 1–5), v Turkey (lost 0–1), v Scotland (lost 0–1), v N. Ireland (lost 0–1), v Iceland (won 4–0)

1981 v Turkey (won 4–0), v Czechoslovakia (won 1–0), v Turkey (won 1–0), v Scotland (won 2–0), v England (0–0), v USSR (0–0)

1982 v Czechoslovakia (lost 0–2), v USSR (lost 0–3)

Leighton Phillips of Aston Villa and Wales was a versatile player who won the first of his 58 caps in 1971 against Czechoslovakia. *(Lancashire Evening Post)*

LEIGHTON PHILLIPS ALWAYS HARBOURED the ambition of becoming a professional footballer. After winning Welsh schoolboy international honours, he joined the ground staff of Cardiff City. He worked his way through the club's junior and reserve teams, making his League debut as a substitute in a 2–2 home draw against Rotherham United in January 1968. He scored with his first touch of the ball to level the scores after City had been 2–0 down. At Ninian Park Phillips had plenty of opportunities to show his versatility, appearing as a striker, defender and in midfield before succeeding Brian Harris in the role of sweeper. His performances led to his winning Welsh under-21 and under-23 caps before he won the first of his 58 full caps, playing against Czechoslovakia in 1971.

In September 1974, having appeared in 216 first-team games for the Bluebirds, he became dissatisfied with Cardiff's lack of success and left to play for Aston Villa, which paid £80,000 for his services.

Phillips went on to captain the club and help them win promotion to the First Division in his first season at Villa Park. He won a League Cup winners' medal in 1977 as Villa beat Everton, forming an excellent defensive partnership with Chris Nicholl. In fact, it was around this time that Phillips was rated 'the best covering centre-half in the country'. Phillips, who read the game brilliantly, did most of his best work off the ball, anticipating dangerous situations. He was a defender of real pace and determination. Phillips returned to South Wales in November 1978 to join Swansea City after appearing in 175 League and Cup games for the Villans.

Phillips became the Swans' record signing at £70,000 and went on to help the club win promotion to the Second Division in his first season with them. By the time he left Swansea to join Charlton Athletic in 1981 for a modest £25,000, he had helped the club into the top flight.

His stay at the Valley was brief because the versatile international was beset with injury problems. His last season in the first-class game was 1982/83, when he played as a non-contract player for Exeter City.

Tom WALLEY

Position	Midfielder
Born	John Thomas Walley, Caernarfon, 27 February 1945
Height	5ft 10in
Weight	11st 6lb
Clubs	Caernarfon Town, Arsenal, Watford, Leyton Orient,
Welsh Caps	1
	1971 v Czechoslovakia (lost 1–3)

A STRONG AND DETERMINED wing-half, Tom Walley joined First Division Arsenal from Caernarfon Town in December 1964. During his first season at Highbury he established himself as an important member of the club's Football Combination side.

It was a full twelve months after his arrival at Highbury that Walley made his League debut against Sheffield Wednesday, but even then he couldn't win a regular place.

He won the first of his four Welsh under-23 caps against England midway through the 1966/67 season. However, he thereafter only made four more appearances for the Gunners before being allowed to join Watford for £5,000 in March 1967.

Walley stayed at Vicarage Road for over four seasons, amassing 266 first-team appearances. His consistency won him his only full cap against Czechoslovakia in 1971. He later played for Orient and had a second spell with the Hornets. Sadly, Walley's career was ended prematurely by injury. He played with the dedication that was to characterise his work as an outstanding youth coach who took Watford and Millwall to two FA Youth Cup Finals each.

Arfon GRIFFITHS

Position	Midfielder
Born	Arfon Trevor Griffiths, Wrexham, 23 August 1941
Height	5ft 6in
Weight	10st 5lb
Clubs	Wrexham, Arsenal
Welsh Caps	17 Goals 6

1971 v Czechoslovakia (lost 1–3)
1975 v Austria (lost 1–2) 1 goal, v Hungary (won 2–0) 1 goal, v Luxembourg (won 5–0) 1 goal, v Hungary (won 2–1), v Luxembourg (won 3–1), v England (2–2) 1 goal, v N. Ireland (lost 0–1)
1976 v Austria (won 1–0) 1 goal, v England (lost 1–2), v Yugoslavia (lost 0–2), v Scotland (lost 1–3) 1 goal, v England (lost 0–1), v N. Ireland (won 1–0), v Yugoslavia (1–1)
1977 v W. Germany (lost 0–2), v Scotland (lost 0–1)

ARFON GRIFFITHS SCORED THE only goal of the 1976 European qualifier against Austria that took Wales through to the quarter-finals of the European Championships. He joined Wrexham straight from school, turning professional in May 1959.

He made his League debut for the Racecourse club in a 2–1 home win over Reading in November 1959 and went on to score eight goals in 42 League appearances. He was later transferred to Arsenal for £15,000 in February 1961. However, after making a disastrous debut towards the end of the 1960/61 season in a 5–1 defeat at Wolves, Griffiths played in just 15 games, mainly as a scheming inside-forward, the following season. Unable to maintain his first-team place, he was subsequently transferred back to the Robins for £8,000.

Arfon Griffiths was a loyal servant to Wrexham and over the next 17 seasons appeared in 713 first-team games. At Arsenal he had made two appearances for the Wales under-23 team and, on his return to the Racecourse Ground, gained two more under-23 caps and made 17 full appearances for Wales. The first of these came in 1971 (when he came on as a substitute against Czechoslovakia), the remainder between 1975 and 1977.

He scored 120 League goals for the Robins, second only to Tommy Bamford in the club's all-time scoring charts. His best season for the club was undoubtedly 1969/70, when he masterminded the club's promotion to the Third Division and scored 16 goals in 44 games.

Arfon Griffiths capped Wales 17 times and was awarded the MBE for his services to football. (*Getty Images*)

In 1975 John Neal appointed him as his assistant manager. When Neal left to manage Middlesbrough, the Wrexham board had no hesitation in appointing Griffiths as his successor. In his first season in charge, he led the club to the Third Division Championship and Welsh Cup, and over the next four years kept the club in the Second Division. In the summer of 1981 he resigned his post following an internal disagreement, but soon returned to management with Crewe Alexandra. The Gresty Road club finished bottom of the Football League in 1981/82 and were still bottom when he was sacked in October 1982.

Griffiths was awarded the MBE for his services to football. He returned to Wrexham to open a newsagent's shop and is now not involved with the game.

John ROBERTS

Position	Central defender/Forward
Born	John Griffith Roberts, Abercynon, 11 September 1946
Height	6ft 0in
Weight	12st 2lb
Clubs	Abercynon Athletic, Swansea City, Northampton Town, Arsenal, Birmingham City, Wrexham, Hull City
Welsh Caps	22
	1971 v Scotland (0–0), v England (0–0), v N. Ireland (lost 0–1), v Finland (won 1–0)
	1972 v Finland (won 3–0), v England (lost 0–3), v N. Ireland (0–0)
	1973 v England (1–1), v Poland (won 2–0), v Scotland (lost 0–2), v England (lost 0–3), v N. Ireland (lost 0–1)
	1974 v Poland (lost 0–3), v England (lost 0–2), v Scotland (lost 0–2), v N. Ireland (won 1–0)
	1975 v Austria (lost 1–2), v Hungary (won 2–1), v Scotland (2–2), v England (2–2)
	1976 v England (lost 1–2), v Scotland (lost 1–3)

JOHN ROBERTS STARTED HIS professional career with his local club, Swansea City, in the summer of 1964, and spent three years at the Vetch Field before joining Northampton Town in November 1967. He made 62 League appearances for the Cobblers before Arsenal paid £30,000 for his services in May 1969.

During his first full season at Highbury he played in 11 League games. Then in 1970/71 he won a League Championship medal and played in 15 League games during Arsenal's double-winning campaign. Also that season he won the first of his 22 Welsh caps when he played against Scotland. In October 1972, having played in 81 League and Cup games for the Gunners, he joined Birmingham City for a fee of £140,000. At St Andrew's Roberts was constantly plagued by injuries and in four years with the club appeared in only 79 games.

In August 1976 Roberts joined Wrexham for £30,000, making his debut in a 2–0 home win over Portsmouth on the opening day of the 1976/77 season. After the Robins finished fifth in his first season at the Racecourse Ground, Roberts inspired the club to the Third Division Championship in 1977/78. Also that season he won a Welsh Cup winners' medal as Bangor City were beaten 3–1 on aggregate. He went on

John Roberts, a member of Arsenal's 'double' winning side, was capped 22 times by Wales. (*Lancashire Evening Post*)

to play in 191 first-team games for Wrexham before moving to Hull City for £15,000 in the summer of 1980.

He spent two seasons at Boothferry Park before having to retire through injury. He then worked as a salesman for a stationery company, and later became a driving instructor in Chester.

Wayne JONES

Position	Midfielder
Born	Philip Wayne Jones, Treorchy, 20 October 1948
Height	5ft 10in
Weight	11st 4lb
Clubs	Bristol Rovers
Welsh Caps	1
	1971 v Finland (won 1–0)

THERE WAS NO ONE WITHIN yards of the talented Welsh international midfielder Wayne Jones when he turned with the ball, twisted his knee and fell to the ground in Bristol Rovers' Third Division encounter with Brentford at Eastville in November 1972. He was in agony. Although cartilage trouble was suspected, when the knee was opened up it was found to be riddled with arthritis. Wayne Jones, who had won his one and only Welsh cap against Finland twelve months previously, never played again.

The 24-year-old had looked set for an outstanding career. He was the subject of intense interest from several of the country's leading clubs and had just been called into the Welsh squad for the forthcoming World Cup qualifier against England.

Jones was one of the most memorable performers to ever grace Eastville. He had superb ball control, tremendous confidence and possessed a fierce shot. Yet his greatest asset was his ability to pass the ball over long distances, both instantly and accurately. He also had a temperamental side, more often than not being annoyed with himself when he made a mistake.

He later served several clubs as a physiotherapist and put in a stint as assistant manager under David Williams at Bristol Rovers, before taking over a similar position with Notts County.

Ray MIELCZAREK

Position	Central defender
Born	Raymond Mielczarek, Caernarfon, 10 February 1946
Height	5ft 11in
Weight	11st 8lb
Clubs	Wrexham, Huddersfield Town, Rotherham United
Welsh Caps	1
	1971 v Finland (won 1–0)

DESPITE HAVING A POLISH grandfather, an Irish grandmother and a father who hailed from Luxembourg, Ray Mielczarek was born in Caernarfon.

The central defender impressed in schoolboy football, and it was Wrexham manager Ken Barnes's assistant Ken Roberts who persuaded him to become an apprentice at the Racecourse Ground. Whilst starring in the club's reserve side, he captained the Welsh youth side. Soon after turning professional in the summer of 1964, he made his League debut against Aldershot. His performances at the heart of the defence in his first season with the Robins earned him selection for Wales at under-23 level and he helped the club reach the Welsh Cup Final in 1965.

In September 1967 Huddersfield Town paid £20,000 for his services, but a knee injury restricted his first-team appearances to just 25 games. He then left to play for Rotherham United. His career took off again at Millmoor and he made his full international debut in a 1-0 win over Finland in 1971. He had made over 100 appearances for the Millers by the time he was forced to retire by a recurrence of his knee injury. Wrexham manager John Neal rated him so highly that he tried to re-sign him for the Robins. However, Mielczarek could give no assurances that his knee would hold out and so the move fell through.

He then returned to Wales to coach local clubs Llay, Druids and Rhos, turning out on a number of occasions.

Malcolm PAGE

Position	Defender
Born	Malcolm Edward Page, Knucklas, 5 February 1947
Height	5ft 9in
Weight	10st 11lb
Clubs	Birmingham City, Oxford United
Welsh Caps	28

1971 v Finland (won 1-0)
1972 v Scotland (lost 0-1), v N. Ireland (0-0)
1973 v England (1-1), v England (lost 0-3), v N. Ireland (lost 0-1)
1974 v Scotland (lost 0-2), v N. Ireland (won 1-0)
1975 v Hungary (won 2-1), v Luxembourg (won 3-1), v Scotland (2-2), v England (2-2), v N. Ireland (lost 0-1)
1976 v England (lost 1-2), v Yugoslavia (lost 0-2), v England (lost 0-1), v N. Ireland (won 1-0), v Yugoslavia (1-1), v W. Germany (lost 0-2)
1977 v Scotland (lost 0-1)
1978 v Kuwait (0-0), v Kuwait (0-0), v W. Germany (1-1), v Iran (won 1-0), v England (lost 1-3), v Scotland (1-1)
1979 v Malta (won 7-0), v W. Germany (lost 0-2)

MALCOLM PAGE APPEARED IN 28 full internationals for Wales. During that eight-year period Page, who made his debut against Finland in 1971, proved his ability to play in a variety of roles at international level by turning out in four different positions.

Malcolm Page appeared 28 times for Wales and is Birmingham City's most-capped player. *(Lancashire Evening Post)*

Page is also Birmingham City's most capped player. He was a marvellous servant to the St Andrew's club, appearing in 394 games in 17 seasons. His first was a 1–1 draw at Everton in February 1965. Between then and his last game against Brighton in September 1980 he played in every position except goalkeeper. He led the Midlands club to promotion to the First Division in 1971/72 and appeared in three FA Cup semi-finals with the City.

He left St Andrew's in February 1981 to join Oxford United. He spent just one season at the Manor Ground before leaving the game to work as an insurance representative.

Brian EVANS

Position	Winger
Born	Brian Clifford Evans, Brynmawr, 2 December 1942
Died	Swansea, 26 February 2003
Height	5ft 8in
Weight	9st 12lb
Clubs	Abergavenny Thistle, Swansea City, Hereford United
Welsh Caps	7
	1972 v Finland (won 3–0), v Czechoslovakia (lost 0–1)
	1973 v England (1–1), v Poland (won 2–0), v Scotland (lost 0–2), v England (lost 0–3)
	1974 v Poland (lost 0–3)

A WINGER IN THE OLD-FASHIONED mode, Brian Evans joined Swansea City from Abergavenny Thistle in the summer of 1963, when Swans' manager Trevor Morris paid the Welsh League club just £650 for his services. Over the next ten seasons, Brian Evans was to give the Vetch Field club great service, missing few games.

Very quick off the mark, he soon won Welsh under-23 honours and in 1972 earned the first of his seven full international caps when he played in a 3–0 win over Finland at Ninian Park. Just prior to that Evans, along with goalkeeper Tony Millington and Dave Gwyther, was selected to tour New Zealand with an FA of Wales party.

Brian Evans scored 58 goals in 355 League appearances for the Swans. Their manager, Harry Gregg, felt obliged to sell him to Hereford United for a fee of £7,000 because he had to offload older players before he could buy new ones.

The flying winger scored nine goals in 48 League outings for the Edgar Street club before leaving to play non-League football with a number of sides. He then returned to Swansea, where he ran a very successful painting and decorating business. He died in February 2003.

Trevor HOCKEY

Position	Midfielder	
Born	Trevor Hockey, Keighley, 1 May 1943	
Died	Keighley, 1 April 1987	
Height	5ft 6in	
Weight	10st 6lb	
Clubs	Bradford City, Nottingham Forest, Newcastle United, Birmingham City, Sheffield United, Norwich City, Aston Villa, Athlone Town	
Welsh Caps	9	Goals 1
	1972 v Finland (won 3–0), v Romania (lost 0–2)	
	1973 v England (lost 0–1), v England (1–1), v Poland (won 2–0) 1 goal, v Scotland (lost 0–2), v England (lost 0–3), v N. Ireland (lost 0–1)	
	1974 v Poland (lost 0–3)	

TREVOR HOCKEY QUALIFIED TO PLAY for Wales because of his father's nationality. He holds the unwanted distinction of being the first Welsh player to be sent off in an international match.

During his early days as a footballer with Bradford City and Nottingham Forest, the diminutive Hockey was a fast-raiding winger and a match-winner on his day but, like many talented forwards, suffered from inconsistency. After joining Newcastle United in November 1963, he began to appear occasionally as a midfielder, just when football was changing into the modern style. He helped the Magpies win promotion to the top flight but in November 1965 he left St James Park to join Birmingham City for a fee of £25,000.

He missed very few games for the Blues over the next six seasons, modelling himself into a midfield general, tenacious and hardworking and characterised by his long hair and bushy beard. He relished a battle on the field. Hockey then moved on to Sheffield United, winning the first of his nine caps while with the Blades. He later had a spell with Norwich City before returning to Bradford City, where he ended his career.

The extrovert Hockey once owned a velvet-covered car and played a pink piano in a rock group. For a while he coached in Germany and at Pontin's holiday camps, later running a hotel in his home town. Hockey was player-manager of Athlone Town before managing Stalybridge Celtic. He collapsed and died in 1987 when he was only 43 years old after taking part in a five-a-side competition.

Mick HILL

Position	Centre-forward
Born	Michael Richard Hill, Hereford, 3 December 1947
Height	6ft 0in
Weight	11st 10lb
Clubs	Cardiff City, Bethesda Athletic, Sheffield United, Ipswich Town, Crystal Palace
Welsh Caps	2
	1972 v Czechoslovakia (lost 0–1), v Romania (lost 0–2)

MICK HILL QUALIFIED TO PLAY FOR Wales on the basis of his father's birthplace. He was called up for his international debut against Czechoslovakia in October 1971 after scoring six goals in six games for his club, Ipswich Town. Although he held his place for Wales's next match against Romania, the national side failed to score in either of Mick Hill's international appearances.

He had begun his career with Cardiff City but was released in 1965 without having made a first-team appearance. He decided to give up soccer and took a job as a clerk in Hereford. His father persuaded him to have another try and he joined Welsh League (North) club Bethesda Athletic.

Sheffield United were very impressed with his goalscoring exploits and the 17-year-old was signed on. In his very first League appearance for the Bramall Lane club, he scored his side's first goal against Chelsea and was voted Man of the Match. Strong in the air and skilful on the ground, Mick Hill hit some spectacular goals.

During the 1970/71 season before the BBC *Match of the Day* cameras, he notched a fine goal against Liverpool following a solo run from the halfway line.

In October 1969 he joined Ipswich Town, continuing to find the net on a regular basis for the Suffolk club in three and a half seasons at Portman Road. Hill then joined Crystal Palace but, following a spate of niggling injuries, his contract was cancelled and he departed for South Africa.

Leighton JAMES

Position	Left-winger
Born	Leighton James, Loughor, 16 February 1953
Height	5ft 9in
Weight	10st 3lb
Clubs	Burnley, Derby County, Queen's Park Rangers, Swansea City, Sunderland, Bury, Newport County
Welsh Caps	54 Goals 10

1972 v Czechoslovakia (lost 0–1), v Romania (lost 0–2), v Scotland (lost 0–1)

1973 v England (lost 0–1), v England (1–1), v Poland (won 2–0) 1 goal, v Scotland (lost 0–2), v England (lost 0–3), v N. Ireland (lost 0–1)

1974 v Poland (lost 0–3), v England (lost 0–2), v Scotland (lost 0–2), v N. Ireland (won 1–0)

1975 v Austria (lost 1–2), v Hungary (won 2–0), v Luxembourg (won 5–0), v Hungary (won 2–1), v Luxembourg (won 3–1) 2 goals, v Scotland (2–2), v England (2–2), v N. Ireland (lost 0–1)

1976 v Austria (won 1–0), v Yugoslavia (lost 0–2), v Scotland (lost 1–3), v England (lost 0–1), v N. Ireland (won 1–0) 1 goal, v Yugoslavia (1–1), v W. Germany (lost 0–2)

1977 v Scotland (lost 0–1), v Czechoslovakia (won 3–0), 2 goals, v Scotland (0–0), v England (won 1–0) 1 goal, v N. Ireland (1–1)

1978 v Kuwait (0–0), v Kuwait (0–0), v W. Germany (1–1)

1979 v Turkey (won 1–0)

1980 v England (won 4–1) 1 goal, v Scotland (lost 0–1), v N. Ireland (lost 0–1), v Iceland (won 4–0)

1981 v Turkey (won 4–0) 2 goals, v Republic of Ireland (won 3–1), v Turkey (won 1–0), v Scotland (won 2–0), v England (0–0)

1982 v Czechoslovakia (lost 0–2), v Iceland (2–2), v USSR (lost 0–3), v England (lost 0–1), v Scotland (lost 0–1), v N. Ireland (won 3–0), v France (won 1–0)

1983 v England (lost 1–2)

LEIGHTON JAMES WON THE FIRST of his 54 Wales caps as a substitute in the European Championship match against Czechoslovakia in Prague in October 1971. At 18 years 238 days old, he was one of the youngest players to appear for Wales in a full international.

Leighton James was one of the game's most naturally gifted players. He was a winger of great speed and skill and always had an eye for goal. The steelworker's son represented the Welsh schoolboys but could quite easily have emerged as a Welsh Rugby Union international, excelling as he did in both codes. He opted for Association Football and in October 1968 signed apprentice forms for Burnley. It wasn't long

At only 18 years 238 days old, Leighton James of QPR and Wales was one of the youngest players to represent Wales when he played against Czechoslovakia in 1971. *(Lancashire Evening Post)*

before he made his League debut for the Clarets; but, still eligible for the club's yout
team, he helped them reach the semi-final of the FA Youth Cup. By 1971/72 Jame
was a regular in the Burnley side and in the following campaign became a househol
name as Burnley won the Second Division Championship. After two good seasons i
the top flight and an appearance in the 1975 FA Cup semi-final, James becam
unsettled and in November 1975 he joined Derby County for £310,000.

He spent two seasons at the Baseball Ground but, despite being the club's top score
in 1976/77 with 15 goals, he didn't seem to figure in manager Tommy Docherty'
long-term plans. In October 1977 he went to Queen's Park Rangers in an exchang
deal which saw Don Masson join the Rams. However, within less than a year he wa
back at Turf Moor after Harry Potts splashed out a club record fee of £165,000.

In his second spell with the Clarets, James was instrumental in their winning th
Anglo-Scottish Cup in 1978. Two years later, following the club's relegation, Jame
was on the move again, this time to ambitious Swansea for a fee of £130,000. He wa
a big favourite with the Vetch Field fans, finishing his first season with the Sout
Wales club as leading scorer as they won promotion to the top flight for the first tim
in their history. He also played a major role in City's victory in the Welsh Cup with i
passport to European football.

In January 1983 James moved to Sunderland, helping to spark something of
revival at Roker Park. In the summer of 1984 he returned to the North-West wit
Bury. After helping the Shakers win promotion to the Third Division, he signed fo
Newport County as player-coach, but shortly afterwards rejoined Burnley for a thir
time. He took his total of first-team outings (in which he scored 81 goals) to 40
before going into coaching with Bradford City.

He later entered non-League management with Gainsborough Trinity and the
Morecambe before becoming a regular contributor on local-radio sports programmes

Cyril DAVIES

Position	Midfielder
Born	Cyril Davies, Swansea, 7 September 1948
Height	5ft 7in
Weight	10st 8lb
Clubs	Swansea City, Carlisle United, Yeovil Town, Charlton Athletic
Welsh Caps	1
	1972 v Romania (lost 0–2)

IN DECEMBER 1970 MIDFIELDER Cyril Davies was selected for the Wales under-2
team by Dave Bowen, who was hoping that Davies's speed would help launch quic
breaks out of defence. Although he was disappointing, he went on to gain one ful
cap in Bucharest against Romania as a substitute for Mick Hill, but never establishe
himself at senior level.

In fact, Cyril Davies had a disappointing start to his professional career, making jus
two League appearances in three years at his first two League clubs. The Swanse
manager had been keen to retain Davies but the board overruled him. At Carlisle h

failed to impress and, when the club decided to reduce the playing staff, Davies was the first to go.

He then drifted into the Southern League with Yeovil Town, where he scored a number of spectacular goals in the club's famous FA Cup run. This put him back in the public eye and, after attracting the attention of a number of leading clubs, he joined Charlton Athletic in the summer of 1970.

Davies was just 25 when he was forced into retirement by a knee ligament injury. He then went to work for the school playing-fields department of a London council.

David ROBERTS

Position	Central defender
Born	David Frazer Roberts, Southampton, 26 November 1949
Height	5ft 11in
Weight	11st 5lb
Clubs	Fulham, Oxford United, Hull City, Cardiff City, Kettering Town, Barry Town, Bridgend Town
Welsh Caps	17
	1973 v Poland (won 2–0), v England (lost 0–3), v N. Ireland (lost 0–1)
	1974 v England (lost 0–2), v Scotland (lost 0–2)
	1975 v Austria (lost 1–2), v Luxembourg (won 3–1), v N. Ireland (lost 0–1)
	1976 v Scotland (lost 1–3), v N. Ireland (won 1–0), v Yugoslavia (1–1)
	1977 v England (won 1–0), v N. Ireland (1–1)
	1978 v Kuwait (0–0), v Kuwait (0–0), v Scotland (1–1), v N. Ireland (won 1–0)

THE SOUTHAMPTON-BORN CENTRAL defender began his career with Fulham, but in four years at Craven Cottage he made just 22 League appearances. In February 1971 he joined Oxford United in the hope of playing regular first-team football.

He was prompted by his team-mates at the Manor Ground to write to the Football Association of Wales, drawing attention to his eligibility based on parental qualification (his college lecturer father had been born in Anglesey). Roberts made his full international debut for Wales in 1973, playing alongside John Roberts (no relation) in the 2–0 World Cup qualifying match win over Poland.

On leaving Oxford United, Roberts joined Hull City, who were managed by John Kaye. After three seasons at Boothferry Park, he left, signing for Cardiff City in the summer of 1978. Although not particularly tall for a central defender, he was nevertheless a highly capable player. Injuries prevented him from giving a full return on the £70,000 fee and he was eventually forced to retire from League football.

He made a comeback with non-League Kettering Town before being reunited with former Cardiff boss Ritchie Morgan at Barry Town. Roberts later became player-coach to Bridgend Town.

Peter O'SULLIVAN

Position	Midfielder
Born	Peter Anthony O'Sullivan, Conway, 4 March 1951
Height	5ft 8in
Weight	10st 0lb
Clubs	Manchester United, Brighton and Hove Albion, Fulham, Charlton Athletic, Reading, Aldershot
Welsh Caps	3 Goals 1
	1973 v Scotland (lost 0–2)
	1976 v Scotland (lost 1–3)
	1979 v Malta (won 7–0) 1 goal

PETER O'SULLIVAN WON HIS THIRD and last Welsh cap in October 1978, 5½ years after making his full international debut.

He began his career with Manchester United but made little headway at Old Trafford and joined Brighton in the summer of 1970. O'Sullivan, who was Freddie Goodwin's last signing, made his Albion debut in the goalless home draw against Torquay United on the opening day of the 1970/71 season. After a few indifferent displays in the early part of the campaign, he settled down to become one of the club's most consistent performers.

In 1971/72, when Albion won promotion to the Second Division, O'Sullivan was ever-present and scored 12 goals from his position on the left-wing. He appeared in 176 consecutive League games before an injury at Charlton Athletic in September 1974 ended the run. O'Sullivan was ever-present again in 1975/76 as Albion just missed out on promotion back to the Second Division, and had an outstanding season in 1976/77 as the Seagulls finally returned to the Second Division as runners-up to Mansfield Town.

In 1977/78 O'Sullivan was named Player of the Season. During the following campaign his midfield creativity provided a number of goalscoring opportunities for Maybank and Poskett as the Seagulls finally won promotion to the First Division. O'Sullivan continued to be one of the club's best players for a further two seasons of top-flight football. However, after scoring 43 goals in 491 games he left the Goldstone Ground to play for Fulham.

After one season with the Cottagers he lost his place in the starting line-up and after loan spells with Charlton Athletic and Reading, he tried his luck in Hong Kong before ending his career with Aldershot.

John PHILLIPS

Position	Goalkeeper
Born	Thomas John Seymour Phillips, Shrewsbury, 7 July 1951
Height	5ft 10in
Weight	10st 5lb
Clubs	Shrewsbury Town, Aston Villa, Chelsea, Crewe Alexandra, Brighton and Hove Albion, Charlton Athletic, Crystal Palace

1973 v England (lost 0–3)
1974 v England (lost 0–2)
1975 v Hungary (won 2–0)
1978 v Kuwait (0–0)

JOHN PHILLIPS WAS THE FIRST 'Anglo' to keep goal for Wales and proved to be a very creditable reserve to both Gary Sprake and later Dai Davies. Although Phillips was born in Shrewsbury, he qualified for Wales by virtue of his father's birthplace – Llanelli – and was first recognised as an under-23 player.

John Phillips learnt his trade under the watchful eye of former Manchester United and Northern Ireland goalkeeper Harry Gregg, who was then manager of Phillips's home-town team Shrewsbury.

Aston Villa manager Tommy Docherty tried to sign him at the start of the 1969/70 season, but the Villa Park directors did not put up the money until the club's Second Division plight had become desperate. The 18-year-old Phillips was considered by Docherty to be a better player than Peter Bonetti had been at that age. Vic Crowe, Docherty's successor at Stamford Bridge, did not share that opinion. When Tommy Hughes, Chelsea's Scottish under-23 international goalkeeper and deputy to Peter Bonetti, broke a leg in August 1970, John Phillips was sold to the London club as cover.

Phillips played a part in Chelsea's reaching the European Cup Winners' Cup Final, but did not play in the final itself. He eventually displaced Bonetti in 1973 to become the Blues' first-choice goalkeeper. He had appeared in 125 League games for the Stamford Bridge club, but then, after a loan spell with Crewe, he joined Brighton and Hove Albion. After just one appearance for the Seagulls, he had two games for Charlton Athletic before ending his career with Crystal Palace.

On his arrival at Selhurst Park, Phillips began his own motor factors company in Mitcham and continues in business to this day.

John EMANUEL

Position	Midfielder
Born	William John Emanuel, Treherbert, 5 April 1948
Height	5ft 8in
Weight	12st 0lb
Clubs	Blaenrhondda, Swansea Town, Ferndale, Bristol City, Swindon Town, Gillingham, Newport County, Barry Town, Ton Pentre
Welsh Caps	2
	1973 v England (lost 0–3), v N. Ireland (lost 0–1)

CAPPED BY WALES THREE TIMES at amateur international level, John Emanuel was one of the last players to use the representative amateur matches as a launching pad for a professional career.

Emanuel was a relatively late starter in League soccer. He played for Blaenrhondda, Swansea Town and Ferndale before Bristol City manager Alan Dicks signed him in the summer of 1971. 'Ivor' made his League debut at home to Millwall at the start of the 1971/72 season and went on to prove himself a tireless worker. He could be relied upon to win the lion's share of possession in midfield with his diligent, no-frills style. A keen tackler, he was usually involved in all of his team's moves and this involvement led to his winning both of his international caps while at Ashton Gate. Both were substitute appearances: he replaced Malcolm Page against England and Trevor Hockey in the match against Northern Ireland.

After loan spells with Swindon Town and Gillingham, Emanuel was signed by Jimmy Scoular for struggling Newport County, and gave them a couple of years' good service before returning to South Wales. Subsequently, with Barry Town and Ton Pentre, he entered non-League management with Maesteg Park.

Tony VILLARS

Position	Winger
Born	Anthony Keith Villars, Pontypool, 24 January 1952
Height	5ft 6in
Weight	9st 10lb
Clubs	Pontnewydd, Panteg, Cwmbran Town, Cardiff City, Newport County
Welsh Caps	3
	1974 v England (lost 0–2), v Scotland (lost 0–2), v N. Ireland (won 1–0)

WINGER TONY VILLARS WAS A member of the Newport County ground staff, but left Somerton Park because the pay was so poor. He then took work as an electrician and began playing for Pontnewydd, a side that was so successful that Welsh League (South) side Panteg signed up the entire team en bloc!

After some impressive displays for his next club, Cwmbran Town, Cardiff City offered him a second stab at League football, which he gladly accepted.

A master at close dribbling, Tony Villars was soon in the Bluebirds' first team. In 1974 he scored the goal against Crystal Palace that secured Cardiff's place in the Second Division for another season, when all had looked lost. Although an undoubted talent, Villars was an enigmatic player, flawed by inconsistency. He made three full international appearances for Wales while with Cardiff. However, dogged by injury problems, he could no longer hold down a first-team place and in June 1976 he moved down the M4 to Newport County.

His stay at Somerton Park was brief and in December of the following year his contract was cancelled. Villars was only 25 – two and a half years after gaining full international honours – when his career in senior soccer ended in enforced premature retirement. He then ran his own milk business while occasionally turning out in charity matches.

Phil ROBERTS

Position	Right-back
Born	Philip Stanley Roberts, Cardiff, 24 February 1950
Height	5ft 11in
Weight	12st 12lb
Clubs	Bristol Rovers, Portsmouth, Hereford United, Exeter City
Welsh Caps	4 Goals 1
	1974 v England (lost 0–2)
	1975 v Austria (lost 1–2), v Hungary (won 2–0), v Luxembourg (won 5–0) 1 goal

CARDIFF-BORN PHIL ROBERTS's ambitions of making the grade in his native city had been hampered when he broke his leg in a schoolboy coaching session with the Ninian Park club. After recovering he tried his luck with Bristol Rovers.

Roberts was a right-back who could also play in midfield or central defence. He was given his League debut by Bristol Rovers' manager Bill Dodgin, the club's former chief scout who discovered Roberts. He made an immediate impact with his strength in the tackle and eye-catching speed on the overlap. His consistency in the Pirates' defence earned him selection for Wales's under-23 encounter with England at the Racecourse Ground in December 1970. A number of First Division scouts saw him snuff out the threat of Mick Channon and Dave Thomas, and transfer rumours began to circulate. Roberts, who troubled many a goalkeeper with his long-range shooting, left Eastville in May 1973 as the club's most expensive footballer Rovers had ever sold.

Joining Portsmouth for a fee of £55,000, Roberts continued to win admirers and, not surprisingly, his displays led to four full international caps while he was with Pompey. But ultimately he did not make the progress many had predicted and, following a brief spell with Hereford United, he completed his playing days with Exeter City.

Les CARTWRIGHT

Position	Midfielder
Born	Leslie Cartwright, Aberdare, 4 March 1952
Height	5ft 9in
Weight	10st 13lb
Clubs	Coventry City, Wrexham, Cambridge United, Southend United
Welsh Caps	7
	1974 v England (lost 0–2), v Scotland (lost 0–2), v N. Ireland (won 1–0)
	1976 v Scotland (lost 1–3)
	1977 v W. Germany (lost 0–2)
	1978 v Iran (won 1–0)
	1979 v Malta (won 7–0)

MIDFIELDER LES CARTWRIGHT began his Football League career as a winger with Coventry City. Although he was to spend eight years at Highfield Road, he only made 68 League appearances, scoring four goals. After being capped by Wales at under-23 level, the Aberdare-born player won the first of seven full international caps when he played against England in May 1974.

He joined Wrexham in the summer of 1977 for a fee of £40,000 and made his debut against Port Vale in the third match of the 1977/78 season, going on to score four goals in 41 League appearances that campaign as the Robins won the Third Division Championship. He also won a Welsh Cup winners' medal, scoring in the 2–1 first leg win at Bangor City. Cartwright also played his part when the club reached the sixth round of the FA Cup, scoring in the 4–1 fourth round replay win over Newcastle United.

However, injuries limited his appearances for Wrexham in the Second Division and in March 1982, after scoring 14 goals in 154 first-team outings, he moved to Cambridge United. After a loan period with Southend United, he ended his first-class career.

He ran a sub-post office but remained involved with the game, coaching Coventry City's junior teams.

David SMALLMAN

Position	Forward
Born	David Paul Smallman, Connahs Quay, 22 March 1953
Height	5ft 8in
Weight	10st 4lb
Clubs	Wrexham, Everton, Newtown, Colwyn Bay.
Welsh Caps	7 Goals 1
	1974 v England (lost 0–2), v Scotland (lost 0–2), v N. Ireland (won 1–0) 1 goal
	1975 v Hungary (won 2–1), v England (2–2), v N. Ireland (lost 0–1)
	1976 v Austria (won 1–0)

DAVID SMALLMAN BURST ON TO the scene in 1972/73 when he scored 15 goals in 40 League and Cup appearances for Wrexham. Having scored against Oldham Athletic and Notts County in successive games, he kept his place for the club's European Cup Winners' Cup second-round first-leg tie against Hajduk Split, and scored in a 3–1 win for the Robins. The following month he netted a hat-trick in a 5–0 FA Cup first-round replay win over Darlington.

The following season was Smallman's best as his goals helped Wrexham reach the sixth round of the FA Cup for the first time in their history. In 1974/75 he topped the club's goalscoring charts with 20 League and Cup goals. He also scored his second hat-trick for the Robins in a 4–0 home win over Aldershot which transpired to be his last appearance in a Wrexham shirt.

Smallman was capped three times by Wales during his Wrexham career, and he netted the only goal of the game against Northern Ireland at Wrexham in May 1974. He joined Everton for a fee of £75,000. Although he scored three goals in the first four games of the 1975/76 season, his five years at Goodison were nothing short of a disaster. Smallman, who had scored 51 goals in 125 first-team games or Wrexham, broke his leg twice on Merseyside and managed just seven goals in 5 games.

After emigrating to Australia, where he played part-time football, he returned to the Racecourse Ground to play in the club's reserve side before playing non-League football with Newtown and Colwyn Bay.

rian FLYNN

Position	Midfielder
Born	Brian Flynn, Port Talbot, 12 October 1955
Height	5ft 3in
Weight	9st 8lb
Clubs	Burnley, Leeds United, Cardiff City, Doncaster Rovers, Bury, Wrexham
Welsh Caps	66 Goals 7

1975 v Luxembourg (won 5–0), v Hungary (won 2–1), v Luxembourg (won 3–1),
v Scotland (2–2) 1 goal, v England (2–2), v N. Ireland (lost 0–1)

1976 v Austria (won 1–0), v England (lost 1–2), v Yugoslavia (lost 0–2), v England (lost 0–1),
v N. Ireland (won 1–0), v Yugoslavia (1–1)

1977 v W. Germany (lost 0–2), v Scotland (lost 0–1), v Czechoslovakia (won 3–0),
v Scotland (0–0), v England (won 1–0), v N. Ireland (1–1)

1978 v Kuwait (0–0), v Kuwait (0–0), v Scotland (lost 0–2), v Czechoslovakia (lost 0–1),
v W. Germany (1–1), v Iran (won 1–0), v England (lost 1–3), v Scotland (1–1),
v N. Ireland (won 1–0)

1979 v Malta (won 7-0) 1 goal, v Turkey (won 1–0), v Scotland (won 3–0), v England (0–0),
v N. Ireland (1–1), v Malta (won 2–0) 1 goal

1980 v Republic of Ireland (won 2–1), v W. Germany (lost 1–5), v England (won 4–1),
v Scotland (lost 0–1), v N. Ireland (lost 0–1), v Iceland (won 4–1) 1 goal

1981 v Turkey (won 4–0) 1 goal, v Czechoslovakia (won 1–0), v Republic of Ireland
(won 3–1), v Turkey (won 1–0), v Scotland (won 2–0), v England (0–0), v USSR
(0–0)

1982 v Czechoslovakia (lost 0–2), v USSR (lost 0–3), v England (lost 0–1), v Scotland
(lost 0–1), v N. Ireland (won 3–0), v France (won 1–0)

1983 v Norway (won 1–0), v Yugoslavia (4–4) 1 goal, v England (lost 1–2), v Bulgaria
(won 1–0), v Scotland (lost 0–2), v N. Ireland (won 1–0), v Brazil (1–1) 1 goal

1984 v Norway (0–0), v Romania (won 5–0), v Bulgaria (lost 0–1), v Yugoslavia (1–1),
v Scotland (lost 1–2), v Norway (lost 0–1), v Israel (0–0)

A WELSH SCHOOLBOY INTERNATIONAL, Brian Flynn was first spotted playing for Neath Boys by Cardiff City. But the Ninian Park club let him slip through the net, and in 1971 Burnley signed him as an apprentice. He turned professional the following year but had to wait until February 1974 before making his Clarets debut in a First Division match at Arsenal. It was early the following season that the 5ft 3in Flynn began to establish himself in the Burnley midfield, his performances earning him a first Welsh cap at the age of 19 when he played against Luxembourg at Swansea in November 1974.

Though not a prolific scorer, Brian Flynn netted at international level before scoring in the Football League. *(Lancashire Evening Post)*

Flynn was not a prolific goalscorer. He scored for his country in his fourth international against Scotland in May 1975 before finding the net in a League match for Burnley, a feat he achieved in a 3–2 win at Everton in January 1976.

Following Burnley's relegation to the Second Division in 1976, it was always going to be difficult for the Turf Moor club to hold on to its stars. In November 1977, Flynn left the Clarets to join Leeds United for a fee of £175,000, and immediately forged a superb midfield partnership with England international Tony Currie.

Although the more flamboyant skills of Currie grabbed the headlines, it was Flynn's voracious appetite for work and his variety of defence-splitting passes that caught the eye. Flynn also had good control and a neat first touch, and had a longer stay at Elland Road than his midfield partner. But, as Allan Clarke made fruitless experiments in an attempt to stave off relegation, Flynn returned to Turf Moor on loan, eventually signing on a permanent basis towards the end of 1982. He took his tally of goals to 27 in 254 League and Cup games before leaving to play for Cardiff City in November 1984. After spells with Doncaster Rovers and Bury he went to Limerick as the club's player-coach. He had another spell with Doncaster and then, after working on the Football in the Community Scheme at Burnley, he joined Wrexham in February 1988.

When the Robins' manager Dixie McNeil resigned in the early part of the 1989/90 season, Flynn was asked to take over as player-manager of the Racecourse Ground club. After Wrexham had finished bottom of the Fourth Division in 1990/91, Flynn began to turn things around. Following their defeat of Flynn the reigning League Champions Arsenal in the third round of the FA Cup, Flynn led them to promotion to the new Second Division in 1992/93. Flynn stayed at the Racecourse Ground until 2001 before parting company with the club.

In September 2002 he took over the reins at Swansea City and against all odds kept the Vetch Field club in the Football League, but later lost out to Kenny Jackett.

Dai DAVIES

Position	Goalkeeper
Born	William David Davies, Ammanford, 1 April 1948
Height	6ft 1in
Weight	13st 3lb
Clubs	Ammanford, Swansea City, Everton, Wrexham, Tranmere Rovers, Bangor City
Welsh Caps	52

1975 v Hungary (won 2–1), v Luxembourg (won 3–1), v Scotland (2–2), v England (2–2), v N. Ireland (lost 0–1)

1976 v Yugoslavia (lost 0–2), v England (lost 0–1), v N. Ireland (won 1–0), v Yugoslavia (1–1)

1977 v W. Germany (lost 0–2), v Scotland (lost 0–1), v Czechoslovakia (won 3–0), v Scotland (0–0), v England (won 1–0), v N. Ireland (1–1)

1978 v Kuwait (0–0), v Scotland (lost 0–2), v Czechoslovakia (lost 0–1), v W. Germany (1–1), v Iran (won 1–0), v England (lost 1–3), v Scotland (1–1), v N. Ireland (won 1–0)

Goalkeeper Dai Davies of Wrexham and Wales overtook Jack Kelsey's record of 41 caps. *(Lancashire Evening Post)*

1979 v Malta (won 7–0), v Turkey (won 1–0), v W. Germany (lost 0–2), v Scotland (won 3–0), v England (0–0), v N. Ireland (1–1), v Malta (won 2–0)
1980 v Republic of Ireland (won 2–1), v W. Germany (lost 1–5), v Turkey (lost 0–1), v England (won 4–1), v Scotland (lost 0–1), v N. Ireland (lost 0–1), v Iceland (won 4–0)
1981 v Turkey (won 4–0), v Czechoslovakia (won 1–0), v Republic of Ireland (won 3–1), v Turkey (won 1–0), v Scotland (won 2–0), v England (0–0), v USSR (0–0)
1982 v Czechoslovakia (lost 0–2), v Iceland (2–2), v USSR (lost 0–3), v Spain (1–1), v England (lost 0–1), v Scotland (lost 0–1), v France (won 1–0)
1983 v Yugoslavia (4–4)

DAI DAVIES WAS A COMMANDING goalkeeper who dominated his penalty area. Although he was prone to the odd mistake, he was a permanent fixture in the Wales side, keeping his place for some eight years. When he turned out against Scotland at Swansea in 1981, Davies overtook Jack Kelsey's record of 41 caps, going on to concede just 51 goals in 52 games, the best record of all modern Wales goalkeepers.

Born in the South Wales mining village of Ammanford, Dai Davies tasted early success with Cardiff College of Education in 1969 when they won the Welsh Amateur Cup.

He began his Football League career with Swansea City, making his debut for the Vetch Field club against Third Division champions Chesterfield in the final game of the 1969/70 season. His first game in 1970/71 was against Preston North End, a match the Swans drew 1–1 before going on to complete a remarkable sequence of 19 matches undefeated, to equal the club record set some ten years earlier.

In December 1970 Davies signed for Everton for £25,000 but, after spending virtually four seasons in the shadows of Gordon West and his understudy David Lawson, he went back to the Vetch Field on loan. Eventually he returned to Goodison Park and went on to appear in 94 League and Cup games before leaving to join Wrexham in September 1977 for £8,000.

In his first season at the Racecourse Ground, Wrexham suffered the lowest number of defeats in their history as they won the Third Division Championship. In 1978/79 the Wrexham keeper helped establish the club's best-ever defensive record of only 42 goals conceded. The Robins won the Welsh Cup and qualified for Europe. At the beginning of that season, Welsh-speaking Davies was accorded a rare honour when he became the first soccer player to be admitted to the Gorsedd circle at the Cardiff National Eisteddfod. He chose the bardic name 'Dai o'r cwm' (Dai of the Valleys) after his native Amman valley.

At the end of the 1980/81 season he returned to play for Swansea, where he was unbeaten in six consecutive matches. In the summer of 1983 Davies joined Tranmere Rovers as the Prenton Park club's player-coach. A year later he retired from the game. However, in 1985 Bangor City qualified for Europe, and Davies came out of retirement to play in the European Cup Winners' Cup matches against Fredrikstad and Atletico Madrid. The following season he turned out in Wrexham's Welsh Cup campaign, winning a medal after Kidderminster Harriers were beaten in the final.

He became involved in a Welsh book and craft stall in Mold and could be heard commenting on football on Welsh TV. Davies now runs a natural healing centre in Llangollen, North Wales.

Derek SHOWERS

Position	Forward
Born	Derek Showers, Merthyr Tydfil, 28 January 1953
Height	5ft 10in
Weight	11st 4lb
Clubs	Cardiff City, Bournemouth, Portsmouth, Hereford United, Barry Town
Welsh Caps	2
	1975 v England (2–2), v N. Ireland (lost 0–1)

DEREK SHOWERS WON TWO full international caps for Wales in 1975.

He joined the Cardiff City ground staff at the age of 15 after being spotted on a coaching course at Whitchurch by John Charles, Colin Baker and Bobby Ferguson. Showers was without doubt a prolific goalscorer at junior level and this led to his early – arguably premature – baptism into League football at the age of just 17, following John Toshack's transfer to Liverpool. Showers found it hard going in the top flight, but the Cardiff manager stuck by him. Showers always gave maximum effort for the Bluebirds' cause, but unfortunately he lacked polish and was made the scapegoat by a section of Cardiff fans when things weren't going well for the Ninian Park club.

On leaving Cardiff, Showers joined Bournemouth. He soon rediscovered his goalscoring touch and netted a number of important goals for the Cherries before moving along the south coast to Portsmouth. He flitted in and out of the Pompey side before joining Hereford United, where he ended his League career having scored 50 goals in 271 League games for his four clubs.

After a spell playing non-League football for Barry Town, he was involved with Cardiff City's junior teams before leaving to join with the Royal Mail in South Wales.

Ian EVANS

Position	Central defender
Born	Ian Peter Evans, Egham, 30 January 1952
Height	6ft 2in
Weight	11st 2lb
Clubs	Queen's Park Rangers, Crystal Palace, Barnsley, Exeter City, Cambridge United
Welsh Caps	13 Goals 1
	1976 v Austria (won 1–0), v England (lost 1–2), v Yugoslavia (lost 0–2), v England (lost 0–1), v N. Ireland (won 1–0), v Yugoslavia (1–1) 1 goal
	1977 v W. Germany (lost 0–2), v Scotland (lost 0–1), v Czechoslovakia (won 3–0), v Scotland (0–0), v England (won 1–0), v N. Ireland (1–1)
	1978 v Kuwait (0–0)

IAN EVANS BEGAN HIS CAREER WITH Queen's Park Rangers. After failing to hold down a regular first-team spot, he joined Crystal Palace in September 1974. He quickly established himself as a favourite among the fans at Selhurst Park with his wholehearted displays at the centre of the Eagles' defence.

He captained Palace to the FA Cup semi-final in 1976 – the first time in the club's history they had reached this stage of the competition – and the following season led the side to promotion to the Second Division. After he had won the first of 13 full caps for Wales in the crunch match against Austria in November 1975, his future looked rosy. But an appalling injury sustained in a tackle with George Best, then of Fulham, put him out of action for two years. His courage and determination in overcoming the double fracture established an empathy between Ian Evans and the fans, and this made him part of the folklore of Crystal Palace Football Club. In fact, it took a revolutionary technique for Ian to be able to play again.

After a spell in the club's reserves, he went north and spent three seasons with Barnsley. He made 102 League appearances for the Tykes before returning to Selhurst Park as assistant manager to Steve Coppell. After helping fashion the side that restored First Division football at The Palace in 1989, Evans left to take over as manager of Swansea City. In recent years he assisted Mick McCarthy in the running of the Republic of Ireland national side.

Joey JONES

Position	Defender
Born	Joseph Patrick Jones, Llandudno, 4 March 1955
Height	5ft 10in
Weight	11st 7lb
Clubs	Wrexham, Liverpool, Chelsea, Huddersfield Town
Welsh Caps	72 Goals 1

1976 v Austria (won 1–0), v England (lost 1–2), v Scotland (lost 1–3)

1977 v W. Germany (lost 0–2), v Scotland (lost 0–1), v Czechoslovakia (won 3–0),
v Scotland (0–0), v England (won 1–0), v N. Ireland (1–1)

1978 v Kuwait (0–0), v Kuwait (0–0), v Scotland (lost 0–2), v Czechoslovakia (lost 0–1),
v W. Germany (1–1), v Iran (won 1–0), v England (lost 1–3), v Scotland (1–1),
v N. Ireland (won 1–0)

1979 v Malta (won 7–0), v Turkey (won 1–0), v W. Germany (lost 0–2), v Scotland
(won 3–0), v England (0–0), v N. Ireland (1–1), v Malta (won 2–0)

1980 v Republic of Ireland (won 2–1), v W. Germany (lost 1–5), v Turkey (lost 0–1),
v England (won 4–1), v Scotland (lost 0–1), v N. Ireland (lost 0–1), v Iceland (won 4–0)

1981 v Turkey (won 4–0), v Republic of Ireland (won 3–1), v Turkey (won 1–0), v Scotland
(won 2–0), v England (0–0), v USSR (0–0)

1982 v Czechoslovakia (lost 0–2), v Iceland (2–2), v USSR (lost 0–3), v Spain (1–1), v England
(lost 0–2), v Scotland (lost 0–1), v N. Ireland (won 3–0), v France (won 1–0)

1983 v Norway (won 1–0), v Yugoslavia (4–4) 1 goal, v England (lost 1–2), v Bulgaria
(won 1–0), v Scotland (lost 0–2), v N. Ireland (won 1–0), v Brazil (1–1)

1984 v Norway (0–0), v Romania (won 5–0), v Bulgaria (lost 0–1), v Yugoslavia (1–1),
v Scotland (lost 1–2), v England (won 1–0), v N. Ireland (1–1), v Norway (lost 0–1),
v Israel (0–0)

1985 v Iceland (lost 0–1), v Norway (1–1), v Scotland (won 1–0), v Norway (lost 2–4)

1986 v Scotland (1–1), v Hungary (lost 0–3), v Republic of Ireland (won 1–0), v Uruguay
(0–0), v Canada (lost 0–2), v Canada (won 3–0)

JOEY JONES IS ONE OF THE GREAT characters of Welsh football. His 72 full international caps remained a record until Peter Nicholas surpassed the total in 1991.

Jones joined Wrexham straight from school. Capped at youth international level, he made his Wrexham debut as a 17-year-old in a 1–1 draw at Rotherham United in January 1973. The Llandudno-born full-back went on to play in 118 first-team games before Liverpool manager Bob Paisley paid £110,000 for him in the summer of 1975.

He was signed to replace the out-of-form Alec Lindsay. His early displays for the Anfield club indicated too many rough edges for the top flight. Phil Neal switched to left-back and Tommy Smith came in on the right; Jones was out of the side. That disappointment, however, was merely a prelude to his finest season with the club, that of 1976/77. Having won a regular place in the Liverpool side, he went on to help them win that season's European Cup and League Championship. They just missed out on the FA Cup, losing 2–1 to Manchester United. During the club's run to the European Cup Final, the Kopites took the tattooed Jones to their hearts. After victories over the French, Swiss and West German champions, the Liverpool fans coined the catchphrase 'Who ate all the Frogs' legs, made the Swiss roll and topped

Liverpool's Joey Jones was a great character who broke Ivor Allchurch's long-standing record of Wales appearances against the Republic of Ireland in 1986. *(Lancashire Evening Post)*

the lot by munching Gladbach?' to immortalise Jones's displays in the Liverpool defence. Jones lost his place in the Liverpool side when manager Bob Paisley shuffled the Reds' defence to accommodate the increasingly impressive Alan Hansen. So it came as no surprise when he returned to Wrexham in September 1978 for a club record fee of £210,000.

Jones's first season in his second spell at the Racecourse Ground was the club's first in the Second Division. He stayed for four years. After the club were relegated in 1981/82, he discovered that his international place was in jeopardy, and so left the Racecourse Ground to link up with his former manager John Neal at Chelsea.

During his three years at Stamford Bridge, Jones won a Second Division Championship medal before leaving to play for Huddersfield Town. While with the Terriers, Jones broke Ivor Allchurch's long-standing record of Welsh international appearances when he played his 69th game for Wales against the Republic of Ireland in March 1986. He had previously announced his retirement from the international arena but, with Mike England's squad decimated through injuries, he offered to help out.

In August 1987 Jones again became a Wrexham player for the ridiculously low fee of £7,000. In 1988/89 he helped the club reach the Fourth Division play-off finals, where they lost to Leyton Orient. In December 1989 Wrexham manager Brian Flynn made Jones the club's player-coach. Since playing the last of his 482 first-team games for the Robins he has concentrated on coaching.

Brian LLOYD

Position	Goalkeeper
Born	Brian William Lloyd, St Asaph, 18 March 1948
Height	6ft 1in
Weight	13st 7lb
Clubs	Rhyl, Stockport County, Southend United, Wrexham, Chester City, Port Vale
Welsh Caps	3
	1976 v Austria (won 1–0), v England (lost 1–2), v Scotland (lost 1–3)

BRIAN LLOYD'S SUCCESSFUL PERIOD for the Wrexham team of the 1970s was further boosted by his selection for the full international side. He won three caps during the course of the 1975/76 season and kept a clean sheet on his debut against Austria.

Beginning his career with Rhyl, Lloyd then joined Stockport County. After two seasons of sharing the goalkeeping duties with Alan Ogley, he left Edgeley Park and joined Southend United for £10,000. However, he was never happy in his 2½-year spell at Roots Hall and was quick to return to North Wales when Wrexham offered to buy him.

Initially he again had to share the goalkeeping role, this time with Dave Gaskell, until 4 March 1972, when he embarked upon a remarkable run, playing in every game until his last appearance on 20 August 1977. This run consisted of 248 League matches and a record 312 appearances in all competitions. However, following the appointment of Arfon Griffiths as manager, Lloyd was dropped, and in September 1977 he moved to Chester.

He made 94 League appearances for Chester and had a loan spell at Port Vale befor
returning to Stockport County for a second stint. During this period Lloyd became th
only County goalkeeper to score a League goal when, with a gale-force wind behind
him, he netted at Bradford City. Lloyd completed his 500th League appearance in th
1982/83 season but retired aged 35 at the end of that campaign.

Alan CURTIS

Position	Forward/Midfielder
Born	Alan Thomas Curtis, Pentre, 16 April 1954
Height	5ft 11in
Weight	12st 8lb
Clubs	Swansea City, Leeds United, Southampton, Stoke City, Cardiff City, Barry Town, Haverfordwest
Welsh Caps	35 Goals 6

1976 v England (lost 1–2) 1 goal, v Yugoslavia (lost 0–2), v Scotland (lost 1–3), v England
(lost 0–1), v N. Ireland (won 1–0), v Yugoslavia (1–1)

1977 v W. Germany (lost 0–2), v Scotland (lost 0–1), v N. Ireland (1–1)

1978 v W. Germany (1–1), v England (lost 1–3), v Scotland (1–1)

1979 v W. Germany (lost 0–2), v Scotland (won 3–0), v England (0–0), v N. Ireland (1–1),
v Malta (won 2–0)

1980 v Republic of Ireland (won 2–1) 1 goal, v W. Germany (lost 1–5) 1 goal, v Turkey
(lost 0–1)

1982 v Czechoslovakia (lost 0–2), v Iceland (2–2) 1 goal, v USSR (lost 0–3), v Spain (1–1),
v England (lost 0–1), v Scotland (lost 0–1), v N. Ireland (won 3–0) 1 goal

1983 v Norway (won 1–0)

1984 v Romania (won 5–0) 1 goal, v Scotland (lost 1–2)

1985 v Spain (lost 0–3), v Norway (1–1), v Norway (lost 2–4)

1986 v Hungary (lost 0–3)

1987 v USSR (0–0)

A NEPHEW OF FORMER SWANSEA, Manchester City and Wales international Ro
Paul, Alan Curtis won a total of 35 full international caps for Wales over a period o
eleven years.

He was taken on to the Swansea ground staff directly from school and soor
emerged as a first-team player of skill, vision and imagination. He made his first-team
debut for the Swans against Charlton Athletic in the final game of the 1972/73
season. Curtis became quite a prolific marksman, netting his first first-team hat-trick
in a 4–1 Welsh Cup win over Newport County in January 1977, and ended the
season with 14 goals. His first League hat-trick came in a 5–0 win over Crewe
Alexandra in November 1977, while five months later both Curtis and Robbie James
scored hat-tricks as the Swans recorded their biggest-ever League win, defeating
Hartlepool United 8–0.

Curtis built his reputation as Swansea surged out of the lower reaches of the
Football League. In May 1979 he joined Leeds United for £400,000, a record for a

Alan Curtis of Southampton and Wales had imagination, vision and skill, winning 35 caps for Wales. (*Lancashire Evening Post*)

player from the lower divisions. Curtis arrived at Elland Road in triumphant form, scoring two goals on his debut against Bristol City. Though injury and a loss of form restricted his career with the Yorkshire club to 18 months, he did provide a handful of memorable moments. In October 1979 Leeds, who had endured six months without an away win, travelled to Southampton. It was here that Curtis scored a glorious individual goal when, in the dying seconds of the game, he ran almost the full length of the pitch to drive home a long-range shot that provided Leeds with a 2–1 victory.

Curtis returned to the Vetch Field in December 1980 as the Swans paid £165,000 to take him back to South Wales. He went on to be an important member of the Swansea side that won promotion to the First Division for the first time in their history.

Curtis left the Vetch Field for a second time in November 1983, following the club's relegation from the top flight. He joined Southampton for £85,000 to ease the Swans' financial plight. At The Dell, he failed to show his best form and in March 1986 he was loaned to Stoke City. Things didn't work out for him at the Victoria Ground and he returned to South Wales to play for Cardiff City, whom he joined on a free transfer.

In 1987/88 Curtis was instrumental in the club winning promotion to the Third Division and the Welsh Cup, in which he scored one of the goals in a 2–0 win over Wrexham. He continued to be a regular member of the Bluebirds' team;. However, during the early part of the 1989/90 campaign he returned to the Vetch Field for a third spell. He announced his retirement at the end of that season, having scored 96 goals in 364 League games for the Swans. He then joined Barry Town as player-coach before a spell playing for Haverfordwest.

After working as a financial consultant for a life insurance company, he returned to the Vetch Field as the club's assistant coach.

Carl HARRIS

Position	Winger
Born	Carl Stephen Harris, Neath, 3 November 1956
Height	5ft 9in
Weight	11st 1lb
Clubs	Leeds United, Charlton Athletic, Bury, Rochdale, Exeter City, Briton Ferry
Welsh Caps	24 Goals 1

1976 v England (lost 1–2), v Scotland (lost 1–3)
1978 v W. Germany (1–1), v Iran (won 1–0), v England (lost 1–3), v Scotland (1–1), v N. Ireland (won 1–0)
1979 v Malta (won 7–0), v Turkey (won 1–0), v W. Germany (lost 0–2), v England (0–0), v Malta (won 2–0)
1980 v N. Ireland (lost 0–1), v Iceland (won 4–0)
1981 v Turkey (won 4–0), v Czechoslovakia (won 1–0), v Republic of Ireland (won 3–1), v Turkey (won 1–0) 1 goal, v Scotland (won 2–0), v England (0–0), v USSR (0–0)
1982 v Czechoslovakia (lost 0–2), v Iceland (2–2), v England (lost 0–1)

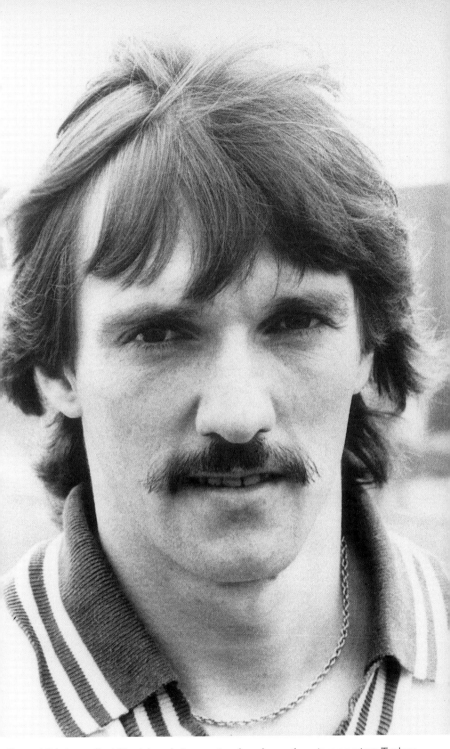

Capped 24 times, Carl Harris's only international goal was the winner against Turkey in 1981. *(Lancashire Evening Post)*

FLYING WINGER CARL HARRIS was first capped by Wales against England in March 1976, adding to under-23 and youth honours even before he had established himself as a regular in the Leeds United side.

Leeds persisted in their pursuit of Harris and were rewarded after moulding him into an international player. Harris had represented Wales's schoolboys. He was rejected by Burnley before joining the Elland Road club. Within days of his arrival at Leeds, he was homesick and left to get a job in a factory in Wales. Leeds persuaded him to return and in November 1973 he signed professional forms. Though he made a goalscoring debut for United in a 2–1 win over Ipswich Town in April 1975, he became the club's regular substitute.

Despite ending the 1980/81 season as the club's leading scorer, he was soon transferred to Charlton Athletic for £100,000. He maintained his form at The Valley, but was unable to add to his tally of international caps. After struggling with injuries he returned to Leeds, but was unable to force his way back into the club's first team. He left for Bury. He later had trials with Swansea and Cardiff. After further trials north of the border with Airdrie, he joined Rochdale in January 1988 and then Exeter City in December 1988. In the summer of 1989 he was given a free transfer by the Grecians and was appointed player-manager of Welsh League club Briton Ferry, later becoming the club's general manager.

Dave JONES

Position	Central defender
Born	David Edward Jones, Gosport, 11 February 1952
Height	6ft 0in
Weight	12st 8lb
Clubs	Bournemouth, Nottingham Forest, Norwich City
Welsh Caps	8 Goals 1
	1976 v Scotland (lost 1–3), v England (lost 0–1)
	1978 v Scotland (lost 0–2), v Czechoslovakia (lost 0–1), v W. Germany (1–1) 1 goal,
	v Iran (won 1–0), v England (lost 1–3)
	1980 v England (won 4–1)

ALTHOUGH HE WAS BORN IN Gosport, centre-half Dave Jones qualified to play for Wales by virtue of his father's birthplace. He won eight full caps, the first against Scotland in 1976. The Scots were Wales's opponents in 1978 in a World Cup qualifier at Anfield, where Jones was without doubt the innocent victim in the alleged handball clash with Scotland's Joe Jordan that cost the Wales side a place in the Finals.

Dave Jones began his Football League career with Bournemouth, where he made 134 appearances for the south-coast club before joining Nottingham Forest in the summer of 1974. Following the appointment of Brian Clough as manager at the City ground, Jones was allowed to leave Forest and signed for Norwich City in September 1975.

He didn't have the best of debuts for the Canaries, for not only did Norwich lose 5–2 against Newcastle United at St James Park, but Jones had the misfortune to score a last-minute own goal.

After suffering knee ligament damage in Wales's 4−1 win over England at the Racecourse Ground in May 1980, Dave Jones was forced to retire from League football. He had made 132 first-team appearances for the Canaries. Jones moved into a printing business, bit later returned to Dean Court to work with Bournemouth's School of Excellence.

David Jones was the innocent victim in the alleged handball clash with Scotland's Joe Jordan in the 1978 World Cup qualifier. *(Lancashire Evening Post)*

Mickey THOMAS

Position	Winger/midfielder
Born	Michael Reginald Thomas, Caersws, 7 July 1954
Height	5ft 6in
Weight	10st 6lb
Clubs	Wrexham, Manchester United, Everton, Brighton and Hove Albion, Stoke City, Chelsea, West Bromwich Albion, Derby County, Wichita (USA), Shrewsbury Town, Leeds United
Welsh Caps	51 Goals 4

1977 v W. Germany (lost 0–2), v Scotland (lost 0–1), v Czechoslovakia (won 3–0),
v Scotland (0–0), v N. Ireland (1–1)

1978 v Kuwait (0–0), v Scotland (lost 0–2), v Czechoslovakia (lost 0–1), v Iran (won 1–0)

1979 v England (lost 1–3), v N. Ireland (won 1–0), v Malta (won 7–0) 1 goal, v Turkey
(won 1–0), v W. Germany (lost 0–2), v Malta (won 2–0)

1980 v Republic of Ireland (won 2–1), v W. Germany (lost 1–5), v Turkey (lost 0–1),
v England (won 4–1) 1 goal, v Scotland (lost 0–1), v N. Ireland (lost 0–1)

1981 v Czechoslovakia (won 1–0), v Scotland (won 2–0), v England (0–0), v USSR (0–0)

1982 v Czechoslovakia (lost 0–2), v USSR (lost 0–3), v Spain (1–1), v England (lost 0–1),
v Scotland (lost 0–1), v N. Ireland (won 3–0)

1983 v Yugoslavia (4–4), v England (lost 1–2), v Bulgaria (won 1–0), v Scotland (lost 0–2),
v N. Ireland (won 1–0), v Brazil (1–1)

1984 v Romania (won 5–0) 1 goal, v Bulgaria (lost 0–1), v Yugoslavia (1–1), v Scotland
(lost 1–2), v England (won 1–0)

1985 v Iceland (lost 0–1), v Spain (lost 0–3), v Iceland (won 2–1) 1 goal, v Scotland
(won 1–0), v Spain (won 3–0), v Norway (lost 2–4)

1986 v Scotland (1–1), v Hungary (lost 0–3), v Saudi Arabia (won 2–1)

MICKEY THOMAS BEGAN HIS long career in League football with Wrexham, making his debut for the Robins on New Year's Day 1972, while he was still an amateur. Over the next seven seasons his bustling style earned him rave reviews. In 1977/78 his darting runs down the left flank helped Wrexham win promotion to the Second Division and earned him the first of 51 caps for Wales when he played against West Germany. Thomas was soon in demand from the bigger clubs and in November 1978 he was transferred to Manchester United for a fee of £300,000.

Although he had been bought to replace Gordon Hill, Thomas was more midfield than winger. The fact that he went a long way towards replacing his crowd-pleasing predecessor says much for the player's ability and application. During his three seasons at Old Trafford, Thomas earned himself a reputation for selfless running, the fans identifying with him as a trier with far more skill than he was given credit for. With United, Thomas also scored his fair share of goals, his most prolific season being 1979/80 when United finished two points behind champions Liverpool.

In July 1981 Thomas joined Everton in a deal involving cash plus John Gidman in exchange. His time at Goodison Park was short and marked by disagreements, and ended when he refused to play in the club's reserve side. A similar position was repeated at his next club, Brighton and Hove Albion, and it was only when he joined Stoke City for £200,000 in August 1982 that he recaptured much of his earlier form.

Mickey Thomas, the much-travelled midfielder, won the first of his 51 caps against West Germany in October 1976. *(Lancashire Evening Post)*

He repaid the Potters by winning the Player of the Year award in his first season at the Victoria Ground. Stoke manager Richie Barker's conversion to the long ball game was a disaster for Mickey Thomas. His alleged off-the-field problems made a transfer inevitable, and he joined Chelsea for £75,000 in January 1984. There, his old Wrexham boss John Neal was in charge. He also renewed acquaintances with former Wrexham colleagues Joey Jones and Eddie Niedzwiecki and became a great favourite with the Stamford Bridge crowd. It was with Chelsea that Thomas produced some of the best football of his career, helping the Pensioners win the Second Division title.

From Chelsea he joined West Bromwich Albion and then Derby County before moving to Wichita, in the United States, for 18 months. On his return he joined Shrewsbury Town, then underwent a remarkable free transfer to Leeds United under Howard Wilkinson as they started their big push to the First Division. However, injuries and illness restricted his first-team appearances to a minimum, and he rejoined Stoke.

Although time was catching up with him, he was again voted the club's Player of the Year before returning to the Racecourse Ground for a second spell with Wrexham.

He continued to make news on and off the field, scoring a brilliant goal against Arsenal in a memorable FA Cup giant-killing win. He was jailed for 18 months in 1993 for his part in a counterfeit currency scheme. He later linked up with Conway United and then managed Porthmadog.

Nick DEACY

Position	Central defender/Forward
Born	Nicholas Simon Deacy, Cardiff, 19 July 1953
Height	6ft 1in
Weight	12st 4lb
Clubs	Merthyr Tydfil, Hereford United, Workington, PSV Eindhoven, Beringen Vitesse Arnhem, Hull City, Happy Valley (Hong Kong), Bury
Welsh Caps	12 Goals 4
	1977 v Czechoslovakia (won 3–0) 1 goal, v Scotland (0–0), v England (won 1–0), v N. Ireland (1–1) 1 goal
	1978 v Kuwait (0–0), v Scotland (lost 0–2), v Czechoslovakia (lost 0–1), v W. Germany (1–1), v Iran (won 1–0), v Scotland (1–1), v N. Ireland (won 1–0) 1 goal
	1979 v Turkey (won 1–0) 1 goal

WALES TEAM MANAGER MIKE SMITH selected Nick Deacy as a replacement for the injured John Toshack for the game against Czechoslovakia at the Racecourse Ground in March 1977. He scored on his debut as Wales beat the Czechs 3–0 and surprised many people with the quality of his football. Eventually, however, the versatile Deacy, who won 12 caps, fell out of favour with Smith, who preferred the ageing Toshack.

Nick Deacy was a steelworker in Merthyr Tydfil when he was signed for the local lub by the legendary John Charles. He then moved to Hereford and made his League lebut for the Edgar Street club before later spending a brief loan period with Vorkington. After impressing in a mini-tournament in Holland in 1975, PSV indhoven paid £20,000 for his services.

With PSV Deacy marked his European Cup debut against Linfield with two goals. fter four successful years with Eindhoven, Deacy moved to Belgium in search of irst-team football but was soon back in Holland with Vitesse Arnhem.

He then returned to these shores and unexpectedly linked up with former Wales eam manager Mike Smith, who was then manager of Hull City. Deacy finally ended is League career with Bury after a spell in Hong Kong with Happy Valley, and then owed out of the game after a spell with his first club Merthyr Tydfil.

He went to work as a computer systems analyst with British Airways at Filton near ristol.

Peter SAYER

osition	Winger
orn	Peter Anthony Sayer, Cardiff, 2 May 1955
leight	5ft 7in
Veight	11st 0lb
.lubs	Cardiff City, Brighton and Hove Albion, Preston North End, Chester City, Northwich Victoria
Velsh Caps	7
	1977 v Czechoslovakia (won 3–0), v Scotland (0–0), v England (won 1–0), v N. Ireland (1–1)
	1978 v Kuwait (0–0), v Kuwait (0–0), v Scotland (lost 0–2)

CARDIFF-BORN PETER SAYER worked his way up through the ranks of his home-own club before making his debut for the Bluebirds against Hull City in September 974. He went on to play in a further nine games that season but, towards the end of hat 1974/75 campaign, he broke his ankle in Cardiff's match at Southampton. He ecovered to play in a number of matches towards the end of the following season as he club won promotion to the Second Division.

In 1976/77 Sayer missed just a handful of matches as the club just avoided elegation back to the Third Division. However, his form was such that he won the irst of seven full international caps when he played against Czechoslovakia. Sayer was ot a profile scorer. Towards the end of that campaign, found the net six times in six ames.

Midway through the 1977/78 season he left Ninian Park to join Brighton and Hove lbion for £100,000. In his first full season at the Goldstone Ground, he helped the eagulls win promotion to the First Division before later moving to play for Preston Jorth End.

He returned to Cardiff on loan in September 1981 before playing in just four games nd scoring in a 3–2 win at Luton Town. He left the Bluebirds after scoring 20 goals n 98 first-team outings, and ended his League career with Chester. He later appeared n non-League football for Northwich Victoria.

The Cardiff-born forward Peter Sayer won his 7 caps while with his home-town club
(Lancashire Evening Post)

Ian EDWARDS

Position	Forward
Born	Robert Ian Edwards, Wrexham, 30 January 1955
Height	6ft 1in
Weight	12st 5lb
Clubs	Rhyl, West Bromwich Albion, Chester City, Wrexham, Crystal Palace
Welsh Caps	4 Goals 4
	1978 v Kuwait (0–0)
	1979 v Malta (won 7–0), 4 goals, v W. Germany (lost 0–2)
	1980 v Turkey (lost 0–1)

IAN EDWARDS WON THE FIRST of his four caps against Kuwait in September 1977. On his next appearance at full international level, the Chester City player scored four times as Wales beat Malta 7–0.

Ian Edwards turned down an apprenticeship with Wrexham and joined West Bromwich Albion. Although he scored on his League debut for the Baggies, he found that his chances at the Hawthorns were limited, and in November 1976 he joined Chester for a fee of £20,000. At Sealand Road Edwards not only found the net himself but made numerous goalscoring chances for his fellow forwards. He had scored 36 goals in 104 League outings for the Cestrians when in November 1979 he joined Wrexham for £125,000.

Although he suffered from injuries throughout his first season with the Robins, he did score a hat-trick in a 5–0 Welsh Cup win over Connah's Quay Nomads. When the Robins lost their Second Division status in 1981/82, Edwards was the club's leading scorer, with 11 goals. In the summer of 1982, after having scored 30 goals in 99 appearances in three years at the Racecourse Ground, he joined Crystal Palace.

However, the knee problem from which he had suffered throughout his career curtailed his playing days after just 18 League appearances and four goals for the Selhurst Park club.

Don NARDIELLO

Position	Winger
Born	Donato Nardiello, Cardigan, 9 April 1957
Height	5ft 10in
Weight	10st 11lb
Clubs	Coventry City, Worcester City
Welsh Caps	2
	1978 v Czechoslovakia (lost 0–1), v W. Germany (1–1)

DON NARDIELLO WAS BROUGHT into the Wales side for the World Cup qualifying matches against Czechoslovakia and West Germany in 1978, just 25 days after making his First Division debut for Coventry City.

Born in Cardigan of Neapolitan parents, he was aged six when his family left Wes
Wales to live in Oldbury in the Midlands.

Nardiello was a winger in the traditional mould, with a most uncomplicated style
On joining Coventry City he provided an accurate supply of crosses for the likes o
Mick Ferguson and Ian Wallace as the Sky Blues' 4–2–4 formation relied heavily o
his fast raiding down either flank. Sadly, Nardiello failed to maintain his earl
promise and much of the remainder of his career at Highfield Road, where he mad
just 33 League appearances, was an anti-climax. In March 1980 he left Leagu
football to join Alliance Premier League Club, Worcester City.

A committed Christian, he served in the police from 1983 to 1988 and was
leading light in the West Midlands Police FC during that period.

Gareth DAVIES

Position	Central defender
Born	Gareth Davies, Bangor, 11 July 1949
Height	5ft 10in
Weight	11st 7lb
Club	Llandudno, Colwyn Bay, Wrexham
Welsh Caps	3
	1978 v Iran (won 1–0), v England (lost 1–3), v N. Ireland (won 1–0)

AFTER SOME IMPRESSIVE PERFORMANCES in the Welsh League for both Llandudn
and Colwyn Bay, Gareth Davies joined Wrexham and made his Football League debu
against Bradford City in February 1968. Davies established himself as a regular in th
Wrexham side during the following season, scoring his first League goal in a 1–
draw at Brentford. In 1969/70 he missed just one game as the Robins wer
promoted from the Fourth Division as runners-up to Chesterfield. In fact, Davie
missed very few games over the next 14 seasons, being ever-present in 1976/77 an
1977/78 and playing in 135 consecutive League matches. In this latter seaso
Wrexham won the Third Division Championship, and it was his performances durin
this campaign that led to full international honours, his first cap being against Iran i
the summer of 1978. The 1977/78 season also saw Third Division Wrexham reac
the quarter-finals of both the FA and League Cups, and Davies was outstanding i
both runs.

Davies won three Welsh Cup winners' medals and shares the record with Me
Sutton for having played in the most European matches for the club – 14 . His onl
goal in the Cup Winners' Cup came in the 2–1 home win over Swedish sid
Djurgardens IF in the opening match of the 1975/76 competition.

He played in 612 first-team games for the Robins, a record second only to Arfo
Griffiths, before injury forced his retirement at the end of the 1982/83 season. H
later went into hotel management in Wrexham.

Phil DWYER

Position	Defender
Born	Philip John Dwyer, Cardiff, 28 October 1953
Height	6ft 0in
Weight	13st 0lb
Clubs	Cardiff City, Rochdale

Cardiff City great Philip Dwyer represented Wales at under-21 and under-23 level before winning the first of 10 full caps. (*Lancashire Evening Post*)

Welsh Caps   10   Goals 2

           1978 v Iran (won 1–0) 1 goal, v England (lost 1–3) 1 goal, v Scotland (1–1), v N. Ireland (won 1–0)

           1979 v Turkey (won 1–0), v Scotland (won 3–0), v England (0–0), N. Ireland (1–1), v Malta (won 2–0)

           1980 v W. Germany (lost 1–5)

ONE OF THE CARDIFF CITY GREATS, Phil Dwyer holds the club record for the greatest number of appearances for the Bluebirds with a total of 573. Never one to shirk a challenge, Dwyer won under-21 and under-23 international honours before securing the first of ten full caps for Wales against Iran in 1978 – a match in which he scored the game's only goal.

A member of the successful Bluebirds' youth team of 1971, the former Welsh schoolboy international made his debut for the Cardiff side in a goalless draw at Orient in October 1972. He held his place for the rest of the season and ended the campaign with his first Welsh Cup winners' medal when Bangor City were beaten over two legs. An ever-present in 1973/74, he won another Welsh Cup winners' medal and played in 76 consecutive matches from his debut until injury forced him to miss a game.

In 1975/76 he missed just one game – a 4–1 defeat at Hereford – as the Bluebirds won promotion to the Second Division. At the end of that season he won his third Welsh Cup winners' medal, scoring two goals in the first leg against Hereford United in a tie that City won 6–5 on aggregate.

Despite a series of niggling injuries, he missed very few games and in 1983/84 he was ever-present. Although the majority of his 573 games were played at full-back or in the centre of defence, he still managed to score 50 goals. City manager Alan Durban let him leave Ninian Park towards the end of the 1984/85 season and he joined Rochdale, where he played in just 15 League games. He then joined the South Wales Police Force at Barry.

Byron STEVENSON

Position	Midfielder
Born	William Byron Stevenson, Llanelli, 7 September 1956
Height	6ft 1in
Weight	11st 0lb
Clubs	Leeds United, Birmingham City, Bristol Rovers, Garforth
Welsh Caps	15

           1978 v N. Ireland (won 1–0)

           1979 v Malta (won 7–0), v Turkey (won 1–0), v Scotland (won 3–0), v England (0–0), v N. Ireland (1–1), v Malta (won 2–0)

           1980 v W. Germany (lost 1–5), v Turkey (lost 0–1), v Iceland (won 4–0)

           1982 v Czechoslovakia (lost 0–2), v Spain (1–1), v Scotland (lost 0–1), v N. Ireland (won 3–0), v France (won 1–0)

During a moment of madness in the match against Turkey in November 1979, Byron Stevenson was sent off for violent conduct, which cost him several Welsh caps. (*Lancashire Evening Post*)

BYRON STEVENSON MADE 15 FULL international appearances for Wales – th opposition failed to score in nine of those matches. However, a moment of madnes in Izmir against Turkey in November 1979 certainly cost him several Welsh caps. H was sent off for violent conduct and was banned by UEFA from the European gam for over four years, although the sentence was later reduced.

Stevenson joined Leeds United as a youngster, turning professional in Septembe 1973. He was earmarked as a replacement for Norman Hunter but found himsel filling a variety of defensive positions. He won three Welsh under-21 caps befor making his full international debut against Northern Ireland at the Racecourse Groun in May 1978.

During the latter stages of the 1981/82 season, as Leeds found themselves i desperate need of a striker as they fought against relegation, Stevenson was traded fo Birmingham City forward Frank Worthington.

At St Andrew's Stevenson resumed his international career before moving on t Bristol Rovers in the summer of 1985. Stevenson appeared in a total of 200 Leagu games for his three clubs. He then assisted Garforth in the Northern Counties Eas League while running a public house.

Robbie JAMES

Position	Midfielder
Born	Robert Mark James, Swansea, 23 March 1957
Died	18 February 1998
Height	5ft 11in
Weight	13st 1lb
Clubs	Swansea City, Stoke City, Queen's Park Rangers, Leicester City, Bradford City, Cardiff City, Merthyr Tydfil, Barry Town, Llanelli
Welsh Caps	47 Goals 7

1979 v Malta (won 7–0), v W. Germany (lost 0–2), v Scotland (won 3–0), v England (0–0), v N. Ireland (1–1) 1 goal, v Malta (won 2–0)

1980 v W. Germany (lost 1–5)

1982 v Czechoslovakia (lost 0–2), v Iceland (2–2) 1 goal, v Spain (1–1) 1 goal, v England (lost 0–1), v Scotland (lost 0–1), v N. Ireland (won 3–0), v France (won 1–0)

1983 v Norway (won 1–0), v Yugoslavia (4–4) 1 goal, v England (lost 1–2), v Bulgaria (won 1–0)

1984 v Norway (0–0), v Romania (won 5–0) 1 goal, v Bulgaria (lost 0–1), v Yugoslavia (1–1) 1 goal, v Scotland (lost 1–2) 1 goal, v England (won 1–0), v N. Ireland (1–1), v Norway (lost 0–1), v Israel (0–0)

1985 v Iceland (lost 0–1), v Spain (lost 0–3), v Iceland (won 2–1), v Norway (1–1), v Scotland (won 1–0), v Spain (won 3–0), v Norway (lost 2–4)

1986 v Scotland (1–1), v Saudi Arabia (won 2–1), v Republic of Ireland (won 1–0), v Uruguay (0–0), v Canada (lost 0–2), v Canada (won 3–0)

1987 v Finland (1–1), v USSR (0–0), v Finland (won 4–0), v Czechoslovakia (1–1)

1988 v Denmark (won 1–0), v Denmark (lost 0–1), v Yugoslavia (lost 1–2)

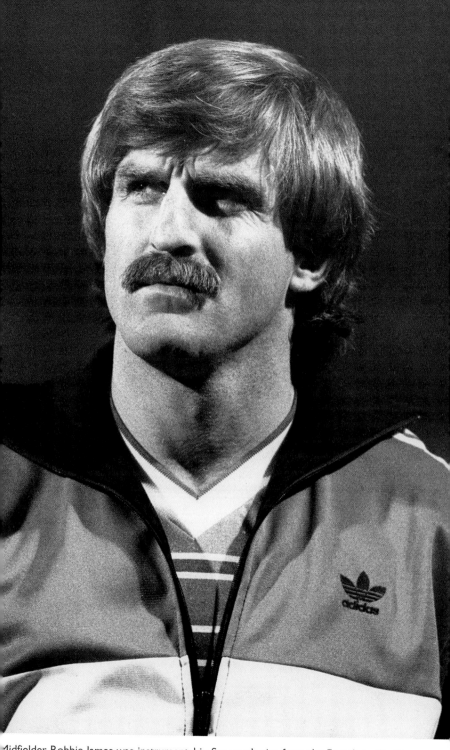

Midfielder Robbie James was instrumental in Swansea's rise from the Fourth to the First Division. *(Lancashire Evening Post)*

A REGULAR AND PASSIONATE WALES international, Robbie James had left school and was working for an electrical firm when he caught the eye of Swansea City manager Harry Gregg. After the youngster had impressed in Welsh League and Football Combination games, he was given his first-team debut in the final match of the 1972/73 season against Charlton Athletic. James, who was just 16 years old, starred in a 2–1 win for the Swans.

The driving midfielder was instrumental in the Vetch Field club's rise from the Fourth to the First Division, and in October 1978 his outstanding form led to the first of 47 full caps when he played in the 7–0 rout of Malta.

Within the space of twelve months during the club's successive promotions, James netted three hat-tricks: against Hartlepool United in the Football League (April 1978), Newport County in the League Cup (August 1978), and Kidderminster Harriers in the Welsh Cup (January 1979).

James was also an integral member of the Swansea side that took the old First Division by storm in 1981/82, when the Welsh club's displays captured the imagination not only of the locals but of the whole country. Arsenal, Liverpool and Manchester United were among the sides to come a cropper at the Vetch. James finished the season as the club's leading scorer with 14 goals as the Swans finished sixth in the table.

James had scored 99 goals in 394 League games for Swansea when, in July 1983, after the club had lost their place in the top flight, he joined Stoke City for £160,000. Unfortunately, he never quite showed the same form for the Potters and in October 1984 Stoke manager Bill Asprey offloaded him to Queen's Park Rangers for £100,000.

At Loftus Road he was used successfully as a full-back before moving in June 1987 to Leicester City, where manager Bryan Hamilton saw in James the sort of experienced campaigner who might help his young Second Division side. Sadly, many of his efforts were negated by lack of pace. After Wales had been eliminated from the European Championships, James seemed to lose some of his enthusiasm for the game and returned to the Vetch Field for a second spell.

Immediately assuming the captaincy, he led the Swans to promotion from the Fourth Division via the play-offs and scored in their Welsh Cup Final win of 1989. A year later he was transferred to Bradford City. After leaving the Valley Parade, James celebrated further Championship success with Cardiff City's Third Division side of 1993, where he also picked up his fifth Welsh Cup winners' medal.

His move to non-League Merthyr Tydfil as the club's player-manager prompted the first instance of the FA of Wales convening a transfer tribunal to set the £10,000 fee. It closed his Football League career of 782 appearances, a total bettered only by Peter Shilton, Terry Paine and Tommy Hutchison. After playing for Barry Town, Robbie James joined Llanelli, for whom he was playing in a Welsh League game when he collapsed and died, aged just 40.

George BERRY

Position	Central defender
Born	George Frederick Berry, Rostrop, W. Germany, 19 November 1957
Height	6ft 0in
Weight	12st 8lb
Clubs	Wolverhampton Wanderers, Stoke City, Doncaster Rovers, Peterborough United, Preston North End, Aldershot, Stafford Rangers
Welsh Caps	5
	1979 v W. Germany (lost 0–2)
	1980 v Republic of Ireland (won 2–1), v W. Germany (lost 1–5), v Turkey (lost 0–1)
	1983 v England (lost 1–2)

BORN IN ROSTROP, WEST GERMANY, central defender George Berry was only the second black player to represent Wales at full international level, winning five caps between May 1979 and February 1983.

He made his Football League debut for Wolves in a vital promotion clash against Chelsea at Molineux in May 1977 in a game that ended all square at 1–1. However, it was to be 1978/79 before he established himself as a first-team regular. Over the next four seasons he went on to take his total of League and Cup appearances for Wolves to 160. In 1980 he won a League Cup winners' medal as the Molineux club beat Nottingham Forest 1–0 in the final.

In the summer of 1982, George Berry joined Stoke City, and within a short period had been made the Potters' team captain. He was to stay at the Victoria Ground for eight seasons and, despite a loan spell at Doncaster Rovers and a brief sojourn in Portuguese football, Berry amassed a total of 269 first-team appearances for the Potters.

He then joined Peterborough United and in his only season at London Road captained the club to promotion from the Fourth Division. He then signed for Preston North End but his legs could not stand the pressure of playing home games on the Deepdale plastic, and he was loaned to Aldershot. Although he never made a League appearance for the Shots, it was while at the Recreation Ground that he decided to end his first-class career.

After playing non-League football for Stafford Rangers, he hung up his boots to take a job with the Professional Footballers' Association.

Peter NICHOLAS

Position	Midfielder	
Born	Peter Nicholas, Newport, 10 November 1959	
Height	5ft 8in	
Weight	11st 8lb	
Clubs	Crystal Palace, Arsenal, Luton Town, Aberdeen, Chelsea, Aberdeen, Watford	
Welsh Caps	73	Goals 2

While with Aberdeen Peter Nicholas became the first player from a Scottish club sinc[e] 1938 to be capped by Wales – when playing against Denmark in 1987. (*Lancashir[e] Evening Post*)

1979 v Scotland (won 3–0), v N. Ireland (1–1), v Malta (won 2–0) 1 goal
1980 v Republic of Ireland (won 2–1), v W. Germany (lost 1–5), v Turkey (lost 0–1),
   v England (won 4–1), v Scotland (lost 0–1), v N. Ireland (lost 0–1), v Iceland (won 4–0)
1981 v Turkey (won 4–0), v Czechoslovakia (won 1–0), v Republic of Ireland (won 3–1),
   v Turkey (won 1–0), v Scotland (won 2–0), v England (0–0), v USSR (0–0)
1982 v Czechoslovakia (lost 0–2), v Iceland (2–2), v USSR (lost 0–3), v Spain (1–1),
   v England (lost 0–1), v Scotland (lost 0–1), v N. Ireland (won 3–0) 1 goal, v France
   (won 1–0)
1983 v Yugoslavia (4–4), v Bulgaria (won 1–0), v Scotland (lost 0–2), v N. Ireland (won 1–0)
1984 v Norway (0–0), v Bulgaria (lost 0–1), v Norway (lost 0–1), v Israel (0–0)
1985 v Spain (lost 0–3), v Norway (1–1), v Scotland (won 1–0), v Spain (won 3–0),
   v Norway (lost 2–4)
1986 v Scotland (1–1), v Hungary (lost 0–3), v Saudi Arabia (won 2–1), v Republic of Ireland
   (won 1–0), v Uruguay (0–0), v Canada (lost 0–2), v Canada (won 3–0)
1987 v Finland (1–1), v USSR (0–0), v Finland (won 4–0), v Czechoslovakia (1–1)
1988 v Denmark (won 1–0), v Denmark (lost 0–1), v Czechoslovakia (lost 0–2),
   v Yugoslavia (lost 1–2), v Sweden (lost 1–4)
1989 v Holland (lost 0–1), v Finland (2–2), v Israel (3–3), v Sweden (lost 0–2),
   v W. Germany (0–0)
1990 v Finland (lost 0–1), v Holland (lost 1–2), v W. Germany (lost 1–2), v Republic of
   Ireland (lost 0–1), v Sweden (lost 2–4), v Costa Rica (won 1–0)
1991 v Denmark (lost 0–1), v Belgium (won 3–1), v Luxembourg (won 1–0), v Republic of
   Ireland (lost 0–3), v Belgium (1–1), v Poland (0–0), v Germany (won 1–0)
1992 v Luxembourg (won 1–0)

PETER NICHOLAS ACHIEVED 73 Welsh international caps.

The hard-tackling midfielder was a member of Crystal Palace's FA Youth Cup
winning sides. He signed professional forms for the Eagles in December 1976 and
made his first-team debut at Millwall on the opening day of the 1977/78 season in a
1–0 victory. Over the next four seasons, Nicholas was a virtual ever-present, and
helped Palace win promotion to the top flight as Second Division champions in
1978/79.

At one stage Palace declared that Nicholas was positively the one player that would
never be allowed to leave the club. But opinions and values change, and after a while
they were persuaded to part with their dominant midfield force. Nicholas was
disillusioned by the managerial upheavals at Selhurst Park that saw Terry Venables
leave and Dario Gradi take over. Those were turbulent times, with Malcolm Allison
and Ernie Walley in turn taking charge before Gradi's appointment.

Nicholas was a hard man in the mould of fearsome adversaries like Nobby Stiles
and Peter Storey. He joined Arsenal in March 1981 for a fee of £400,000. Combining
his natural toughness in the challenge with a deft skill and penchant for attacking, he
quickly established himself as a favourite with the Highbury crowd. When he arrived
at Arsenal the Gunners were wallowing ineffectively in mid-table and had won just
three of their previous 14 League games. With Nicholas in the side, they proceeded to
drop only two points in the last nine games of the season, moving up to third spot
and claiming a place in Europe.

After making such a positive early impression, Nicholas was tipped for a long-term Highbury future. But, following two steady campaigns, he found himself on the sidelines as the Gunners' manager experimented with other players.

Nicholas moved back to Crystal Palace, originally on loan. He made more international appearances while playing for the Eagles, but still registered with Arsenal, a fact which confuses the issue over whether he is Palace's most-capped player. He eventually joined Palace on a permanent basis in October 1983 for a fee of £150,000. He had scored 16 goals in 199 games for the South London club when, following a row between Palace and the Welsh FA over injury payments, he left to join Luton Town in January 1985.

He later signed for Aberdeen for £350,000. In 1987 he became the first player from a Scottish club since Freddie Warren in 1938 to be capped by Wales when he played against Denmark.

In August 1988, following the illness of his child, Nicholas returned south to play for Chelsea. He was appointed club captain and played an important part in the Pensioners' promotion-winning season of 1988/89 when the Stamford Bridge club returned to the top flight as Second Division champions. Nicholas ended his League career with Watford before returning to Selhurst Park for a third spell, this time as Crystal Palace's first-team coach. He then moved to his home-town club, Newport County, as manager.

1980–89

So Near and Yet So Far

Although Wales failed to qualify for any of the major tournaments throughout the decade, they could argue that they were extremely unlucky. The match that proved to be their undoing in the 1982 World Cup qualifiers was the home tie against Iceland at Swansea on 14 October 1981. The floodlights failed, temporarily stopping the match and unsettling Wales, who dropped a crucial point.

Wales did themselves proud in attempting to qualify for the 1984 European Championships, and a victory against Yugoslavia in Cardiff on 14 December 1983 would have sent them on their way to France. Instead, a 1–1 draw meant that everything hinged on the final match between Yugoslavia and Bulgaria in Split. A draw would have put Wales through; any victory would do for the Yugoslavs; but a win for Bulgaria would be sufficient for them to leap-frog into first place. With seconds remaining, the score was 2–2 and it looked as if Wales were through. Then the Yugoslav defender Radanovic headed a winning goal and Wales were out.

Wales also had just cause for complaint for not reaching the 1986 World Cup Finals in Mexico. In the final match of the group, they had to beat Scotland at Ninian Park to qualify for a play-off. Wales were 1–0 ahead at half-time and the Scots were despondent. With just 10 minutes to go, a dubious handball in the Welsh penalty area was adjudged by the French referee to be a penalty to Scotland. Cooper scored from the spot.

Wales's failure to qualify for the 1988 European Championships cost Mike England his job and brought a new twist to the club-versus-country debate. When England was sacked in February 1988 there were rumours that Wales might turn to Brian Clough. Intense speculation reached fever pitch when Clough said he would leave Forest if they stopped him running the Wales team on a part-time basis. Clough had talks with the Welsh FA and, although Forest refused to allow him to take the job, he did not quit the City Ground.

190 *Wales Footballers - Ian Walsh*

Ian WALSH

Position	Forward
Born	Ian Patrick Walsh, St Davids, 4 September 1958
Height	5ft 9in
Weight	11st 6lb
Clubs	Crystal Palace, Swansea City, Barnsley, Grimsby Town, Cardiff City
Welsh Caps	18 Goals 7

1980 v Republic of Ireland (won 2–1) 1 goal, v Turkey (lost 0–1), v England (won 4–1) 1 goal, v Scotland (lost 0–1), v Iceland (won 4–0), 2 goals

1981 v Turkey (won 4–0) 1 goal, v Czechoslovakia (won 1–0), v Republic of Ireland (won 3–1), v Turkey (won 1–0), v Scotland (won 2–0), 2 goals, v England (0–0), v USSR (0–0)

1982 v Czechoslovakia (lost 0–2), v Iceland (2–2), v Spain (1–1), v Scotland (lost 0–1), v N. Ireland (won 3–0), v France (won 1–0)

WITH HIS CLUB, CRYSTAL PALACE, in the First Division, Ian Walsh became a regular choice for the Wales squad. After scoring on his international debut in a 2–1 win over the Republic of Ireland in September 1979, he went on to find the net seven times in 18 appearances, including scoring both goals in a 2–0 defeat of Scotland in May 1981.

Walsh helped Palace juniors win the FA Youth Cup in 1977, and then forced his way into the Eagles' League side and became a key member of the Selhurst Park club's 1979 Second Division Championship winning team. During the course of that campaign he scored several invaluable goals, including the first one in the decisive victory over Burnley which clinched the title in the final game of the season.

He had scored 23 goals in 117 League outings for the Eagles when in February 1982 he moved to Swansea, playing in the Vetch Field club's First Division side. He averaged a goal every three games for the Swans but, following their relegation in 1982/83, he left to continue his career with Barnsley.

He spent two seasons at Oakwell, netting at a similar rate as at the Vetch. His best season was 1986/87, when he scored 15 goals in 33 games, before joining Grimsby Town. Walsh helped the Mariners win promotion in his first season at Blundell Park, scoring some vital goals along the way. However, midway through the 1987/88 season Walsh suffered a spate of niggling injuries and was allowed to join Cardiff City. Injuries again hampered his progress and he was forced into premature retirement.

He lives and works in Cardiff, where he sells insurance, and can often be heard on BBC Radio Wales.

Crystal Palace central defender Ian Walsh was part of Wales's successful side for many years. (*Lancashire Evening Post*)

192 *Wales Footballers - Gordon Davies*

Gordon DAVIES

Position	Forward
Born	Gordon Jones Davies, Merthyr Tydfil, 3 August 1955
Height	5ft 7in
Weight	10st 6lb
Clubs	Merthyr Tydfil, Fulham, Chelsea, Manchester City, Wrexham
Welsh Caps	16 Goals 2

1980 v Turkey (lost 0–1), v Iceland (won 4–0)

1982 v Spain (1–1), v France (won 1–0)

1983 v England (lost 1–2), v Bulgaria (won 1–0), v Scotland (lost 0–2), v N. Ireland (won 1–0) 1 goal, v Brazil (1–1)

1984 v Romania (won 5–0), v Scotland (lost 1–2), v England (won 1–0), v N. Ireland (1–1)

1985 v Iceland (won 2–1), v Norway (1–1)

1986 v Saudi Arabia (won 2–1) 1 goal.

GORDON DAVIES, FULHAM's greatest-ever goalscorer, began his career with Manchester City, joining the club as an apprentice in 1972. However, he failed to make the grade and decided to train as a teacher while playing non-League football for his home-town team of Merthyr Tydfil.

In March 1978 Fulham manager Bobby Campbell paid just £4,000 for his services and, after making his debut against Mansfield Town, Davies became an automatic choice. In 1979/80 he topped the club's goalscoring charts for the first time – his total of 15 goals in 39 games included hat-tricks against Birmingham City and Leicester City. Not surprisingly, his prolific goalscoring attracted the national selectors and in November 1979 he won the first of 16 full caps when he played against Turkey.

Davies was Fulham's leading scorer for the next four seasons, helping the club win promotion to the Second Division in 1981/82 when he netted 24 goals. During the course of the 1983/84 season Davies scored four of Fulham's goals in a 5–1 rout of Manchester City and all three in the 5–3 home defeat by Chelsea.

In November 1984 Chelsea gave Davies the opportunity to prove himself in the First Division but, despite scoring a hat-trick in a 4–3 win at Everton, most of his stay at Stamford Bridge was as understudy to David Speedie.

In October 1985 he left to play for Manchester City. After scoring nine goals in 31 games, he returned to Craven Cottage to play for Fulham. He took his tally of goals in his two spells with Fulham to 178 in 448 League and Cup games before ending his first-class career with Wrexham. Davies later managed Tornado of Norway before working as a pest control officer for Rentokil.

Fulham's greatest-ever goalscorer, Gordon Davies, won the first of 16 caps against Turkey in November 1979. (*Lancashire Evening Post*)

The much-travelled David Giles won 9 of his 12 caps with Swansea, whom he helped win promotion to the top flight. *(Lancashire Evening Post)*

David GILES

Position	Winger
Born	David Charles Giles, Cardiff, 21 September 1956
Height	5ft 7in
Weight	10st 4lb
Clubs	Cardiff City, Wrexham, Swansea City, Leyton Orient, Crystal Palace, Birmingham City, Newport County, Barry Town
Welsh Caps	12 Goals 2

1980 v England (won 4–1), v Scotland (lost 0–1), v N. Ireland (lost 0–1), v Iceland (won 4–0)
   1 goal
1981 v Turkey (won 4–0), v Czechoslovakia (won 1–0) 1 goal, v Turkey (won 1–0),
   v England (0–0), v USSR (0–0)
1982 v Spain (1–1)
1983 v N. Ireland (won 1–0), v Brazil (1–1)

A MUCH-TRAVELLED PLAYER, David Giles won 9 of his 12 full international caps and helped Swansea win promotion to the First Division during his two-year stay at the Vetch Field.

He was a Welsh schoolboy international when he joined Cardiff City, making his debut for the Bluebirds in a goalless draw at Nottingham Forest in February 1975. He had played in 70 first-team games, scoring ten goals, when in December 1978 Wrexham paid £20,000 to take him to the Racecourse Ground. In two seasons with the Robins he played in 48 games before Swansea paid £40,000 for his services. Despite his success at the Vetch, Giles was loaned out to Orient before moving on to Crystal Palace.

At Selhurst Park his form was such that he continued to play for his country. Eventually he moved on again, this time to Birmingham City. But in two months at St Andrew's he didn't play a game. After a season with Newport County, he left Somerton Park to return to his home-town club Cardiff City in September 1985. Ending his first-class career where he had started it, Giles had appeared in 324 League games for his six clubs before leaving to play part-time football for Barry Town in the Welsh League.

After a spell as a double-glazing salesman, he entered management with Ebbw Vale.

Paul PRICE

Position	Central defender
Born	Paul Terence Price, St Albans, 23 March 1954
Height	5ft 11in
Weight	12st 0lb
Clubs	Welwyn Garden United, Luton Town, Tottenham Hotspur, Minnesota Kicks, Swansea City, Saltash United, Peterborough United, Chelmsford City, Wivenhoe, St Albans City, Hitchin Town

Defender Paul Price battled back from two broken legs to win 25 caps for his country
(Lancashire Evening Post)

Welsh Caps   25   Goals 1

1980 v England (won 4–1), v Scotland (lost 0–1), v N. Ireland (lost 0–1), v Iceland (won 4–0)

1981 v Turkey (won 4–0), v Czechoslovakia (won 1–0), v Republic of Ireland (won 3–1)
    1 goal, v Turkey (won 1–0), v Scotland (won 2–0), v England (0–0), v USSR (0–0)

1982 v USSR (lost 0–3), v Spain (1–1), v France (won 1–0)

1983 v Norway (won 1–0), v Yugoslavia (4–4), v England (lost 1–2), v Bulgaria (won 1–0),
    v Scotland (lost 0–2), v N. Ireland (won 1–0)

1984 v Norway (0–0), v Romania (won 5–0), v Bulgaria (lost 0–1), v Yugoslavia (1–1),
    v Scotland (lost 1–2)

PAUL PRICE QUALIFIED TO PLAY for Wales because his father was born in Merthyr Vale. He made his full international debut against England in May 1980, a match the Welsh won 4–1.

After joining Luton Town, Paul Price twice broke his leg while playing for the Hatters' reserves. But he battled back and eventually developed into a cool, cultured defender. Price made his League debut for Luton as a substitute at Oxford United on the final day of the 1972/73 season. However, he didn't figure in the club's promotion-winning season of 1973/74 or relegation in 1974/75. Over the next few seasons, Price built a reputation as a reliable player who performed his duties with the minimum of fuss. He left Kenilworth Road in the summer of 1981, having made 230 appearances, and joined Tottenham Hotspur for a fee of £250,000.

Although good enough to play in most First Division defences, he failed to displace Graham Roberts and Paul Miller, until, that is, Roberts moved into midfield. Price played in the Spurs team that won the FA Cup in 1982.

In the summer of 1984 Price left White Hart Lane and went to America to join the Minnesota Kicks. On his return to these shores he played for Swansea City. He moved to Saltash United and then to Peterborough United. He later returned to non-League circles, appearing for Chelmsford City, Wivenhoe and his home-town side of St Albans City. He then had a spell as player-manager of Hitchin Town.

Keith PONTIN

Position	Central defender
Born	Keith Pontin, Pontyclun, 14 June 1956
Height	6ft 1in
Weight	12st 7lb
Clubs	Cardiff City, Merthyr Tydfil, Barry Town
Welsh Caps	2
	1980 v England (won 4–1), v Scotland (lost 0–1)

A ONE-CLUB MAN, CENTRAL DEFENDER Keith Pontin worked his way up through the Cardiff City ranks before making his first-team debut in a 2–0 win for the Bluebirds at Charlton Athletic on the opening day of the 1976/77 season. But, following the arrival of Paul Went from Portsmouth, he went back to playing reserve-team football. He was recalled to Cardiff's first team in September 1977 after Went was moved into the attack. Over the next four seasons, the Pontyclun-born defender missed very few matches and his form was such that he won two full caps for Wales: the first was in the 4–1 win over England.

During the 1981/82 season, when the Bluebirds were relegated from the Second Division, Keith Pontin played in 40 matches, more than anyone else. One of Cardiff's most experienced players at that time, he left Ninian Park during the early part of the following season after an argument with City manager Len Ashurst. Pontin, who had played in 231 first-team games for the Bluebirds, was aged just 26 when he joined Merthyr Tydfil in the Southern League. He later signed for Barry Town, playing out his career with the successful Welsh League club.

Ian RUSH

Position	Forward
Born	Ian James Rush, St Asaph, 20 October 1961
Height	6ft 0in
Weight	12st 6lb
Clubs	Chester City, Liverpool, Juventus, Leeds United, Newcastle United, Sheffield United, Wrexham
Welsh Caps	73 Goals 28

1980 v Scotland (lost 0–1), v N. Ireland (lost 0–1)

1981 v England (0–0)

1982 v Iceland (2–2), v USSR (lost 0–3), v England (lost 0–1), v Scotland (lost 0–1), v N. Ireland (won 3–0) 1 goal, v France (won 1–0), 1goal

1983 v Norway (won 1–0) 1 goal, v Yugoslavia (4–4) 1 goal, v England (lost 1–2) 1 goal, v Bulgaria (won 1–0)

1984 v Norway (0–0), v Romania (won 5–0), 2 goals, v Bulgaria (lost 0–1), v Yugoslavia (1–1), v Scotland (lost 1–2), v England (won 1–0), v N. Ireland (1–1)

1985 v Iceland (won 2–1), v Norway (1–1) 1 goal, v Scotland (won 1–0) 1 goal, v Spain (won 3–0), 2 goals

1986 v Scotland (1–1), v Saudi Arabia (won 2–1), v Republic of Ireland (won 1–0) 1 goal, v Uruguay (0–0)

1987 v Finland (1–1), v USSR (0–0), v Finland (won 4–0) 1 goal, v Czechoslovakia (1–1) 1 goal

1988 v Denmark (lost 0–1), v Czechoslovakia (lost 0–2), v Yugoslavia (lost 0–2), v Sweden (lost 1–4), v Malta (won 3–2) 1 goal, v Italy (won 1–0) 1 goal

1989 v Holland (lost 0–1), v Finland (2–2), v Sweden (lost 0–2), v W. Germany (0–0)

1990 v Finland (lost 0–1), v Republic of Ireland (lost 0–1)

1991 v Denmark (lost 0–1), v Belgium (won 3–1) 1 goal, v Luxembourg (won 1–0) 1 goal, v Republic of Ireland (lost 0–3), v Belgium (1–1), v Poland (0–0), v Germany (won 1–0) 1 goal.

1992 v Germany (lost 1–4), v Luxembourg (won 1–0), v Romania (lost 1–5) 1 goal.

1993 v Faroe Islands (won 6–0), 3 goals, v Cyprus (won 1–0), v Belgium (lost 0–2), v Belgium (won 2–0) 1 goal, v RCS (1–1), v Faroe Islands (won 3–0) 1 goal

1994 v RCS (2–2) 1 goal, v Cyprus (won 2–0) 1 goal, v Romania (lost 1–2), v Norway (lost 1–3), v Sweden (lost 0–2), v Estonia (won 2–1) 1 goal

1995 v Albania (won 2–0), v Georgia (lost 0–5), v Bulgaria (lost 0–3), v Germany (1–1), v Georgia (lost 0–1)

1996 v Moldova (won 1–0), v Italy (lost 0–3)

THE GREATEST GOALSCORER IN WELSH international football history, Ian Rush made his debut for Wales six months before playing in Liverpool's first team.

One of ten children, he began his career with Chester City, where his goalscoring abilities were spotted by Liverpool. Bob Paisley paid £300,000 for the youngster in April 1980. Many doubted the shrewdness of this acquisition and in his early days at Anfield he could hardly find the net in Central League games – there was even talk of moving him on. However, by the time he scored his first goal at international level for Wales against Northern Ireland at Wrexham, he had become a firm favourite with the Kop.

Mark Hughes (right) and Ian Rush, two of Wales's greatest goalscorers, celebrate, 1994. (*Getty Images*)

In the 1981/82 season he scored 30 goals in 49 games, to win his first League Championship medal, including one of his first appearances in the Merseyside derby as Liverpool beat Everton 3−1. His best individual performance in the derby game came exactly a year later in Liverpool's 5−0 humiliation of the old enemy at Goodison; his four-goal haul was only the third time this feat had been achieved. Rush's goals record in the derbies is unparalleled, his total of 21 being the best of either side. There were further League titles in 1982/83 and 1983/84, European Cup victory in 1984 and League Cup wins in 1981, 1982, 1983 and 1984.

Unlike some run-of-the-mill strikers, Ian Rush was the focal point of the Liverpool attacks, collecting the ball out of defence and laying it off simply but effectively before speeding off to a new position. The sight of him breaking free to leave defenders in his wake before slotting home the ball is one that will linger long in the memory.

Perhaps the peak of his career was 1985/86, when the Reds lifted the near impossible League and Cup double. His 23 goals were crucial in helping Liverpool to win the First Division title for a record 16th time, while he also scored twice in the 3−1 FA Cup Final victory over Everton.

Rush's reputation as one of the world's most feared strikers had clubs battling for his signature. Juventus succeeded in a deal worth £3.2 million. There was one consolation for the Anfield faithful in that he would be staying for one more season. Rush showed his greatness by playing his heart out and scoring 30 goals in 42 League games, although Liverpool ended trophy-less.

The move to Juventus, where he had to come to terms with the man-to-man marking of the Italian game, provided him with a fresh and intriguing challenge − and financial security for life. But he didn't receive the service that he needed and the goals dried up. On the eve of the 1988/89 season, Kenny Dalglish surprised the soccer world by paying £2.8 million to bring Rush back to Anfield.

Although he took some time to readjust, he eventually broke Roger Hunt's record haul of 286 goals for the club with his first-ever goal against Manchester United and his first in the Premier League. Rush continued to terrorise defences throughout the Premiership, taking his tally of goals to 346 in 659 games for the Anfield club before joining Leeds United in May 1996. At Elland Road he hit the worst goalscoring drought of his career. Soon he was on the move again, this time to Newcastle United. He helped the Magpies on their way to Wembley with the FA Cup third-round winner against Everton, extending his record as the top FA Cup goalscorer in the last century with 43 goals.

Released in May 1998 he joined Wrexham as player-coach, but the goalscoring legend struggled with injuries and, after passing on his vast experience to the Racecourse youngsters, he left the club the following summer.

Jeremy CHARLES

Position	Forward
Born	Jeremy Melvyn Charles, Swansea, 26 September 1959
Height	6ft 1in
Weight	13st 1lb
Clubs	Swansea City, Queen's Park Rangers, Oxford United

Son of Mel and nephew of John, Jeremy Charles of Swansea City and Wales won 19 caps for Wales. *(Lancashire Evening Post)*

Welsh Caps   19   Goals 1

              1981 v Czechoslovakia (won 1–0), v Turkey (won 1–0), v Scotland (won 2–0), v USSR
                 (0–0)

              1982 v Iceland (2–2)

              1983 v Norway (won 1–0), v Yugoslavia (4–4), v Bulgaria (won 1–0) 1 goal, v Scotland
                 (lost 0–2), v N. Ireland (won 1–0), v Brazil (1–1)

              1984 v Bulgaria (lost 0–1), v Yugoslavia (1–1), v Scotland (lost 1–2)

              1985 v Iceland (lost 0–1), v Spain (lost 0–3), v Iceland (won 2–1)

              1986 v Republic of Ireland (won 1–0)

              1987 v Finland (1–1)

SON OF MEL AND NEPHEW OF THE legendary John, Jeremy Charles made his League debut for Swansea City before his 17th birthday. The first game of the 1976/77 season was a League Cup tie against Newport County. Jeremy Charles came on as a substitute for Robbie James and scored twice in a 4–1 win, his first coming after he had been on the field for just two minutes. He ended his first season at the Vetch Field with a total of 23 goals.

Charles was a member of the Swansea side that rose from Division Four to Division One in four seasons. After helping the club win promotion from the Third Division, he scored the all-important third goal in the 3–1 win at Preston North End in the final game of the 1980/81 season to take Swansea into the First Division for the first time in their history.

It was Jeremy Charles who scored the club's first-ever goal in the First Division, when he netted against Leeds United in a 5–1 win. But he missed quite a few matches during that 1981/82 season as he underwent two cartilage operations. During his time at the Vetch Field, Swansea received a number of offers for Charles from top-flight clubs, but he refused all overtures until November 1983, when he was transferred to Queen's Park Rangers for £100,000.

Charles had scored 53 goals in 247 League games for the Swans. He stayed at Loftus Road only a short time before joining Oxford United and helping them win the Second Division Championship in 1984/85. Injury brought his career to a premature end, his last League appearance coming against Arsenal at Highbury when he was sent off.

Charles later returned to the Vetch Field as one of Swansea's Football Development Officers before leaving to work as an insurance salesman.

Kevin RATCLIFFE

Position	Central defender
Born	Kevin Ratcliffe, Deeside, 12 November 1960
Height	5ft 11in
Weight	12st 7lb
Clubs	Everton, Dundee, Cardiff City, Derby County, Chester City
Welsh Caps	59

              1981 v Czechoslovakia (won 1–0), v Republic of Ireland (won 3–1), v Turkey (won 1–0),
                 v Scotland (won 2–0), v England (0–0), v USSR (0–0)

Capped 59 times by Wales, Kevin Ratcliffe is also the most successful captain in Everton's history. *(Lancashire Evening Post)*

1982 v Czechoslovakia (lost 0–2), v Iceland (2–2), v USSR (lost 0–3), v Spain (1–1),
v England (lost 0–1)
1983 v Yugoslavia (4–4), v England (lost 1–2), v Bulgaria (won 1–0), v Scotland (lost 0–2),
v N. Ireland (won 1–0), v Brazil (1–1)
1984 v Norway (0–0), v Romania (won 5–0), v Bulgaria (lost 0–1), v Yugoslavia (1–1),
v Scotland (lost 1–2), v England (won 1–0), v N. Ireland (1–1), v Norway (lost 0–1),
v Israel (0–0)
1985 v Iceland (lost 0–1), v Spain (lost 0–3), v Iceland (won 2–1), v Norway (1–1),
v Scotland (won 1–0), v Spain (won 3–0), v Norway (lost 2–4)
1986 v Hungary (lost 0–3), v Saudi Arabia (won 2–1), v Uruguay (0–0)
1987 v Finland (1–1), v USSR (0–0), v Finland (won 4–0), v Czechoslovakia (1–1)
1988 v Denmark (won 1–0), v Denmark (lost 0–1), v Czechoslovakia (lost 0–2)
1989 v Finland (2–2), v Israel (3–3), v Sweden (lost 0–2), v W. Germany (0–0)
1990 v Finland (lost 0–1)
1991 v Denmark (lost 0–1), v Belgium (won 3–1), v Luxembourg (won 1–0), v Republic of
Ireland (lost 0–3), v Belgium (1–1), v Iceland (won 1–0), v Poland (0–0), v Germany
(won 1–0)
1992 v Brazil (won 1–0), v Germany (lost 1–4)
1993 v Belgium (won 2–0)

KEVIN RATCLIFFE CAPTAINED Wales in many of his 59 international appearances. He made his international debut against Czechoslovakia at Ninian Park in November 1980 and completely marked dangerman Masny out of the game. Wales won 1–0. The international side with Ratcliffe at the heart of the defence conceded only one goal in the Everton defender's first six games.

The most successful captain in Everton's history, Kevin Ratcliffe played in the same Flintshire schools side as Ian Rush. They grew up together and could have gone to Chester together as apprentices. Rush chose Chester as the launching pad for his career. Although a number of top clubs offered Ratcliffe apprentice forms, only one club interested him, and that was the team he had supported as a schoolboy, Everton. For on the rare occasions he was not kicking a ball about as a boy, he could be found cheering on the likes of Ball and Royle from the Goodison terraces.

After kicking his heels in Everton's Central League side for a couple of seasons, Ratcliffe made his League debut against Manchester United in March 1980. Despite managing to subdue the fearsome Joe Jordan in a goalless draw, Ratcliffe spent the next two seasons in and out of the Everton side. When he did play, most of his games were at left-back. Upset by such lack of apparent recognition and by being played out of position, Ratcliffe confronted new manager Howard Kendall. At one stage there was even talk of a move to Ipswich Town when Bobby Robson showed an interest.

In December 1982 Ratcliffe's fortunes took a decisive upturn when he replaced the overweight Billy Wright alongside Mark Higgins in the heart of the Everton defence. Within 12 months he had succeeded the injury-ravaged Higgins as captain, and the following March he was leading his country. After that, Ratcliffe became the calming influence on both the Everton and Wales teams. His role in the Everton side, whose game was built on a very sound defensive system, was crucial. The Blues often played a tight and rigid offside game but, if a striker did break through, Ratcliffe's speed was such that the danger was snuffed out immediately. Strong in the tackle, Ratcliffe possessed quite a ruthless streak that meant he couldn't be intimidated.

In May 1984, after Watford had been beaten 2–0, at the age of 23 Ratcliffe became the youngest man since Bobby Moore some 20 years earlier to receive the FA Cup. He also played in the League Cup Final against Liverpool and Rush, but this time finished on the losing side. Having been threatened with relegation at Christmas, Everton ended the season in seventh place.

Within the next year, he had led the Blues forward to pick up the FA Charity Shield, the League Championship and the European Cup Winners' Cup in Rotterdam after a 3–1 win over Rapid Vienna. Thereafter he skippered Everton to the runners-up spot in both the League and FA Cup in 1985/86 and to another League title in 1986/87.

Ratcliffe could read the game with instinctive shrewdness and could close down opponents instantly in moments of danger, often averting crises by clever positional play. Despite losing some of his astonishing speed, he continued to retain the style and consistency that made him one of the world's classiest defenders. Kevin Ratcliffe played in 461 League and Cup games for the Blues. However, after losing his place to Martin Keown he joined Cardiff City and helped them win promotion to the new Second Division.

In April 1995 he was appointed player-manager of Chester City and in his first two seasons with the club came close to taking them to promotion to the Second Division. He later took charge of Shrewsbury Town but parted company with the club in the summer of 2003 after the Gay Meadow side lost their League status.

Terry BOYLE

Position	Central defender
Born	Terence David John Boyle, Ammanford, 29 October 1958
Height	5ft 10in
Weight	12st 4lb
Clubs	Tottenham Hotspur, Crystal Palace, Wimbledon, Bristol City, Newport County, Cardiff City, Swansea City, Merthyr Tydfil, Barry Town, Ebbw Vale, Inter Cardiff, Cinderford Town
Welsh Caps	2 Goals 1
	1981 v Republic of Ireland (won 3–1) 1 goal, v Scotland (won 2–0)

A WELSH SCHOOLBOY INTERNATIONAL, Terry Boyle began his career at Tottenham Hotspur. But he failed to make the grade with the White Hart Lane club and moved across London to play for Crystal Palace. At Selhurst Park he made 26 League appearances and had a short spell on loan at Wimbledon as well as being capped twice for Wales. In fact, the tough-tackling defender scored on his international debut in a 3–1 win over the Republic of Ireland.

On leaving the Eagles, Boyle joined Bristol City, playing in 37 League games for the Ashton Gate club before being given a free transfer and joining Newport County to ease the club's financial difficulties.

One of the best defenders ever to play for the Somerton Park club, he scored 11 goals in 166 League games before joining Cardiff City for £22,000, a fee fixed by an independent tribunal.

Ever-present in 1986/87, his first season at Ninian Park, he also played in all the games the following season as the Bluebirds won promotion to the Third Division and won the Welsh Cup, beating Wrexham in the final. He went on to appear in 101 consecutive League games from his debut and in 167 first-team matches altogether before leaving to end his League career with Swansea City. He subsequently played for Merthyr Tydfil and Barry Town, whom he helped win the Welsh League and Cup double in 1993/94. He then took up player-manager roles at Ebbw Vale, Inter Cardiff and Cinderford Town.

Steve LOVELL

Position	Forward
Born	Stephen John Lovell, Swansea, 16 July 1960
Height	5ft 9in
Weight	11st 3lb
Clubs	Crystal Palace, Stockport County, Millwall, Swansea City, Gillingham, Bournemouth
Welsh Caps	6 Goals 1
	1982 v USSR (lost 0–3)
	1985 v Norway (lost 2–4) 1 goal
	1986 v Scotland (1–1), v Hungary (lost 0–3), v Canada (lost 0–2), v Canada (won 3–0)

IN THE SUMMER OF 1986, Steve Lovell came out of the international wilderness to go on the Wales tour of Canada. He returned with a knee injury that required major surgery and kept him out of the game for a long period.

Steve Lovell had the option of joining either his home-town team Swansea or Crystal Palace. With the Swans in the Fourth Division and at a low ebb, he decided to join the South London club. At Selhurst Park he was primarily regarded as a defender but he always had an inclination to push forward.

Following a loan spell with Stockport County, he joined Millwall, initially also on loan. Towards the end of the 1983/84 season, manager George Graham moved him into midfield. He began to get his name on the scoresheet and in October 1984, after being moved up to striker, he began a record sequence of scoring in 11 successive matches. He topped the Lions' scoring charts in 1984/85 and 1985/86, helping Millwall to become established in the Second Division.

Following his long absence from the game, he was unable to win his place back in the Millwall side and moved to Swansea on loan. But, as the Vetch Field club couldn't afford the asking price, he joined Gillingham instead.

He topped the Gills' scoring lists in his first three seasons at the Priestfield Stadium going on to score 94 goals in 233 League games for the Kent club before later ending his career as a non-contract player with Bournemouth.

Chris MARUSTIK

Position	Midfielder
Born	Christopher Marustik, Swansea, 10 August 1961
Height	5ft 8in
Weight	12st 7lb
Clubs	Swansea City, Cardiff City, Barry Town
Welsh Caps	6
	1982 v Spain (1–1), v England (lost 0–1), v Scotland (lost 0–1), v N. Ireland (won 3–0), v France (won 1–0)
	1983 v Norway (won 1–0)

Son of a Czech immigrant, Chris Marustik appeared for both Cardiff and Swansea. *(Lancashire Evening Post)*

THE SON OF A CZECH IMMIGRANT, Chris Marustik was unlucky to lose his place in the national side, for in his last three appearances not only was he on the winning side each time but also he helped his side keep consecutive clean sheets.

Marustik caught the eye of Swansea City's Harry Griffiths while playing for the town's schoolboys side. Signed on as an apprentice at the Vetch, he later turned professional and made his first-team debut as a substitute in the second round of the League Cup as the Swans drew 2–2 at home to Tottenham Hotspur in August 1978. His full League debut didn't come until seven months later, when the Swans visited Peterborough United.

Quick and very versatile, Marustik's talent was nurtured by John Toshack, John Mahoney and Les Chappell. Over the next seasons at the Vetch, he scored 11 goals in 153 games before leaving to join Swansea's arch-rivals Cardiff City in October 1985.

Injuries hampered his progress at Ninian Park and, after making 43 League appearances in two years with the Bluebirds, he left to play non-League football for Barry Town. He later ran a wine bar with his brother.

Nigel STEVENSON

Position	Central defender
Born	Nigel Charles Ashley Stevenson, Swansea, 2 November 1958
Height	6ft 2in
Weight	12st 10lb
Clubs	Swansea City, Cardiff City, Reading
Welsh Caps	4
	1982 v England (lost 0–1), v Scotland (lost 0–1), v N. Ireland (won 3–0)
	1983 v Norway (won 1–0)

THE TALL CENTRE-HALF WAS instrumental in Swansea's promotion in three out of four seasons. When they played in the top flight, his form was such that he was awarded his first international cap when he played against England at Ninian Park. He made further appearances against Scotland at Hampden Park, Northern Ireland at the Racecourse Ground, and finally Norway at the Vetch Field.

Nigel Stevenson joined Swansea City as a schoolboy and remained with the club during their dramatic rise and fall through the Football League. He made his first-team debut for the Swans in a Fourth Division match at Southport in 1976, and thereafter became an established member of the Vetch Field side.

After ten seasons with the Swans, 'Speedy', as he was known to friends and fans alike, was awarded a testimonial match against Real Sociedad of Spain, managed by his former boss John Toshack. It was around this time that he lost his place in the Swansea side and had loan spells at both Cardiff and Reading before returning to the Vetch to complete 259 League appearances for the club.

In the summer of 1987 he joined Cardiff City on a free transfer and played in a further 68 League games for the Bluebirds before deciding to hang up his boots.

Having contributed to Swansea's dramatic rise through the Football League, Nigel Stevenson won the first of his four caps against England in April 1982. *(Lancashire Evening Post)*

Neville SOUTHALL

Position   Goalkeeper
Born   Neville Southall, Llandudno, 16 September 1958
Height   6ft 1in
Weight   12st 0lb
Clubs   Winsford United, Bury, Everton, Port Vale, Southend United, Stoke City, Doncaster Rovers,
                Torquay United, Bradford City
Welsh Caps   92
                1982 v N. Ireland (won 3–0)
                1983 v Norway (won 1–0), v England (lost 1–2), v Bulgaria (won 1–0), v Scotland (lost 0–2),
                v N. Ireland (won 1–0), v Brazil (1–1)
                1984 v Norway (0–0), v Romania (won 5–0), v Bulgaria (lost 0–1), v Yugoslavia (1–1),
                v Scotland (lost 1–2), v England (won 1–0), v N. Ireland (1–1), v Norway (lost 0–1),
                v Israel (0–0)
                1985 v Iceland (lost 0–1), v Spain (lost 0–3), v Iceland (won 2–1), v Norway (1–1), v Scotland
                (won 1–0), v Spain (won 3–0), v Norway (lost 2–4)
                1986 v Scotland (1–1), v Hungary (lost 0–3), v Saudi Arabia (won 2–1), v Republic of Ireland
                (won 1–0)
                1987 v USSR (0–0), v Finland (won 4–0), v Czechoslovakia (1–1)
                1988 v Denmark (won 1–0), v Czechoslovakia (lost 0–2), v Yugoslavia (lost 1–2), v Sweden
                (lost 1–4)
                1989 v Holland (lost 0–1), v Finland (2–2), v Sweden (lost 0–2), v W. Germany (0–0)
                1990 v Finland (lost 0–1), v Holland (lost 1–2), v W. Germany (lost 1–2), v Republic of Ireland
                (lost 0–1), v Sweden (lost 2–4), v Costa Rica (won 1–0)
                1991 v Denmark (lost 0–1), v Belgium (won 3–1), v Luxembourg (won 1–0), v Republic of Ireland
                (lost 0–3), v Belgium (1–1), v Iceland (won 1–0), v Poland (0–0), v Germany (won 1–0)
                1992 v Brazil (won 1–0), v Germany (lost 1–4), v Luxembourg (won 1–0), v Republic of Ireland
                (won 1–0), v Austria (1–1), v Romania (lost 1–5), v Holland (lost 0–4), v Argentina (lost 0–1),
                v Japan (won 1–0)
                1993 v Faroe Islands (won 6–0), v Cyprus (won 1–0), v Belgium (lost 0–2), v Republic of Ireland
                (lost 1–2), v Belgium (won 2–0), v RCS (1–1), v Faroe Islands (won 3–0)
                1994 v RCS (2–2), v Cyprus (won 2–0), v Romania (lost 1–2), v Norway (lost 1–3), v Sweden
                (lost 0–2), v Estonia (won 2–1)
                1995 v Albania (won 2–0), v Moldova (lost 2–3), v Georgia (lost 0–5), v Bulgaria (lost 0–3),
                v Bulgaria (lost 1–3), v Germany (1–1), v Georgia (lost 0–1)
                1996 v Moldova (won 1–0), v Germany (lost 1–2), v Albania (1–1), v Italy (lost 0–3), v San
                Marino (won 5–0),
                1997 v San Marino (won 6–0), v Holland (lost 1–3), v Holland (lost 1–7), v Turkey (0–0),
                v Belgium (lost 1–2)
                1998 v Turkey (lost 4–6)

THE MOST CAPPED PLAYER in the history of Welsh international football, goalkeeper Neville Southall frequently produced saves that proved to be the turning point in crucial matches. His anticipation was superb and he was an excellent shot-stopper. But what gave him the edge was an astonishing capacity to change direction at the last moment, sometimes even in mid-air, and an instinct for improvising unorthodox saves.

One of the game's most outstanding keepers, Neville Southall holds the Wales appearance record, having played 92 times for his country. *(Lancashire Evening Post)*

As a boy, Neville Southall played for the Caernarfon District side as a centre-half. But, after turning out as an emergency goalkeeper for Llandudno Swifts against Rhos Aelwyd, he shelved any thoughts of being an outfield player to concentrate on goalkeeping. Southall was just 14 years old, making him one of the youngest players to appear in the Welsh League (North). When he left school Southall took a job with the local council, demolishing gun emplacements built during the Second World War. After working as a dustman, he found employment in the Ritz Café in Llandudno before spending several years working on building sites as a hod carrier.

While living in Llandudno he kept goal for both Bangor City and Conwy United. But it was his fine form for Winsford United that caused Bury to pay £6,000 for him in June 1980. In the summer of 1981, after only 44 first-team appearances for the Gigg Lane club, he signed for Everton in a £150,000 deal. However, following a 5–0 defeat in the Merseyside derby, Southall was dropped. He was loaned to Port Vale but was recalled to Goodison Park after just nine appearances for the Valiants.

He made his international debut for Wales on 27 May 1982, keeping a clean sheet in a 3–0 win over Northern Ireland. It was 1984 before he got his first taste of glory at club level. That year Everton beat Watford 2–0 to win the FA Cup for the first time in 18 years. The following season Everton won the League Championship and the European Cup Winners' Cup, and were runners-up in the FA Cup. At the end of the season Southall became only the fourth goalkeeper to win the Player of the Year award, following in the footsteps of Bert Trautmann, Gordon Banks and Pat Jennings. One save that season from Mark Falco, which effectively ended Spurs' challenge, had experienced writers going back for comparison to Gordon Banks's famous save from Pelé in the 1970 World Cup.

Southall suffered severe dislocation of the ankle and ligament damage playing for Wales against the Republic of Ireland in March 1986. The injury was so acute that it was wondered if he would ever be able to get back to his brilliant best. He recovered in time to collect his second League Championship medal as Everton won the title again in 1987. His world-class performances played a major part in Everton's rise to become one of England's top clubs.

Time finally began to catch up with the Welsh goalkeeping wizard midway through the 1996/97 season. He made a record-breaking 700th first-team appearance for the Blues on the opening day of the season and received an MBE from the Queen in the Birthday Honours list. But then he found himself dropped for the first time in 15 years after an FA Cup upset against Bradford City. However, the following season saw Southall establish new records at Goodison. Having become the first footballer to appear in 200 Premiership matches, he made his 750th appearance in an Everton jersey, a figure unlikely to be matched.

After a loan spell with Southend United, he joined Stoke City, also on loan before the move became permanent. Freed by the Potters in the summer of 1998, Southall played non-League football for Doncaster Rovers before returning to League action with Torquay United. In March 2000 Southall returned to the Premiership for Bradford City but was on the losing side in a 2–1 home defeat by Leeds United.

As his Welsh team-mate and former Liverpool centre-forward Ian Rush said: 'For sheer consistency, there's no one to touch Neville.'

Kenny JACKETT

Position	Midfielder/Left-Back
Born	Kenneth Francis Jackett, Watford, 5 January 1962
Height	5ft 10in
Weight	11st 3lb
Clubs	Watford
Welsh Caps	31

1983 v Norway (won 1–0), v Yugoslavia (4–4), v England (lost 1–2), v Bulgaria (won 1–0), v Scotland (lost 0–2)

1984 v Norway (0–0), v Romania (won 5–0), v Yugoslavia (1–1), v Scotland (lost 1–2), v N. Ireland (1–1), v Norway (lost 0–1), v Israel (0–0)

1985 v Iceland (lost 0–1), v Spain (lost 0–3), v Iceland (won 2–1), v Norway (1–1), v Scotland (won 1–0), v Spain (won 3–0), v Norway (lost 2–4)

1986 v Scotland (1–1), v Hungary (lost 0–3), v Saudi Arabia (won 2–1), v Republic of Ireland (won 1–0), v Canada (lost 0–2), v Canada (won 3–0)

1987 v Finland (1–1), v Finland (won 4–0)

1988 v Denmark (lost 0–1), v Czechoslovakia (lost 0–2), v Yugoslavia (lost 1–2), v Sweden (lost 1–4)

KENNY JACKETT, WHOSE Caerphilly-born father was a Watford and Leyton Orient player in the late 1940s and early 1950s, qualified to play for both England and Wales but opted to play for the latter.

Jackett, who alternated between defence and midfield for club and country throughout his career, suffered his fair share of injuries. A bad knee injury sidelined him for almost half of Watford's promotion-winning campaign of 1981/82, but the following season he missed only one League match as they finished runners-up in the First Division to Liverpool. Although he was defensively minded, scoring just 25 goals including seven penalties, Jackett provided good service to the front men and plenty of through balls for Luther Blissett to chase.

When Watford manager Graham Taylor moved to Villa Park, he tried unsuccessfully to recruit Jackett.

Jackett was a dedicated player and holder of a full FA coaching badge. He was awarded a testimonial match against Aston Villa in August 1989. Just over a year later, Jackett, who was in sight of the club appearance record aged just 28, was forced to retire because of a persistent knee injury. He became Watford's youth team coach, but is now manager of Swansea City.

Nigel VAUGHAN

Position	Midfielder
Born	Nigel Mark Vaughan, Caerleon, 20 May 1959
Height	5ft 5in
Weight	8st 10lb
Clubs	Newport County, Cardiff City, Reading, Wolverhampton Wanderers, Hereford United

Welsh Caps	10

1983 v Yugoslavia (4–4), v Brazil (1–1)

1984 v Norway (0–0), v Romania (won 5–0), v Bulgaria (lost 0–1), v Yugoslavia (1–1),
v N. Ireland (1–1), v Norway (lost 0–1), v Israel (0–0)

1985 v Spain (lost 0–3)

NIGEL VAUGHAN BEGAN HIS Football League career with Newport County and went on to score 32 goals in 224 League appearances for the Somerton Park club. While with County he won the first of ten Welsh caps when he played in the 4–4 draw against Yugoslavia. In fact, six of the ten internationals in which Vaughan played were draws.

He joined Cardiff City in September 1983 as part of an unusual five-man exchange deal between the two clubs. But he suffered a disappointing debut as the Bluebirds lost at home to Barnsley 3–0. He then played in all the remaining 36 games of the season as the club finished 15th in the Second Division. In 1984/85 the diminutive forward was Cardiff's top scorer with 16 League goals. But, despite his efforts, the club were relegated to the Third Division. He was the club's top scorer again the following season, but the Bluebirds were relegated for a second successive season and dropped into the League's basement. In 1986/87 he became dissatisfied with Fourth Division football and played on a weekly contract until, after scoring 54 goals in 178 games, he left to join Wolverhampton Wanderers for a fee of £12,000.

He made his debut for the Molineux club at Ninian Park, where he came on as a substitute and scored in a 3–2 win for the Bluebirds. He went on to score ten goals in 93 League outings for Wolves before ending his first-class career with Hereford United. He then became player-manager for his first club, Newport County, combining the role with work as a production controller for Bundy UK.

Neil SLATTER

Position	Defender
Born	Neil John Slatter, Cardiff, 30 May 1964
Height	5ft 11in
Weight	10st 10lb
Clubs	Bristol Rovers, Oxford United, Bournemouth
Welsh Caps	22 Goals 2

1983 v Scotland (lost 0–2)

1984 v Norway (lost 0–1), v Israel (0–0)

1985 v Iceland (lost 0–1), v Spain (lost 0–3), v Iceland (won 2–1), v Norway (1–1),
v Scotland (won 1–0), v Spain (won 3–0), v Norway (lost 2–4)

1986 v Hungary (lost 0–3), v Saudi Arabia (won 2–1) 1 goal, v Canada (lost 0–2),
v Canada (won 3–0)

1987 v Finland (1–1) 1 goal, v Czechoslovakia (1–1)

1988 v Denmark (won 1–0), v Denmark (lost 0–1), v Czechoslovakia (lost 0–2),
v Malta (won 3–2), v Italy (won 1–0)

1989 v Israel (3–3)

NEIL SLATTER WON HIS FIRST full cap against Scotland two days before his 19th birthday. He had been Bristol Rovers' youngest postwar debutant at 16 years old and won ten of his 22 international caps while at Eastville.

Slatter arrived, like so many before him, from Rovers' Cardiff nursery. Although at first acquaintance he seemed hardly likely to flourish in the rough and tumble of league football, it was soon obvious that he was a class above his fellow apprentices. He was fast, had a sure touch with both feet and tackled with a power that belied his apparent frailty. After displaying so much promise with his initial taste of senior football, he soon established a regular place in the Pirates' side. Able to play at both right-and left-back, he had a preference for playing himself out of tight situations at the back rather than launching the ball indiscriminately downfield.

Such flair was hardly likely to go unnoticed, and in the summer of 1985 he joined first Division Oxford United for a fee of £100,000. Unfortunately he did not enjoy the best of fortune, with a succession of injuries and with his new club returning to the Second Division. He had a brief loan spell with Bournemouth but ultimately had to retire from the game, aged just 25.

Steve LOWNDES

Position	Winger
Born	Stephen Robert Lowndes, Cwmbran, 17 June 1960
Height	5ft 7in
Weight	10st 7lb
Clubs	Newport County, Millwall, Barnsley, Hereford United, Newport AFC
Welsh Caps	10
	1983 v Scotland (lost 0–2), v Brazil (1–1)
	1985 v Norway (lost 2–4)
	1986 v Saudi Arabia (won 2–1), v Republic of Ireland (won 1–0), v Uruguay (0–0), v Canada (lost 0–2), v Canada (won 3–0)
	1987 v Finland (1–1)
	1988 v Sweden (lost 1–4)

STEVE LOWNDES (who won ten full caps for Wales) and his Millwall team-mate Steve Lovell were the first players from the London club to appear in the same international side when, in May 1986, they lined up to face Canada in Toronto.

Lowndes made his League debut for Newport County at Scunthorpe United in April 1978, and developed into a fine attacking right-sided wide player under Len Ashurst's regime. He became an important member of the County side that won the Welsh Cup for the first time in 1979/80, scoring a number of vital goals in the earlier rounds of the competition. Lowndes was much underrated at Somerton Park, and in the summer of 1983 he was very surprisingly allowed to leave and join Millwall.

At the Den, with his pacey runs down the right flank, Lowndes gave more width to the London side. Although he contributed his fair share of goals as well as creating a host of goalscoring opportunities for the club's strikers, he was allowed to join Barnsley for a fee of £40,000 in August 1986.

He began his first season at Oakwell confidently but then suffered an injury that forced him to miss the rest of the campaign. He returned the following season to head the Yorkshire club's scoring charts, and for a while his displays put him back on the fringe of the national side. However, he left Oakwell in October 1990 to see out his first-class career with Hereford United.

Lowndes, who scored 79 goals in 469 League appearances for his four clubs, now runs his own physiotherapy clinic.

Alan DAVIES

Position	Winger
Born	Alan Davies, Manchester, 5 December 1961
Died	Horton near Swansea, 4 February 1992
Height	5ft 8in
Weight	11st 0lb
Clubs	Manchester United, Newcastle United, Charlton Athletic, Carlisle United, Swansea City, Bradford City
Welsh Caps	13
	1983 v N. Ireland (won 1–0), v Brazil (1–1)
	1984 v England (won 1–0), v N. Ireland (1–1)
	1985 v Iceland (lost 0–1), v Iceland (won 2–1), v Norway (1–1)
	1986 v Hungary (lost 0–3)
	1988 v Malta (won 3–2), v Italy (won 1–0)
	1989 v Holland (lost 0–1)
	1990 v Finland (lost 0–1), v Republic of Ireland (lost 0–1)

ALAN DAVIES WAS BORN IN England of Welsh parents. He had a meteoric rise to fame as one of Manchester United's modern 'babes'. He joined the Old Trafford club as a schoolboy and started out as a skilful outside-right before later moving into a general midfield role. Davies was catapulted into the headlines when he was chosen for two major fixtures, a European Cup Winners' Cup semi-final and the FA Cup Final in place of Steve Coppell. He played well in both games, netting and laying on goals for others. He was also capped by Wales but, just as his career was about to take off, he broke an ankle and the chance to claim a regular position in the United side was lost.

He then joined Newcastle United but showed only a brief glimpse of his true capabilities. After loan spells with Charlton Athletic and Carlisle United, he was transferred to Swansea City.

Davies was a virtual ever-present at the Vetch Field for two seasons before leaving to join Bradford City. But, after just one year at the Valley Parade, he returned to Swansea, where he took his tally of goals to 12 in 127 League games.

Tragically overwhelmed by personal problems, Alan Davies committed suicide. He was found dead in his car on the same day as he was due to play for the Swans in the South Wales derby against Cardiff City.

Alan Davies keeps an eye on the ball during a match against Northern Ireland at Cardiff Arms Park. The match ended in a 1–1 draw. *(Getty Images)*

Jeff Hopkins was a dedicated professional who won 16 caps for Wales. His career was cut short by injury. (*Lancashire Evening Post*)

Jeff HOPKINS

Position	Central defender
Born	Jeffrey Hopkins, Swansea, 14 April 1964
Height	6ft 0in
Weight	11st 9lb
Clubs	Fulham, Crystal Palace, Plymouth Argyle, Bristol Rovers, Reading
Welsh Caps	16
	1983 v N. Ireland (won 1–0), v Brazil (1–1)
	1984 v Norway (0–0), v Romania (won 5–0), v Bulgaria (lost 0–1), v Yugoslavia (1–1),
	v Scotland (lost 1–2), v England (won 1–0), v N. Ireland (1–1), v Norway (lost 0–1),
	v Israel (0–0)
	1985 v Iceland (lost 0–1), v Iceland (won 2–1), v Norway (lost 2–4)
	1990 v Holland (lost 1–2), v Costa Rica (won 1–0)

SWANSEA-BORN CENTRAL DEFENDER Jeff Hopkins won 16 full caps for Wales. He was still an apprentice when he made his League debut for Fulham in a 4–2 defeat at Huddersfield Town on the final day of the 1980/81 season. The following season he missed just a handful of games as the Cottagers won promotion from the Third Division.

Hopkins initially played at right-back, but moved to centre-half following the departure of Roger Brown to Bournemouth. Although he struggled in the air against some of the larger opposition forwards, he went on to be a fine central defender for Fulham. He had scored six goals – all from set pieces – in 257 League and Cup games when, in the summer of 1988, Crystal Palace paid £240,000 for his services.

He played in 93 games for the Eagles. Then, following a loan spell with Plymouth Argyle, he joined Bristol Rovers on a free transfer. His stay at Twerton Park was brief and in the summer of 1992 he moved to Reading, where this dedicated professional not only captained the side but helped out with the coaching of the younger players. Injury forced him to quit the first-class game after 123 appearances for the Royals.

Dudley LEWIS

Position	Central defender
Born	Dudley Keith Lewis, Swansea, 17 November 1962
Height	5ft 10in
Weight	10st 9lb
Clubs	Swansea City, Huddersfield Town, Halifax Town, Wrexham, Torquay United.
Welsh Caps	1
	1983 v Brazil (1–1)

IT WAS DUDLEY LEWIS's consistent displays at the heart of the Swansea City defence that earned him full international honours when he came on as a substitute for Jeremy Charles in Wales's 1–1 draw with Brazil at Ninian Park in June 1983. Surprisingly, it was to be his only cap.

A Welsh schoolboy international, Dudley Lewis became an apprentice at the Vetch Field before turning professional some six months later. Swans' manager John Toshack gave the central defender his first-team debut in the 1980/81 season at Notts County. He returned to the club's reserve side, where his displays were outstanding. He was restored to the first team as sweeper for the visit by Bolton Wanderers, a match the Swans won 3−0. Lewis then had a great game at Deepdale as the Welsh side beat Preston North End 3−1 to clinch promotion to the First Division.

He soon established himself in the Swansea defence and over the next nine seasons went on to appear in 230 League games. He was usually the first name on the team-sheet. Lewis left the Vetch in the summer of 1989 to play for Huddersfield Town. After 34 appearances and a loan spell at Halifax Town, he returned to Wales to play for Wrexham. He then rejoined Halifax as a non-contract player before seeing out his League career with Torquay United.

Dave FELGATE

Position	Goalkeeper
Born	David Wynne Felgate, Blaenau Ffestiniog, 4 March 1960
Height	6ft 2in
Weight	13st 10lb
Clubs	Bolton Wanderers, Rochdale, Crewe Alexandra, Lincoln City, Cardiff City, Grimsby Town, Bury, Wolverhampton Wanderers, Chester City, Wigan Athletic, Leigh RMI
Welsh Caps	1
	1984 v Romania (won 5−0)

GOALKEEPER DAVE FELGATE won his only full international cap when he replaced Neville Southall at half-time during Wales's 5−0 hammering of Romania.

Though he began his career with Bolton Wanderers, he couldn't force his way into the club's first team and was loaned out to Rochdale and Crewe Alexandra to gain experience. Still unable to break into the Wanderers' side, he was transferred to Lincoln City for £25,000. It was while he was at Sincil Bank that he won full international honours. He went on to play in 198 League games for Lincoln and in December 1984 had a short loan spell with Cardiff City. In the summer of 1985 he joined Grimsby Town in a £27,000 deal but early the following year he returned to Burnden Park, making his long-awaited Bolton debut.

He helped the Wanderers reach the Freight Rover Trophy Final, only to miss out on a Wembley appearance as his loan period had expired. He rejoined Grimsby for a couple of months before signing for the Wanderers on a permanent basis. Though the Lancashire club were relegated in his first season at Burnden Park, he was ever-present in 1987/88, when the club bounced back into the Third Division at the first attempt. He won a winners medal in the 1989 Sherpa Van Trophy Final. He went on to make 300 League and Cup appearances for Bolton before brief spells with Bury and Wolves.

His next League appearances came with Chester City before he ended his first-class career with Wigan Athletic. He then signed for Unibond League side Leigh RMI and was a regular in their promotion-winning side.

Mark HUGHES

Position	Forward
Born	Leslie Mark Hughes, Wrexham, 1 November 1963
Height	5ft 11in
Weight	12st 13lb
Clubs	Manchester United, Barcelona, Bayern Munich, Chelsea, Southampton, Everton, Blackburn Rovers
Welsh Caps	72 Goals 16

1984 v England (won 1–0) 1 goal, v N. Ireland (1–1) 1 goal

1985 v Iceland (lost 0–1), v Spain (lost 0–3), v Iceland (won 2–1) 1 goal, Norway (1–1), v Scotland (won 1–0), v Spain (won 3–0) 1 goal, v Norway (lost 2–4) 1 goal

1986 v Scotland (1–1) 1 goal, v Hungary (lost 0–3), v Uruguay (0–0)

1987 v USSR (0–0), v Czechoslovakia (1–1)

1988 v Denmark (won 1–0) 1 goal, v Denmark (lost 0–1), v Czechoslovakia (lost 0–2), v Sweden (lost 1–4), v Malta (won 3–2) 1 goal, v Italy (won 1–0)

1989 v Holland (lost 0–1), v Finland (2–2), v Israel (3–3), v Sweden (lost 0–2), v W. Germany (0–0)

1990 v Finland (lost 0–1), v W. Germany (lost 1–2), v Costa Rica (won 1–0)

1991 v Denmark (lost 0–1), v Belgium (won 3–1) 1 goal, v Luxembourg (won 1–0), v Belgium (1–1), v Iceland (won 1–0), v Poland (0–0), v Germany (won 1–0)

1992 v Brazil (won 1–0), v Germany (lost 1–4), v Luxembourg (won 1–0), v Republic of Ireland (won 1–0), v Romania (lost 1–5), v Holland (lost 0–4), v Argentina (lost 0–1), v Japan (won 1–0)

1993 v Faroe Islands (won 6–0), v Cyprus (won 1–0) 1 goal, v Belgium (lost 0–2), v Republic of Ireland (lost 1–2) 1 goal, v Belgium (2–2), v RCS (1–1) 1 goal, v Faroe Islands (won 3–0)

1994 v RCS (2–2), v Cyprus (won 2–0), v Norway (lost 1–3)

1995 v Georgia (lost 0–5), v Bulgaria (lost 0–3), v Germany (1–1), v Georgia (lost 0–1)

1996 v Moldova (won 1–0), v Italy (lost 0–3), v San Marino (won 5–0) 2 goals

1997 v San Marino (won 6–0) 2 goals, v Holland (lost 1–3), v Turkey (0–0), v Republic of Ireland (0–0), v Belgium (lost 1–2)

1998 v Turkey (lost 4–6)

1999 v Italy (lost 0–2), v Denmark (won 2–1), v Belarus (won 3–2), v Switzerland (lost 0–2), v Italy (lost 0–4), v Denmark (lost 0–2)

MARK HUGHES IS PROBABLY the only player in recent years to have played in two important matches on the same day. On 11 November 1987 he played for Wales against Czechoslovakia in Prague in a European Championship match before being rushed from the changing room to a waiting car which took him to a plane. He reached Bayern Munich's Olympic Stadium with the match already under way, but went on in the second-half to help Bayern to victory.

Although he had had to wait for his chance at Old Trafford, Hughes made an encouraging start, scoring four goals in his first seven appearances towards the end of the 1983/84 season. He also played in Manchester United's European Cup Winners' Cup tie against Barcelona at the Nou Camp Stadium. He crowned a remarkable first season by scoring on his Wales debut against England at the Racecourse Ground.

222 *Wales Footballers - Mark Hughes*

The following season he was United's number-one striker, scoring 25 goals in all competitions, the best individual scoring performance at Old Trafford for 13 years. It wasn't just the number of goals that he scored but the style of them. The glorious leaping volley which flew past Spain's Arconada will linger long in the memory, while his winner in the FA Cup semi-final against Liverpool was a perfectly placed low shot. He ended the campaign with an FA Cup winners' medal and, not unexpectedly, was voted the Professional Footballers' Association (PFA) Young Player of the Year.

At the start of the 1985/86 season, United went 15 games before suffering their first defeat – Hughes scored ten goals in that run as the Reds raced to the top of the League. It is little wonder that soon every scout in Europe was visiting Old Trafford to see his talents. When United's results fell away, Sparky was sold to Barcelona for £2.3 million. But he did keep one foot in the Old Trafford camp, stating that when he did come back to England he would join only one club, Manchester United.

In fact, Hughes found Spanish football difficult and in his second season he was loaned out to Bayern Munich, where he was much happier. United manager Alex Ferguson had wanted to sign Hughes just before he was loaned to Bayern, and in June 1988 he clinched the deal on a player that many felt should never have been allowed to leave Old Trafford in the first place.

Hughes soon readjusted to the Football League and was duly honoured by his peers when he was elected Player of the Year by the PFA. He added a second FA Cup winners' medal to his collection in 1990 as United beat Crystal Palace. In 1991 he was part of a United team that won the European Cup Winners' Cup, scoring the crucial goal in the 2–1 win over Barcelona in the final. Also that year he became the only British player to have twice been voted the PFA Player of the Year.

As he was a great favourite with the United fans, his £1.5 million transfer to Chelsea in the summer of 1995 came as a great shock, particularly as he was thought to have signed a new two-year contract at old Trafford. At Stamford Bridge he formed an almost telepathic understanding with Zola, but was often left on the bench by Ruud Gullit. However, after coming on as a substitute against Liverpool, he remained in the side and created a 20th-century record by winning his fourth FA Cup winners' medal as Chelsea beat Middlesbrough 2–0 in the final.

Hughes was awarded the MBE in the 1998 New Year's Honours List. He helped the Blues win the European Cup Winners' Cup before joining Southampton. After helping the Saints retain their Premiership status, he had a brief spell with Everton before moving to Blackburn Rovers. Hughes helped Rovers win the League Cup Final at the Millennium Stadium in 2002 before hanging up his boots. He was appointed Wales's manager in 1999.

Wales's national team manager Mark Hughes marked his international debut with the only goal of the game against England. *(Lancashire Evening Post)*

David PHILLIPS

Position	Midfielder/Right-back
Born	David Owen Phillips, Wegberg, Germany, 29 July 1963
Height	5ft 9in
Weight	11st 2lb
Clubs	Plymouth Argyle, Manchester City, Coventry City, Norwich City, Nottingham Forest, Huddersfield Town, Lincoln City, Stevenage Borough
Welsh Caps	62 Goals 2

1984 v England (won 1–0), v N. Ireland (1–1), v Norway (lost 0–1)

1985 v Spain (lost 0–3), v Iceland (won 2–1), v Scotland (won 1–0), v Spain (won 3–0), v Norway (lost 2–4)

1986 v Scotland (1–1), v Hungary (lost 0–3), v Saudi Arabia (won 2–1), v Republic of Ireland (won 1–0), v Uruguay (0–0)

1987 v Finland (won 4–0) 1 goal, v Czechoslovakia (1–1)

1988 v Denmark (won 1–0), v Denmark (lost 0–1), v Czechoslovakia (lost 0–2), v Yugoslavia (lost 1–2), v Sweden (lost 1–4)

1989 v Sweden (lost 0–2), v W. Germany (0–0)

1990 v Finland (lost 0–1), v Holland (lost 1–2), v W. Germany (lost 1–2), v Republic of Ireland (lost 0–1), v Sweden (lost 2–4)

1991 v Denmark (lost 0–1), v Belgium (1–1), v Iceland (won 1–0), v Poland (0–0), v Germany (won 1–0)

1992 v Luxembourg (won 1–0), v Republic of Ireland (won 1–0), v Austria (1–1), v Romania (lost 1–5), v Holland (lost 0–4), v Argentina (lost 0–1), v Japan (won 1–0)

1993 v Faroe Islands (won 6–0), v Cyprus (won 1–0), v Belgium (lost 0–2), v Republic of Ireland (lost 1–2), v Belgium (won 2–0), v RCS (1–1), v Faroe Islands (won 3–0)

1994 v RCS (2–2), v Cyprus (won 2–0), v Romania (lost 1–2), v Norway (lost 1–3), v Sweden (lost 0–2), v Estonia (won 2–1) 1 goal

1995 v Albania (won 2–0), v Moldova (lost 2–3), v Georgia (lost 0–5), v Bulgaria (lost 0–3), v Bulgaria (lost 1–3), v Germany (1–1), v Georgia (lost 0–1)

1996 v Moldova (won 1–0), v Albania (1–1), v Italy (lost 0–3)

DAVID PHILLIPS WAS BORN IN Wegberg, Germany, because his Caerphilly-born father was stationed there with the RAF. He joined Plymouth Argyle when he was 18 and soon established himself as a regular in the Home Park club's side.

His early performances for the Pilgrims included the goal that won the FA Cup quarter-final match against Derby County direct from a corner-kick in injury time. He was selected for Wales at under-21 level in 1984 when he did enough to convince the national selectors that he was ready for senior honours.

Phillips won the first of his 62 caps for Wales in May 1984 when he gave an outstanding display at full-back in the 1–0 win over England at the Racecourse Ground.

Phillips left Plymouth in the summer of 1984 after playing in 93 first-team games to join Manchester City for £65,000 plus £15,000 after 25 appearances, another £20,000 after 50 appearances and a further £20,000 should he score 20 goals. Although he didn't score 20 goals, he helped the then Maine Road club win promotion in 1984/85, when he was ever-present. He missed only a few matches the following season before moving to Coventry City in exchange for goalkeeper Perry Suckling.

Capped 62 times, David Phillips's greatest game was against Scotland in a World Cup qualifier at Hampden in March 1985. *(Lancashire Evening Post)*

Phillips had an outstanding game for Wales against Scotland's Graeme Souness in the World Cup qualifying match at Hampden Park in March 1985, which Wales won 1−0. However, six months later he was controversially adjudged to have handled the ball and the subsequent penalty was converted to give the Scots a draw.

In his first season with the Sky Blues, Phillips won an FA Cup winners' medal following Coventry's 3−2 victory over Spurs at Wembley. After three seasons at Highfield Road, in which he made 123 appearances, he was allowed to join Norwich City for £525,000 − a figure fixed by a tribunal.

He was very popular at Carrow Road and was ever-present in each of his first two campaigns with the club, helping the Canaries finish third in the Premiership's first season. But, after failing to agree terms for a new contract, he was on the move again, this time to Nottingham Forest. His decision to join Forest was a good one because in his first season at the City ground they won promotion to the Premier League behind Crystal Palace.

Phillips then joined Huddersfield Town, but injuries hampered his progress at the McAlpine Stadium, and he was released. He joined Lincoln City where at the age of 36 he maintained his enthusiasm for the game before moving into non-League football with Stevenage Borough.

Colin PASCOE

Position	Left-winger
Born	Colin James Pascoe, Bridgend, 9 April 1965
Height	5ft 9in
Weight	10st 0lb
Clubs	Swansea City, Sunderland, Blackpool
Welsh Caps	10
	1984 v Norway (lost 0−1), v Israel (0−0)
	1989 v Finland (2−2), v Israel (3−3), v W. Germany (0−0)
	1990 v Holland (lost 1−2), v W. Germany (lost 1−2)
	1991 v Republic of Ireland (lost 0−3), v Iceland (won 1−0)
	1992 v Brazil (won 1−0)

COLIN PASCOE JOINED SWANSEA CITY as a 16-year-old apprentice in 1981, when the Vetch Field club were members of the First Division of the Football League. After making his debut as a substitute for the injured John Mahoney against Brighton in March 1983, he played his first full game against Liverpool at Anfield.

During his first season with the Swans, he represented the Wales youth side and in 1983/84 he was chosen for the Welsh under-21 side on four occasions. Two years after winning his Wales youth cap, he was selected for the Wales senior side against Norway. Pascoe had played in 201 first-team games for the Swans when in March 1988 he was transferred to Sunderland for £70,000.

After scoring the Wearsiders' goal in a 2−1 defeat at York City on his debut, Pascoe netted the winner against Chesterfield in a 3−2 win for Sunderland. He also scored in his third game for the North-East club in a 4−1 win at Southend United. He helped Sunderland reach the First Division via the 1989/90 play-offs even though it was at

A great favourite at the Vetch, Colin Pascoe won 10 caps for Wales. (*Lancashire Evening Post*)

the expense of Swindon Town, who were found guilty of financial irregularities and relegated from the top flight.

Pascoe went on to score 26 goals in 151 games. He returned to Swansea for a fee of £120,000 after a loan spell with the Vetch Field club. He took his total of goals for the Swans to 67 in 324 League and Cup games before being released by the club after suffering damage to his ankle ligaments.

Tony REES

Position	Forward
Born	Anthony Andrew Rees, Merthyr Tydfil, 1 August 1964
Height	5ft 9in
Weight	11st 13lb
Clubs	Aston Villa, Birmingham City, Peterborough United, Shrewsbury Town, Barnsley, Grimsby Town, West Bromwich Albion
Welsh Caps	1
	1984 v Norway (lost 0–1)

TONY REES BUILT UP QUITE a reputation in Villa's FA Youth Cup winning side until a broken leg forced him to miss a complete season. After recovering he couldn't force his way into the Villa first team and opted to join Birmingham City.

Stepping straight into the Blues' first team, he initially played wide on the right, where he displayed an ability to take on defenders. Having won schoolboy, youth, under-21 and 'B' caps for Wales, his form for the St Andrew's club over the next few seasons won him full international recognition when he played the last half-hour of Wales's match against Norway in Trondheim. He came on as a substitute for Swansea's Colin Pascoe.

Rees had scored 12 goals in 95 League outings for the Blues when, following loan spells with Peterborough United and Shrewsbury Town, he joined Barnsley. His career seemed to stagnate at Oakwell and it was only when he moved to Grimsby Town, managed by Alan Buckley, that his form started to pick up again. He helped the Blundell Park club win successive promotions in 1989/90 and 1990/91 as the club moved from the Fourth to the Second Division. Rees scored 33 goals in 141 League games for the Mariners before leaving to end his first-class career with West Bromwich Albion.

Glyn HODGES

Position	Left-midfielder
Born	Glyn Peter Hodges, Streatham, 30 April 1963
Height	6ft 0in
Weight	12st 3lb
Clubs	Wimbledon, Newcastle United, Watford, Crystal Palace, Sheffield United, Derby County, Sin Tao (Hong Kong), Hull City, Nottingham Forest, Scarborough

Wimbledon star Glyn Hodges played in all four divisions of the Football League with the Dons. *(Lancashire Evening Post)*

Welsh Caps	18	Goals 2

1984 v Norway (lost 0–1), v Israel (0–0)

1987 v USSR (0–0), v Finland (won 4–0) 1 goal, v Czechoslovakia (1–1)

1988 v Denmark (won 1–0), v Denmark (lost 0–1), v Czechoslovakia (lost 0–2), v Sweden
(lost 1–4) 1 goal, v Malta (won 3–2), v Italy (won 1–0)

1990 v Sweden (lost 2–4), v Costa Rica (won 1–0)

1992 v Brazil (won 1–0), v Republic of Ireland (won 1–0), v Austria (1–1)

1996 v Germany (lost 1–2), v Italy (lost 0–3)

GLYN HODGES BEGAN HIS LONG career with Wimbledon. He made his Football League debut in September 1980 when he came on as a substitute in the match against Halifax Town while still an apprentice. The youngster went on to play in 27 games that season as Wimbledon were promoted to the Third Division. Although the side was relegated the following season, he won a Fourth Division Championship medal in 1982/83 as the Dons bounced straight back.

In 1983/84 Hodges played in 39 League matches as Wimbledon won promotion to the Second Division as runners-up to Oxford United. At the end of that season, Hodges won the first of 18 full caps for Wales – his last came 12 years later – when he came on as a substitute for Nigel Vaughan in the match against Norway. In 1985/86 he helped the Dons win promotion to the First Division and, in so doing, scored his first hat-trick for the club in a 3–0 home win over Sunderland.

Hodges had now played in all four divisions of the Football League with the same club and had scored 54 goals in 264 games in achieving that feat.

He left Wimbledon in the summer of 1987 to join Newcastle United for a fee of £200,000 but was unable to settle at St James Park. He played in just seven League games for the Magpies before leaving to join Watford only three months after his arrival on Tyneside. Watford were relegated at the end of his first season with them. After three years at Vicarage Road, in which he scored 19 goals in 102 League outings, he joined Crystal Palace; but after just a handful of appearances his career was rescued by former Wimbledon boss Dave Bassett, who signed him for Sheffield United.

He scored some vital goals as the Blades managed to avoid relegation. But he then suffered a loss of form and lost his place in the side before returning to first-team action and going on to score 22 goals in 171 games. He joined Derby County on a free transfer and made a number of effective appearances, mainly as a substitute, before going to play in Hong Kong. He returned to the Football League with Hull City but, after taking his tally of League goals to 100, he joined Nottingham Forest to provide experienced cover for Dave Bassett's Premiership-bound side. Not required to play at first-team level, he joined his ninth League club Scarborough but lasted just 25 minutes of one game before being forced to retire from football.

Andy HOLDEN

Position	Central defender
Born	Andrew Ian Holden, Flint, 14 September 1962
Height	6ft 1in
Weight	13st 2lb
Clubs	Rhyl, Chester City, Wigan Athletic, Oldham Athletic
Welsh Caps	1
	1984 v Israel (0–0)

IT IS EXTREMELY RARE FOR A player, particularly a Fourth Division one, to gain a full international cap in his first season in League football. But Andy Holden managed the feat in the summer of 1984, when he came on as a substitute for Colin Pascoe in the friendly against Israel.

Having started his career with North-West Counties side Rhyl, he joined Chester City, where he became a great favourite with the Sealand Road crowd for his fiercely competitive attitude and hunger for goals. Despite being a central defender, he was always on the lookout for a goalscoring opportunity, and in 1983/84 was Chester's joint-top scorer. When John McGrath took over as Chester boss, he harnessed Holden's leadership qualities by appointing him captain. He had played in exactly 100 League games for the Cestrians, scoring 17 goals, when in October 1986 he left to join Wigan Athletic.

He soon ran into injury problems on his arrival at Springfield Park. Torn knee ligaments kept him out for seven months; and, just a few weeks after his comeback, he chipped a bone in the same knee and was out of action for a further seven months.

His fight-back and rediscovered form induced Oldham manager Joe Royle to pay £130,000 for Holden's services in January 1989. His rehabilitation seemed complete when Wales's boss Terry Yorath recalled him to the Wales squad later that year after a five-year gap. Selected to play against Finland in September 1989, he had to withdraw from the team through injury and returned to club action only in April of the following year. He took up the positions of team coach and reserve team manager, but was recalled to the Oldham side in 1994/95 during an injury crisis. He later followed Royle to Everton to take up a post on the Goodison Park club's coaching staff.

Howard PRITCHARD

Position	Winger
Born	Howard Keith Pritchard, Cardiff, 18 October 1958
Height	5ft 10in
Weight	12st 7lb
Clubs	Bristol City, Swindon Town, Gillingham, Walsall, Maidstone United, Yeovil Town
Welsh Caps	1
	1985 v Norway (1–1)

HOWARD PRITCHARD'S SOLE international appearance was as a substitute for Gordon Davies in a 1–1 draw with Norway in February 1985. He joined Bristol City as an apprentice in the summer of 1976 and later signed professional forms for the Ashton Gate club.

His first game in City's colours was in an Anglo-Scottish cup tie against Partick Thistle at Firhill, which City lost 2–0. But he had to wait until the visit of Aston Villa in August 1978 before making his Football League debut. Over the next three seasons, Pritchard was in and out of the City team and in August 1981 he was allowed to join Swindon Town on a free transfer.

In two years at the County ground, Pritchard scored 11 goals in 65 League games, prompting Bristol City manager Terry Cooper to bring him back to Ashton Gate for a second spell. He was ever-present in 1983/84 when the club finished fourth in the Fourth Division, scoring 10 goals. When City won the Freight Rover Trophy in 1986, Pritchard scored one of the goals in the 3–0 win over Bolton Wanderers.

He went on to score 29 goals in 182 League and Cup games for Bristol City before joining Gillingham for a fee of £22,500 in August 1986. After two seasons at the Priestfield Stadium, he moved on to play for Walsall, Maidstone United and finally Yeovil Town.

Pat VAN DEN HAUWE

Position	Full-Back
Born	Patrick William Roger Van Den Hauwe, Belgium, 16 December 1960
Height	5ft 11in
Weight	11st 5lb
Clubs	Birmingham City, Everton, Tottenham Hotspur, Millwall
Welsh Caps	13
	1985 v Spain (won 3–0)
	1986 v Scotland (1–1), v Hungary (lost 0–3)
	1987 v USSR (0–0), v Finland (won 4–0), v Czechoslovakia (1–1)
	1988 v Denmark (won 1–0), v Denmark (lost 0–1), v Czechoslovakia (lost 0–2), v Yugoslavia (lost 1–2), v Italy (won 1–0)
	1989 v Finland (2–2), v Sweden (lost 0–2)

ALTHOUGH HE WAS BORN IN Belgium, where his father René had been a professional goalkeeper, Pat van den Hauwe had opted out of National Service and was therefore ineligible to play for his country of birth. He chose to play for Wales and made his international debut in a 3–0 defeat of Spain at Wrexham's Racecourse Ground in April 1985.

Pat van den Hauwe was an uncompromising hard-tackling defender who began his Football League career with Birmingham City. When the St Andrew's club were relegated at the end of the 1983/84 season, van den Hauwe left to play for Everton, who paid £100,000 for his services.

By the end of his first season at Goodison Park, he had helped Everton win the League Championship and the European Cup Winners' Cup. Over the next four years

Belgian-born defender Pat van den Hauwe of Everton was capped 13 times by Wales. He helped the Goodison Park side win the League title and the European Cup Winners' Cup. *(Lancashire Evening Post)*

van den Hauwe was a regular in the Everton sides that won the League Championship again in 1986/87 and reached the FA Cup Final in 1985, 1986 and 1989. Van Den Hauwe had played in 190 League and Cup games for the Toffees when in August 1989 he left Merseyside to join Tottenham Hotspur for £575,000.

He finally collected an FA Cup winners' medal in May 1991 when Spurs beat Nottingham Forest, and went on to play in 140 first-team games for the White Hart Lane club before ending his first-class career with Millwall.

Clayton BLACKMORE

Position	Midfielder/Full-back
Born	Clayton Graham Blackmore, Neath, 23 September 1964
Height	5ft 9in
Weight	11st 3lb
Clubs	Manchester United, Middlesbrough, Bristol City, Barnsley, Notts County, Leigh RMI
Welsh Caps	39 Goals 1

1985 v Norway (lost 2–4)

1986 v Scotland (1–1), v Hungary (lost 0–3), v Saudi Arabia (won 2–1), v Republic of Ireland (won 1–0), v Uruguay (0–0)

1987 v Finland (1–1), v USSR (0–0), v Finland (won 4–0), v Czechoslovakia (1–1)

1988 v Denmark (won 1–0), v Denmark (lost 0–1), v Czechoslovakia (lost 0–2), v Yugoslavia (lost 1–2), v Sweden (lost 1–4), v Malta (won 3–2), v Italy (won 1–0)

1989 v Holland (lost 0–1), v Finland (2–2), v Israel (3–3), v W. Germany (0–0)

1990 v Finland (lost 0–1), v Holland (lost 1–2), v W. Germany (lost 1–2), v Costa Rica (won 1–0)

1991 v Belgium (won 3–1), v Luxembourg (won 1–0)

1992 v Republic of Ireland (won 1–0), v Austria (1–1), v Romania (lost 1–5), v Holland (lost 0–4), v Argentina (lost 0–1), v Japan (won 1–0)

1993 v Faroe Islands (won 6–0) 1 goal, v Cyprus (won 1–0), v Belgium (lost 0–2), v RCS (1–1)

1994 v Sweden (lost 0–2)

1997 v Belgium (lost 1–2)

CLAYTON BLACKMORE HAD MADE only two appearances for Manchester United when he made his full international debut for Wales, coming on as a substitute for Fulham's Jeff Hopkins in a 4–2 defeat against Norway in Bergen in June 1985.

He appeared in Manchester United's 1982 FA Youth Cup Final side before making his League debut in the final game of the 1983/84 season at Nottingham Forest. Gradually he began to get more opportunities and in 1985/86 established himself as a first-team regular in the United side. With United he won a Premier League Championship medal and a European Cup Winners' Cup medal. But in the summer of 1994, after playing in 249 games for United and scoring 27 goals, he joined Middlesbrough on a free transfer.

Blackmore was one of Bryan Robson's first signings. He helped Boro win the First Division Championship in his first season on Teesside. Although his first-team appearances got fewer with each passing season, Blackmore lent his vast experience to

Midfielder Clayton Blackmore of Manchester United appeared for Wales at schoolboy, youth and under-21 level, going on to win 39 full caps. (*Lancashire Evening Post*)

the club's reserve side, where he helped them win the Pontin's League Second Division Championship. However, following a loan spell with Bristol City, he returned to the Boro side, collecting an FA Cup runners-up medal in 1997.

In February 1999 Blackmore was allowed to join Barnsley. But his stay at Oakwell was brief, and a few months later he moved to Notts County. His early displays were outstanding, but he seemed to lose form in the second half of the season. On being given a free transfer in the summer of 2000, he joined non-League Leigh RMI.

Eddie NIEDZWIECKI

Position	Goalkeeper
Born	Andzej Edward Niedzwiecki, Bangor, 3 May 1959
Height	6ft 0in
Weight	11st 0lb
Clubs	Wrexham, Chelsea
Welsh Caps	2
	1985 v Norway (lost 2–4)
	1988 v Denmark (lost 0–1)

GOALKEEPER EDDIE NIEDZWIECKI was the son of a Pole who came to Britain during the Second World War. He was a Welsh schoolboy and youth international, and won his first full cap when he replaced the injured Neville Southall after 67 minutes of Wales's 4–2 defeat in Norway in the summer of 1985.

He had made his Wrexham debut in a 2–2 home draw against Oxford United in August 1977. He then played in only 27 League games over the next four seasons, as he deputised for the more experienced keepers on Wrexham's books, Brian Lloyd and Dai Davies. When the latter returned to the Vetch Field to play for Swansea City at the end of the 1980/81 season, Niedzwiecki replaced him between the posts and was ever-present the following season when he kept 12 clean sheets. Despite his efforts, Wrexham were relegated from the Second Division. In 1982/83 he missed just four games as the Robins suffered another relegation into the League's basement.

However, Niedzwiecki's performances led to Chelsea paying £45,000 for his services. In five seasons at Stamford Bridge he made 136 League appearances and won a Second Division Championship medal. Sadly, he had to quit the game at the age of 29 after five operations on his knee. He stayed at Stamford Bridge as youth team coach before becoming assistant manager and later reserve-team coach.

In 1990 he went to coach Reading and later became assistant manager to Ian Porterfield at Elm Park. When the Berkshire club decided that they could not afford an assistant manager, he returned to Chelsea, where he resumed his former role of reserve-team manager. Nowadays he is involved with Wales at national level.

Mark AIZLEWOOD

Position	Central Defender
Born	Mark Aizlewood, Newport, 1 October 1959
Height	6ft 0in
Weight	12st 8lb
Clubs	Newport County, Luton Town, Charlton Athletic, Leeds United, Bradford City, Bristol City, Cardiff City, Merthyr Tydfil
Welsh Caps	39

1986 v Saudi Arabia (won 2–1), v Canada (lost 0–2), v Canada (won 3–0)
1987 v Finland (1–1), v USSR (0–0), v Finland (won 4–0)
1988 v Denmark (won 1–0), v Sweden (lost 1–4), v Malta (won 3–2), v Italy (won 1–0)
1989 v Holland (lost 0–1), v Finland (2–2), v Sweden (lost 0–2), v W. Germany (0–0)
1990 v Finland (lost 0–1), v W. Germany (lost 1–2), v Republic of Ireland (lost 0–1),
     v Costa Rica (won 1–0)
1991 v Denmark (lost 0–1), v Belgium (won 3–1), v Luxembourg (won 1–0),
     v Republic of Ireland (lost 0–3), v Belgium (1–1), v Iceland (won 1–0), v Poland (0–0),
     v Germany (won 1–0)
1992 v Brazil (won 1–0), v Luxembourg (won 1–0), v Republic of Ireland (won 1–0),
     v Austria (1–1), v Romania (lost 1–5), v Holland (lost 0–4), v Argentina (lost 0–1),
     v Japan (won 1–0)
1993 v Republic of Ireland (lost 1–2), v Belgium (won 2–0), v Faroe Islands (won 3–0)
1994 v RCS (2–2), v Cyprus (won 2–0)

MARK AIZLEWOOD WAS A FINE performer at baseball, cricket and golf. He won Welsh schoolboy and under-23 football honours before achieving the first of 39 full caps for his country in a 2–1 win over Saudi Arabia in Dhahran.

Mark Aizlewood followed his elder brother Steve to Newport County, making his League debut as a 16-year-old schoolboy after getting permission from his head teacher to play. He soon established himself as a regular member of the Somerton Park club's side, but in April 1978 he was transferred to Luton Town for £50,000. During his stay at Kenilworth Road, Aizlewood helped the Hatters win promotion. In November 1982 another £50,000 deal took him to Charlton Athletic.

He was the Addicks' Player of the Year in 1984/85 and 1985/86, but he was stripped of the captaincy and suspended for 14 days for giving a rude gesture to the crowd after being barracked. It came as no surprise when Aizlewood, who had appeared in 152 League games for Charlton, left to join Leeds United for a fee of £200,000 where he almost won a third promotion to the First Division. However, taunts from the terraces caused him to react in the same way again, so he was transferred to Bradford City. After just one season at the Valley Parade he was on the move again, this time to Bristol City, who paid £125,000 for his services.

He played a major role in the Robins' FA Cup run of 1991/92 as they beat Wimbledon and Leicester City before losing to Nottingham Forest. He was later released and allowed to join Cardiff City. It was while he was at Ninian Park that Aizlewood won the last of his international caps, some eight years after he was first capped. On leaving the Bluebirds he became player-coach at Merthyr Tydfil and had a spell coaching Newport before becoming involved in media work.

A determined defender, Mark Aizlewood helped both Luton Town and Charlton Athletic win promotion. *(Lancashire Evening Post)*

David WILLIAMS

Position	Midfielder
Born	David Michael Williams, Cardiff, 11 March 1955
Height	5ft 10in
Weight	11st 8lb
Clubs	Clifton Athletic, Bristol Rovers, Norwich City, Bournemouth
Welsh Caps	5
	1986 v Saudi Arabia (won 2–1), v Uruguay (0–0), v Canada (lost 0–2), v Canada (won 3–0)
	1987 v Finland (1–1)

DAVID WILLIAMS TOOK CHARGE of Wales as caretaker-manager for their match against Yugoslavia in March 1988. He came late to the full-time professional game, having combined his teaching career with a long part-time spell with Bristol Rovers.

When he made his Football League debut against Oldham Athletic in August 1975, he was the first amateur in 13 years to play for Rovers in a League match. During his time at Eastville he was employed variously in central defence, at full-back and even up front. But his most effective position was unquestionably midfield, where he had a penchant for blasting long-range goals.

The challenge of the player-manager's role at Eastville persuaded him to relinquish the classroom. Williams acquitted himself well, leading the Pirates to fifth and sixth place in the Third Division in his two seasons in charge. At the age of 30 he felt he was too young to embark on full-time management. So, after scoring 65 goals in 352 League matches, he joined ambitious Norwich City as a player.

In 1985/86, his first season at Carrow Road, he helped the Canaries win the Second Division Championship. His fine passing and constructive play for the East Anglian side helped him realise his ambition of playing international football, and he won the first of five caps against Saudi Arabia. On leaving Norwich, he had a brief spell with Bournemouth as a non-contract player. Since hanging up his boots, he has held the assistant manager's job at Norwich, Bournemouth and Everton, and was first-team coach at Leeds United.

Malcolm ALLEN

Position	Forward
Born	Malcolm Allen, Caernarfon, 21 March 1967
Height	5ft 9in
Weight	10st 8lb
Clubs	Watford, Aston Villa, Norwich City, Millwall, Newcastle United
Welsh Caps	14 Goals 3
	1986 v Saudi Arabia (won 2–1), v Canada (lost 0–2), v Canada (won 3–0) 1goal
	1989 v Israel (3–3) 1 goal
	1990 v Holland (lost 1–2), v W. Germany (lost 1–2) 1 goal, v Republic of Ireland (lost 0–1),
	v Sweden (lost 2–4), v Costa Rica (won 1–0)
	1991 v Luxembourg (won 1–0), v Republic of Ireland (lost 0–3)

Malcolm Allen had made 14 appearances for Wales when a knee injury forced his premature retirement at the age of 28. *(Lancashire Evening Post)*

1992 v Austria (1–1)
1993 v Republic of Ireland (lost 1–2)
1994 v Romania (lost 1–2)

MALCOLM ALLEN WAS REJECTED by Watford and then by Manchester United as a trialist, but was grateful to receive another chance at Vicarage Road and carved out a decent career in the game. He scored Watford's goal in the 1985 FA Youth Cup Final and made his League debut in November of that year. He had played in only four games under Graham Taylor's guidance before being called into the Wales squad at the age of 18 for the game in Saudi Arabia.

Malcolm Allen was skilful on the ball, with a sure pass and shot. He had impressed more in cup games than League fixtures when, following a loan period with Aston Villa, he joined Norwich City in the summer of 1988. It was at Carrow Road that Allen's problems with his knees first flared up, and in a season and a half he appeared in 35 League games, scoring eight goals. Allen moved on to Millwall, where he had a little more luck, finding the net 24 times in 81 games.

In August 1993 he joined Newcastle United as cover for the injured Peter Beardsley as the Magpies embarked on their inaugural season in the Premiership. He made a good start, finding the net with confidence. But he was then badly injured and found himself on the sidelines for almost a year with knee ligament problems. By the time he returned from injury, he not only found a host of multi-million-pound stars barring his way but suffered an injury relapse. At the age of 28, after seven knee operations, he was forced to leave the game. He then took up a post in North Wales as Welsh FA Schools Coach.

Dean SAUNDERS

Position	Forward
Born	Dean Nicholas Saunders, Swansea, 21 June 1964
Height	5ft 8in
Weight	10st 0lb
Clubs	Swansea City, Cardiff City, Brighton and Hove Albion, Oxford United, Derby County, Liverpool, Aston Villa, Galatasaray, Nottingham Forest, Sheffield United, Benfica, Bradford City
Welsh Caps	75 Goals 22

1986 v Republic of Ireland (won 1–0), v Canada (lost 0–2), v Canada (won 3–0) 2 goals
1987 v Finland (1–1), v USSR (0–0)
1988 v Yugoslavia (lost 1–2) 1 goal, v Sweden (lost 1–4), v Malta (won 3–2), v Italy (won 1–0)
1989 v Holland (lost 0–1), v Finland (2–2) 1 goal, v Israel (3–3), v Sweden (lost 0–2),
   v W. Germany (0–0)
1990 v Finland (lost 0–1), v Holland (lost 1–2), v W. Germany (lost 1–2), v Sweden (lost 2–4),
   2 goals, v Costa Rica (won 1–0) 1 goal
1991 v Denmark (lost 0–1), v Belgium (won 3–1) 1 goal, v Luxembourg (won 1–0),
   v Republic of Ireland (lost 0–3), v Belgium (1–1) 1 goal, v Iceland (won 1–0), v Poland (0–0),
   v Germany (won 1–0)
1992 v Brazil (won 1–0) 1 goal, v Germany (lost 1–4), v Republic of Ireland (won 1–0),
   v Romania (lost 1–5), v Holland (lost 0–4), v Argentina (lost 0–1), v Japan (won 1–0)

1993 v Faroe Islands (won 6–0) 1 goal, v Cyprus (won 1–0), v Belgium (lost 0–2), v Belgium
  (won 2–0), v RCS (1–1), v Faroe Islands (won 3–0) 1 goal
1994 v RCS (2–2), v Cyprus (won 2–0) 1 goal, v Romania (lost 1–2) 1 goal, v Norway (lost 1–3)
1995 v Georgia (lost 0–5), v Bulgaria (lost 0–3), v Bulgaria (lost 1–3) 1 goal, v Germany (1–1)
  1 goal, v Georgia (lost 0–1)
1996 v Germany (lost 1–2), v Albania (1–1), v San Marino (won 5–0), v San Marino
  (won 6–0) 2 goals
1997 v Holland (lost 1–3) 1 goal, v Holland (lost 1–7) 1 goal, v Turkey (0–0), v Belgium (lost
  1–2), v Scotland (won 1–0)
1998 v Turkey (lost 4–6) 1 goal, v Belgium (lost 2–3), v Brazil (lost 0–3), v Malta (won 3–0),
  v Tunisia (lost 0–4)
1999 v Italy (lost 0–2), v Denmark (won 2–1), v Belarus (won 3–2), v Switzerland (lost 0–2),
  v Italy (lost 0–4), v Denmark (lost 0–2)
2000 v Belarus (won 2–1) 1 goal, v Switzerland (lost 0–2), v Finland (lost 1–2), v Brazil (lost 0–3)
2001 v Armenia (2–2), v Ukraine (1–1)

WITH 75 INTERNATIONAL APPEARANCES, Dean Saunders held the Welsh record for an outfield player until surpassed by Gary Speed. He won his first cap against the Republic of Ireland in 1986 and his last against the Ukraine some 15 years later.

The son of Roy, who played for Liverpool and Swansea City, Dean Saunders was thrown into League action in October 1983 with the Swans just relegated from the First Division. With Swansea struggling, Saunders was an ever-present for the last 15 games of the season but could not prevent them dropping into the Third Division. John Bond took over from Colin Appleton in December 1984, and top-scorer Saunders was loaned to rivals Cardiff City before he was given a free transfer and joined Brighton and Hove Albion.

He quickly justified the Seagulls' confidence, scoring 19 League and Cup goals in a side that was in the top half of the Second Division and reached the FA Cup fifth round. His form convinced Wales's manager Mike England to include him in the squad for the close season tour of Canada, Saunders having already made his international debut. Midway through the following season, the hard-up south-coast club accepted a bid of £60,000 from Oxford United.

His six goals in the last dozen matches of that 1986/87 season helped Oxford secure their First Division status in the penultimate game of the campaign. The 1987/88 season was particularly successful for Saunders, whose 21 goals included six in the League Cup and helped Oxford to a second semi-final in three seasons. In October 1988 Saunders was transferred to Derby County for £1 million, the repercussions of which led to an angry Mark Lawrenson being sacked as manager.

Saunders immediately set about repaying the massive fee with some spectacular goals for both the Rams and Wales, thus dispelling any doubts about the inflated fee. He was the club's leading scorer in each of his three seasons at the Baseball Ground. This led to Liverpool paying £2.9 million for his services in the summer of 1991– a record for a transfer between two English clubs.

Saunders never really showed his usual sharpness at Anfield as he did not receive the kind of service he needed. Just over a year later he was sold to Aston Villa for £2.3 million and his career was resurrected, scoring twice in a 4–2 win over Liverpool on his debut! He finished his first season at Villa Park as the club's leading scorer with 1

The much-travelled forward Dean Saunders scored some spectacular goals for his clubs and Wales. *(Liverpool Daily Post and Echo)*

goals, helping Villa finish as runners-up in the Premier League to Manchester United. He continued to top Villa's scoring charts until in the summer of 1995 he joined the Turkish club Galatasaray.

He later returned to the Premiership with Nottingham Forest. Although he didn't have the best of times at the City Ground, he kept his place in the Wales side and scored in the World Cup qualifiers. Eventually he was allowed to move on to Sheffield United, where his form was outstanding. But, because of a clause in his contract, the Bramall Lane club were powerless to prevent him joining Benfica in December 1998.

In the summer of 1999 Saunders returned to top-flight action with Premiership new boys Bradford City. After two seasons at Valley Parade, in which he took his total of League and Cup games for his ten clubs to 713, he decided to retire.

Tony NORMAN

Position	Goalkeeper
Born	Anthony Joseph Norman, Deeside, 24 February 1958
Height	6ft 2in
Weight	12st 8lb
Clubs	Burnley, Hull City, Sunderland, Huddersfield Town
Welsh Caps	5
	1986 v Republic of Ireland (won 1–0), v Uruguay (0–0), v Canada (lost 0–2)
	1988 v Malta (won 3–2), v Italy (won 1–0)

GOALKEEPER TONY NORMAN's last appearance in a Wales shirt saw him keep a clean sheet against the might of Italy.

He began his career with Burnley. But he failed to make the grade with the Turf Moor club, and joined Hull City for a fee of £30,000 in February 1980. At Boothferry Park he set a new club record of 226 consecutive League appearances. Although receivership cast a shadow over the keeper's future with the Tigers, he stayed to help the club win promotion to the Third Division in 1982. He went on to appear in 442 League and Cup games for Hull City before joining Sunderland in December 1989 in a record £400,000 deal.

He helped the Wearsiders into the Second Division play-offs in 1989/90, where he kept clean sheets in both legs of the semi-final tie against arch-rivals Newcastle United. In the final against Swindon Town he was in magnificent form. Although Sunderland lost 1–0 the margin would have been greater had it not been for Tony Norman.

The Sunderland keeper did, however, eventually play in the top flight. After investigations by the Inland Revenue and the Football League, Swindon Town were relegated and Sunderland were promoted in their place. Norman missed just one game in that 1990/91 campaign. Although the club were relegated, he kept nine clean sheets in his 37 games. Norman played in 227 first-team games for the Wearsiders, including an appearance in the 1992 FA Cup Final debut against Liverpool, before leaving to see out his first-class career with Huddersfield Town.

While with the Yorkshire club, Norman doubled up as the club's goalkeeping coach and radio summariser.

Mark BOWEN

Position	Left-back
Born	Mark Rosslyn Bowen, Neath, 7 December 1963
Height	5ft 8in
Weight	11st 13lb
Clubs	Tottenham Hotspur, Norwich City, West Ham United, Shimizu SP (Japan), Charlton Athletic, Wigan Athletic, Reading

Mark Bowen, Norwich City's most-capped player, won 35 of his 41 caps while with the anaries. *(Lancashire Evening Post)*

Welsh Caps   41   Goals 3

1986 v Canada (lost 0–2), v Canada (won 3–0)
1988 v Yugoslavia (lost 1–2)
1989 v Finland (2–2), v Israel (3–3), v Sweden (lost 0–2), v W. Germany (0–0)
1990 v Finland (lost 0–1), v Holland (lost 1–2) 1 goal, v W. Germany (lost 1–2), v Sweden (lost 2–4)
1992 v Brazil (won 1–0), v Germany (lost 1–4), v Luxembourg (won 1–0), v Republic of Ireland (won 1–0), v Austria (1–1), v Romania (lost 1–5), v Holland (lost 0–4), v Japan (won 1–0) 1 goal
1993 v Faroe Islands (won 6–0) 1 goal, v Cyprus (won 1–0), v Belgium (lost 0–2), v Belgium (won 2–0), v RCS (1–1)
1994 v RCS (2–2), v Sweden (lost 0–2)
1995 v Moldova (lost 2–3), v Georgia (lost 0–5), v Bulgaria (lost 0–3), v Bulgaria (lost 1–3), v Germany (1–1), v Georgia (lost 0–1)
1996 v Moldova (won 1–0), v Germany (lost 1–2), v Albania (1–1), v Switzerland (lost 0–2), v San Marino (won 5–0)
1997 v San Marino (won 6–0), v Holland (lost 1–3), v Holland (lost 1–7), v Republic of Ireland (0–0)

MARK BOWEN HAD PLAYED FOR Wales at both youth and under-21 levels by the time he made his first-team debut for Tottenham Hotspur. He won his first international cap during Wales's summer tour of Canada in 1986, twice appearing as a substitute in games against the home nation. However, during his time at White Hart Lane he could never quite lay claim to a regular place in the side because of its surfeit of stars. In July 1987 he joined Norwich City for a fee of £90,000.

Linking up with former Spurs players Ian Crook and Ian Culverhouse, he had a short run on the left-side of midfield before making his mark at left-back. He made a huge contribution from the left in 1988/89 as City led the First Division for the early part of the season, eventually finishing fourth. In 1992/93, when the club finished third in the newly formed Premier League, Bowen was the only ever-present and over the next four seasons he hardly missed a game. He gained more international caps than anyone else while at Carrow Road. But the 1995/96 season ended in controversy for the Neath-born player. He was dropped from the first team and given a free transfer. He joined West Ham United after 399 appearances for the East Anglian club.

At Upton Park he had to be content with the role of squad player before being released in March 1997 to take up an offer from Shimizu SP of Japan. He later returned to these shores to play for Charlton Athletic. After a couple of seasons with the Addicks he was recruited by ambitious Wigan Athletic. The Latics were unbeaten in the seven games in which Bowen played for them before ending his first-class career with Reading.

Mark Bowen joined Mark Hughes's backroom staff, taking up a role as coach to the Wales under-21 side. He later coached Birmingham City until parting company with the club in the summer of 2004.

Andy DIBBLE

Position	Goalkeeper
Born	Andrew Gerald Dibble, Cwmbran, 8 May 1965
Height	6ft 3in
Weight	16st 8lb
Clubs	Cardiff City, Luton Town, Sunderland, Huddersfield Town, Manchester City, Aberdeen, Middlesbrough, Bolton Wanderers, West Bromwich Albion, Glasgow Rangers, Altrincham, Hartlepool United, Carlisle United, Stockport County, Wrexham
Welsh Caps	3
	1986 v Canada (lost 0–2), v Canada (won 3–0)
	1989 v Israel (3–3)

MUCH-TRAVELLED GOALKEEPER ANDY DIBBLE made his international debut as a replacement for Andy Norman during Wales's first match of their summer tour to Canada in 1986. He kept his place for the second meeting, which Wales won 3–0.

He began his League career with Cardiff City, making his debut on his 17th birthday as the Bluebirds went down to a single-goal home defeat by Crystal Palace. Cardiff were relegated that season. Dibble was the club's first-choice keeper, the following season helped his side return at the first attempt.

In July 1984 Luton Town paid £125,000 to take him to Kenilworth Road. His early displays were disappointing. He was loaned out to Sunderland and Huddersfield Town but returned to help the Hatters win the League Cup in 1988, when his save from Nigel Winterburn's penalty helped Luton beat Arsenal 3–2.

In June 1988 Manchester City secured his services for £240,000. Although while at Maine Road he made more appearances for the club than he did anywhere else, he still had loan spells with Aberdeen, Bolton, Middlesbrough and West Bromwich Albion.

In March 1997 he joined Glasgow Rangers, making his debut in a 1–0 win over Celtic in the Old Firm derby and so recording a ninth consecutive Championship.

After that he had loan spells with former clubs Luton and Middlesbrough before playing non-League football for Altrincham. He then returned to League action with Hartlepool United, Carlisle United and Stockport County before joining Wrexham. As well as inspiring his colleagues at the Racecourse Ground to promotion, he acted as goalkeeping coach to the Robins.

Martin THOMAS

Position	Goalkeeper
Born	Martin Richard Thomas, Senghenydd, 28 November 1959
Height	6ft 1in
Weight	13st 0lb
Clubs	Bristol Rovers, Cardiff City, Southend United, Newcastle United, Middlesbrough, Birmingham City, Cheltenham Town
Welsh Caps	1
	1987 v Finland (1–1)

THERE WAS A TIME WHEN MARTIN THOMAS seemed set for an illustriou international future. He had established second place in the pecking order of Wels goalkeepers, even being rated above a young Neville Southall. But the Bristol Rover keeper, who was understudy to Dai Davies, made only one appearance at fu international level.

He made his League debut as a 17-year-old against Charlton Athletic at The Valle in January 1977. Although he made an elementary error to concede an early goal, h went on to show the form that soon won him the first-team berth at the expense o Jim Eadie. There followed three and a half seasons of splendid performances as Second Division regular before a dislocated finger required an operation. On h return he was unable to dislodge Phil Kite and, after turning down Spurs, joine Newcastle United.

Although he won his long-awaited cap while at St James Park, more injuries led t frustration and a move to Birmingham City. He turned in a number of memorab performances, but the Blues were relegated at the end of his first season at ' Andrew's. Thomas's penalty saves against Swansea in 1991 were instrumental in th club's winning the Leyland Daf Cup. He then began to suffer from a spate of nigglir injuries and left the club in the summer of 1993.

After a spell playing non-League football for Cheltenham Town, he became goalkeeping coach for Birmingham, Norwich, Swindon and the FA at Lilleshall.

Andy JONES

Position	Forward
Born	Andrew Mark Jones, Wrexham, 9 January 1963
Height	5ft 11in
Weight	12st 7lb
Clubs	Wrexham, Rhyl, Port Vale, Charlton Athletic, Bristol City, Bournemouth, Leyton Orient, Poole Town, Havant Town
Welsh Caps	6 Goals 1
	1987 v Finland (won 4–0) 1 goal, v Czechoslovakia (1–1), v Denmark (won 1–0), v Denmar (lost 0–1), v Czechoslovakia (lost 0–2)
	1990 v Holland (lost 1–2)

ANDY JONES WAS A POWERFUL striker who was capped six times by Wales. He w rejected by Wrexham as not being good enough, yet he subsequently made remarkable rise to First Division soccer!

Jones was released by the Robins into non-League football and in four seasons wit Rhyl netted 92 goals. He worked as a cabinet maker and then as a supervisor at Corwen health foods factory. He was taken back into the League by Port Vale and aft scoring 12 goals in 1985/86, he began to score on a regular basis. When Ma Hughes was suspended, Jones was watched by Welsh scouts and, after scoring a ha trick against Fulham, he was chosen to win his first cap against Finland. Jones score his side's last goal in a 4–0 win. In 1986/87 he broke Vale's postwar scoring recor finishing the season as the Third Division's leading scorer.

A strong, bustling type of forward, he was signed by Charlton Athletic's Lennie Lawrence, who stepped in with a successful £350,000 bid to take the striker into the top flight. He developed fitness problems at The Valley and also a few differences of opinion with the manager. But on the field Jones certainly had the knack of being in the right place at the right time, despite lacking a little in pace.

After a loan spell back at Port Vale, he looked set to join Bristol City. But as the Ashton Gate club couldn't come up with the necessary £100,000 fee, Charlton accepted a bid of £80,000 from Bournemouth. He netted after just seconds into his debut for the Cherries, but his time at Dean Court was hampered by injuries and he eventually moved on to end his first-class career with Leyton Orient. Jones later played non-League football for Poole Town and Havant Town before working as a financial adviser.

Barry HORNE

Position	Midfielder
Born	Barry Horne, St Asaph, 18 May 1962
Height	5ft 10in
Weight	11st 6lb
Clubs	Rhyl, Wrexham, Portsmouth, Southampton, Everton, Birmingham City, Huddersfield Town, Sheffield Wednesday, Kidderminster Harriers, Walsall, Belper Town
Welsh Caps	59 Goals 2

1988 v Denmark (won 1–0), v Yugoslavia (lost 1–2), v Sweden (lost 1–4), v Malta (won 3–2) 1 goal, v Italy (won 1–0)

1989 v Holland (lost 0–1), v Finland (2–2), v Israel (3–3) 1 goal, v Sweden (lost 0–2), v W. Germany (0–0)

1990 v W. Germany (lost 1–2), v Republic of Ireland (lost 0–1), v Sweden (lost 2–4), v Costa Rica (won 1–0)

1991 v Denmark (lost 0–1), v Belgium (won 3–1), v Luxembourg (won 1–0), v Republic of Ireland (lost 0–3), v Belgium (1–1), v Iceland (won 1–0), v Poland (0–0), v Germany (won 1–0)

1992 v Brazil (won 1–0), v Germany (lost 1–4), v Luxembourg (won 1–0), v Republic of Ireland (won 1–0), v Austria (1–1), v Romania (lost 1–5), v Holland (lost 0–4), v Argentina (lost 0–1), v Japan (won 1–0)

1993 v Faroe Islands (won 6–0), v Cyprus (won 1–0), v Belgium (lost 0–2), v Republic of Ireland (lost 1–2), v Belgium (won 2–0), v RCS (1–1), v Faroe Islands (won 3–0)

1994 v RCS (2–2), v Cyprus (won 2–0), v Romania (lost 1–2), v Norway (lost 1–3), v Sweden (lost 0–2), v Estonia (won 2–1)

1995 v Moldova (lost 2–3), v Georgia (lost 0–5), v Bulgaria (lost 1–3), v Germany (1–1), v Georgia (lost 0–1)

1996 v Moldova (won 1–0), v Germany (lost 1–2), v Italy (lost 0–3), v Switzerland (lost 0–2), v San Marino (won 5–0)

1997 v San Marino (won 6–0), v Holland (lost 1–3), v Turkey (0–0), v Republic of Ireland (0–0), v Belgium (lost 1–2)

Although a late starter in League football, Barry Horne went on to win 59 caps for Wales. *(Getty Images)*

A LATE STARTER IN LEAGUE FOOTBALL, Barry Horne completed a chemistry degree at Liverpool University while playing part-time football for Rhyl in the Northern Premier League. On leaving university, he joined Fourth Division Wrexham and made his debut for the Robins against Swindon Town in August 1984. In three years at the Racecourse Ground, Horne won a Welsh Cup winners' medal and impressed in the club's European run when he scored one of the goals in the defeat of FC Porto on the away goal rule. After scoring 29 goals in 184 first-team games, he joined Portsmouth in the summer of 1987.

Within a month of his arrival at Fratton Park, he made his first appearance for the Welsh national side, coming on as a substitute for Robbie James in a 1–0 win over Denmark. Horne went on to win 59 caps for his country in a ten-year period following his debut.

He had made 79 appearances for Pompey when Southampton paid £700,000 to take the tough-tackling Welshman to The Dell, making him the Saints' most expensive signing. He missed very few games for the south-coast club before being unexpectedly snapped up by Everton during the summer of 1992.

Horne added steel to the Goodison club's midfield. His spirited performances and great leadership qualities proved that he was an astute buy. However, after making 148 appearances for the Toffees, including helping them win the FA Cup in 1995, he was allowed to join Birmingham City for £250,000, a somewhat surprising move for such an experienced international.

A year later Horne was on the move again, this time to Huddersfield Town on a free transfer before staying in Yorkshire with a brief spell at Sheffield Wednesday. Horne, who was PFA Chairman, then joined League newcomers Kidderminster Harriers and played in their first-ever Football League game against Torquay United, scoring with a long-range shot that clinched victory over the Devon club. He then wound down his League career with Walsall before joining non-League side Belper Town.

Geraint WILLIAMS

Position	Midfielder
Born	David Geraint Williams, Treorchy, 5 January 1962
Height	5ft 7in
Weight	12st 6lb
Clubs	Bristol Rovers, Derby County, Ipswich Town, Colchester United
Welsh Caps	13
	1988 v Czechoslovakia (lost 0–2), v Yugoslavia (lost 1–2), v Sweden (lost 1–4), v Malta (won 3–2), v Italy (won 1–0)
	1989 v Holland (lost 0–1), v Israel (3–3), v Sweden (lost 0–2), v W. Germany (0–0)
	1990 v Finland (lost 0–1), v Holland (lost 1–2)
	1993 v Republic of Ireland (lost 1–2)
	1996 v Germany (lost 1–2)

MIDFIELDER GERAINT WILLIAMS, popularly known as 'George', easily adjusted to the demands of First Division football and was rewarded with his first call-up to the Welsh

Geraint Williams was a hard-tackling, competitive midfielder who won 13 Welsh caps. *(Lancashire Evening Post)*

national squad. He made his international debut against Czechoslovakia in November 1987 and remained a regular choice up until 1989.

Williams was always in the thick of the action. He made his Football League debut for Bristol Rovers in a 3–3 home draw against Sheffield Wednesday in October 1980. He held his place for the rest of the season despite Rovers' eventual relegation to the Third Division. He was a regular performer during his five seasons with the Pirates. He left Eastville after making 166 League and Cup appearances to join Derby County for a fee of £40,000 in March 1985.

He quickly established himself in a defensive midfield anchor role at the Baseball Ground, assisting the Rams to two consecutive promotion seasons. Williams went on to appear in 321 League and Cup games for Derby. After the Rams missed out on the First Division play-offs, he joined Ipswich Town for a fee of £650,000 in the summer of 1992.

He scored on his Town debut on the opening day of the season in a 1–1 draw with Aston Villa. Although he was not a prolific scorer from midfield, he did net a number of memorable goals, perhaps none better than his goal at Reading midway through the 1995/96 season when he ran half the length of the Elm Park pitch to score in a 4–1 win for Ipswich. He remained an important member of the Ipswich side until the summer of 1998 when, after appearing in 267 games for the Portman Road club, he joined Colchester United. He ended his career after just one season with the Layer Road club.

Gareth HALL

Position	Right-back
Born	Gareth David Hall, Croydon, 12 March 1969
Height	5ft 8in
Weight	10st 7lb
Clubs	Chelsea, Sunderland, Brentford, Swindon Town, Havant and Waterlooville
Welsh Caps	9
	1988 v Yugoslavia (lost 1–2), v Malta (won 3–2), v Italy (won 1–0)
	1989 v Holland (lost 0–1), v Finland (2–2), v Israel (3–3)
	1990 v Republic of Ireland (lost 0–1)
	1991 v Republic of Ireland (lost 0–3)
	1992 v Austria (1–1)

GARETH HALL, A YOUNG CHELSEA starlet, was snatched by Wales from under England's noses in March 1988 when he was named in the Welsh squad for the friendly against Yugoslavia. Hall was a former England schoolboy international player, but his mother's birthplace of Caerphilly also qualified him for Wales. At the same time as his selection for Wales, he was given the chance to tour Brazil with the England under-20 side, but he saw greater opportunities for senior international honours with Wales.

He made his Chelsea debut against Wimbledon at Plough Lane in May 1987. The next couple of seasons he found it difficult to hold down a regular place in the side, with Steve Clark being preferred in Hall's position of right-back. His real break-through came in February 1990, when he finally managed to secure a first-team place at his rival's expense. However, following the appointment of Ian Porterfield as Chelsea manager, Hall lost his place to Clarke and asked for a transfer. Throughout a succession of Chelsea managers – including David Webb and Glenn Hoddle – Hall found himself in and out of the side. In January 1996, after a loan spell with Sunderland, he joined the Wearsiders on a permanent basis.

He helped the Black Cats win the First Division title in his first season in the North-East, but then began to suffer from criticism from the terraces. As he lost confidence, he lost his place in the Sunderland line-up. Following a loan spell with Brentford, Hall joined Swindon Town under the Bosman ruling.

Although part of a struggling team, he showed his versatility by playing in a variety of positions. After three seasons at the County Ground, he left the first-class scene to play non-League football for Havant and Waterlooville.

Alan KNILL

Position	Central defender
Born	Alan Richard Knill, Eton, 8 October 1964
Height	6ft 2in
Weight	12st 10lb
Clubs	Southampton, Halifax Town, Swansea City, Bury, Cardiff City, Scunthorpe United, Rotherham United
Welsh Caps	1
	1989 v Holland (lost 0–1)

ALAN KNILL WAS A FORMER APPRENTICE with Southampton. He failed to make the grade with the south-coast club, and in the summer of 1984 he joined Halifax Town. He made his League debut for the Shaymen against Blackpool in August 1984, and ended the season playing in 44 games. Knill was a virtual ever-present in his three seasons with the Yorkshire club. In the summer of 1987, after appearing in 136 games for Halifax, he joined Swansea City for a tribunal-fixed fee of £15,000.

Knill formed an effective central defensive partnership with Andy Melville and then Dudley Lewis. He helped the Swans win promotion to the Third Division via the play-offs in his first season at the Vetch. In 1988/89 they came close to winning another play-off place. Also during that season, Knill's performances led to full international recognition when he played for Wales against Holland in Amsterdam in a World Cup qualifying game. At the end of that season, Knill decided to take up an offer of a contract with Bury, claiming that Swansea lacked ambition. Once again, his fee – this time £95,000, Bury's record outgoing transfer fee – was settled by a tribunal.

In four seasons at Gigg Lane Knill played in two consecutive play-off finals, suffered relegation to the League's basement, and then appeared in another play-off match against York City. Knill then had a short loan spell with Cardiff City before joining Scunthorpe United. The tall central defender served the Irons well for almost four seasons. Then he moved to Rotherham United, where he took his total of first-class games for his six League clubs to 659 before hanging up his boots.

1990-99

Rollercoaster Ride

The first season of the decade finished with Wales firmly on top of Group 5 at the 1992 European Championships with three wins and a draw from four matches, including a creditable 1−0 victory over West Germany in Cardiff. However, a 4−1 defeat in the return game saw Wales finish one point behind the eventual beaten finalists. In that game Ryan Giggs became Wales's youngest player at 17 years 332 days. (His record was broken on 3 June 1998 when Ryan Green of Wolves, aged just 17 years 226 days, played for Wales in their 2−0 win over Malta.)

The writing was on the wall for Wales's manager Terry Yorath when they just missed out on qualifying for the 1994 World Cup Finals. Determined to do better in the following European Championships, Wales turned to John Toshack. Toshack agreed to run the national team while still managing Real Sociedad. But, during his first match in charge − a 3−1 defeat by Norway − he was jeered by the fans, who chanted Yorath's name. Toshack promptly quit after just 47 days in charge.

After a good start to the 1996 European Championships, including beating Albania 2−0, Wales suffered four successive defeats. They then produced the result of the competition − a 1−1 draw against Germany in Düsseldorf. This lifted Wales off the bottom of the table.

Wales began their 1998 World Cup campaign with two resounding defeats of San Marino in 5−0 and 6−0 victories. Mark Hughes scored twice in each match. Although Neville Southall gave an outstanding display in the match against Holland, he couldn't prevent the Dutch from scoring three times in an eight-minute spell in the second half. In the return match in Eindhoven Wales suffered their worst-ever World Cup defeat, going down 7−1, with Dennis Bergkamp netting a hat-trick. Wales then blew their chances of qualifying for the finals, losing 2−1 against Belgium in the last-ever match at the Cardiff Arms Park, prompting Neville Southall to retire from international football. Wales then lost a ten-goal thriller in Turkey 6−4 (Hakan Suker scored four of the home side's goals), but salvaged some pride in an academic trip to Belgium. Wales pulled two goals back after being 3−0 down at half-time.

In the qualifying matches for the European Championships in 2000, Wales went down 2−0 against Italy before beating Denmark 2−1 and Belarus 3−2, coming back from the dead to record two victories in the space of five days. After Wales's 4−0 defeat in Italy, an angry Bobby Gould resigned as team manager. But, despite a series of saves from Paul Jones against Denmark, Wales, under Neville Southall, rarely threatened and lost 2−0 at a half-empty Anfield.

Gavin MAGUIRE

Position	Central defender
Born	Gavin Terence Maguire, Hammersmith, 24 November 1967
Height	5ft 8in
Weight	11st 4lb
Clubs	Queen's Park Rangers, Portsmouth, Newcastle United, Millwall, Scarborough
Welsh Caps	7
	1990 v Finland (lost 0−1), v Holland (lost 1−2), v W. Germany (lost 1−2), v Republic of Ireland (lost 0−1), v Sweden (lost 2−4)
	1992 v Brazil (won 1−0), v Germany (lost 1−4)

GAVIN MAGUIRE, WHOSE MOTHER comes from Ystrad Rhondda, was drawn to the attention of the Football Association of Wales by the Queen's Park Rangers assistant manager Peter Shreeves, who held a similar position with the Wales senior team. The Hammersmith-born defender, whose father hails from Ireland, was eligible to play for any one of three countries. He chose Wales and made his full international debut against Finland in September 1989.

Maguire was a hard, uncompromising defender. Although in his early days with Queen's Park Rangers he had a poor disciplinary record, he worked hard at this aspect of his game. Maguire possessed undoubted skills and was adept at creating attacks by long and accurate passes out of defence. His speed and timing enabled him to perform well as a sweeper while Wales team manager Terry Yorath greatly admired his ability to mark men out of the game.

By the time he won his first international cap, Maguire had joined Portsmouth. His displays at the heart of the Pompey defence were outstanding. But after suffering a serious knee injury he found he couldn't win his place back in the side and joined Newcastle United on loan. Sadly, another knee injury set him back and, after a brief spell with Millwall and a loan period with Scarborough, he went to play in the United States.

Iwan ROBERTS

Position	Forward
Born	Iwan Wyn Roberts, Bangor, 26 June 1968
Height	6ft 3in
Weight	14st 0lb
Clubs	Watford, Huddersfield Town, Leicester City, Wolverhampton Wanderers, Norwich City

Iwan Roberts made his debut against Holland in October 1989, and won the last of his 15 caps in 2002. *(Lancashire Evening Post)*

Welsh Caps	15
	1990 v Holland (lost 1–2)
	1992 v Austria (1–1), v Argentina (lost 0–1), v Japan (won 1–0)
	1994 v Sweden (lost 0–2)
	1995 v Albania (won 2–0), v Moldova (lost 2–3)
	2000 v Finland (lost 1–2), v Brazil (lost 0–3), v Portugal (lost 0–3)
	2001 v Belarus (lost 1–2), v Norway (1–1), v Armenia (2–2)
	2002 v Armenia (0–0), v Belarus (won 1–0)

WATFORD WERE ABLE TO ENTICE IWAN ROBERTS from school because they had a Welsh-speaking coach in Tom Walley. Throughout his playing career Roberts has remained in demand for media work as one of very few contemporary internationals able to converse in his native tongue. He memorably scored his first goal for the Hornets as a substitute against Manchester United and won his first cap against Holland in October 1989.

He didn't receive any further international calls until he had left Vicarage Road and joined Huddersfield Town for a fee of £275,000 in the summer of 1990. His decent strike-rate with the Terriers – 50 goals in 141 League games – brought him to the attention of a number of top clubs. In November 1993 Leicester City manager Brian Little paid £300,000 for his services.

A 12-minute hat-trick against local rivals Derby County sealed his place in City folklore. Then in 1995/96 Roberts became the first Leicester player since Alan Smith in 1987 to score 20 goals in a season as Leicester returned to the Premiership via the play-offs. Not surprisingly, the former Leicester manager Mark McGhee, who had replaced Little as the Foxes' boss but had since joined Wolverhampton Wanderers, came back to Filbert Street and paid £1.3 million to take Roberts to Molineux.

He endeared himself to Wolves fans early on by becoming the first man to score a hat-trick in a Wolves v West Bromwich Albion derby at the Hawthorns. Unexpectedly, after just one season at Molineux he was allowed to join Norwich City for £900,000.

The big, bustling centre-forward didn't have the best of times during his early days at Carrow Road. But in 1998/99 he rediscovered his goalscoring touch and was named in several Welsh 'B' squads and put on standby for the full international side. He was hugely popular with Canaries' fans, especially after he scored both goals in a 2–0 East Anglian derby win over Ipswich in 1999/2000. Roberts was appointed the Canaries' captain at the start of the 2000/01 season. He topped the Norwich scoring charts for four consecutive seasons, and his total of 89 goals took him to third place in the club's all-time records, before being released in the summer of 2004 after helping the Canaries win the First Division Championship.

Andy MELVILLE

Position	Central defender
Born	Andrew Roger Melville, Swansea, 29 November 1968
Height	6ft 0in
Weight	13st 10lb
Clubs	Swansea City, Oxford United, Sunderland, Bradford City, Fulham
Welsh Caps	63 Goals 3

1990 v West Germany (lost 1–2), v Republic of Ireland (lost 0–1), v Sweden (lost 2–4),
  v Costa Rica (won 1–0)
1991 v Iceland (won 1–0), v Poland (0–0), v Germany (won 1–0)
1992 v Brazil (won 1–0), v Germany (lost 1–4), v Luxembourg (won 1–0),
  v Romania (lost 1–5), v Holland (lost 0–4), v Japan (won 1–0)
1993 v RCS (1–1), v Faroe Islands (won 3–0)
1994 v RCS (2–2), v Romania (lost 1–2), v Norway (lost 1–3), v Sweden (lost 0–2),
  v Estonia (won 2–1)
1995 v Albania (won 2–0), Moldova (lost 2–30, v Georgia (lost 0–5), v Bulgaria (lost 0–3)
1996 v Germany (lost 1–2), v Albania (1–1), v San Marino (won 5–0) 1 goal
1997 v San Marino (won 6–0) 1 goal, v Holland (lost 1–3), v Holland (lost 1–7),
  v Turkey (0–0)
1998 v Turkey (lost 4–6) 1 goal
1999 v Italy (lost 0–4), v Denmark (lost 0–2)
2000 v Belarus (2–2), v Qatar (won 1–0), v Finland (lost 1–2), v Brazil (lost 0–3),
  v Portugal (lost 0–3)
2001 v Belarus (lost 1–2), v Norway (1–1), v Poland (0–0), v Armenia (2–2), v Ukraine (1–1),
  v Poland (lost 1–2), v Ukraine (1–1)
2002 v Armenia (0–0), v Belarus (won 1–0), v Argentina (1–1), v Czech Republic (0–0),
  v Germany (won 1–0)
2003 v Croatia (1–1), v Finland (won 2–0), v Italy (won 2–1), v Azerbaijan (won 2–0),
  v Bosnia-Herzegovina (2–2), v Azerbaijan (won 4–0), v United States (lost 0–2)
2004 v Finland (1–1), v Russia (0–0), v Russia lost (0–1), v Scotland (won 4–0),
  v Hungary (won 2–1)

ONE OF WALES'S MOST CAPPED defenders, Andy Melville began his career with his home-town club Swansea City and progressed from the youth training scheme to make his senior debut against Bristol City in November 1985. In his early days with the Swans there was something of a problem in that his best position was not readily apparent. He was tried in most positions before settling into the back four. He won a permanent place in the Swansea side in 1986/87 and helped the win promotion the following season.

He was appointed the Swansea captain at the age of 20. In the summer of 1990, after scoring 29 goals in 213 games for the Vetch Field club, he joined Oxford United for £275,000 plus a percentage of any future transfer fee. In three seasons at the Manor Ground he appeared in 159 games before being transferred to Sunderland in the summer of 1993.

His first three seasons in the North-East were spent in relegation battles. But in 1995/96 Melville helped the Wearsiders win the First Division Championship.

Powerful in the air and always dangerous at set pieces, he acquitted himself well in the Premiership. A broken nose ruled him out of the last seven games of the season when his experience could have helped the club in their attempt to avoid the drop. An injury ended his virtual monopoly of a back-four position, but following a loan spell with Bradford City he returned to help Sunderland win the First Division title for a second time. Melville spent just one more season with Sunderland before unexpectedly being released and joining Fulham.

Although it took him a while to win over the crowd, he remained a regular in the Wales side and in 2000/01 he helped the Cottagers run away with the First Division Championship. The following season he captained both club and country, leading Wales for the first time on the occasion of his 50th cap against the Czech Republic. In 2002/03 he had an outstanding season, playing especially well in Fulham's European games, at which his vast international experience stood him and the Cottagers in good stead.

Robert Page, John Hartson, Andy Melville, Ryan Giggs and Robert Earnshaw of Wales line up for the national anthems before the International Friendly match between Wales and Germany played at the Millennium Stadium, 14 May 2002. Wales won the match 1–0. (Getty Images)

Brian LAW

Position	Central defender
Born	Brian John Law, Merthyr Tydfil, 1 January 1970
Height	6ft 2in
Weight	11st 10lb
Clubs	Queen's Park Rangers, Wolverhampton Wanderers, Millwall
Welsh Caps	1
	1990 v Sweden (lost 2–4)

ALTHOUGH IMPRESSIVE WHEN PLAYING for the Queen's Park Rangers reserve side, Brian Law's chances of regular first-team football at Loftus Road were restricted. However, Peter Shreeve, the club's coach and Wales team manager Terry Yorath's number two, had seen enough to recommend him to the Wales boss. He had played in only a handful of Football League games when in April 1990 he was drafted into the Wales team after a number of players cried off with injuries. He withdrew at first because of a very heavy cold but then recovered and stepped in for the injured Mark Aizlewood in the game against Sweden.

A strong, powerful, and very quick youngster, Brian Law was forced to retire in 1992. He later realised that his tendon injury was standing up well to arduous hobbies such as climbing and trekking, and he decided to try again.

Wolverhampton Wanderers gave him a trial but had to pay £34,000 to the insurers for compensation he had received and £100,000 to his former club. His form was such that he was called up into the Wales squad for the game against Bulgaria. Then there followed a catalogue of disasters. He was sent off for handball in the FA Cup win over Birmingham and then finished the season on the sidelines with an injury. Although he had his ankle reconstructed, he could not force his way back into the Wolves' side and left to join Millwall.

Nicknamed 'Mr Consistency', he missed very few games for the Lions until, following a knee injury midway through the 1998/99 season, he was released.

Paul BODIN

Position	Left-back
Born	Paul John Bodin, Cardiff, 13 September 1964
Height	6ft 0in
Weight	10st 11lb
Clubs	Chelsea, Newport County, Cardiff City, Bath City, Swindon Town, Crystal Palace, Newcastle United, Reading, Wycombe Wanderers
Welsh Caps	23 Goals 3
	1990 v Costa Rica (won 1–0)
	1991 v Denmark (lost 0–1), v Belgium (won 3–1), v Luxembourg (won 1–0), v Republic of Ireland (lost 0–3), v Belgium (1–1), v Iceland (won 1–0) 1 goal, v Poland (0–0), v Germany (won 1–0)
	1992 v Brazil (won 1–0), v Germany (lost 1–4) 1 goal, v Luxembourg (won 1–0) 1 goal,

v Republic of Ireland (won 1–0), v Holland (lost 0–4), v Argentina (lost 0–1)

1993 v Republic of Ireland (lost 1–2), v Belgium (won 2–0), v RCS (1–1), v Faroe Islands (won 3–0)

1994 v Romania (lost 1–2), v Sweden (lost 0–2), v Estonia (won 2–1)

1995 v Albania (won 2–0)

ALONG WITH HIS SWINDON team-mates, Paul Bodin was denied top-flight football following financial irregularities committed some years earlier by the Wiltshire club. But he won the first of 23 full caps for Wales when he played against Costa Rica. He was the side's regular penalty-taker, and was named third, behind Ryan Giggs and Mark Hughes, in a 1992/93 poll of Welsh footballers.

Paul Bodin began his career as an associated schoolboy with Chelsea. After not being offered apprentice terms when he left school two years later, he joined Newport County. However, he was freed by the Somerton Park club without making a first-team appearance, and joined his home-town club. Bodin immediately won a place in the Cardiff side and made his League debut against Wrexham on the opening day of the 1982/83 season. After three seasons at Ninian Park, he won selection for Wales at under-21 level.

Having received no offers from League clubs, he joined Bath City and stayed with them for two years. He was given another chance to resurrect his League career with Newport County, of all clubs. However, within two months the Welsh club were wound up and in March 1988 Bodin joined Swindon Town for £30,000.

In his first full season with the Robins, he helped them reach the play-offs and 'qualify' for the First Division by beating Sunderland. They were then demoted to the Third Division for their past financial irregularities. His consistent displays for Swindon led to Crystal Palace paying £550,000 for his services in March 1991. But his style of play wasn't suited to the Eagles, and after a loan spell with Newcastle United he rejoined Swindon for just £225,000, ten months after leaving the County Ground.

He was one of the stars of a Swindon side that won promotion to the Premiership via the play-offs, and scored the winner from the penalty-spot in the play-off final at Wembley. Although he later suffered successive relegations with the Wiltshire club, Bodin took his total of goals in his two spells with the club to 40 in 297 games before being given a free transfer and joining Reading. After a loan spell at Wycombe Wanderers, he rejoined his former club Bath City as player-manager.

Eric YOUNG

Position	Central defender
Born	Eric Young, Singapore, 25 March 1960
Height	6ft 2in
Weight	12st 6lb
Clubs	Slough Town, Brighton and Hove Albion, Wimbledon, Crystal Palace, Wolverhampton Wanderers
Welsh Caps	21 Goals 1
	1990 v Costa Rica (won 1–0)

Singapore-born defender Eric Young was called up to the national side in May 1990 when the Wales squad was plagued by injuries. *(Lancashire Evening Post)*

1991 v Denmark (lost 0–1), v Belgium (won 3–1), v Luxembourg (won 1–0), v Republic of
    Ireland (lost 0–3), v Belgium (1–1)

1992 v Germany (lost 1–4), v Luxembourg (won 1–0), v Republic of Ireland (won 1–0),
    v Austria (1–1)

1993 v Faroe Islands (won 6–0), v Cyprus (won 1–0), v Belgium (lost 0–2), v Republic of
    Ireland (lost 1–2), v Belgium (won 2–0), v Faroe Islands (won 3–0) 1 goal

1994 v RCS (2–2), v Cyprus (won 2–0), v Romania (lost 1–2), v Norway (lost 1–3)

1996 v Albania (1–1)

BORN IN SINGAPORE OF WEST INDIAN parents, Eric Young was eligible to play for
any of the Home International countries. When in May 1990 the Wales squad was
devastated by injuries and withdrawals, he was called up to win the first of 21 caps
against Costa Rica.

Eric Young began his League career with Brighton and Hove Albion, who he joined
from Slough Town. His form for the Seagulls, where he scored ten goals in 126
League games, prompted Wimbledon manager Bobby Gould to pay £70,000 for his
services in the summer of 1987.

Young, who was a danger at set pieces during his first season with the Dons. He
netted the equaliser in the FA Cup sixth-round match against Watford. Wimbledon
went all the way to Wembley, where Young was outstanding at the heart of the
defence as they beat Liverpool 1–0. He had achieved a similar playing record for the
Dons, ten goals in 125 games, when in August1990 he left to join Crystal Palace for a
fee of £850,000.

He was a great servant for the Eagles, scoring 17 goals in 204 games before
deciding to retire. However, in September 1995 he joined Wolverhampton
Wanderers, replacing Peter Shirtliff who had left the Molineux club because of his
age. Young, who was actually older, appeared in 40 games for Wolves before being
released.

Gary SPEED

Position	Midfielder
Born	Gary Andrew Speed, Deeside, 8 September 1969
Height	5ft 10in
Weight	12st 10lb
Clubs	Leeds United, Everton, Newcastle United
Welsh Caps	80 Goals 6

1990 v Costa Rica (won 1–0)

1991 v Denmark (lost 0–1), v Luxembourg (won 1–0), v Republic of Ireland (lost 0–3),
    v Iceland (won 1–0), v Germany (won 1–0)

1992 v Brazil (won 1–0), v Germany (lost 1–4), v Luxembourg (won 1–0), v Republic of
    Ireland (won 1–0), v Romania (lost 1–5), v Holland (lost 0–4), v Argentina (lost 0–1),
    v Japan (won 1–0)

1993 v Faroe Islands (won 6–0), v Cyprus (won 1–0), v Belgium (lost 0–2), v Republic of
    Ireland (lost 1–2), v Belgium (won 2–0), v Faroe Islands (won 3–0)

1994 v RCS (2–2), v Cyprus (won 2–0), v Romania (lost 1–2), v Norway (lost 1–3), v Sweden (lost 0–2)

1995 v Albania (won 2–0), v Moldova (lost 2–3) 1 goal, v Georgia (lost 0–5), v Bulgaria (lost 0–3), v Bulgaria (lost 1–3), v Germany (1–1)

1996 v Moldova (won 1–0) 1 goal, v Germany (lost 1–2), v Italy (lost 0–3), v Switzerland (lost 0–2)

1997 v San Marino (won 6–0), v Holland (lost 1–3), v Holland (lost 1–7), v Turkey (0–0), v Republic of Ireland (0–0), v Belgium (lost 1–2) 1 goal, v Scotland (won 1–0)

1998 v Turkey (lost 4–6), v Brazil (lost 0–3), v Jamaica (0–0), v Malta (won 3–0), v Tunisia (lost 0–4)

1999 v Italy (lost 0–2), v Denmark (won 2–1), v Switzerland (lost 0–2), v Italy (lost 0–4), v Denmark (lost 0–2)

2000 v Belarus (won 2–1), v Switzerland (lost 0–2), v Qatar (won 1–0), v Finland (lost 1–2), v Brazil (lost 0–3), v Portugal (lost 0–3)

2001 v Belarus (lost 1–2) 1 goal, v Norway (1–1), v Poland (0–0), v Armenia (2–2), v Ukraine (1–1), v Poland (lost 1–2), v Ukraine (1–1)

2002 v Belarus (won 1–0), v Argentina (1–1), v Germany (won 1–0)

2003 v Finland (won 2–0), v Italy (won 2–1), v Azerbaijan (won 2–0) 1 goal, v Bosnia-Herzegovina (2–2), v Azerbaijan (won 4–0) 1 goal

2004 v Serbia-Montenegro (lost 0–1), v Italy (lost 0–4), v Finland (1–1), v Serbia-Montenegro (lost 2–3), v Russia (0–0), v Russia (lost 0–1), v Scotland (won 4–0)

GARY SPEED WAS CALLED UP FOR Wales in October 1989 as a late replacement in the squad for a World Cup qualifier at Wrexham. On that occasion he sat out the game on the substitute's bench. But at the end of the season, after helping Leeds United to the Second Division title, he made his full international debut. On 19 May 1990 he played for the Wales under-21 side against Poland at Merthyr, and the following day turned out for the full side against Costa Rica. That was the start of a long international career.

Welsh youth international Gary Speed joined Leeds United straight from school in 1987, and earned his chance in the Yorkshire club's first team in May 1989 when he played against Oldham Athletic after scoring in 12 consecutive Northern Intermediate League games.

He started the 1989/90 season on the bench but became a regular in the Championship run-in and scored a memorable goal against Sheffield United following a 60-yard dash with the ball. For Leeds, Speed had a truly remarkable League Championship-winning season in 1991/92 when his forays down the left wing brought him and others plenty of goals. Although he preferred to play in a more central role, Speed's versatility allowed him to take on a variety of roles, and towards the end of that League Championship-winning season he replaced Tony Dorigo at left-back. After a couple of lean seasons, Speed seemed to have regained all his old consistency and goalscoring ability. However, towards the end of the 1995/96 season he suffered a fractured cheekbone in a match against Port Vale, but such was his commitment to the Elland Road club that he returned to first-team action five weeks later.

It was around this time that Everton made a £3.5 million bid for Speed's services. This was turned down, but three months later the deal went through, enabling Speed

Gary Speed challenges Dragan Mladenovic of Serbia-Montenegro during the Euro 2004 Group 9 qualifying match at the Millennium Stadium, 11 October 2003. *(Getty Images)*

to join the side he had supported as a youngster. In fact, Speed was once a paper boy for former Everton and Wales captain Kevin Ratcliffe.

In his first season with the Blues, he recorded his best total of goals since winning the League Championship with Leeds in 1991/92. His total of 11 included his first senior hat-trick in the 7–1 defeat of Southampton at Goodison Park. Manager Howard Kendall named Speed as Everton's new captain for the 1997/98 season, and he responded with some of the most consistent displays of his career as he found himself employed in a more central midfield role. However, there were rumours that he was unhappy at the club he had supported as a boy, and the situation came to a head when he refused to travel to West Ham United. Soon afterwards he was sold to Newcastle United for £5.5 million, being prevented from telling his side of the story by signing a non-disclosure agreement.

He ended his first season at St James Park with a runners-up medal following the Magpies FA Cup Final defeat at the hands of Arsenal. With David Batty's return to Leeds, Speed moved into a more central midfield role. A constant threat at set pieces, he continued to score his fair share of goals as well as tracking back to help out his defence when they were under pressure. After his arrival on Tyneside, he suffered a number of injuries but he continues to be a leading player for both Newcastle and Wales, having appeared in 246 League and Cup games for the Magpies.

Jeremy GOSS

Position	Midfielder
Born	Jeremy Goss, Cyprus, 11 May 1965
Height	5ft 9in
Weight	10st 7lb
Clubs	Norwich City
Welsh Caps	9
	1991 v Iceland (won 1–0), v Poland (0–0)
	1992 v Austria (1–1)
	1994 v Cyprus (won 2–0), v Romania (lost 1–2), v Sweden (lost 0–2)
	1995 v Albania (won 2–0)
	1996 v Switzerland (lost 0–2), v San Marino (won 5–0)

AS A YOUNGSTER, JEREMY GOSS had played for the England schoolboys side, but he graduated to become a full Welsh international when he played against Iceland in May 1991. His birth in Cyprus entitled him to play for any of the home countries.

He was a member of Norwich City's FA Youth Cup Final team against Everton in 1983, and joined the Carrow Road club on a manpower work experience scheme before turning professional. Although he made his League debut against Coventry City in May 1984, he had to wait until December 1987 before winning a regular place in the Canaries' side. He then suffered a knee injury, followed by a hernia operation, both of which restricted his opportunities. However, when he did return to first-team action, the hardworking enthusiastic midfielder, could always be relied upon to give total commitment.

After he starred in the club's excellent UEFA Cup run of 1993/94, when his goals in each leg helped defeat Bayern Munich, another hernia injury disrupted his 1994/95 campaign. He was awarded a testimonial in 1994 and, although he was given little opportunity at first-team level under Martin O'Neill, he was recalled under new manager Gary Megson. At the end of the 1995/96 season, after playing in 238 first-team games, the dedicated one-club professional was released despite still figuring in Wales's plans.

Mark PEMBRIDGE

Position	Midfielder
Born	Mark Anthony Pembridge, Merthyr Tydfil, 29 November 1970
Height	5ft 8in
Weight	12st 0lb
Clubs	Luton Town, Derby County, Sheffield Wednesday, Benfica, Everton
Welsh Caps	51 Goals 6

1992 v Brazil (won 1–0), v Republic of Ireland (won 1–0) 1 goal, v Romania (lost 1–5), v Holland (lost 0–4), v Japan (won 1–0)
1993 v Belgium (lost 0–2), v Republic of Ireland (lost 1–2)
1994 v Norway (lost 1–3)
1995 v Albania (won 2–0), v Moldova (lost 2–3), v Georgia (lost 0–1)
1996 v Moldova (won 1–0), v Germany (lost 1–2), v Albania (1–1) 1 goal, v Switzerland (lost 0–2), v San Marino (won 5–0) 1 goal
1997 v San Marino (won 6–0), v Holland (lost 1–3), v Holland (lost 1–7), v Turkey (0–0), v Republic of Ireland (0–0), v Belgium (lost 1–2), v Scotland (won 1–0)
1998 v Belgium (lost 2–3) 1 goal, v Brazil (lost 0–3), v Jamaica (0–0), v Malta (won 3–0) 1 goal, v Tunisia (lost 0–4)
1999 v Denmark (won 2–1), v Belarus (won 3–2), v Switzerland (lost 0–2), v Italy (lost 0–4), v Denmark (lost 0–2)
2000 v Belarus (won 2–1), v Qatar (won 1–0), v Finland (lost 1–2)
2001 v Armenia (2–2), v Poland (lost 1–2), v Ukraine (1–1) 1 goal
2002 v Belarus (won 1–0), v Argentina (1–1), v Germany (won 1–0)
2003 v Croatia (1–1), v Finland (won 2–0), v Italy (won 2–1), v Bosnia-Herzegovina (2–2), v Azerbaijan (won 4–0), v United States (lost 0–2)
2004 v Serbia-Montenegro (lost 0–1), v Italy (lost 0–4), v Finland (1–1)

PREDOMINANTLY LEFT-FOOTED, Mark Pembridge began his career with Luton Town where his strong performances in the middle of the park led to Derby County paying £1.25 million for his services in the summer of 1992.

Capped by Wales at under-21 and 'B' international levels, Pembridge made his full international debut while with the Hatters as Wales beat Brazil 1–0.

At the Baseball Ground, he suffered from a series of niggling injuries before a more serious knee problem forced him to miss a number of matches. However, when restored to full fitness, the small, combative midfielder was most impressive. In three seasons with the Rams he scored 37 goals in 140 first-team games. He then left to play for Sheffield Wednesday, who paid £900,000 to take him to Hillsborough.

Mark Pembridge slips past Elvir Baljic of Bosnia-Herzegovina during the international friendly match between Wales and Bosnia-Herzegovina at the Millennium Stadium, 12 February 2003. *(Getty Images)*

Struggling to make an impact in his early games for the Owls, he regained his form in 1996/97 when he found the net five times in four successive games. Not a prolific scorer from midfield, he was recognised for his long-range shooting; one of his best strikes that season beat Wales and Everton keeper Neville Southall all ends up. Adding strength and power to the side, Pembridge was very much a regular in the Welsh national side during his time at Hillsborough. After his contract expired he decided to leave the Premiership and play for Portuguese giants Benfica.

The dream move turned sour because of in-fighting at the Portuguese club, and Pembridge was delighted when on the eve of the 1999/2000 season Everton paid £800,000 to bring him back to these shores. His down-to-earth qualities of hard work and determination helped the Blues maintain their Premiership status. When he was absent through injury his contribution to the Everton team was missed. In subsequent seasons a calf injury has on occasions ruled him out of matches for both club and country.

Ryan GIGGS

Position	Forward
Born	Ryan Joseph Giggs, Cardiff, 29 November 1973
Height	5ft 11in
Weight	10st 9lb
Clubs	Manchester United
Welsh Caps	48 Goals 8

1992 v Germany (lost 1–4), v Luxembourg (won 1–0), v Romania (lost 1–5)

1993 v Faroe Islands (won 6–0), v Belgium (lost 0–2), v Belgium (won 2–0) 1 goal, v RCS (1–1), v Faroe Islands (won 3–0)

1994 v RCS (2–2) 1 goal, v Cyprus (won 2–0), v Romania (lost 1–2)

1995 v Albania (won 2–0) 1 goal, v Bulgaria (lost 1–3)

1996 v Germany (lost 1–2), v Albania (1–1), v San Marino (won 5–0) 1 goal

1997 v San Marino (won 6–0), v Turkey (0–0), v Belgium (lost 1–2)

1998 v Turkey (lost 4–6), v Belgium (lost 2–3) 1 goal

1999 v Italy (lost 0–2), v Italy (lost 0–4), v Denmark (lost 0–2)

2000 v Belarus (won 2–1) 1 goal, v Finland (lost 1–2) 1 goal

2001 v Belarus (lost 1–2), v Norway (1–1), v Poland (0–0), v Ukraine (1–1), v Poland (lost 1–2), v Ukraine (1–1)

2002 v Armenia (0–0), v Norway (lost 2–3), v Argentina (1–1), v Germany (won 1–0)

2003 v Finland (won 2–0), v Italy (won 2–1), v Azerbaijan (won 2–0), v Azerbaijan (won 4–0) 1 goal

2004 v Serbia-Montenegro (lost 0–1), v Italy (lost 0–4), v Finland (1–1), v Serbia-Montenegro (lost 2–3), v Russia (0–0), v Russia (lost 0–1), v Scotland (won 4–0), v Canada (won 1–0)

RYAN GIGGS'S APPEARANCE FOR Wales as a substitute in their European Championship qualifying game against Germany in Nuremberg on 16 October 1991 made him the youngest-ever player to be capped by Wales until Ryan Green. He was just 17 years and 332 days old. Giggs's first start in an international match came in 1993 in the World Cup qualifier against Belgium, when he slammed a free kick from outside the penalty area into the roof of the net for Wales's opening goal.

Although he was born in Cardiff, Ryan Giggs was brought up in Manchester, where his father played rugby league after a successful career in rugby union. Before United snapped him up as a trainee in the summer of 1990, he was actually at Manchester City's School of Excellence and captained England schoolboys against Scotland at Old Trafford.

Although Ryan's talent was obvious, United were careful to develop him slowly. They were reluctant to throw him into the first team week after week, and it wasn't until 1991 that he became a permanent member of the United side.

He made his League debut for United as a substitute against Everton at Old Trafford in March 1991. He played just once more that season in the local derby against Manchester City on 4 May 1991, when he scored the only goal of the game.

As well as becoming Wales's youngest-ever debutant, he set another record when he became the first player to win the PFA's Young Player of the Year award in successive seasons, a feat he achieved in 1991/92 and 1992/93.

Ryan Giggs runs with the ball during the European Championships 2004 Group 9 qualifying match between Wales and Azerbaijan at the Millennium Stadium, 29 March 2003. Wales won the match 4–0. *(Getty Images)*

Giggs is blessed with the pace to outstrip most full-backs and with the two-footed ability to go inside or outside his marker whenever he chooses. He also has the confidence and the power to go on and finish his own good work when the opportunity arises, and has scored a number of spectacular goals.

In 1996, at the age of 22, he became the youngest player to appear in two double-winning sides (he won the first with United in 1994, aged 20). One of his greatest games for United came in the 1996/97 season against Porto at Old Trafford, a performance that was compared to George Best's legendary night against Benfica some 31 years earlier. In 1998/99 he scored the all-important equaliser against Juventus in the European Cup semi-final at Old Trafford before netting after a wondrous 60-yard run against Arsenal in the FA Cup semi-final replay. It prompted United manager Sir Alex Ferguson to say 'It was the goal of a genius', while Ryan described it as probably the best he has scored for the club.

There is no finer sight in football than Ryan Giggs tearing down the left flank in search of goals. At the peak of his form, and having scored his 100th goal for the club, he was an inspirational figure during United's treble-winning season in 1999, and has since helped the Reds to further success in winning three Premiership titles and the 2003/04 FA Cup Final.

Kit SYMONS

Position	Central defender
Born	Christopher Jeremiah Symons, Basingstoke, 8 March 1971
Height	6ft 2in
Weight	13st 7lb
Clubs	Portsmouth, Manchester City, Fulham, Crystal Palace
Welsh Caps	37 Goals 2

1992 v Republic of Ireland (won 1–0), v Holland (lost 0–4), v Argentina (lost 0–1), v Japan (won 1–0)

1993 v Faroe Islands (won 6–0), v Cyprus (won 1–0), v Belgium (lost 0–2), v Republic of Ireland (lost 1–2), v RCS (1–1), v Faroe Islands (won 3–0)

1994 v RCS (2–2), v Cyprus (won 2–0), v Romania (lost 1–2)

1995 v Moldova (lost 2–3), v Georgia (lost 0–5), v Bulgaria (lost 1–3), v Germany (1–1), v Georgia (lost 0–1)

1996 v Moldova (won 1–0), v Germany (lost 1–2) 1 goal, v Italy (lost 0–3), v Switzerland (lost 0–2)

1997 v Holland (lost 1–3), v Holland (lost 1–7), v Republic of Ireland (0–0), v Belgium (lost 1–2), v Scotland (won 1–0)

1999 v Italy (lost 0–2), v Denmark (won 2–1), v Belarus (won 3–2) 1 goal, v Switzerland (lost 0–2)

2000 v Qatar (won 1–0)

2001 v Poland (lost 1–2)

2002 v Armenia (0–0), v Norway (lost 2–3), v Belarus (won 1–0)

2004 v Scotland (won 4–0)

KIT SYMONS WAS A REGULAR MEMBER of the Wales side for ten years. He began his League career with Portsmouth, where his strong all-round displays in the heart of the Pompey defence made him the subject of much discussion regarding expensive transfers to Premier League clubs. As club captain he formed an effective central defensive partnership with Guy Butters. But in August 1995, after making 204 League and Cup appearances for Pompey, he joined Manchester City for £1.6 million.

In his first two seasons at Maine Road, Symons missed just three games, two through injury and one when getting married. In 1997/98 his form suffered and he was forced to relinquish the responsibility of captaincy in an effort to regain some stability in his game. However, new manager Joe Royle reinstated him. Although he continued to play with skill and foresight, he couldn't prevent City from dropping out of the Premiership.

Unexpectedly allowed to leave Maine Road, he joined Fulham and in his first season at Craven Cottage he helped them win the Second Division Championship. The club's success was undoubtedly built on the rock-like foundation at the heart of the defence, in which Symons and his fellow Welsh international Chris Coleman were outstanding.

Symons in fact found time to net 11 League goals at the other end. Yet the following season Symons found himself one of three top-class defenders – all Welsh internationals – vying for three places at the back. With Coleman and Melville appearing in all games for which they were available, he shared the third spot with Simon Morgan. When Jean Tigana took over as manager, he switched to a back four instead of a formation of three central defenders and he missed out. But he did return to the side following Chris Coleman's horrific injury suffered in a car crash.

Symons left Fulham in December 2001, joining Crystal Palace for £400,000 – Trevor Francis's first signing for the Eagles. He was soon out, falling victim to a complicated muscle strain. On his return to action, however, he quickly found his best form and even won a recall to the Wales international squad, although he failed to add to his tally of 36 caps, until being recalled for the friendly against Scotland in February 2004.

Alan NEILSON

Position	Full-back
Born	Alan Bruce Neilson, Wegberg, W. Germany, 26 September 1972
Height	5ft 11in
Weight	12st 10lb
Clubs	Newcastle United, Southampton, Fulham, Grimsby Town, Luton Town
Welsh Caps	5
	1992 v Republic of Ireland (won 1–0)
	1994 v Sweden (lost 0–2), v Estonia (won 2–1)
	1995 v Georgia (lost 0–5)
	1997 v Holland (lost 1–7)

ALAN NEILSON WAS BORN IN GERMANY while his father was serving with the RAF. He also lived in Cyprus before writing to Newcastle United for a trial. His letter was answered positively and he went on to earn a contract with the Magpies. He was capped by Wales at under-21 and full international levels while in the Magpies' reserve line-up. But he found it difficult to win a regular place in the Newcastle side, and it came as no surprise when in May 1995 he moved to Southampton for £400,000.

In his first season at The Dell Neilson found himself in and out of the Saints' side as the manager continually shuffled players and changed formations in order to secure the rearguard. An excellent passer of the ball, one of Neilson's greatest strengths is getting into forward positions to create chances for others. Despite his lack of regular first-team football, he added to his total of Welsh caps when he came back into the side for the World Cup qualifier against Holland, which Wales lost 7–1.

Midway through the 1997/98 season, Neilson became one of Ray Wilkins's first signings when he joined Fulham for £125,000. Although he impressed in his first season at Craven Cottage, he had a disappointing 1998/99 season. Even though Fulham won the Second Division Championship, he played in too few matches to warrant a medal. After that a series of hamstring-related injuries dogged his progress, and for the rest of his time with the Cottagers he was no more than a fringe player.

In four years at Craven Cottage, Neilson had made just 24 League starts, and so it was not unexpected that when his contract expired he joined Grimsby Town. However, he was unable to settle at Blundell Park and signed for Luton Town, where his experience is a great asset to a young Hatters' side.

Chris COLEMAN

Position	Defender
Born	Christopher Coleman, Swansea, 10 June 1970
Height	6ft 2in
Weight	12st 10lb
Clubs	Manchester City, Swansea City, Crystal Palace, Blackburn Rovers, Fulham
Welsh Caps	32 Goals 4

1992 v Austria (1–1) 1 goal
1993 v Republic of Ireland (lost 1–2)
1994 v Norway (lost 1–3) 1 goal, v Estonia (won 2–1)
1995 v Albania (won 2–0) 1 goal, v Moldova (lost 2–3), v Georgia (lost 0–5), v Bulgaria (lost 0–3), v Bulgaria (lost 1–3), v Germany (1–1)
1996 v Moldova (won 1–0), v Italy (lost 0–3), v Switzerland (lost 0–2), v San Marino (won 5–0)
1997 v San Marino (won 6–0)
1998 v Brazil (lost 0–3), Jamaica (0–0), v Malta (won 3–0), v Tunisia (lost 0–4)
1999 v Italy (lost 0–2), v Denmark (won 2–1), v Belarus (won 3–2) 1 goal, v Switzerland (lost 0–2), v Denmark (lost 0–2)
2000 v Belarus (won 2–1), v Switzerland (lost 0–2), v Qatar (won 1–0), v Finland (lost 1–2)
2001 v Belarus (lost 1–2), v Norway (1–1), v Poland (0–0)
2002 v Germany (won 1–0)

Chris Coleman won 24 Wales caps in a career curtailed by injury. *(Lancashire Evening Post)*

CHRIS COLEMAN SCORED ON HIS WALES debut in a 1–1 draw against Austria and in fact went on to score three goals in his first five games at full international level. Not a bad return for a defender!

Swansea-born Coleman joined his home-town club from Manchester City juniors in September 1987. In his first season with the Swans he helped them win promotion to the Third Division via the play-offs. He also won Welsh Cup winners' medals in 1989 and 1991. After four seasons at the Vetch, in which he appeared in 196 first-team games, he left to join Crystal Palace for a fee of £275,000.

Forming a good understanding with Richard Shaw, he helped the Eagles win the First Division Championship in 1993/94 and continued to impress in the Premier League. Coleman possessed all the attributes of a top-class defender, and was the subject of a number of enquiries from top clubs. In December 1995 he left Selhurst Park to join Premiership Champions Blackburn Rovers for £2.8 million.

Although he took a little time to settle in alongside Colin Hendry at the heart of the Rovers' defence, he improved rapidly as the season progressed. However, in 1996/97 an Achilles tendon injury restricted his first-team appearances, and when Roy Hodgson was appointed manager Coleman was allowed to join Kevin Keegan's Fulham for £2.1 million.

In an impressive first season at Craven Cottage, Coleman was voted by his fellow professionals into the PFA award-winning Second Division. Appointed club captain, he was selected for the PFA side for a second successive year as the Cottagers won the Second Division title. A defender of real class, he was selected for the PFA First Division side in 1999/2000. The following season he captained Fulham to the First Division Championship. The only blot on the club's fantastic season was the horrific car accident that left Chris Coleman's future career in doubt. He required a series of operations on his badly damaged leg and was still on crutches when he received the Championship trophy at the end of the season. However, he had played so well up to the time of his accident in January that he was named in the PFA Divisional awards for a fourth successive season.

Although he was determined to be back in action during the club's first season in the Premiership, it wasn't to be. The popular Coleman was appointed the Cottagers' manager in April 2003 following the departure of Jean Tigana.

Lee NOGAN

Position	Forward
Born	Lee Martin Nogan, Cardiff, 27 May 1969
Height	5ft 9in
Weight	11st 0lb
Clubs	Oxford United, Brentford, Southend United, Watford, Reading, Notts County, Grimsby Town, Darlington, Luton Town, York City
Welsh Caps	2
	1992 v Austria (1–1)
	1996 v Moldova (won 1–0)

MUCH-TRAVELLED FORWARD LEE NOGAN began his career with Oxford United. Steve Perryman, the former Spurs player, knew him at the Manor Ground, took him on loan for Brentford, and then signed him on a permanent basis for Watford when he was in charge at Vicarage Road. The highly promising forward cost the Hornets just £350,000 as Oxford were in desperate need of money immediately after Robert Maxwell's death.

Soon after his arrival at Vicarage Road, Nogan won his first full international cap when he came on as a substitute for Malcolm Allen in a 1–1 draw with Austria. Although he scored on a regular basis for Watford – 30 goals in 114 League and Cup games – he was loaned out to Southend, for a second time, prior to joining Reading in January 1995.

He proved to be a shrewd investment at Elm Park, forming a prolific striking partnership with Stuart Lovell. His goalscoring feats, including a spectacular opener at Wembley in the play-off final, earned him a recall into the Wales squad. In 1995/96 he netted his first League hat-trick in a 3–3 draw with Southend, and although not the biggest of front players he proved very difficult to mark. The following season was a disappointment for Lee Nogan. He lost confidence in front of goal and then in a loan spell with Notts County, failed to find the net in six League outings for the Meadow Lane club. A parting of the ways seemed inevitable and in the summer of 1997 he joined Grimsby Town.

In his first season at Blundell Park he helped the Mariners to return to the First Division at the first attempt via the play-offs and to win the Auto Windscreen Shield. However, the following season he found himself in and out of Alan Buckley's side and moved on to his ninth League club, Darlington.

Although he didn't find the net as much as he would have liked, he formed a good understanding with leading scorer Marco Gabbiadini. However, he was allowed to join Luton Town, where his brother Kurt had started his career. His stay at Kenilworth Road was short and he returned north to play for York City.

In his first full season at Bootham Crescent he was the club's leading scorer, notching his 100th League goal in the process before dropping back into midfield where his exceptional work-rate continues to be an important feature of the Minstermen's play.

Jason REES

Position	Winger
Born	Jason Mark Rees, Aberdare, 22 December 1969
Height	5ft 5in
Weight	10st 6lb
Clubs	Luton Town, Mansfield Town, Portsmouth, Exeter City, Cambridge United, Torquay United, Tiverton Town
Welsh Caps	1
	1992 v Austria (1–1)

SON REES HAD ONE OF THE shortest international careers ever: he played just
ree minutes of football for Wales when he came on as a substitute for Jeremy Goss
the match against Austria in Vienna in April 1992.

Rees began his career with Luton Town, where he was capped by Wales at youth
' and under-21 levels. He joined Portsmouth in the summer of 1994 following an
xtended loan period with Mansfield Town. He was a tenacious, hard-working ball
inner and, finding himself in and out of the Pompey side, he joined Exeter City on
an. He immediately made a strong impression on the left side of midfield for the
evon club. Although they intended to put in an offer for his services, it didn't
aterialise and he returned to Fratton Park for a season of reserve football.

Freed by Pompey, he moved to Cambridge United in the summer of 1997, but
ayed for just one season before joining Exeter City on a permanent basis. He was a
rtual ever-present at St James Park, where his tenacity and never-say-die attitude
ade him a great favourite with the Exeter fans. Unexpectedly released after two
ccessful seasons, he began the 2000/01 season with Tiverton Town before joining
eter's arch-rivals, Torquay United.

He confirmed his value to the Plainmoor club when he scored the opening goal in
e crucial last day victory at Barnet that secured another season of Third Division
otball for United. He continued to be a regular member of the Torquay side in
01/02. He then rejoined non-League Tiverton Town.

eri HUGHES

sition	Midfielder
rn	Ceri Morgan Hughes, Pontypridd, 26 February 1971
ight	5ft 9in
eight	11st 6lb
ubs	Luton Town, Wimbledon, Portsmouth, Cardiff City
elsh Caps	8
	1992 v Holland (lost 0–4)
	1994 v Norway (lost 1–3), v Sweden (lost 0–2), v Estonia (won 2–1)
	1996 v Albania (1–1)
	1997 v Republic of Ireland (0–0)
	1998 v Turkey (lost 4–6), v Belgium (lost 2–3)

RI HUGHES WORKED HIS WAY UP through the junior teams at Kenilworth Road
fore making his League debut for Luton Town against Aston Villa in March 1990. It
as his only appearance that season, while over the next couple of campaigns he was
and out of the Luton side. He had already won his first full international cap against
olland when he won a regular place in the Hatters' side. Unfortunately, his progress
as hampered by injuries and suspensions.

His strong battling midfield qualities were sorely missed. Although he did return to
e Luton side for virtually the whole of the 1996/97 season, he was then allowed to
ave the club and join Wimbledon for an initial fee of £400,000. Hughes had scored

20 goals in 205 games for Luton. He soon settled into the Dons' side but the suffered a hamstring strain.

In January 2000 he moved to Portsmouth for a fee of £150,000. He made a excellent contribution during the second half of the season, helping to guide the clu away from the relegation zone with a series of solid performances. However, he the began to suffer from a series of niggling injuries and was finally sidelined in Februar 2001. The versatile midfielder then left Fratton Park and joined Cardiff City, but I left Ninian Park without playing for the Bluebirds' first team.

Tony ROBERTS

Position	Goalkeeper
Born	Anthony Mark Roberts, Holyhead, 4 August 1969
Height	6ft 0in
Weight	12st 0lb
Clubs	Queen's Park Rangers, Millwall, St Albans City
Welsh Caps	2
	1993 v Republic of Ireland (lost 1–2)
	1997 v San Marino (won 6-0)

TONY ROBERTS'S TWO FULL international appearances for Wales were as substitute goalkeeper for Neville Southall.

He began his League career with Queen's Park Rangers and made his debut for tl Loftus Road club against Coventry City in December 1987, replacing the injure David Seaman. When the England international left to join Arsenal, Roberts shared tl goalkeeping duties with Jan Stejskal before becoming the club's first-choice keeper 1992/93.

It was his form this season that led to selection for the Wales squad and h international debut against the Republic of Ireland.

Tony Roberts was a good shot-stopper and an accurate long kicker from his hand He continually gave instructions to his defenders. He faced further stiff competitic from American keeper Juergen Sommer and later Lee Harper. Although he played 144 League and Cup games in a 12-year stay with Rangers, he was generally tl club's second-choice keeper. Released in the summer of 1998, he joined Millw because of an injury to Nigel Spink.

Roberts had played in only eight League games for the Lions when a serious ha injury prevented him from playing any more games in the 1998/99 seaso Allowed to leave the Den in the close season, he moved into non-League footb with St Albans City.

Nathan BLAKE

Position	Forward
Born	Nathan Alexander Blake, Cardiff, 27 January 1972
Height	5ft 11in
Weight	13st 2lb
Clubs	Newport County, Chelsea, Cardiff City, Sheffield United, Bolton Wanderers, Blackburn Rovers, Wolverhampton Wanderers
Welsh Caps	29 Goals 4

1994 v Norway (lost 1–3), v Sweden (lost 0–2)
1995 v Albania (won 2–0), v Moldova (lost 2–3) 1 goal
1996 v Germany (lost 1–2), v Italy (lost 0–3)
1998 v Turkey (lost 4–6) 1 goal
1999 v Italy (lost 0–2), v Denmark (won 2–1), v Belarus (won 3–2), v Switzerland (lost 0–2)
2000 v Belarus (won 2–1), v Switzerland (lost 0–2), v Qatar (won 1–0), v Finland (lost 1–2)
2001 v Belarus (lost 1–2), v Norway (1–1) 1 goal, v Poland (0–0), v Poland (lost 1–2) 1 goal, v Ukraine (1–1)
2002 v Norway (lost 2–3), v Czech Republic (0–0)
2003 v Italy (won 2–1)
2004 v Serbia-Montenegro (lost 0–1), v Italy (lost 0–4), v Finland (1–1), v Serbia-Montenegro (lost 2–3), v Russia (0–0, v Russia (lost 0–1)

NATHAN BLAKE STARTED OUT WITH Newport County before being taken on as a trainee by Chelsea. He returned to South Wales to his home-town club, Cardiff City, and made his League debut against Bristol Rovers in March 1990. He became a regular in the Bluebirds' side, playing in defence and midfield as well as up front.

He netted 11 goals to help Cardiff win the Third Division Championship in 1992/93. He rose to national prominence the following season when his goal knocked Manchester City out of the FA Cup as the Welsh Cup winners reached the fifth round. He had netted 35 goals in 131 League outings for Cardiff when Sheffield United paid £300,000 to take him to Bramall Lane in February 1994.

He hit five goals in seven Premiership starts for the Blades that season, but couldn't prevent them being relegated on the final day at Chelsea. He was United's leading scorer in 1994/95 with 17 League goals, and was leading the way again the following season when he made a £1.35 million move to Bolton Wanderers.

He became the club's first Welsh international since Wyn Davies when he came on as a substitute against Italy in January 1996. He then lost his place in the squad following a much publicised quarrel with manager Bobby Gould. Although he took time to settle, he soon formed a prolific strike partnership, first with John McGinlay and then with Dean Holdsworth. He was then unexpectedly allowed to join neighbours Blackburn Rovers for a fee of £4.25 million.

Having sorted his differences out with Bobby Gould, he returned to international duty. But then he suffered a spate of niggling injuries that restricted his effectiveness. Rovers' fans rarely saw his pace and power and, as his confidence slowly ebbed away, he was allowed to move to Wolverhampton Wanderers for £1.4 million.

After a good first season, he netted his first hat-trick for the Molineux club against Gillingham to help them reach the Premiership through the play-offs. To show that his international career was far from over, he came on as a substitute for Craig Bellamy in the 2–1 win over Italy in 2003 before playing in the six internationals leading up to the end of the year. At domestic level, Blake was a regular in the Wolves side until sidelined by injury early in the new year.

Jason PERRY

Position	Central defender
Born	Jason Perry, Caerphilly, 2 April 1970
Height	5ft 11in
Weight	10st 4lb
Clubs	Cardiff City, Bristol Rovers, Lincoln City, Hull City, Newport County
Welsh Caps	1
	1994 v Norway (lost 1–3)

AFTER WINNING UNDER-21 AND 'B' international honours, the strong-tackling defender was capped at full level when he played against Norway at Ninian Park in March 1994.

Jason Perry began his League career with Cardiff City, making his debut for the Bluebirds in a goalless draw at home to Exeter City in March 1987. But it was 1989/90 before he established himself as a regular first-team member. After helping the club win the Third Division Championship in 1992/93, he hardly missed a game until 1995/96, when he suffered the worst injury crisis of his career. A giant of a player though small in stature, he bounced back the following season, missing very few games in helping the club reach the play-offs. His tigerish tackling and commanding presence were sorely missed when in the summer of 1997, after almost ten years and 344 first-team appearances, he was allowed to join Bristol Rovers.

The all-action defender became a cult figure among Rovers' fans as he proved to be a wholehearted player who added steel to the club's back line. But suspensions ruined his run of appearances. Freed after just one season with the club, he moved to Lincoln City, but his stay at Sincil Bank was short. He then joined Hull City and, along with fellow new signing Jon Witney, helped to shore up the Tigers' defence. He damaged ankle ligaments the following season and found it hard to return to first-team action. Turning down a move to Chester City, he returned to South Wales to play non-League football for Newport County.

Nathan Blake of Wales gets the better of Poland's Michal Zewtakow during the 2002 World Cup qualifying Group 5 match at the Millennium Stadium, 2 June 2001. (Getty Images)

Jason BOWEN

Position	Winger
Born	Jason Peter Bowen, Merthyr Tydfil, 24 August 1972
Height	5ft 7in
Weight	11st 0lb
Clubs	Swansea City, Birmingham City, Southampton, Reading, Cardiff City
Welsh Caps	2
	1994 v Estonia (won 2–1)
	1997 v Holland (lost 1–7)

HAVING ALREADY BEEN CAPPED by Wales at schoolboy, youth, under-21 and 'B' levels, Jason Bowen's form for Swansea led to his first full international cap when he played in a 2–1 win over Estonia in Tallinn in May 1994.

Able to play in midfield or on the wing, Jason Bowen began his career with Swansea. After a couple of outings as a substitute, he made his full first-team debut in a 2–1 FA Cup win over arch-rivals Cardiff City in November 1991. With his speed taking him past defenders and into shooting positions, he became a great favourite with the Vetch crowd. In March 1993 he scored his first hat-trick for the club in 4–2 home win over Chester City. He helped the Swans win the Autoglass Trophy in 1994, and the following season he netted another hat-trick in a 7–0 Welsh Cup win over Taffs Well. But in the close season, after scoring 37 goals in 160 games, he was transferred to Birmingham City for £350,000.

After making an immediate impact at St Andrew's, scoring a number of spectacular goals, his progress was hampered by a series of unfortunate injuries. When he recovered full fitness, he found himself out of favour and, after a loan spell with Southampton, he joined Reading for a fee of £200,000.

His stay with the Royals was brief and he returned to South Wales to play for Cardiff City, helping the Bluebirds gain promotion from the Third Division in his first season at Ninian Park. Although the 1999/2000 season was a disappointing one for Cardiff, Bowen ended the campaign as the club's leading scorer with 17 goals. He is talented player with pace, movement and good ball control used in a role just behind the front two, and his balance and skill can pull defences apart.

Ryan JONES

Position	Midfielder
Born	Ryan Anthony Jones, Sheffield, 23 July 1973
Height	6ft 1in
Weight	13st 10lb
Clubs	Sheffield Wednesday, Scunthorpe United
Welsh Caps	1
	1994 v Estonia (won 2–1)

LEFT-SIDED MIDFIELDER RYAN JONES was strong in the tackle and possessed a great shot. He began his League career with his home-town club Sheffield Wednesday after joining the Owls as a trainee in the summer of 1989. He came on in leaps and bounds from an occasional member of the club's reserve side in 1991/92 to a regular in the first-team squad towards the end of the 1992/93 season.

Jones made his Premier League debut for Wednesday against Coventry City in March 1993 and impressed in a further eight games that season. Rated very highly by the club, he then had a very disappointing time of it. Over the next couple of seasons he was never really free from injury although, after representing Wales at under-21 and 'B' levels, he won a full international cap in a 2–1 defeat of Estonia.

Having come back from injury, he struggled initially to ease his way back to fitness and at the same time re-establish himself in the Wednesday first team. He was loaned out to Scunthorpe United and scored three goals in 11 outings for the Irons despite finding it difficult to adapt to lower-division football. On his return to Hillsborough, he continued to play for the club's reserve side for a couple of seasons before he was forced into premature retirement.

Adrian WILLIAMS

Position	Central defender
Born	Adrian Williams, Reading, 16 August 1971
Height	6ft 2in
Weight	13st 2lb
Clubs	Reading, Wolverhampton Wanderers
Welsh Caps	13 Goals 1
	1994 v Estonia (won 2–1)
	1995 v Albania (won 2–0), v Moldova (lost 2–3), v Germany (1–1), v Georgia (lost 0–1)
	1996 v Moldova (won 1–0), v Italy (lost 0–3)
	1998 v Jamaica (0–0), v Malta (won 3–0)
	1999 v Italy (lost 0–2), v Denmark (won 2–1) 1 goal, v Italy (lost 0–4)
	2003 v United States (lost 0–2)

ADRIAN WILLIAMS WON HIS 13th international cap against the United States in 2003. He was the first player to progress from Reading's Centre of Excellence to full international level.

The Reading club captain was a powerful and dominant centre-back, and was sought by many Premier clubs. Williams played in every position for the club including goalkeeper. During his first spell with the Royals he netted one of the goals in the 1995 First Division play-off final against Bolton Wanderers. However, it wasn't enough to take the Berkshire club into the Premiership. Following another good season in 1995/96, Williams left Elm Park to join his former manager Mark McGhee at Wolverhampton Wanderers, who paid £750,000 for his services.

He had played in only a handful of games for the Molineux club when he damaged a cruciate knee ligament on the club's tour of Austria and missed most of the 1996/97 season. On his return to first-team action, he was called into the Wales squad for the games against Italy and Denmark, scoring his first goal at this level in the 2–1 defeat of the Danes. However, he was injured during his stay with the squad, rupturing a disc in his neck.

Powerful and commanding at the back, Williams could also be used effectively in midfield or up front, where his physique often allowed him to get into dangerous areas.

After three injury-ravaged seasons at Molineux, he had a couple of loan spells with Reading before rejoining the club on a permanent basis.

In his first season back with his former club, now playing at the Madejski Stadium, he helped them reach the play-off final against Walsall at the Millennium but was disappointed to be on the losing side. In 2001/02 Williams won a Second Division runners-up medal as the Royals were promoted to the First Division. The following season he became the club's captain, and has since proved he still has all the embition, fitness and enthusiasm of a youngster.

Vinnie JONES

Position	Midfielder
Born	Vincent Peter Jones, Watford, 5 January 1965
Height	5ft 11in
Weight	11st 10lb
Clubs	Wealdstone, Wimbledon, Leeds United, Sheffield United, Chelsea, Queen's Park Rangers
Welsh Caps	9
	1995 v Bulgaria (lost 0–3), v Bulgaria (lost 1–3), v Germany (1–1), v Georgia (lost 0–1)
	1996 v Switzerland (lost 0–2)
	1997 v Holland (lost 1–7), v Turkey (0–0), v Republic of Ireland (0–0), v Belgium (lost 1–2)

VINNIE JONES QUALIFIED TO PLAY for Wales through his grandparents. He represented his country on nine occasions but was dismissed in only his fourth international against Georgia. Jones captained both Wimbledon and Wales, displaying great motivational skills.

He was a bricklayer playing part-time football for Wealdstone when Dave Bassett signed him for Wimbledon in November 1986. He made his debut for the Dons at Nottingham Forest. The following week, in only his second game for the club, he scored the winning goal against Manchester United – all this from a man who the previous month could not get a game for Wealdstone. Jones went on to score four goals from midfield in his first eight games for the Dons. But, also in his early days with the club, he was sent off three times, including in a friendly on the Isle of Wight! Although he shared the No. 4 shirt with Vaughan Ryan in 1987/88, he played in all of the FA Cup rounds, which culminated with the Dons beating Liverpool in the final.

Jones, who was continuously dogged by disciplinary problems, could not manage full set of appearances in 1988/89. But it was still a surprise when Bobby Gould sold him to Leeds United in the summer of 1989 for a fee of £650,000.

Dubbed 'Psycho' by the media, Jones cleaned up his act at Elland Road, where his enormous throw-ins were a regular source of goals for the Yorkshire club during the 1989/90 Second Division Championship winning campaign. The arrival of Gary McAllister saw Jones lose his first-team place, and his former manager Dave Bassett

Wimbledon's Vinnnie Jones, who qualified to play for Wales through his grandparents, was sent off in the match against Georgia. *(Lancashire Evening Post)*

signed him for Sheffield United for £700,000. He was soon appointed captain at Bramall Lane and helped the Blades climb up the table. It was therefore something of a puzzle when Bassett agreed to transfer Jones to Chelsea in the second week of the 1991/92 season.

His career came full circle when in September 1992 he was transferred to Wimbledon. His arrival at Selhurst Park was clouded by his involvement in the video 'Soccer's Hard Men', for which he was later fined £20,000 by the FA for bringing the game into disrepute.

His first game in his second spell with the club was against Blackburn Rovers, a match marred by three players – Jones among them – being sent off. He was later hauled up before the FA after collecting ten yellow cards and a red one. A mis-understanding over the time of the hearing saw him arrive almost an hour and a half late, after which he was suspended indefinitely. The FA later lifted the ban. He took his tally of goals for Wimbledon to 25 in 322 first-team games before leaving the Dons to become player-coach with Queen's Park Rangers.

Having earlier been involved in public speaking at universities and presenting his own chat show on television, Jones left the game to pursue a career in films. He has been involved in a number of box office hits after making his debut in *Lock, Stock and Two Smoking Barrels* (1998).

John HARTSON

Position	Forward
Born	John Hartson, Swansea, 5 April 1975
Height	5ft 11in
Weight	12st 0lb
Clubs	Luton Town, Arsenal, West Ham United, Wimbledon, Coventry City, Glasgow Celtic
Welsh Caps	40 Goals 11

1995 v Bulgaria (lost 1–3), v Germany (1–1), v Georgia (lost 0–1)
1996 v Moldova (won 1–0), v Switzerland (lost 0–2)
1997 v Holland (lost 1–7), v Turkey (0–0), v Republic of Ireland (0–0), v Belgium (lost 1–2), v Scotland (won 1–0) 1 goal
1998 v Belgium (lost 2–3), v Jamaica (0–0), v Malta (won 3–0) 1 goal, v Tunisia (lost 0–4)
1999 v Switzerland (lost 0–2), v Italy (lost 0–4), v Denmark (lost 0–2)
2000 v Switzerland (lost 0–2)
2001 v Norway (1–1), v Poland (0–0), v Armenia (2–2) 2 goals, v Ukraine (1–1) 1 goal, v Poland (lost 1–2), v Ukraine (1–1)
2002 v Norway (lost 2–3), v Belarus (won 1–0) 1 goal, v Argentina (1–1), v Czech Republic (0–0), v Germany (won 1–0)
2003 v Croatia (1–1), v Finland (won 2–0) 1 goal, v Italy (won 2–1), v Azerbaijan (won 2–0) 1 goal, v Bosnia-Herzegovina (2–2) 1 goal, v Azerbaijan (won 4–0) 1 goal
2004 v Italy (lost 0–4), v Finland (1–1), v Serbia-Montenegro (lost 2–3) 1 goal, v Russia (0–0), v Russia (lost 0–1)

ONE OF WALES'S MOST PASSIONATE players, John Hartson is a big, bustling centre forward. He won the first of his 40 caps against Bulgaria in Sofia in March 1995.

ohn Hartson celebrates after scoring the second equalising goal during the international riendly match between Wales and Bosnia-Herzegovina on 12 February 2003. The match ended in a 2–2 draw. *(Getty Images)*

He began his career with Luton Town, where his early performances led to Welsh under-21 honours. However, after two seasons at Kenilworth Road, he was unsure of a regular place in the Hatters' side and joined Arsenal for a fee of £2.5 million. In fact, the Gunners broke the British record fee for a teenage transfer. Standing in for the injured Alan Smith, Hartson soon demonstrated that it had been money well spent. It was while he was at Highbury that he won his first full cap. But, with Ian Wright and Dennis Bergkamp scoring regularly, his first-team opportunities at Arsenal were limited, although he did score their goal in the 1995 European Cup Winners Cup Final against Zaragoza. As well, his disciplinary record was poor and in February 1997 Arsene Wenger accepted West Ham United's offer of £5 million for Hartson's services.

It was the last throw of the dice for the beleaguered Harry Redknapp but, happily for Hammers' fans, Hartson got among the goals to help the club on their way to Premiership safety. In 1997/98, his first full season at Upton Park, Hartson scored 24 goals, including his first hat-trick in club football as the Hammers beat Huddersfield Town in the Coca Cola Cup. The following season the goals dried up and, with a well-publicised training ground quarrel with Eyal Berkovic not helping his cause, he parted company with the club.

Hartson joined Wimbledon for a fee of £7 million, the Dons smashing the club transfer record by nearly £5 million. Much was made of Joe Kinnear's decision to buy Hartson. But the big Welshman, who initially had to miss matches through suspension, came good towards the end of the 1998/99 season by scoring some vital goals and thus ensuring the Dons safety. A cartilage operation then forced him to miss much of the following season, when the club lost their top-flight status. On his return, a proposed move to Spurs fell through before he was again sidelined, this time requiring a hernia operation. Despite being appointed club captain, he left Wimbledon in February 2001, joining Coventry City. Although he scored six goals in his 12 outings for the Sky Blues, he couldn't keep them in the Premiership.

In the close season, Hartson joined Glasgow Celtic and, in his first season with the Scottish giants, formed a prolific strike force with Henrik Larsen. Hartson scored 19 goals including a hat-trick in a 5–0 defeat of Dundee United, and helped the Bhoys win the Scottish Premier League. Though injuries hampered his progress in 2003–04, he was outstanding in the first half of a season that saw the Parkhead club retain the title.

John CORNFORTH

Position	Midfielder
Born	John Michael Cornforth, Whitley Bay, 7 October 1967
Height	6ft 1in
Weight	11st 5lb
Clubs	Sunderland, Doncaster Rovers, Shrewsbury Town, Lincoln City, Swansea City, Birmingham City, Wycombe Wanderers, Peterborough United, Cardiff City, Scunthorpe United, Exeter City
Welsh Caps	2
	1995 v Bulgaria (lost 1–3), v Georgia (lost 0–1)

JOHN CORNFORTH PLAYED HIS EARLY football for Sunderland. When he couldn't hold down a regular first-team place, he had loan spells with Doncaster Rovers hrewsbury Town and Lincoln City. He joined Swansea City for a fee of £50,000 in the ummer of 1991.

He had the misfortune to break his leg during the early stages of his time at the etch Field, but recovered to become a major influence in the Swansea midfield. He ecame the first Swansea captain in the history of the club to lead a team out at Vembley in the Autoglass Trophy Final against Huddersfield Town, where he scored wansea's first goal in the penalty shoot-out. His outstanding passing skills led to full nternational honours for Wales in 1995 when he played against Bulgaria and Georgia.

In 1995/96 Cornforth suffered a knee injury, and his absence coincided with the lub's slide down the Second Division table and eventual relegation. He had scored 18 oals in 193 games for the Swans when in March 1996 he was allowed to join irmingham City for £350,000.

Unable to establish himself at St Andrew's, he was transferred to Wycombe Vanderers. But in 1997/98, when further payments of the £50,000 fee were due to irmingham City, he was dropped. A proposed return to Swansea did not materialise. lthough Cornforth had a loan spell at Peterborough United, he remained with Vycombe until joining Cardiff City in the summer of 1999. His stay at Ninian Park vas brief, and was followed by an equally brief spell with Scunthorpe United. He then oined Exeter City, becoming their player-coach before retiring at the end of the 000/01 season.

teve JENKINS

osition	Right-back
orn	Stephen Robert Jenkins, Merthyr Tydfil, 16 July 1972
eight	5ft 11in
Veight	12st 3lb
lubs	Swansea City, Huddersfield Town, Birmingham City, Cardiff City
Velsh Caps	16
	1996 v Germany (lost 1–2), v Albania (1–1), v Italy (lost 0–3)
	1997 v Holland (lost 1–3), v Turkey (0–0), v Scotland (won 1–0)
	1998 v Turkey (lost 4–6), v Belgium (lost 2–3), v Brazil (lost 0–3), v Jamaica (0–0)
	1999 v Italy (lost 0–4), v Denmark (lost 0–2)
	2001 v Poland (lost 1–2), v Ukraine (1–1)
	2002 v Armenia (0–0), v Norway (lost 2–3)

TEVE JENKINS IS A SOLID DEFENDER who turned professional in the summer of 1991 fter a two-year apprenticeship with Swansea City. He made his debut for the Swans as substitute against Cambridge United in the last game of the 1990/91 season. In his arly days with the club, he played in midfield but was later converted into a right-ack. In just over five seasons at the Vetch, the dependable Jenkins played in 215 first-eam games, his only goal coming in a 1–1 home draw against Hartlepool United in anuary 1991. Having won Welsh youth and under-21 honours, he made his first full ppearance for Wales against Germany at Ninian Park in October 1995. It was an mpressive debut, but shortly afterwards, after appearing in 215 games, he left the

Vetch to join Huddersfield Town for a ridiculously low tribunal judgement set £275,000.

On his debut for the Yorkshire club he was played on the right wing and scored in 3–2 home win over Norwich City. He then settled into the Terriers' side at right-back Over the next couple of seasons he not only established himself at international lev but was also rewarded with the captaincy of Huddersfield Town. His progress was the hampered by a series of injuries and suspensions, but in 1998/99 he enjoyed one his best seasons of League football. Despite a couple of sendings-off, he gave solid an lively performances throughout the campaign, and was rewarded with continu involvement with the Welsh national side. He was called into the Wales squad on thr separate occasions and made captain of the 'B' team, only to miss all three matches do to injury problems.

Following a loan spell with Birmingham City, it seemed that Jenkins would I joining the St Andrew's club. But he returned to the McAlpine Stadium to take his to number of appearances for Huddersfield to 295 before leaving to join Cardiff C towards the end of the 2002/03 season.

Paul MARDON

Position	Central defender
Born	Paul Jonathan Mardon, Bristol, 14 September 1969
Height	6ft 0in
Weight	11st 10lb
Clubs	Bristol City, Doncaster Rovers, Birmingham City, West Bromwich Albion, Oldham Athletic, Plymouth Argyle, Wrexham
Welsh Caps	1
	1996 v Germany (lost 1–2)

A FAST, STRONG, ELEGANT CENTRAL defender, Paul Mardon started his career und manager Terry Cooper at Bristol City. He then moved with his boss to Birmingha City. His performances for the St Andrew's club attracted the attention of Liverpo manager Graeme Souness, but Mardon missed out on a possible move to Anfield I injuring his ankle while on trial with the Merseyside club.

In November 1993 Mardon joined West Bromwich Albion and slotted straig into a fragile Baggies' defence. But he arrived at the Hawthorns with a reputatic from St Andrew's as a defender prone to making expensive mistakes, which too him a couple of years to live down. While he was at the Hawthorns, not only d he win his one full international cap when he replaced Steve Jenkins after 7 minutes of the match against Germany at Cardiff Arms Park, but his inju problems began.

He was a dominant player, powerful in the air, sound and capable on the groun He formed a fine partnership at the heart of the Albion defence with Paul Rav until a facial injury forced him to miss the remainder of that 1994/95 season. Aft that, a succession of injuries limited his first-team appearances, and he had a lo spell with Oldham Athletic in an effort to get match fit. Mardon represented t

Welsh 'B' team that played Northern Ireland midway through the 1998/99 season. He later had loan spells with Plymouth Argyle and Wrexham.

Mardon had made just 139 League appearances for the Baggies in eight seasons at the Hawthorns. He was unable to resurrect his career, and announced his retirement from the game following recurring knee problems.

Gareth TAYLOR

Position	Forward
Born	Gareth Keith Taylor, Weston-super-Mare, 25 February 1973
Height	6ft 2in
Weight	13st 8lb
Clubs	Southampton, Bristol Rovers, Crystal Palace, Sheffield United, Manchester City, Port Vale, Queen's Park Rangers, Burnley
Welsh Caps	14 Goals 1
	1996 v Albania (1–1), v Italy (lost 0–3), v Switzerland (lost 0–2)
	1997 v San Marino (won 6–0), v Holland (lost 1–7), v Republic of Ireland (0–0)
	1998 v Belgium (lost 2–3), v Jamaica (0–0)
	2002 v Czech Republic (0–0)
	2003 v Croatia (1–1), v Bosnia-Herzegovina (2–2), v United States (lost 0–2)
	2004 v Scotland (won 4–0) 1 goal, v Hungary (won 2–1)

A REGULAR SCORER THROUGHOUT his Football League career, Gareth Taylor has yet to find the net for Wales at full international level, but he has come close on a number of occasions.

Gareth Taylor began his career with Bristol Rovers where, as a result of his displays, he became a regular member of the Welsh under-21 side. An effective targetman and goalscorer, he made a remarkable recovery from a career-threatening knee injury before moving to Crystal Palace for £750,000. But he failed to settle at Selhurst Park, and moved to Sheffield United in the deal that saw Dave Tuttle and Carl Veart move in the opposite direction.

Taylor formed a good strike partnership with Andy Walker and later Jan-Aage Fjortoft. His sheer physical presence brought him 12 goals in his first season at Bramall Lane. Following the arrival of Brian Deane, Taylor found himself relegated to the substitute's bench for much of the 1997/98 season, and was linked with moves to Huddersfield Town, Stoke City, Utrecht, Genoa and Sochaux before he joined Manchester City for a fee of £400,000 in November 1998.

Settling in quickly at Maine Road, Taylor struck up a good understanding with Shaun Goater. Although he scored fewer goals than he would have liked, he created problems for the opposition, which in turn relieved other strikers. After being pushed further down the pecking order, he had loan spells with Port Vale, Queen's Park Rangers and Burnley before he joined the Clarets on a permanent basis in February 2001.

His striking partnership with Ian Moore was a key factor in the Turf Moor club's revival towards the end of the 2000/01 season, and the following season he was the club's leading scorer, netting a hat trick in the 7–4 defeat by Watford!

Robbie SAVAGE

Position   Midfielder
Born   Robert William Savage, Wrexham, 18 October 1974
Height   6ft 1in
Weight   11st 11lb
Clubs   Manchester United, Crewe Alexandra, Leicester City, Birmingham City
Welsh Caps   35   Goals 2
                1996 v Albania (1–1), v Switzerland (lost 0–2), v San Marino (won 5–0)
                1997 v Republic of Ireland (0–0), v Scotland (won 1–0)

1998 v Turkey (lost 4–6) 1 goal, v Belgium (lost 2–3), v Jamaica (0–0), v Tunisia (lost 0–4)
1999 v Italy (lost 0–2), v Denmark (won 2–1), v Belarus (won 3–2), v Switzerland
    (lost 0–2)
2000 v Switzerland (lost 0–2), v Finland (lost 1–2), v Brazil (lost 0–3)
2001 v Belarus (lost 1–2), v Norway (1–1), v Poland (0–0), v Poland (lost 1–2)
2002 v Armenia (0–0), v Norway (lost 2–3) 1 goal, v Argentina (1–1), v Czech Republic
    (0–0), v Germany (won 1–0)
2003 v Finland (won 2–0), v Italy (won 2–1), v Bosnia-Herzegovina (2–2), v Azerbaijan (won 4–0)
2004 v Serbia-Montenegro (lost 0–1), v Italy (lost 0–4), v Russia (0–0), v Russia (lost 0–1),
    Scotland (won 4–0), v Hungary (won 2–1)

ROBBIE SAVAGE HAS WON 35 full caps for Wales. Despite occasionally being singled out for rough treatment by opponents, his energy levels and will to win have inspired those around him at both club and country to greater heights.

He was a member of Manchester United's FA Youth Cup-winning team of 1992. He left Old Trafford in the summer of 1994 to join Crewe Alexandra and, although in his first season at Gresty Road he made only a handful of appearances, he represented Wales at under-21 level. His early games for Crewe saw him playing up front, but in 1995/96 he settled down in a new midfield role and won the first of his full international caps when he played against Albania. In 1996/97 he helped Crewe reach the play-offs, the aftermath of which saw the club reach the First Division for the first time in its history. Even though he had re-signed for Alex during the close season, he started the 1997/98 campaign at Leicester City after the then Filbert Street club had paid £400,000 for his services.

He started the season on the bench, but soon forced his way into the Leicester side with a series of committed performances. During the 1999/2000 season, the Leicester midfielder showed some of his best-ever form. Not only did he provide the pin-point cross for Matt Elliott to head home the winner against Aston Villa in the Worthington Cup semi-final, but he slotted home

Robbie Savage is tackled by Italy's Christian Panucci during the Euro 2004 Group 9 qualifying match between Wales and Italy, 16 October 2002. Wales won the match 2–1. *(Getty Images)*

vital penalties in two shoot-outs and was an important contributor to the Foxes' victory in the League Cup Final at Wembley. He continued to be inspirational at Leicester, where he became a cult figure. Although in 2000/01 he had to undergo a cartilage operation, he was back playing just 17 days after going under the surgeon's knife. He went on to appear in 205 games for the Foxes. Following their relegation from the Premiership, he joined Birmingham City for £2.5 million. Savage provided a real heartbeat to the Blues side on their return to top-flight football and was deservedly voted Birmingham's Player of the Season in his first campaign at St Andrew's. Since then he has continued to impress with his wholehearted displays, helping the Blues consolidate their place in the top flight.

John ROBINSON

Position	Winger
Born	John Robert Campbell Robinson, Bulawayo, Zimbabwe, 29 August 1971
Height	5ft 10in
Weight	11st 7lb
Clubs	Brighton and Hove Albion, Charlton Athletic, Cardiff City
Welsh Caps	30 Goals 3

1996 v Albania (1–1), v Switzerland (lost 0–2), v San Marino (won 5–0)

1997 v San Marino (won 6–0) 1 goal, v Holland (lost 1–3), v Holland (lost 1–7), v Republic of Ireland (0–0), v Scotland (won 1–0)

1998 v Belgium (lost 2–3), v Brazil (lost 0–3)

1999 v Italy (lost 0–2), v Denmark (won 2–1), v Belarus (won 3–2) 1 goal, v Switzerland (lost 0–2), v Italy (lost 0–4), v Denmark (lost 0–2)

2000 v Belarus (won 2–1), v Switzerland (lost 0–2), v Qatar (won 1–0) 1 goal, v Finland (lost 1–2), v Brazil (lost 0–3), v Portugal (lost 0–3)

2001 v Belarus (lost 1–2), v Norway (1–1), v Poland (0–0), v Armenia (2–2)

2002 v Norway (lost 2–3), v Belarus (won 1–0), v Argentina (1–1), v Czech Republic (0–0)

WHEN JOHN ROBINSON ANNOUNCED his retirement at the start of the 2002/03 season, his total of 30 full international caps for Wales put him second in Charlton Athletic's all-time international honours list.

The tricky winger who can play on either side, although predominantly right-footed, began his career with Brighton and Hove Albion. He possessed a good burst of speed and was a good crosser of the ball. He had appeared in 73 games for the Seagulls when Charlton Athletic paid £75,000 for his services in September 1992.

Able to perform equally well at right-back as on either flank, it was in this position that he made an encouraging start for Wales and ended that 1995/96 season as the Addicks' Player of the Year. Over the next couple of seasons, Robinson scored vital goals for the club. But midway through the 1997/98 season he suffered a hairline fracture of his right leg, which kept him out of the Charlton side until the play-off final at Wembley, when he came on as a substitute. His performances that season for both club and country were recognised by his fellow professionals when they voted him into the award-winning PFA First Division select side.

John Robinson on the ball during the 2002 World Cup qualifier against Belarus played at the Millennium Stadium, 6 October 2001. Wales won the match 1–0. (Getty Images)

Damaged ankle ligaments restricted his first-team appearances the following season. However, in 1999/2000 he was not only selected again for the PFA award-winning First Division side but won a First Division Championship medal as Charlton returned to top-flight action. That season also saw Robinson become the most capped Charlton player when he made his 20th appearance for Wales (the club record is now held by the Republic of Ireland's Mark Kinsella).

Although he found his first-team opportunities limited at The Valley, John Robinson took his total of appearances to 382 before being released in the summer of 2003, and joining Cardiff City, where his performances helped the Bluebirds retain their First Division status.

Marcus BROWNING

Position	Midfielder
Born	Marcus Trevor Browning, Bristol, 22 April 1971
Height	6ft 0in
Weight	12st 10lb
Clubs	Bristol Rovers, Hereford United, Huddersfield Town, Gillingham, Bournemouth
Welsh Caps	5
	1996 v Italy (lost 0–3), v San Marino (won 5–0)
	1997 v San Marino (won 6–0), v Holland (lost 1–3), v Scotland (won 1–0)

A CULTURED MIDFIELD PLAYER, Marcus Browning began his career with his home-town club, Bristol Rovers, where his ball-winning qualities and promptings improved over his first few seasons with the club. A contractual dispute that was eventually settled during the early part of the 1994/95 season clearly unsettled him, but by the end of the season he was back to his best. His consistent performances led to his first full international cap when he played against Italy in Terni.

Although not a prolific scorer from midfield for Rovers, he did score a most unusual goal during the 1996/97 season in the match against Brentford. Bees' keeper Kevin Dearden, who believed he had heard the referee's whistle for an infringement, placed the ball for the kick and Browning promptly despatched it into the empty net to claim an important victory for the Pirates.

Browning was the subject of an unsuccessful bid by Wimbledon, but left Rovers to join Huddersfield Town in February 1997, the Terriers paying £500,000 for his services. However, during his first five months at the McAlpine Stadium he was sidelined by a troublesome hamstring injury. Although he forced his way back into the side, the industrious midfielder suffered a spate of niggling injuries. He was unable to win back his first-team place on a regular basis, and joined Gillingham on loan.

After just 69 minutes of his debut for the Gills at Manchester City, he suffered a cruciate ligament injury. Manager Tony Pulis kept a check on his fitness, and in March 1998 he arrived at the Priestfield Stadium on a permanent basis. Further injuries then restricted him to just a handful of appearances before in 2000/01 he won a regular place following injuries to Andy Hessenthaler and Ty Gooden. The following season he was back to his best form and there was even talk of a return to the Wales squad. But, unexpectedly, at the end of that campaign he was allowed to leave and join Bournemouth.

His experience in the middle of the park helped the young Cherries' side win promotion via the play-offs. During the course of the season he had the unusual experience of taking over in goal on two occasions.

Danny COYNE

Position	Goalkeeper
Born	Daniel Coyne, Prestatyn, 27 August 1973
Height	5ft 11in
Weight	13st 0lb
Clubs	Tranmere Rovers, Grimsby Town, Leicester City
Welsh Caps	2
	1996 v Switzerland (lost 0–2)
	2002 v Czech Republic (0–0)
	2004 v Hungary (won 2–1), v Norway (0–0), v Canada (won 1–0)

A PRODUCT OF TRANMERE ROVERS' impressive youth policy, goalkeeper Danny Coyne made his League debut for the Prenton Park club at Peterborough United in May 1993. But it was only towards the end of the 1994/95 season that he replaced the long-serving Eric Nixon on a regular basis. His bravery and safe handling brought the Premier League scouts flocking to Prenton Park, and his consistency between the posts led to his full international debut for Wales against Switzerland at Lugano in April 1996.

On New Year's Day 1997 he was involved in an accidental clash in the match at West Bromwich Albion and was left with badly torn neck ligaments. Thereafter he was plagued by a series of persistent injuries and, even when he had recovered full fitness, he found himself second choice behind Steve Simonsen. When Simonsen left to join Everton, Coyne's return was short-lived due to the recurrence of a persistent groin injury. A free agent under the Bosman ruling, Coyne decided to leave Tranmere and in the summer of 1999 he joined Grimsby Town.

His first season at Blundell Park was almost marred in bizarre circumstances when he received a three-match ban for an alleged incident at Crystal Palace, which was reported by two police officers but went unnoticed by any of the crowd or the Palace player concerned. This penalty was suspended pending an appeal and was ultimately quashed.

Coyne was a fine shot-stopper with excellent positioning and lightning reactions. He became the first Grimsby player for ten years to win the Player of the Year award in successive seasons, and in 2001/02 he won his second cap when he came on as a substitute keeper in the match against the Czech Republic. Transferred to Leicester City in the summer of 2003, Coyne found it difficult to replace Ian Walker, but added to his international appearances late in the season.

Andy LEGG

Position	Left-winger
Born	Andrew Legg, Neath, 28 July 1966
Height	5ft 8in
Weight	10st 7lb
Clubs	Briton Ferry, Swansea City, Notts County, Birmingham City, Ipswich Town, Reading, Peterborough United, Cardiff City
Welsh Caps	6
	1996 v Switzerland (lost 0–2), v San Marino (won 5–0)
	1997 v Holland (lost 1–3), v Republic of Ireland (0–0)
	1999 v Denmark lost 0–2)
	2001 v Armenia (2–2)

ANDY LEGG IS A FAST AND SKILFUL winger who enjoys taking on defenders. He won the first of his six full international caps against Switzerland in 1996. He began his career with Briton Ferry before joining Swansea City in August 1988. He was an important member of the Swans' side for five seasons, scoring 38 goals in 207 League and Cup games before leaving the Vetch to join Notts County for a fee of £275,000.

After appearing in 126 first-team games in two and a half seasons at Meadow Lane, he was transferred to Birmingham City along with Paul Devlin and soon settled down on the left side of the St Andrew's club's midfield. A long throw specialist, his world record throw of 44.54 metres was beaten in 1996/97 by Tranmere's Dave Challinor.

His form with Birmingham was such that he won four of his Welsh caps while with the Midlands club. But midway through the 1997/98 season he failed to agree terms with Birmingham and, after a loan spell with Ipswich Town, he joined Reading in February 1998 for £75,000.

Early the following season, after failing to impress the manager, he was placed on the transfer list and excluded from training with the other players. He then spent a month on loan with Peterborough, where he was hugely popular, before returning to South Wales with Cardiff City.

Legg was given a great reception by Bluebirds' fans when showing total commitment to the team and an ability to take on the opposition. He won the 1999/2000 season Player of the Year award. Reportedly taking a big pay cut to join the Ninian Park club, he switched to playing as a sweeper the following season and again won the club's Player of the Year award. Recalled to the national side for the match against Armenia, Legg was also made the Cardiff club captain. Although many people thought his playing days were coming to an end, he played an important part in Cardiff's promotion to the First Division in the 2002/03 season.

Simon DAVIES

Position	Midfielder
Born	Simon Ithel Davies, Winsford, 23 April 1974
Height	5ft 11in
Weight	10st 2lb
Clubs	Manchester United, Exeter City, Huddersfield Town, Luton Town, Macclesfield, Rochdale, Bangor City
Welsh Caps	1
	1996 v Switzerland (lost 0–2)

SIMON DAVIES IS A FORMER MANCHESTER United youth team captain. He made a great impression on Alan Ball when he was on loan at Exeter City in December 1993. He made a bigger name for himself at Old Trafford when he scored a wonderful goal against Galatasaray in the European Cup the following season. Although he remained an active member of the United squad, he mostly appeared as a substitute in the Premiership or European Cup.

Possessing both skill and vision in his footballing make-up, he was recognised by Wales for the Switzerland game, winning his first full cap along with three other newcomers.

As he continued to find first-team chances hard to come by at Old Trafford, he had a further loan spell, this time with Huddersfield Town, before joining Luton Town for a cut-price fee of £150,000.

He made a poor start to his career at Kenilworth Road, finding it difficult to react to the pace of the game. After an initial run in the side, he was used primarily as a substitute. Continuing to suffer from a loss of form and a number of minor injuries, he left the Hatters to continue his career with Macclesfield Town. He was the subject of a bizarre sending-off while playing for the Silkmen against York City, being dismissed a full two minutes after the incident.

On leaving Moss Rose, Davies joined Rochdale, where he ended his first-class career before moving into non-League football with Bangor City.

Andy MARRIOTT

Position	Goalkeeper
Born	Andrew Marriott, Sutton-in-Ashfield, 11 October 1970
Height	6ft 0in
Weight	12st 7lb
Clubs	Arsenal, Nottingham Forest, West Bromwich Albion, Blackburn Rovers, Colchester United, Burnley, Wrexham, Sunderland, Wigan Athletic, Barnsley, Birmingham City
Welsh Caps	5
	1996 v Switzerland (lost 0–2)
	1997 v Scotland (won 1–0)
	1998 v Belgium (lost 2–3), v Brazil (lost 0–3), v Tunisia (lost 0–4)

ALTHOUGH HE HAD PREVIOUSLY WON international honours for England at schoolboy, youth and under-21 levels, it was Wales that handed Andy Marriott his first full cap when he replaced Tranmere's Danny Coyne during a 2–0 defeat against Switzerland in Lugano in April 1996.

Andy Marriott began his career at Arsenal before Brian Clough paid £50,000 to bring him to Nottingham Forest. Initially he was unable to break into the Forest team and had loan spells with West Bromwich Albion, Blackburn Rovers, Colchester United and Burnley. He spent three months on loan at Turf Moor and won a championship medal as the Clarets won the 1991/92 Fourth Division title.

Eventually he made the breakthrough at the City Ground, albeit briefly because of disciplinary action taken against Forest's regular keeper Mark Crossley. He also appeared twice at Wembley, picking up a Zenith Data Systems Cup winners' medal and a League Cup runners-up medal. However, following Forest's relegation from the Premier League in 1993, Marriott found himself out on loan again, this time at Wrexham. He eventually signed for the Robins in December 1993 for £200,000.

Marriott was an automatic choice at the Racecourse Ground for the next five seasons, playing in 143 consecutive games after making his debut. A superb shot-stopper, he won a Welsh Cup winners' medal in 1995. He put in a number of transfer requests because he wanted to play in a higher grade of football, and in the summer of 1998 Sunderland paid £200,000 for his services.

He had played in 266 games for Wrexham, while he had been signed by Sunderland primarily to act as cover for Thomas Sorensen. Unable to get into the Black Cats team on a regular basis, he had a loan spell with Wigan Athletic before joining Barnsley on a free transfer as back-up to Kevin Miller. When Miller was injured, Marriott made the most of his opportunity and kept his place in the side. Despite some heroic displays, he failed to prevent the Oakwell club from being relegated. During the early part of the 2002/03 season his consistent displays led to his joining Premiership newcomers Birmingham City as cover for Nico Vaesen.

Chris EDWARDS

Position	Central defender
Born	Christian Nicholas Horwells Edwards, Caerphilly, 23 November 1975
Height	6ft 2in
Weight	12st 8lb
Clubs	Swansea City, Nottingham Forest, Bristol City, Oxford United, Crystal Palace, Tranmere Rovers, Bristol Rovers
Welsh Caps	1
	1996 v Switzerland (lost 0–2)

CAERPHILLY-BORN CENTRAL DEFENDER Chris Edwards joined Swansea City in July 1992 under the Youth Training Scheme after being spotted by scout Cliff Morris. He was given his chance in the Swansea first team midway through the 1994/95 season when manager Frank Burrows adopted a triple central defensive formation in away games. He made his first appearance for the Wales under-21 team in October 1995, and the following April came on as a replacement for Chris Coleman in the friendly game against Switzerland.

Edwards continued to impress in the heart of the Swansea defence, where his performances alerted the scouts of a number of top clubs. He eventually became unsettled at the Vetch and, after having been placed on the transfer list, spent a ten-day trial at Nottingham Forest. Having just played for the Wales 'B' side against Scotland, Edwards signed for Forest on transfer deadline day in March 1998 for a fee of £175,000.

Initially he was unable to break into Forest's first team and went on loan to Bristol City before returning to the City Ground. He made a handful of appearances towards the end of the 1998/99 season but couldn't prevent Forest from being relegated to the First Division. There followed another loan spell, this time with Oxford United, before Edwards won a recall to both the Forest side and the Wales squad. He wasn't in the Forest side in 2001/02 and, after loan spells with Crystal Palace, Tranmere Rovers and Oxford United again, he remained on the books of Nottingham Forest before joining Bristol Rovers in the summer of 2003.

Robert PAGE

Position	Central defender
Born	Robert John Page, Rhondda, 3 September 1974
Height	6ft 9in
Weight	12st 5lb
Clubs	Watford, Sheffield United
Welsh Caps	28

1997 v Turkey (0–0), v Belgium (lost 1–2), v Scotland (won 1–0)
1998 v Turkey (lost 4–6), v Belgium (lost 2–3), v Brazil (lost 0–3)
1999 v Italy (lost 0–4)
2000 v Belarus (won 2–1), v Switzerland (lost 0–2), v Qatar (won 1–0), v Finland (lost 1–2), v Brazil (lost 0–3), v Portugal (lost 0–3)
2001 v Belarus (lost 1–2), v Norway (1–1), v Poland (0–0), v Armenia (2–2), v Ukraine (1–1), v Poland (lost 1–2), v Ukraine (1–1)
2002 v Armenia (0–0), v Belarus (won 1–0), v Argentina (1–1), v Czech Republic (0–0), v Germany (won 1–0)
2003 v Azerbaijan (won 2–0), v Bosnia-Herzegovina (2–2), v Azerbaijan (won 4–0)
2004 v Serbia-Montenegro (lost 0–1), v Italy (lost 0–4), v Finland (1–1), v Scotland (won 4–0), v Hungary (won 2–1)

ROBERT PAGE BEGAN HIS CAREER with Watford, where in his first season in the Hornets' first team he won representative honours for Wales at under-21 level. Strong in the tackle and dominant in the air, he was made Watford club captain at the start of the 1996/97 season, aged only 21. That season he gained personal reward when winning his first full Welsh cap, making an outstanding debut against Turkey.

In 1997/98 he had the unusual distinction of playing for Wales against Brazil and for Watford against Barnet in the same week, before winning a Second Division Championship medal when the Hornets finished top of the table. Following Watford's

promotion to the top flight, Page was one of only a few Watford players to emerge with any credit from the club's Premiership season of 1999/2000, and was voted the club's Player of the Year. Furthermore, after several seasons of trying, he scored his first League goal for the club against Sheffield Wednesday at Hillsborough. He continued to provide inspirational leadership for the Vicarage Road club. However, in the summer of 2001, after making 252 appearances for the Hornets, he was placed on the open to offers list.

Sheffield United paid £350,000 for his services and he soon became a committed and reliable central defender for the Blades. Appointed the Bramall Lane club captain, Robert Page remained a regular in the Wales side, and although injury has restricted his appearances, he has played in 33 internationals for Wales and made 122 League and Cup appearances for Sheffield United.

Mark CROSSLEY

Position	Goalkeeper
Born	Mark Geoffrey Crossley, Sheffield, 16 June 1969
Height	6ft 0in
Weight	16st 0lb
Clubs	Nottingham Forest, Millwall, Middlesbrough, Stoke City, Fulham
Welsh Caps	7
	1997 v Republic of Ireland (0–0)
	1999 v Switzerland (lost 0–2)
	2000 v Finland (lost 1–2)
	2002 v Argentina (1–1), v Germany (won 1–0)
	2003 v Bosnia-Herzegovina (2–2)
	2004 v Scotland (won 4–0)

MARK CROSSLEY WAS ONE OF THE BEST goalkeepers in the top flight on his day. He was disappointed at being overlooked by the England management and declared his eligibility for Scotland and Wales through the ancestry of his grandparents. He made his full debut for Wales after representing England at under-21 level and kept a clean sheet in a goalless draw against the Republic of Ireland in 1997.

He was a big, strong goalkeeper who was at his best in one-to-one situations. He began his career with Nottingham Forest. He made his debut as a replacement for the injured Steve Sutton against Liverpool in October 1988, but it wasn't until the 1990/91 season that he claimed a regular place. He had a good game in the 1991 FA Cup Final against Tottenham Hotspur, saving a Gary Lineker penalty in a game Forest lost 2–1. Although he lost his place to Andy Marriott following a well-publicised off-the-field incident in his home town, Crossley was restored to favour and, until losing his place to Dave Beasant midway through the 1997/98 season, was virtually an ever-present.

Robert Page heads the ball away from Finland's Mika Vayrynen in a Euro 2004 Group 9 qualifying match, 10 September 2003. The match ended 1–1. *(Getty Images)*

Following a loan spell with Millwall, he bided his time in Forest's reserve side before replacing Beasant after a couple of heavy defeats. He was awarded a testimonial in 2000 and over 15,000 turned out at the City ground – a measure of his popularity with the Reds' supporters. Out of contract in the summer of 2000, Crossley joined Middlesbrough on a free transfer. He had appeared in 393 games for Forest.

He received few chances at the Riverside because of the fine form of Mark Schwarzer, and had a couple of loan spells with Stoke City before being recalled. Crossley won a series of man-of-the-match awards and was rewarded with a substitute appearance for Wales in their match against Bosnia-Herzegovina in February 2003. Joining Premiership Fulham in the summer of 2003, he made just one League appearance for the Cottagers.

Karl READY

Position	Full-back
Born	Karl Ready, Neath, 14 August 1972
Height	6ft 1in
Weight	12st 0lb
Clubs	Queen's Park Rangers, Motherwell, Aldershot
Welsh Caps	5
	1997 v Republic of Ireland (0–0)
	1998 v Belgium (lost 2–3), v Brazil (lost 0–3), v Malta (won 3–0), v Tunisia (lost 0–4)

DEFENDER KARL READY CAN PLAY anywhere across the back four. His early performances for Queen's Park Rangers led to under-21 and 'B' honours for Wales. He made his full international debut in a goalless draw against the Republic of Ireland in Cardiff in February 1997.

Good in the air and comfortable on the ball, Ready was made Rangers' captain in the absence of Gavin Peacock and held on to the armband after a change in management. Although he didn't score too many goals for Rangers, one of his most satisfying came against Bristol City in the first home game of the 1998/99 campaign. In order to try and retrieve something from a lost cause, he was moved up to the left-hand side of the forward line and ended the match by scoring in injury time with a remarkable curling shot from just outside the box.

Over the next couple of seasons, the only games he missed were through suspensions, until in the third game of the 2000/01 season he suffered a broken leg playing against Crewe Alexandra. On his return he went down with an ankle injury. Although he was back in first-team action towards the end of the season, Ready was one of 15 players to be released by the club in the close season. He had appeared in 246 games for Rangers in his time at Loftus Road. Ready then went north of the border to play for Scottish Premier League club, Motherwell, but a year later moved back south to play for Aldershot.

Paul TROLLOPE

Position	Midfielder
Born	Paul Jonathan Trollope, Swindon, 3 June 1972
Height	6ft 0in
Weight	12st 5lb
Clubs	Swindon Town, Torquay United, Derby County, Grimsby Town, Crystal Palace, Fulham, Coventry City, Northampton Town
Welsh Caps	9
	1997 v Scotland (won 1–0)
	1998 v Brazil (lost 0–3), v Jamaica (0–0), v Malta (won 3–0), v Tunisia (lost 0–4)
	2002 v Czech Republic (0–0)
	2003 v Croatia (1–1), v Azerbaijan (won 2–0), v Azerbaijan (won 4–0)

THE SON OF JOHN TROLLOPE, the holder of the Swindon Town club appearance record, Paul too began his career at the County Ground but wasn't able to make the grade. He joined Torquay United and his impressive displays for the Devon club led to First Division Derby County paying £100,000 for his services in December 1994.

His ability to link defence and attack made him a key member of the County side. After adding to his other abilities that of man-marking successfully in a central position in 1996/97, he won his first full international cap in Wales's friendly against Scotland. Trollope had gained valuable experience in loan spells with Grimsby Town and Crystal Palace. After helping the Rams win promotion to the Premiership, he had appeared in just 13 top-flight games when he was transferred to Fulham for a fee of £600,000.

He went on to pick up a Second Division Championship medal in 1998/99 as he played some of his best-ever football. However, in the following season because of the number and quality of the midfielders at Fulham manager Paul Bracewell's disposal, he was often on the fringes of first-team action. Although he played in occasional games as cover for the left-back and left-midfield positions, he played the majority of his football the following season in the club's reserve side, helping them win the Avon Insurance Combination for the first time in their history.

He joined Coventry City on a free transfer in March 2002 and found himself restored to the Wales side for the match against the Czech Republic. At the end of the season he left Highfield Road to play for Northampton Town, where he was immediately appointed captain.

Simon HAWORTH

Position	Forward
Born	Simon Owen Haworth, Cardiff, 30 March 1977
Height	6ft 2in
Weight	13st 8lb
Clubs	Cardiff City, Coventry City, Wigan Athletic, Tranmere Rovers

Recalled to the Wales squad in the summer of 2003, Simon Haworth couldn't tour as he was still on his honeymoon! *(Wigan Athletic FC)*

Welsh Caps	5
	1997 v Scotland (won 1–0)
	1998 v Brazil (lost 0–3), v Jamaica (0–0), v Malta (won 3–0), v Tunisia (lost 0–4)

SIMON HAWORTH BEGAN HIS FOOTBALL League career with his home-town club Cardiff City, being pitched into the Bluebirds' side following an injury crisis at the start of the 1995/96 season. However, it was midway through the following season before he established himself as a first-team regular, scoring some superb goals. A proposed transfer to Norwich City on deadline day fell through. But, after winning full international honours for Wales when he played against Scotland, he left Ninian Park to join Coventry City for £500,000.

Although he scored on his debut for the Sky Blues in a Coca-Cola Cup game against Everton, his subsequent performances were not so impressive. In October 1998 he joined Wigan Athletic for £600,000, then the club's record signing.

His early progress with the Latics was hampered by hamstring problems. However, he came back strongly towards the end of the campaign to play at Wembley as part of the Wigan side that won the Auto Windscreen Shield.

Strong in the air with an excellent first touch, he captained Wales's under-21 side before scoring the first-ever Football League goal at the club's new JJB Stadium as Wigan beat Scunthorpe United 3–0. He finished the 1999/2000 season with 20 goals, his tremendous strike in the Wembley Second Division play-off final demonstrating his potential. Haworth topped the club's scoring charts the following season including netting the first-ever hat-trick in a match at the JJB Stadium as Latics beat Colchester United 3–1. Haworth scored 58 goals in 141 games for Wigan. In February 2002 he left to play for Tranmere Rovers, who paid £125,000 for his services.

At Prenton Park, he resumed his old striking partnership with Stuart Barlow with some success and ended the 2002/03 season as the club's top scorer with 22 goals – the first player to reach the 20-goal mark in one season since John Aldridge. Haworth was also called up to the Wales international squad in the close season but was unable to join them as he was still on his honeymoon!

Lee JONES

Position	Forward
Born	Philip Lee Jones, Wrexham, 29 May 1973
Height	5ft 9in
Weight	10st 8lb
Clubs	Wrexham, Liverpool, Crewe Alexandra, Tranmere Rovers, Barnsley
Welsh Caps	2
	1997 v Scotland (won 1–0)
	1998 v Turkey (lost 4–6)

VERY FEW 17-YEAR-OLDS MAKE THEIR first-team debut watched by a television audience of millions. Yet this is what happened to Wrexham's Lee Jones. As a result of the 'foreigners rule' (each side is restricted to two non-Welsh players), he was selected for the Robins' second leg European Cup Winners' Cup tie against Manchester United. Two days later he made his League debut and over the next year or so scored a number of vital goals, including a burst of six in six games. Shortly after this he was signed by Liverpool manager Graeme Souness for £300,000 with an equivalent amount to follow if he made the grade.

Bought with an eye to the future, he made a couple of substitute appearances in 1994/95 following a brief loan spell with Crewe. Although he continued to score prolifically for the Reds' reserve side, he couldn't force his way into the Liverpool first team. Further loan spells, first with Wrexham and then Tranmere Rovers, where he teamed up well with John Aldridge, led to his first full international cap against Scotland.

Despite being tracked by a number of top-flight clubs, he joined Tranmere on a permanent basis in May 1997 after he was presented with a petition by Rovers' fans.

Although troubled by injury throughout his time at Prenton Park, he managed to score 18 goals in 96 League and Cup games plus many more assists before joining Barnsley in the summer of 2000.

As a result of managerial changes at Oakwell, he appeared in a variety of positions. He then rejoined Wrexham. In his first match back at the Racecourse Ground he scored five goals in the match against Cambridge United to equal a club record set 68 years earlier by Tommy Bamford. Sadly, this was not enough to save the Robins from being relegated on the same day.

Paul JONES

Position	Goalkeeper
Born	Paul Steven Jones, Chirk, 18 April 1967
Height	6ft 3in
Weight	14st 8lb
Clubs	Kidderminster Harriers, Wolverhampton Wanderers, Stockport County, Southampton, Liverpool
Welsh Caps	38

1997 v Scotland (won 1–0)
1998 v Turkey (lost 4–6), v Brazil (lost 0–3), v Jamaica (0–0), v Malta (won 3–0)
1999 v Italy (lost 0–2), v Denmark (won 2–1), v Belarus
   (won 3–2), v Switzerland (lost 0–2), v Italy (lost 0–4), v Denmark (lost 0–2)
2000 v Belarus (won 2–1), v Switzerland (lost 0–2), v Qatar (won 1–0)
2001 v Belarus (lost 1–2), v Norway (1–1), v Poland (0–0), v Armenia (2–2), v Ukraine (1–1),
   v Poland (lost 1–2), v Ukraine (1–1)
2002 v Armenia (0–0), v Norway (lost 2–3), v Belarus (won 1–0), v Argentina (1–1)
2003 v Croatia (1–1), v Finland (won 2–0), v Italy (won 2–1), v Azerbaijan (won 2–0),
   v Azerbaijan (won 4–0), v United States (lost 0–2)
2004 v Serbia-Montenegro (lost 0–1, v Italy (lost 0–4), v Finland (1–1), v Serbia-Montenegro
   (lost 2–3), v Russia (0–0), v Russia (lost 0–1), v Hungary (won 2–1)

PAUL JONES BEGAN HIS CAREER PLAYING non-League football for Kidderminster Harriers before Wolverhampton Wanderers paid £40,000 to take him to Molineux in the summer of 1991. Signed as Mike Stowell's deputy, he spent five years in his shadow, appearing in 40 League and Cup games before a £60,000 transfer took him to Stockport County.

He had a stunning 1996/97 season for the Edgeley Park club, helping County reach the League Cup semi-final, as a result of which he was called up to the Wales squad and appeared against Scotland. Instrumental in the club's promotion to the First Division, he kept seven consecutive clean sheets during the critical last few weeks of the campaign. In the close season he followed former Stockport boss Dave Jones to Southampton, the Saints paying £900,000 for his signature.

His signing proved to be a masterstroke as his displays in the Saints' goal demonstrated his ability as one of the Premiership's top keepers. In 1998/99 he suffered a freak back injury in the warm-up before an international game, and it was thought he would not play again that season. However, he showed great powers of recovery, returned to first-team action, and helped the Saints remain in the top flight by the skin of their teeth. Voted the Welsh Player of the Year for 1999, he continued to give Southampton outstanding service until another back injury in April 2000 threatened his career.

Goalkeeper Paul Jones in action during the Euro 2004 Group 9 Qualifying match between Wales and Italy on 16 October 2002. Wales won the match 2–1. *(Getty Images)*

In 2000/01 Jones established a new postwar club record with a run of seven straight Premiership clean sheets and 667 minutes without conceding a goal. The following season at the Millennium Stadium he became the first goalkeeper to be brought on as a substitute in an FA Cup Final. In January 2004 after making 222 appearances for Southampton and following a spell on loan with Liverpool, he joined Wolves for £250,000. Though he turned in several outstanding performances, he couldn't prevent their relegation from the Premiership.

Rob EDWARDS

Position	Midfielder
Born	Robert William Edwards, Cockermouth, 1 July 1973
Height	6ft 0in
Weight	12st 2lb
Clubs	Carlisle United, Bristol City, Preston North End
Welsh Caps	4
	1998 v Turkey (lost 4–6), v Belgium (lost 2–3), v Malta (won 3–0), v Tunisia (lost 0–4)

MIDFIELDER ROB EDWARDS MADE HIS Wales international debut as a substitute for Ceri Hughes in the 6–4 defeat by Turkey in 1998 and then started the next game against Belgium.

His career began with his local club Carlisle United. Then in March 1991 a £135,000 transfer took him to Bristol City. Although he initially found it difficult to hold down a regular place with the Ashton Gate club, he then found his form, only for the club to be relegated to the Second Division in 1994/95. Early the following season illness in the guise of glandular fever intervened, but in 1996/97 Edwards had his best season since his arrival at the club. Not only a ball winner but intelligent in distribution, he was called up into the full Welsh squad, this after making 17 appearances at under-21 level and playing in two games for the 'B' side.

It was after making his first two full international appearances that he began to suffer from a spate of niggling injuries, and he missed a number of games in which his experience would have been a help to the side. In the summer of 1999 Edwards, declined a new contract and joined Preston North End. He had appeared in 263 games for the Robins.

At Deepdale he was used more as a left-back than in his usual position of midfield, and ended his first season with the club by winning a Second Division Championship medal. The following season his experience proved vital in helping the club adapt to the higher grade of football. Injuries such as a broken rib and a punctured lung forced him to miss matches including an international call-up in August 2001. His 2002/03 season was also affected by injury, this time a broken hand, though he has since returned to first-team action.

Darren Barnard prepares to deliver a cross during the Euro 2004 Group 9 qualifying match between Wales and Serbia-Montenegro, 11 October 2003. (Getty Images)

Darren BARNARD

Position	Midfielder/Left-back
Born	Darren Sean Barnard, Rinteln, Germany, 30 November 1971
Height	5ft 10in
Weight	12st 3lb
Clubs	Wokingham Town, Chelsea, Reading, Bristol City, Barnsley, Grimsby Town
Welsh Caps	22

1998 v Jamaica (0–0)
1999 v Italy (lost 0–2), v Denmark (won 2–1), v Belarus (won 3–2), v Italy (lost 0–4),
   v Denmark (lost 0–2)
2000 v Belarus (won 2–1), v Switzerland (lost 0–2), v Qatar (won 1–0), v Finland (lost 1–2),
   v Brazil (lost 0–3), v Portugal (lost 0–3)
2001 v Ukraine (1–1), v Poland (lost 1–2), v Ukraine (1–1)
2002 v Armenia (0–0)
2003 v Croatia (1–1), v Azerbaijan (won 2–0)
2004 v Serbia-Montenegro (lost 2–3), v Russia (0–0), v Russia (lost 0–1), v Norway (0–0)

THE SON OF A SERVICEMAN (hence his foreign birthplace), Darren Barnard join Chelsea from Wokingham Town in the summer of 1990. His talent was recognis early by the FA, which selected him for the England schoolboys under-18 side 1989/90.

After waiting patiently for a first-team chance, he made his League debut for Chels against West Ham United in April 1992 but had to wait towards the latter part of t following season before getting an extended run in the team. Over the next couple seasons he found himself in and out of the Chelsea side. Following a loan spell wi Reading, he joined Bristol City in October 1995 for a fee of £175,000.

Barnard had the skill to go past an opponent and was a good crosser of the ball wl ably demonstrated his long-range shooting ability. He soon became a great favouri with the City fans. Moving from midfield to left-back, he continued to find the net both the club's penalty-taker and dead-ball expert. Robins' fans were dismayed when the summer of 1997 he was allowed to join Barnsley for £750,000.

He made giant strides forward with the Oakwell club and was rewarded with his fi full international cap for Wales when he played in the goalless draw against Jamaica.

His outstanding displays for the Tykes attracted interest from a number of top-flig clubs and, after turning down a requested move to Southampton, Barnsley manag Dave Bassett moved him back into a midfield role. Barnard responded by scoring : League and Cup goals, the best return of his career. Injuries then began to hamper l progress at Oakwell, and in the 2002 close season he was released.

Picked up by Grimsby Town, he was initially unable to win a regular place Blundell Park despite regular selection for the Wales squad and a stunning first goal f the club – he lobbed Derby keeper Matt Poom from 40 yards out! In the 2003/(season he was a virtual ever-present.

John OSTER

Position	Winger
Born	John Morgan Oster, Boston, 8 December 1978
Height	5ft 9in
Weight	10st 8lb
Clubs	Grimsby Town, Everton, Sunderland, Barnsley
Welsh Caps	11
	1998 v Belgium (lost 2–3), v Brazil (lost 0–3), v Jamaica (0–0)
	2000 v Switzerland (lost 0–2)
	2003 v Bosnia-Herzegovina (2–2), v Azerbaijan (won 4–0), v United States (lost 0–2)
	2004 v Serbia-Montenegro (lost 2–3), v Scotland (won 4–0), Norway (0–0), v Canada (won 1–

JOHN OSTER HAS THE DISTINCTION of winning his first international cap for Wal without touching the ball after coming on as a late substitute in Belgium in 1998. F was selected to play against Brazil and Jamaica the same year before being sent off successive matches for the under-21 team.

Oster made his under-21 debut for Wales before his initial appearance at Leag level. Beginning his career with Grimsby Town, he showed a football maturity f eyond his years, with speed, ball control and the ability to deliver telling balls into the box. The gifted out-and-out winger was tracked by both Manchester United and Newcastle United before Everton manager Howard Kendall paid £1.5 million to take Oster to Goodison Park.

Like so many other young players at Goodison Park, he struggled to impress in a side constantly battling against relegation before enduring another frustrating season in 1998/99. He was allowed to leave Everton and joined Sunderland for £1 million. Although he was right-sided, he was used by the Black Cats on the left, and it wasn't long before he lost his place to Gavin McCann. He continued to struggle to win a place in the Sunderland first team, and there followed loan spells with Barnsley and then Grimsby Town. His excellent form for the Mariners prompted Sunderland manager Howard Wilkinson to recall him and he spent the remaining months of the 2002/03 season in and out of the side. A regular in Mick McCarthy's Sunderland side of 2003/04, he was instrumental in the Black Cats reaching the First Division play-offs and the FA Cup semi-final.

Craig BELLAMY

Position	Forward
Born	Craig Douglas Bellamy, Cardiff, 13 July 1979
Height	5ft 9in
Weight	10st 12lb
Clubs	Norwich City, Coventry City, Newcastle United
Welsh Caps	25 Goals 6

1998 v Jamaica (0–0), v Malta (won 3–0) 1 goal, v Tunisia (lost 0–4)

1999 v Denmark (won 2–1) 1 goal, v Switzerland (lost 0–2), v Italy (lost 0–4), v Denmark (lost 0–2)

2000 v Brazil (lost 0–3), v Portugal (lost 0–3)

2001 v Belarus (lost 1–2), v Armenia (2–2), v Ukraine (1–1)

2002 v Armenia (0–0), v Norway (lost 2–3) 1 goal, v Belarus (won 1–0), v Argentina (1–1) 1 goal

2003 v Finland (won 2–0), v Italy (won 2–1) 1 goal, v Bosnia-Herzegovina (2–2), v Azerbaijan (won 4–0) 1 goal

2004 v Serbia-Montenegro (lost 0–1), v Italy (lost 0–4), v Serbia-Montenegro (lost 2–3), v Norway (0–0), v Canada (won 1–0)

CRAIG BELLAMY IS ONE OF WALES's most important players. He netted the winner against Italy in the home 2004 European Championships qualifier and then scored after only 13 seconds against Azerbaijan in March 2003 to record the fastest goal in Welsh international history.

He had not played in a League game for his first club Norwich City when he became the youngest-ever player to represent Wales at under-21 level in a match against San Marino. He ended the 1997/98 season, his first in the Norwich side, as the club's leading scorer with 13 goals, prompting Crystal Palace to offer £1 million for his services in December 1997. Three months later he won his first full

international cap against Jamaica and, in so doing, became the third-youngest debutant behind John Charles and Ryan Giggs. He had a fantastic 1998/99 season at Carrow Road and would have scored more than his 19 goals but for a terrible knee injury at Wolverhampton Wanderers. Then he sustained a cruciate ligament injury in a pre-season friendly at Southend and missed all but the final two weeks of the 1999/2000 season.

He left the Canaries early the following season, sold to Coventry City for £6.5 million and arriving at Highfield Road as a replacement for Robbie Keane. A fast and instinctive striker, he netted twice in his first three games but played his best football when he was moved to the left-side of midfield. Despite the club's relegation worries, he always gave of his best but, after just one season with the Sky Blues, he joined Newcastle United for a fee of £6 million.

He made a major contribution to the Magpies, becoming an exciting force near the top of the Premiership as he formed a prolific strike partnership with Alan Shearer. Rested for the League Cup tie against Brentford, he came off the bench to score a hat-trick and so become the first Newcastle player to score three goals both in extra time and when coming on as a substitute. Bellamy's performances throughout the season earned him the PFA Young Player of the Year award.

After undergoing an operation for a torn patella tendon, he missed the start of the 2002/03 season and then he was disrupted by a period of suspension. He returned as a substitute against Feyenoord and scored in the last minute to earn the Magpies their first win in the Champions League and their passport to the second phase.

Bellamy's electric pace makes him a constant threat to opposition defences as he both creates opportunities and scores regularly himself. Though injuries again disrupted his progress in the 2003/04 season, he continues to be hugely popular with the Toon Army.

Ryan GREEN

Position	Full-back
Born	Ryan Michael Green, Cardiff, 20 October 1980
Height	5ft 8in
Weight	11st 0lb
Clubs	Wolverhampton Wanderers, Torquay United, Millwall, Cardiff City, Sheffield Wednesday, Hereford United
Welsh Caps	2
	1998 v Malta (won 3–0), v Tunisia (lost 0–4)

WALES'S YOUNGEST-EVER DEBUTANT in 1998, Ryan Green had played twice for his country by the age of 17, yet he had not even been close to a Wolves'

Craig Bellamy applauds the fans as he leaves the field during the Euro 2004 qualifying Group 9 match between Italy and Wales on 6 September 2003 at the San Siro stadium in Milan. Italy won the match 4–0. (*Getty Images*)

debut. Although his international career continued at under-21 level in 1998/99, the young right-back had still not made the Wolves' first team. He eventually got his chance when Kevin Muscat was suspended in November 1998. He showed remarkable confidence against a Sheffield United team until going off injured in the second half.

He failed to make a first-team appearance the following season but was given more of a run in 2000/01. However, on losing his place he asked for a transfer and linked up with his former boss Colin Lee at Torquay United. While at Plainmoor, he continued to represent Wales at under-21 level, but on his return to Molineux he found that he was still unable to force his way into the Wolves' side.

In October 2001 he joined Millwall on a free transfer, rejoining another former Wolves' boss in Mark McGhee. He acquitted himself well when called upon. Eventually finding himself out of favour, he joined Cardiff City but, after just one substitute appearance for his home-town club, he moved to Sheffield Wednesday.

Chris LLEWELLYN

Position	Forward
Born	Christopher Mark Llewellyn, Swansea, 29 August 1979
Height	5ft 11in
Weight	11st 6lb
Clubs	Norwich City, Bristol Rovers, Wrexham
Welsh Caps	2
	1998 v Malta (won 3–0), v Tunisia (lost 0–4)

IN 1997/98, CHRIS LLEWELLYN's first season in League football, he won three under-21 caps and gained 'B' recognition before in the close season being called up to the Welsh full squad and playing against Malta and Tunisia. He was also eligible for the Norwich City youth team.

During that campaign, Llewellyn demonstrated that he posed a danger from any position in the last third of the pitch, scoring three goals in the last six games from an attacking midfield role. Although not a wide player, he liked to run at defenders using his pace and dribbling skills, and provided many crosses for fellow Welsh international Iwan Roberts during the course of the next few seasons.

He considered himself a central striker, but his versatility allowed him to play in a number of positions for the Canaries. In 1999/2000 he was given the unenviable task of filling Darren Eadie's boots when the former Carrow Road favourite left for Leicester City in December 1999. He was the regular captain of the Wales under-21 side. But for the misfortune of fracturing his cheekbone when playing on his 21st birthday, he would have been ever-present in 2000/01. Injuries then hampered his progress at Carrow Road and he was sent on loan to Bristol Rovers before returning to end the season with the Canaries. Llewellyn later joined Wrexham.

Andy JOHNSON

Position	Midfielder
Born	Andrew James Johnson, Bristol, 2 May 1974
Height	6ft 0in
Weight	13st 0lb
Clubs	Norwich City, Nottingham Forest, West Bromwich Albion
Welsh Caps	14

1999 v Italy (lost 0–2), v Denmark (won 2–1), v Belarus (won 3–2), v Switzerland (lost 0–2)
2000 v Finland (lost 1–2), v Brazil (lost 0–3), v Portugal (lost 0–3)
2003 v Croatia (1–1), v Finland (won 2–0), v United States (lost 0–2)
2004 v Italy (lost 0–4), v Finland (1–1), v Russia (0–0), v Russia (lost 0–1)

AN ENGLAND YOUTH INTERNATIONAL, Andy Johnson qualified to play for Wales through his grandmother and made his full international debut in a 2–0 defeat at the hands of Italy in 1999.

He began his career with Norwich City and had a most interesting first couple of seasons with the Carrow Road club. He was sent off by a substitute referee for a foul he did not commit and then nearly scored after losing a boot in a challenge with Arsenal's Steve Bould on April Fool's Day 1995. He was plagued by suspensions in 1995/96, having been dismissed in consecutive games, and by injuries in 1996/97. Never on the losing side when he scored 15 goals in 75 League and Cup outings, he was sold to Nottingham Forest for £2.2 million in the summer of 1997.

The strong and aggressive midfielder had a good first season at the County Ground, helping Forest win the First Division Championship. Returning to the Premiership, Johnson linked up well with his team-mates, getting forward whenever the opportunity arose. He was fast off the mark, a good passer of the ball and a key figure in Forest's engine-room. He missed a number of games over the next couple of seasons due to a series of niggling injuries before being sold to West Bromwich Albion in a cut-price deal in September 2001.

He slotted straight into Albion's style of play and had an outstanding first season at the Hawthorns, helping the Baggies win promotion to the Premiership. He continued to work hard the following season. Although Albion were relegated after just one season in the top flight, Andy Johnson's form was such that he was selected by Wales on three occasions. Continuing to represent Wales, he was an integral member of the Albion side that returned to the Premiership after just one season of First Division football, netting a vital goal in the 1–1 draw at promotion rivals Millwall.

2000

and Beyond

A New Millennium

On 29 March 2000 a sell-out 66,500 crowd packed into Cardiff's Millennium Stadium; but Wales lost 2–1 to Finland. Then on 23 May the first major international in Britain in an enclosed dome attracted 72,000 to the £125 million stadium to see Brazil beat Wales 3–0.

Wales's 2002 World Cup qualification bid started badly with a 2–1 defeat in Belarus, where also Craig Bellamy was sent off. It was a thoroughly disappointing campaign: Wales failed to win any of their first nine games and in Norway captain Ryan Giggs was sent off for the first time in his career. A goal by John Hartson gave Wales victory over Belarus and prevented them going a record 13 games without a win.

Wales got their 2004 European Championship campaign off to a flying start with a 1–0 win in Finland, and followed this up with an extraordinary 2–1 defeat of Italy. Spurs' Simon Davies scored in both matches. After winning in Azerbaijan, Wales completed the double over them with a comprehensive 4–0 win at the Millennium Stadium. Speed and Hartson got on the scoresheet both home and away.

On 27 May 2003 Wales's ten-game, 20-month unbeaten run ended with a 2–0 defeat in a friendly against the United States at San José. Though Wales failed to reproduce their earlier form in the second half of their European Championship campaign, they were involved in a play-off game against Russia. After giving perhaps their greatest performance under Mark Hughes in Moscow to hold the Russians to a goalless draw, they looked forward to the return in Cardiff with cautious optimism. However, Russia won 1–0, breaking Welsh hearts. Though the Welsh FA appealed to UEFA for a place in the European Finals after a Russian player tested positive for a banned substance, it wasn't to be.

Despite the disappointment, football in Wales has never been on such a high and support for the national team has never been stronger.

Carl ROBINSON

Position	Midfielder
Born	Carl Phillip Robinson, Llandrindod Wells, 13 October 1976
Height	5ft 10in
Weight	12st 10lb
Clubs	Wolverhampton Wanderers, Shrewsbury Town, Portsmouth, Sheffield Wednesday, Walsall, Rotherham United, Sheffield United, Sunderland
Welsh Caps	17
	2000 v Belarus (won 2–1), v Portugal (lost 0–3)
	2001 v Armenia (2–2), v Ukraine (1–1)
	2002 v Armenia (0–0), v Norway (lost 2–3), v Belarus (won 1–0), v Argentina (1–1)
	2003 v Croatia (1–1), v Azerbaijan (won 2–0), v Azerbaijan (won 4–0), v United States (lost 0–2)
	2004 v Serbia-Montenegro (lost 2–3), v Scotland (won 4–0), v Hungary (won 2–1), v Norway (0–0), v Canada (won 1–0)

NOT HAVING PLAYED A GAME in the Wolves' first team, midfielder Carl Robinson went on loan to Shrewsbury Town and within three weeks of his arrival at Gay Meadow was playing for Shrewsbury in the Auto Windscreens Final at Wembley!

Returning to Molineux, he made an appearance for the Wales under-21 side before he was given his first-team debut for the Midlands club. The aggressive side to his game was soon to the fore and, as he adjusted to the pace of the higher grade of football, he grew in confidence. His competitive nature, which led to a number of bookings, also helped him win a place in the Wales 'B' side. But then he was switched from his preferred role in the centre of midfield to playing wide on the right, and his level of performance dropped. Although he was not at his best for Wolves, he won the first of his 12 full caps when he came off the substitute's bench in the match against Belarus in September 1999. Thereafter he found himself in and out of the Wolves' side and, following exploratory surgery on his knee, he was allowed to join Portsmouth, having appeared in 191 games in seven years with the club.

He impressed with his work rate and neat distribution in his early games for Pompey before being allowed to join Sheffield Wednesday on loan. There he made his debut in the local derby against Sheffield United. He later rejoined his former boss Colin Lee at Walsall, again on loan. During the course of the 2003/04 season he had further lean spells with Rotherham United, Sheffield United and Sunderland, helping the Wearsiders to the First Division play-offs.

Mark DELANEY

Position	Right-back
Born	Mark Anthony Delaney, Fishguard, 13 May 1976
Height	6ft 1in
Weight	11st 7lb
Clubs	Carmarthen Town, Cardiff City, Aston Villa

2000 v Switzerland (lost 0–2), v Qatar (won 1–0), v Brazil (lost 0–3), v Portugal (lost 0–3)
2001 v Norway (1–1), v Poland (0–0), v Armenia (2–2), v Ukraine (1–1), v Ukraine (1–1)
2002 v Armenia (0–0), v Norway (lost 2–3), v Belarus (won 1–0), v Argentina (1–1),
    v Czech Republic (0–0), v Germany (won 1–0)
2003 v Croatia (1–1), v Finland (won 2–0), v Italy (won 2–1), v Azerbaijan (won 2–0)
2004 v Serbia-Montenegro (lost 0–1), v Italy (lost 0–4), v Serbia-Montenegro (lost 2–3),
    v Russia (0–0), v Russia (lost 0–1), v Norway (0–0), v Canada (won 1–0)

Mark Delaney looks to control the ball during the World Cup 2002 Group 5 qualifying match against Ukraine played at the Millennium Stadium, 28 March 2001. The match ended in a 1–1 draw. *(Getty Images)*

MARK DELANEY WAS PLUCKED FROM the League of Wales side, Carmarthen Town, by Cardiff City manager Frank Burrows in the summer of 1998. Although most Bluebirds' fans thought his signing was unwise, he soon won them over with some exciting displays. Towards the end of his first season, in which he was selected by his peers for the PFA award-winning Third Division team, Delaney received a shock call-up for the Wales squad to play Switzerland, but he was not called upon.

He left Ninian Park before the season was over, joining Aston Villa for a fee of £500,000. The Cardiff fans complained bitterly because the club had let him go.

He soon established himself as a first-team regular at Villa Park. He went on to make an appearance in the FA Cup Final against Chelsea to crown a fine first full season in the Premiership – a campaign in which he won his first full international cap for Wales. He began the 2000/01 season with some disciplinary problems, having received a red card for his country during the summer and another in the Inter Toto Cup. Although he continued to appear for Wales, he found himself in and out of the Villa side as he spent time out with two separate knee injuries.

Eventually he won back his regular spot at right-back with a string of assured performances. A hard-working, committed player, Delaney then suffered from another bout of injuries, including a broken right foot sustained while he was playing for Wales against Azerbaijan in November 2002. He then had a cartilage operation; and, shortly after returning to action, suffered cruciate ligament damage which brought his 2002/03 season to a premature end. Though injuries hampered his progress in 2003/04 he helped Villa to their best season for a long time and captained Wales in friendlies against Norway and Canada.

Matt JONES

Position	Midfielder
Born	Matthew Graham Jones, Llanelli, 1 September 1980
Height	5ft 11in
Weight	11st 5lb
Clubs	Leeds United, Leicester City
Welsh Caps	13
	2000 v Switzerland (lost 0–2), v Qatar (won 1–0), v Brazil (lost 0–3), v Portugal (lost 0–3)
	2001 v Poland (0–0), v Armenia (2–2), v Ukraine (1–1), v Poland (lost 1–2)
	2002 v Armenia (0–0), v Norway (lost 2–3), v Belarus (won 1–0)
	2003 v Bosnia-Herzegovina (2–2), v United States (lost 0–2)

BY THE TIME MATT JONES MADE HIS first-team debut for Leeds United in an FA Cup victory at Portsmouth midway through the 1998/99 season, he already had a string of Welsh youth and under-21 caps to his name.

Jones was a member of the Leeds United FA Youth Cup winning team of 1997. He had the honour of captaining Wales under-21s against Switzerland in October 1999, and then made his full international debut when coming off the substitute's bench to replace John Oster in the match against Switzerland. The following season he found himself very much on the fringes of the Leeds team. After playing in the Premiership game against Leicester City at Filbert Street in December 2000, he joined the Foxes later in the month for a fee of £3.25 million.

Jones was seen by Leicester boss Peter Taylor as a replacement for Neil Lennon in the central midfield anchor role. He continued to play for Wales, but a foot injury suffered in the World Cup qualifier against Ukraine forced him to miss a number of games for his club. He had just returned to full fitness and was beginning to establish himself under Dave Bassett when he suffered a cruciate ligament injury that put him on the sidelines for over a year.

The Foxes' injury crisis saw him return to action sooner than he should have, but he still managed to acquit himself creditably, and he quickly earned a recall to the full Wales squad. An ankle problem then forced him to miss more games before a closing-day injury crisis led to a late recall to the Leicester starting line-up. A further call to international duty came at the end of the season. Despite this, the midfielder was made available on a free transfer, but later injuries forced his premature retirement.

Neil ROBERTS

Position	Forward
Born	Neil Wyn Roberts, Wrexham, 7 April 1978
Height	5ft 10in
Weight	11st 0lb
Clubs	Wrexham, Wigan Athletic, Hull City
Welsh Caps	3
	2000 v Switzerland (lost 0–2)
	2003 v Azerbaijan (won 2–0), v United States (lost 0–2)

NEIL ROBERTS WAS A PRODUCT of the much-respected Wrexham youth system. He set the Racecourse Ground alight with five goals in his first five games after coming into the Robins' side in September 1997.

While he was never as prolific thereafter, he continued to show immense promise for one so young. Roberts found his second season of League football much harder. He appeared in two representative games for Wales, against Italy at under-21 level and Northern Ireland in a 'B' international. He also suffered an unusual injury. The problem started with a dead leg which turned into a blood clot that calcified. The only cure for this condition was complete rest.

In October 1999 Roberts made his full international debut for Wales when he came on as a substitute for Nathan Blake in the match against Switzerland.

Impressing with his high work rate and willingness to probe hard for openings, he moved to Wigan Athletic for a fee of £450,000 in February 2000. Although he took time to settle into his new surroundings, his ability to use his body to hold the ball up was soon apparent. The majority of his first-team appearances in 2000/01 were as a substitute, and when Paul Jewell took over the reins as Latics manager his first-team appearances diminished somewhat. Roberts was loaned out to Hull City before returning to the JJB Stadium to finish the season as the reserves' leading scorer.

Following his transfer from Wrexham to Wigan, Neil Roberts (right) impressed with his high work rate and won his first cap against Switzerland. *(Wigan Athletic FC)*

The 2002/03 season was his best since his move to Wigan – he replaced leading scorer Andy Liddell in the Latics side, bringing the best out of fellow striker Nathan Ellington. Roberts was also recalled to international duties with Wales, making a substitute appearance in the 2004 European Championships qualifying game against Azerbaijan.

Gareth ROBERTS

Position	Full-back
Born	Gareth Wyn Roberts, Wrexham, 6 February 1978
Height	5ft 7in
Weight	12st 6lb
Clubs	Liverpool, Panionios (Greece), Tranmere Rovers
Welsh Caps	6
	2000 v Finland (lost 1–2), v Brazil (lost 0–3), v Portugal (lost 0–3)
	2001 v Belarus (lost 1–2)
	2004 v Hungary (won 2–1), v Hungary (0–0)

FULL-BACK GARETH ROBERTS WAS unable to make the grade with Liverpool, with whom he won an FA Youth Cup winners' medal in 1996. He joined Tranmere Rovers on loan at the beginning of the 1999/2000 season, and quickly signed on a permanent basis after a series of outstanding displays.

Roberts made a miraculous recovery after suffering what was believed to be a broken leg in the match against Newcastle United. A week before the Worthington Cup Final at Wembley he appeared in the Tranmere starting line-up for the match against Leicester City. Already capped by Wales at under-21 level, he won the first of his four full caps when coming on as a substitute against Finland in March 2000. Something of an unsung hero at Prenton Park, he continued to turn in a series of solid, steady displays for the Wirral club despite their relegation to the Second Division.

He continued to establish himself at international level and, although Rovers' promising attempt to reach the Second Division play-offs was ultimately unsuccessful, he was fully committed to the Tranmere cause. By the end of the 2003/04 season he had appeared in 221 games for the Prenton Park side.

Roger FREESTONE

Position	Goalkeeper
Born	Roger Freestone, Newport, 19 August 1968
Height	6ft 3in
Weight	14st 6lb
Clubs	Newport County, Chelsea, Swansea City, Hereford United
Welsh Caps	1
	2000 v Brazil (lost 0–3)

GOALKEEPER ROGER FREESTONE was first called into the Wales squad in 1995, but had to wait until the summer of 2000 before making his belated international debut against Brazil at Cardiff's Millennium Stadium.

He began his career with his home-town team Newport County in 1986, but within ninth months he had moved to Chelsea for a fee of £95,000. An excellent shot-stopper, he went on to appear in 53 games for the Stamford Bridge club. After loan spells with Swansea City and Hereford United, he joined the Swans on a permanent basis in September 1991.

Freestone was one of the club's most consistent goalkeepers. He did not miss a single League game until April 1995, when he was called up to a Wales international squad for the match against Germany. In 1995/96 he converted a couple of penalties for the Swans during the first month of the season and missed just one game. His consistency for the Swans has been a major factor in the club reaching the play-offs on three occasions and winning the Autoglass Trophy at Wembley.

Following his 500th League and Cup appearance for Swansea at Christmas 1998, he was set to break the Swans' 368 League appearance record held by Johnny King. But for the first time in his career he was forced to miss a number of League games through injury. Recognised as one of the best keepers outside the top flight, Freestone

2002 v Armenia (0–0), v Norway (lost 2–3), v Belarus (won 1–0), v Argentina (1–1), v Czech Republic (0–0), v Germany (won 1–0)

2003 v Croatia (1–1) 1 goal, v Finland (won 2–0) 1 goal, v Italy (won 2–1) 1 goal, v Azerbaijan (won 2–0), v Bosnia-Herzegovina (2–2), v Azerbaijan (won 4–0), v United States (lost 0–2)

2004 v Serbia-Montenegro (lost 0–1), v Italy (lost 0–4), v Finland (1–1), 1 goal, v Scotland (won 4–0)

ONE OF THE HOTTEST PROPERTIES in the Premiership, midfielder Simon Davies made a dramatic impact on his entry into international football against Ukraine in

Simon Davies takes the ball past Samir Aliyev of Azerbaijan during the Euro 2004 qualifying Group 9 match, 29 March 2003. Wales won the match 4–0. *(Getty Images)*

2001. He scored in three successive games in 2003 to become a real factor in the turn-around in his country's fortunes.

He began his career with Peterborough United, starring in the club's junior side that ultimately reached the semi-final stage of the 1997/98 FA Youth Cup. One of the home-grown talents to emerge from the Barry Fry academy, he soon won Wales under-21 and 'B' level recognition to mark his promise. Possessing vision, touch and pace, the young midfielder was recognised by his fellow professionals when he was selected for the PFA Third Division team of 1998/99. He entered the Peterborough United record books when, amid mounting speculation, he was transferred to Tottenham Hotspur in January 2000 for £700,000. The move was perhaps inevitable as Posh were reported to be losing around £30,000 a week.

He broke into the Spurs' team on a regular basis midway through the 2000/01 season. His form also led to his first full cap as a substitute in the World Cup qualifier against Ukraine in March 2001. He then replaced the injured Robbie Savage in the starting line-up for the return game in Kiev. Sadly, he missed much of the 2003/04 season through injury, though he did return to both club and international duty towards the end of the campaign.

Jason KOUMAS

Position	Midfielder
Born	Jason Koumas, Wrexham, 25 September 1979
Height	5ft 10in
Weight	11st 0lb
Clubs	Tranmere Rovers, West Bromwich Albion
Welsh Caps	9 Goals 1
	2001 v Ukraine (1–1)
	2002 v Czech Republic (0–0)
	2003 v Bosnia-Herzegovina (2–2), v United States (lost 0–2)
	2004 v Italy (lost 0–4), v Finland (1–1), v Russia (0–0), v Russia (lost 0–1), v Hungary (won 2–1) 1 goal

JASON KOUMAS MADE HIS LEAGUE debut for Tranmere Rovers midway through the 1998/99 season when he came on as a substitute at Sunderland. Two weeks later he scored the first of a number of unstoppable thunderbolts against Huddersfield Town at Prenton Park. Although he made only 11 starts in his first season, his form was such that he attracted scouts from a number of top clubs.

A hard-running, creative midfield player, Koumas demonstrated good all-round skills in dribbling, passing and shooting. Although Tranmere struggled in 2000/01, Koumas developed into the main focus for the Rovers' attack and ended the campaign as the club's leading scorer with ten goals. At the beginning of June 2001 he made his debut in international football for Wales, when he came off the substitute's bench in the closing stages of the World Cup qualifier against Ukraine. The following season he was rewarded with a place in the PFA award-winning Second Division side. Although he was the subject of much transfer speculation, he

remained at Prenton Park until August 2002, when West Bromwich Albion paid £2.5 million to take him to the Hawthorns. He quickly became a great favourite with Baggies' fans with his driving runs from midfield and his powerful shooting, and in 2003/04 helped Albion return to the top flight at the first time of asking.

Danny GABBIDON

Position	Defender
Born	Daniel Leon Gabbidon, Cwmbran, 8 August 1979
Height	6ft 1in
Weight	11st 2lb
Clubs	West Bromwich Albion, Cardiff City
Welsh Caps	4
	2002 v Czech Republic (0–0)
	2003 v Croatia (1–1), v Finland (won 2–0), v Italy (won 2–1)
	2004 v Serbia-Montenegro (lost 0–1), Serbia-Montenegro (lost 2–3), v Russia (0–0),
	v Russia (lost 0–1), v Scotland (won 4–0), v Hungary (won 2–1), v Norway (0–0),
	v Canada (won 1–0)

DANNY GABBIDON STARTED OUT WITH West Bromwich Albion, where in his first couple of seasons at the Hawthorns he was a regular for Wales at under-21 level. After making his first-team debut against Ipswich Town at a difficult stage of the 1998/99 season, he won a regular place in the side the following season. Then he fell victim to a niggling shin injury and made few appearances in the second half of the campaign. Unable to make much headway at the Hawthorns, appearing in just 27 League and Cup games in two years with the club, he joined Cardiff City for a fee of £175,000.

He immediately established himself in the Bluebirds' first team, playing in every position across the club's back four. A quality defender, Gabbidon made an impressive debut for Wales in a goalless draw against the Czech Republic at the Millennium Stadium. A virtual ever-present in his first two seasons at Ninian Park, he made a very disappointing start to the 2002/03 season. For more than four months he was ruled out by a back injury. It was April before he returned to the Cardiff side, but when he did the campaign at least ended on a high note. He was a member of the side that won promotion to the First Division by beating Queen's Park Rangers 1–0 in the Second Division play-off final at the Millennium Stadium. However, because of the play-off dates he was forced to pull out of the Wales game against the United States in San José. In 2003/04, he was a virtual ever-present in the Bluebirds's side and continued to represent Wales, being one of the side's unsung heroes.

Jason Koumas makes a break forward during the Euro 2004 Group 9 qualifying match between Wales and Finland, 10 September 2003. The match ended in a 1–1 draw. *(Getty Images)*

Paul EVANS

Position	Midfielder
Born	Paul Simon Evans, Oswestry, 1 September 1974
Height	5ft 8in
Weight	11st 6lb
Clubs	Shrewsbury Town, Brentford, Bradford City, Blackpool
Welsh Caps	1
	2002 v Czech Republic (0–0)

A VERY BUSY, STRONG-TACKLING midfielder, Paul Evans began his career with Shrewsbury Town where in his first season with the club he won international recognition, being selected by Wales at under-21 level.

Possessing a very strong shot, he scored a number of spectacular goals for the Gay Meadow club. Over the next few seasons, Evans missed very few games. In 1997/98, seeking to step up the divisions, he spent much of the campaign on the transfer list. Manager Jake King regarded him so well that he was more than happy to see him retain the captaincy. Evans was so grateful for the grounding he had received at Shrewsbury that, on being transferred to Brentford in March 1999, he chose to be 'sold' for a fee of £110,000 rather than await a summer 'Bosman'.

The all-action midfielder scored 30 goals in 237 League and Cup games for Shrewsbury. He was appointed captain on his arrival at Griffin Park. He ended his first season with the Bees with a Third Division Championship medal and a place in the PFA award-winning Third Division side. The following season he lobbed the Preston North End keeper from 50 yards, and after Brentford supporters dubbed it 'Goal of the Decade' it was subsequently shown on BBC television's *A Question of Sport*. In 2000/01 Evans won a runners-up medal in the LDV Vans Trophy as a member of the Bees side that were defeated 2–1 by Port Vale at the Millennium Stadium. In 2001/02 he helped Brentford to the play-off final, where they were beaten by Stoke City, and he was selected for the PFA Second Division side.

Replacing Robbie Savage, he won his first cap for Wales in the goalless draw against the Czech Republic in 2002 before leaving Brentford to join Bradford City. After a good start, he struggled in the second half of the season and left Valley Parade to play on loan for Blackpool.

Rob EARNSHAW

Position	Forward
Born	Robert Earnshaw, Zambia, 6 April 1981
Height	5ft 8in
Weight	10st 10lb
Clubs	Cardiff City, Greenock Morton
Welsh Caps	13 Goals 7
	2002 v Germany (won 1–0) 1 goal
	2003 v Croatia (1–1), v Azerbaijan (won 2–0), v Bosnia-Herzegovina (2–2) 1 goal

Rob Earnshaw prepares to strike the ball during the Euro 2004 Group 9 qualifying match between Wales and Serbia-Montenegro at the Millennium Stadium, 11 October 2003. Serbia-Montenegro eventually won the match 3–2. *(Getty Images)*

2004 v Serbia-Montenegro (lost 0–1), v Italy (lost 0–4), v Finland (1–1), Serbia-Montenegro (lost 2–3) 1 goal, v Russia (lost 0–1), v Scotland (won 4–0) 3 goals, v Hungary (won 2–1) 1 goal, v Norway (0–0), v Canada (won 1–0)

DURING HIS EARLY DAYS IN FOOTBALL, Zambian-born Rob Earnshaw wanted to play international football for the country of his birth. His mother was a Zambian women's international while his uncle played football for a top Belgian club.

He joined Cardiff City and scored 47 goals for the club's youth team in 1997/98, including a hat-trick in the Midland Bank Welsh Youth Cup Final against Llanelli. It was from this point that he started to celebrate all his goals with a somersault. Earnshaw's first goal for the first team came at Hartlepool United on the opening day of the 1998/99 season – a stunning overhead kick. As the season unfolded, he had loan spells with Fulham and Middlesbrough without being called into either club's first team. It was during this season that the pacey young striker won recognition for Wales at under-21 level.

There followed a further loan spell with Scottish League side Morton, where Earnshaw scored twice in his three games, before he finally established himself in the Cardiff team in 2000/01. It was a season in which he top-scored for the Bluebirds with 25 goals, including a hat-trick in the FA Cup tie against Bristol Rovers and another in the Third Division game with Torquay United. Voted Cardiff's Young Player of the Year, he was also selected for the PFA's Third Division team.

The 2001/02 season was a frustrating one for Rob Earnshaw. Yet, despite suffering from a spate of injuries, he still managed to finish the campaign with 15 goals. Undoubtedly the highlight of this talented player's injury-hit campaign came on his full debut for Wales against Germany at the Millennium Stadium, where he produced an outstanding forward display and scored the game's only goal.

The 2002/03 season was a phenomenal one for Earnshaw. Starting the campaign on the bench, he made his first start in the League Cup tie against Boston United, and after netting a hat-trick he went on to score 35 goals in all competitions. In so doing he broke two of the club's long-standing records – his tally of 31 League goals beat Stan Richards' total of 30 set in the first season after the Second World War, and his total of 35 in all games broke Hughie Ferguson's record of 32 set in 1926/27. He continued to feature for Wales and was voted into the PFA Second Division team just as the Bluebirds won promotion to the First Division. In the 2003/04 season, Earnshaw, who netted a hattrick in a 4–0 defeat of Scotland, continued to score with great regularity for Cardiff, netting four against Gillingham in a total of 26 goals.

Rob EDWARDS

Position	Right-back
Born	Robert Owen Edwards, Telford, 25 December 1982
Height	6ft 1in
Weight	12st 0lb
Clubs	Aston Villa, Crystal Palace, Derby County

Welsh Caps	6
	2003 v Azerbaijan (won 4–0)
	2004 v Serbia-Montenegro (lost 2–3), v Scotland (won 4–0), v Hungary (won 2–1), v Norway (0–0), v Canada (won 1–0)

FOLLOWING SOME SOLID DISPLAYS for Aston Villa's reserve and youth teams in 2001/02, Rob Edwards was handed a first-team squad number midway through the following season. Almost immediately he was plunged into first-team action as an emergency right-back for Villa against Middlesbrough because of injuries, illness and suspensions at the club. The Villans won the game 1–0. It was a highly impressive debut by the young Villa player and he went on to appear in a further eight games during the course of the 2002/03 season.

His displays prompted Mark Hughes to give Edwards his international debut in the European Championships qualifier against Azerbaijan at the Millennium Stadium in March 2003, when he came on as a substitute for Craig Bellamy in a 4–0 win. Though still unable to command a place in the Villa side, he impressed on loan spells with Crystal Palace and Derby County.

David VAUGHAN

Position	Midfielder
Born	David Owen Vaughan, Rhuddlan, 18 February 1983
Height	5ft 7in
Weight	10st 10lb
Clubs	Crewe Alexandra
Welsh Caps	2
	2003 v United States (lost 0–2)
	2004 v Hungary (won 2–1)

A LEFT-SIDED MIDFIELDER, David Vaughan is just one of the many players to have developed through Crewe Alexandra's successful youth scheme. He made his Football League debut at the beginning of the 2000/01 season in the goalless draw against Blackburn Rovers but his game lasted just 45 minutes before he was replaced at half-time by Kevin Street. He did not play again that season, and it was midway through the following campaign before he appeared again in the first team. The Welsh youth international impressed the observers and scored his first goal for the club in the 4–2 FA Cup defeat of Rotherham United at Millmoor.

In 2002/03 Vaughan recovered well from a minor operation to have a good season in the Gresty Road midfield. He continued to represent Wales at under-21 level before making his full international debut against the United States during the summer of 2003. Since then he has established himself as a regular in the Crewe side, having appeared in 88 games for the Railwaymen.

David PIPE

Position	Midfielder/forward
Born	David Ronald Pipe, Caerphilly, 5 November 1983
Height	5ft 9in
Weight	12st 4lb
Clubs	Coventry City
Welsh Caps	1
	2003 v United States (lost 0–2)

THE CAERPHILLY-BORN YOUNGSTER worked his way up through the ranks at Highfield Road to make his first appearance as a substitute for Coventry City against Nottingham Forest in August 2002. He scored on his full debut in the 2–0 win over Gillingham. Playing on either the right-side of midfield or up front, David Pipe impressed all onlookers with his non-stop running and aggressive style of play. He dropped out of first-team reckoning for a while but returned to appear in 24 League and Cup matches for the Sky Blues, although half of this total was when he came off the bench.

During the course of his first season he appeared for Wales at under-21 level, and in the close season made his full international debut when he replaced John Oster in Wales's 2–0 defeat by the United States in San José.

Carl FLETCHER

Position	Midfielder
Born	Carl Neil Fletcher, Surrey Heath, 7 April 1980
Height	5ft 10in
Weight	11st 7lb
Clubs	Bournemouth
Welsh Caps	4
	2004 v Scotland (won 4–0, v Hungary (won 2–1), v Norway (0–0), v Canada (won 1–0)

THOUGH CARL FLETCHER WAS STILL A TRAINEE, Bournemouth thought him promising enough to make his Football League debut at Grimsby in February 1998. He made another substitute appearance the following season before in 1999/2000 establishing himself as a regular member of the Cherries' side. Operating in the centre of midfield he proved to have good passing skills and was willing to get forward when opportunities arose.

Rarely missing a game, the combative midfielder became Bournemouth's youngest-ever captain when he led the side out against Blackpool in January 2002. The campaign also saw him manage to tame his fiery nature, but he still picked up too many disciplinary points for the likes of the club's management team.

At the start of the 2003/03 season, Fletcher was named as the Cherries' team captain. In a campaign which saw Bournemouth win promotion via the play-offs in a 5–2 Millennium Stadium win over Lincoln City, he made a clean sweep of the club's Player of the Year awards. His form for the Dean Court club in 2003/04 led to his winning the first of four full caps for Wales when he played in the 4–0 win over Scotland. He kept his place in the side, helping Wales to further victories over Hungary and Canada and a draw against Norway.

Paul PARRY

Position	Midfielder
Born	Paul Parry, Hereford, 19 August 1980
Height	5ft 10in
Weight	11st 4lb
Clubs	Hereford United, Cardiff City
Welsh Caps	3 Goals 1
	2004 v Scotland (won 4–0), v Norway (0–0), v Canada (won 1–0), 1 goal

MIDFIELDER PAUL PERRY BEGAN his career with local club Hereford United, joining them as a trainee in the summer of 1998. It was 1999/2000 before he established himself with the Nationwide Conference side. His best season for the Edgar Street club was 2002/03 when he netted ten goals from midfield as Hereford just missed out on a play-off place. He continued to impress at the start of the 2003/04 season and had just netted a well-taken hat-trick in a 7–1 win at Forest Green when Cardiff manager Lennie Lawrence paid £75,000 to take him to Ninian Park.

He made his Bluebirds' debut in a 3–2 defeat of Rotherham United and had played in only five First Division games when Mark Hughes gave him his full international debut in the friendly against Scotland. He replaced the injured Simon Davies and the Cardiff youngster's first touch released Ryan Giggs down the left. His cross was bundled in at the near post by Rob Earnshaw, who netted a hat-trick in a 4–0 win. Parry continued to hold down a regular place for Cardiff and at the end of the season scored the only goal of the game as Wales beat Canada 1–0.

Ben THATCHER

Position	Defender
Born	Benjamin David Thatcher, Swindon, 30 November 1975
Height	5ft 10in
Weight	11st 10lb
Clubs	Millwall, Wimbledon, Tottenham Hotspur, Leicester City
Welsh Caps	3
	2004 v Hungary (won 2–1), v Norway (0–0), v Canada (won 1–0)

AFTER GRADUATING THROUGH the youth ranks at Millwall and the Lilleshall School of Excellence, Ben Thatcher became a regular in the Lions' defence. At the end of the 1994/95 season he was called up to the England under-21 squad and elected by his fellow professionals to the PFA award-winning First Division side. The following season he represented the Endsleigh League under-21 side against an Italian Serie B XI and was voted the club's Player of the Year. However, in June 1996 he left the New Den to join Wimbledon in a £1.8 million transfer.

An intelligent defender who can read a dangerous situation well, he continued to represent England at under-21 level, though his first couple of seasons with the Dons saw him hampered by ankle injuries. He returned to full fitness and an outstanding season in 1998/99, performing to a consistently high level. The following season saw him pushing for a place in the full England side in their problem left-back spot, yet he was unable to prevent the Dons' relegation to the First Division and in the close season moved to Spurs for £5 million.

He struggled to make an impact in his first season at White Hart Lane, but eventually rediscovered his form to win a place in the side for the 2002 League Cup Final. Then a hip injury kept him out of action for a year and in July 2003, after making just 46 League and Cup appearances for Spurs, he joined newly promoted Leicester City on a free transfer.

His form for the Foxes led to his winning three full caps for Wales, the first in a 2–1 defeat of Hungary. Though he couldn't prevent Leicester from being relegated from the Premiership, he took great delight in netting his first goal for the club in a remarkable 4–4 draw against his former club, Spurs.

Statistics

MOST-CAPPED POSTWAR PLAYERS

1.	Neville Southall	92	11.	David Phillips	62
2.	Gary Speed	80	12.	Barry Horne	59
3.	Dean Saunders	75		Cliff Jones	59
4.	Peter Nicholas	73		Kevin Ratcliffe	59
	Ian Rush	73		Terry Yorath	59
6.	Mark Hughes	72	16.	Leighton Phillips	58
	Joey Jones	72	17.	Leighton James	54
8.	Ivor Allchurch	68	18.	Dai Davies	52
9.	Brian Flynn	66	19.	John Mahoney	51
10.	Andy Melville	63		Mickey Thomas	51
				Mark Penbridge	51

TOP POSTWAR GOALSCORERS

1.	Ian Rush	28		Ryan Giggs	8
2.	Ivor Allchurch	23	13.	Rob Earnshaw	7
	Trevor Ford	23		Brian Flynn	7
4.	Dean Saunders	22		Robbie James	7
5.	Mark Hughes	16		Ian Walsh	7
	Cliff Jones	16	17.	Mel Charles	6
7.	John Charles	15		Alan Curtis	6
8.	John Toshack	12		Wyn Davies	6
9.	John Hartson	11		Arfon Griffiths	6
10.	Leighton James	10		Bryn Jones	6
11.	Ron Davies	9		Terry Medwin	6
12.	Roy Vernon	8		Mark Pembridge	6

Index of Player Entries